The Good Hegemon

The Good Hegemon

US Power, Accountability as Justice, and the Multilateral Development Banks

SUSAN PARK

OXFORD
UNIVERSITY PRESS

OXFORD
UNIVERSITY PRESS

Oxford University Press is a department of the University of Oxford. It furthers
the University's objective of excellence in research, scholarship, and education
by publishing worldwide. Oxford is a registered trade mark of Oxford University
Press in the UK and certain other countries.

Published in the United States of America by Oxford University Press
198 Madison Avenue, New York, NY 10016, United States of America.

© Oxford University Press 2022

All rights reserved. No part of this publication may be reproduced, stored in
a retrieval system, or transmitted, in any form or by any means, without the
prior permission in writing of Oxford University Press, or as expressly permitted
by law, by license, or under terms agreed with the appropriate reproduction
rights organization. Inquiries concerning reproduction outside the scope of the
above should be sent to the Rights Department, Oxford University Press, at the
address above.

You must not circulate this work in any other form
and you must impose this same condition on any acquirer.

Library of Congress Cataloging-in-Publication Data
Names: Park, Susan, 1976– author.
Title: The good hegemon : US power, accountability as justice,
and the multilateral development banks / Susan Park.
Description: New York, NY : Oxford University Press, [2022] |
Includes bibliographical references and index.
Identifiers: LCCN 2021045601 (print) | LCCN 2021045602 (ebook) |
ISBN 9780197626481 (hardback) | ISBN 9780197626504 (epub)
Subjects: LCSH: Development banks. | Economic policy. |
International economic relations. |
United States—Foreign economic relations.
Classification: LCC HG1975 .P37 2022 (print) | LCC HG1975 (ebook) |
DDC 332.1/53—dc23/eng/20211109
LC record available at https://lccn.loc.gov/2021045601
LC ebook record available at https://lccn.loc.gov/2021045602

DOI: 10.1093/oso/9780197626481.001.0001

1 3 5 7 9 8 6 4 2

Printed by Integrated Books International, United States of America

For Matt, who has been there from the beginning, and for William and Christopher, whose arrivals interrupted this book in the best way possible.

Contents

Illustrations

Tables

Figures

Foreword

In 1993 the World Bank created a precedent under international law, allowing people to seek recourse for harm resulting from the projects it finances in developing countries. This was the first time that a universal international organization (IO) recognized and responded to its impact on individuals. Within a decade of the World Bank Inspection Panel, the other multilateral development banks (MDBs, or banks) would create similar mechanisms. These accountability mechanisms embody a norm of "accountability as justice" that seeks to provide recourse for environmentally and socially damaging behavior through a formal sanctioning process. The norm has spread to other development financiers including the Asian Investment Infrastructure Bank (AIIB) and the European Investment Bank, bilateral development agencies, export credit agencies, and private banks. How was the emergence and spread of this norm possible? Although international law scholars/practitioners have expended considerable effort mapping the differences among the accountability mechanisms, no explanation has been provided for their creation, how they function, and whether they hold the banks to account.

This book tackles all three questions, making three central arguments: first, the United States acted as a norm entrepreneur during debates over how to maintain MDB efficiency and effectiveness in the 1990s. Building on its history of using "accountability as control" the United States sought to establish a norm of "accountability as justice" for all of the MDBs, to enable recourse for communities and ecosystems harmed by projects financed by the banks. As the most powerful shareholder, the United States used three strategies to garner support for the norm: its "power of the purse," its "vote," and its "voice" in the banks. Second, the MDBs used a range of passive and active strategies to resist conforming to the norm, leading the United States to invoke the same practices to demand the banks reformulate the mechanisms in egregious cases. Third, the book demonstrates how the MDBs have institutionalized the norm over time: improving the accountability mechanisms' accessibility, transparency, independence, responsiveness to affected people, and the effectiveness of compliance investigations and MDB monitoring. Despite these gains, the accountability as justice norm is a corrective rather than preemptive justice norm adhered to by the MDBs.

Acknowledgments

I have had the very good fortune of interviewing many people over the years, and I thank all the practitioners and activists for the time they gave to tell me exactly how the emergence of accountability for people became possible. A special thank you to David Hunter at American University for letting me trawl through his treasure trove of documents (including faxes!) from the 1990s. Your help has been invaluable. Funding was provided by the Australian Research Council Discovery Project (DP140100868) and the University of Sydney SOAR Fellowship (2017–2018). Both gave me the time and funding to undertake field work at the Asian Development Bank, and I thank Bruce Purdue for being my guide. I started this project on sabbatical at the Grantham Research Institute at the London School of Economics and benefited greatly from discussions with Robert Falkner and colleagues there, while undertaking interviews at the European Bank for Reconstruction and Development. In 2013 I took sabbatical at the Elliott School of International Affairs at George Washington University to conduct many interviews at the World Bank, International Finance Corporation, and the Inter-American Development Bank and attend the annual meeting of the international accountability mechanisms. Thank you to Michael Barnett for commenting on a full draft of this manuscript years ago during a manuscript development workshop here in Sydney, and to all my Government and International Relations colleagues for their feedback and support. During my last sabbatical at the Blavatnik School of Government at Oxford University, and my Hans Senior Fellowship at the Technical University of Munich, I was able to put the finishing touches to this manuscript and present the findings. All errors are mine alone.

Some parts of this work draw on material already published. Part of the analysis of the ADB that appears throughout chapters 3 to 6 were first developed in Park, 2014, "Institutional Isomorphism and the Asian Development Bank's Accountability Mechanism: Something Old, Something New; Something Borrowed, Something Blue?" *Pacific Review* 27 (2): 217–239. I am grateful to Taylor and Francis for their permission to reuse some of the material. Likewise, part of the analysis of the EBRD that appears in chapters 3 to 6 was first published in Park., 2021, "Policy Norms, the Development Finance Regime Complex, and Holding the EBRD to Account," *Global Policy* 12 (4): 90–100. I am grateful to John Wiley and Sons for permission to use this material. Finally, parts of the theoretical argument that appears in chapter 2 and 3 were first published in

Park, 2017, "Accountability as Justice for the Multilateral Development Banks? Borrower Opposition and Bank Avoidance to US Power and Influence," *Review of International Political Economy* 24 (5): 776–801. Again I am grateful to Taylor and Francis for the permission to reuse parts of this material.

As you can see, this project has been in development for a very long time. Much has changed in the world, not least the United States' role in multilateralism and comparatively in the MDBs. I also experienced major life changes while writing this book. I acknowledge the work of, and deeply thank, the pediatric neurologist Dr. Ian Andrews and surgeon Dr. Erica Jacobson at the Sydney Children's Hospital and everyone in his medical team for giving my son a quality of life he would not otherwise have had. I am extremely grateful to live in a country that has such medical care, and despite the problems, do still see a role for development finance to contribute to a better quality of life for all.

Susan Park
Sydney, May 2021

Abbreviations

ADB	Asian Development Bank
ADF	Asian Development Fund
AfDB	African Development Bank
AfDF	African Development Fund
AM	Accountability Mechanism of the ADB
BCRC	Board Compliance Review Committee of the ADB
BIC	Bank Information Center
BIC	Board Inspection Committee of the ADB
CAO	Compliance Advisor/Ombudsman for IFC and MIGA
CIEL	Center for International Environmental Law
CODE	Committee of Development Effectiveness, the World Bank Group
CRMU	Compliance Review and Mediation Unit
CRP	Compliance Review Panel of the ADB AM, and Compliance Review Panel of the IDB's MICI
EBRD	European Bank for Reconstruction and Development
ED	executive director
ESP	Environment and Social Policy of the EBRD
FSO	Fund for Special Operations of the IDB
GABB	Grupo de Accion por el Bibio
IBRD	International Bank for Reconstruction and Development
ICIM	Independent Consultation and Investigation Mechanism of the IDB (MICI in Spanish)
IDA	International Development Association
IDB	Inter-American Development Bank
IFC	International Finance Corporation
IFI	international financial institution
IIM	Independent Investigation Mechanism of the IDB
IMF	International Monetary Fund
IO	international organization
IPAM	Independent Project Accountability Mechanism of the EBRD
IRM	Independent Recourse Mechanism of the EBRD/Independent Review Mechanism of the AfDB
MAP	Management Action Plans
MDB	multilateral development bank
MICI	Mecanismo Independiente de Consulta e Investigación, see ICIM
MIGA	Multilateral Investment Guarantee Agency
NGO	nongovernmental organization

NRDC	Natural Resources Defense Council
NWF	National Wildlife Federation
OCRP	Office of the Compliance Review Panel of the ADB's AM
ODA	overseas development assistance
OECD	Organization for Economic Cooperation and Development
OSPF	Office of the Special Project Facilitator of the ADB's AM
PCM	Project Complaint Mechanism of the EBRD
PR	Performance Requirement of the EBRD
UN	United Nations
US-ED	United States executive director

1

The Good Hegemon

Demanding Accountability as Justice for the Multilateral Development Banks

In 1993 the World Bank created a precedent under international law by establishing its Inspection Panel. The Panel provides recourse for people negatively affected by World Bank–funded projects in developing countries (these are now known as project-affected people). Within a decade the rest of the multilateral development banks (MDBs) would follow with their own accountability mechanisms.[1] The MDBs are relatively autonomous international organizations (IOs) that remain one of the primary means for states to channel international development assistance to developing states (OECD 2018).[2] The International Bank for Reconstruction and Development (World Bank), the World Bank Group composed of the International Finance Corporation (IFC) and the Multilateral Investment Guarantee Agency (MIGA),[3] the African Development Bank (AfDB), the Asian Development Bank (ADB), the European Bank for Reconstruction and Development (EBRD), and the Inter-American Development Bank (IDB) all dispense loans, technical assistance, and guarantees to member states and companies in developing countries at or near market interest rates for development projects and programs.[4] The creation of accountability mechanisms is important because, despite numerous safeguards, extractive, energy, agriculture, and infrastructure projects can have significant consequences for local communities and ecosystems. Physical violence, loss of property, livelihoods, and ecosystem integrity continue to occur because of projects financed by the banks.

In response, communities have challenged being forcibly moved from their homes and livelihoods, receiving inadequate compensation, and witnessing the devastation of their local environment (Park 2019). As the book details, the World Bank–financed Narmada dam in India sparked the need for accountability mechanisms for the MDBs, as opposition to the dam mounted. These included acts of civil disobedience, mass protests (with one event gathering 60,000 protesters from 250 organizations in the state of Madhya Pradesh), rallies, petitions, marches, and a hunger strike involving high-profile Indian celebrities and clergy (Khagram 2004: 123). The Indigenous Pehuenche people also challenged the secrecy surrounding their removal and the environmental and social

The Good Hegemon. Susan Park, Oxford University Press. © Oxford University Press 2022.
DOI: 10.1093/oso/9780197626481.003.0001

implications of the IFC-financed Pangue dam in Chile (Park 2010a). As detailed throughout the book, once established, the accountability mechanisms would struggle to provide recourse for initial claims by communities facing toxic effluent from the Samut Prakarn waste water plant in Thailand (ADB), failures to conduct environmental and social planning and evaluation for the Yacyreta dam and reservoir across Argentina and Paraguay (IDB), failures in environmental impact assessment in the Bujugali dam in Uganda (AfDB), and adequately disclosing information and allowing participation in environmental and social matters regarding the Vlore power plant in Albania (EBRD). Although many of claims are against hydroelectric projects, the accountability mechanisms cover a range of project financing, from roads and railways to farming and mining.[5]

The rise of accountability mechanisms constitutes an international norm of "accountability as justice" (Dubnick 2014),[6] which has now spread to other international financial institutions including the China-led Asian Infrastructure Investment Bank (AIIB 2016) and the European Union's European Investment Bank among other MDBs (Zappile 2016); bilateral development agencies; export credit agencies; and private banks (Hunter 2008). Championed by the United States, the World Bank's Inspection Panel was the first time that a universal IO recognized that it had a relationship with individuals (Bradlow 1994). While this has been sufficiently covered in the academic literature (Hunter 2008; Naude Fourie 2009), what remains unexplained is why, within a decade, the other MDBs also created accountability mechanisms that allow themselves to be "held to account by those affected by the actions" of the banks (Koenig-Archibugi 2004: 236). This is striking, considering how radical a change the norm is for the MDBs and for IOs more broadly. Constitutively, it created new ways of thinking: acknowledging that MDB-financed development projects can lead to environmental and social harm and that this should be addressed by the banks. It created new actors in the form of accountability mechanism officers that independently investigate the MDBs. It also created new categories of action: "problem solving" to address community grievances, and "compliance audits" to assess whether bank policy noncompliance led to harm. The norm is also regulative: bank management or member states on the boards of executive directors must now respond to findings of bank noncompliance (Finnemore and Sikkink 1998: 891).

To explain the rise of the norm, the book makes three central arguments: First, it proposes that powerful states can generate international norms that become accepted behavior for the MDBs, triggering change in international development finance. This can be understood through recognizing power as social and relational, which enables us to examine how and why the hegemon used its predominant shareholder status to push for the norm for all of the MDBs against the concerns of borrowers and the interests of the banks.[7] Building on Babb (2009) and Lavelle's (2011) accounts of US legislative demands for the accountability mechanisms the book details how, over a decade, the United States invoked three strategies to demand accountability mechanisms for the MDBs: its "power of the purse," "vote," and "voice" in the banks. Second, it documents how the MDBs resisted demands for reform; opposing a norm that holds them to account to stakeholders as well as shareholders. The book documents the different strategies all five banks used to resist a norm that challenges their autonomy and banking culture: compromise, acquiescence, avoidance, defiance, and manipulation (Oliver 1991). In response, the United States invoked the same mechanisms in egregious cases where the mechanisms were prevented from providing recourse. Third, despite entrenched MDB resistance, the book shows how the accountability mechanisms became accepted as part of the banks' governance structures, including regularized reviews that continue to strengthen their operations. Although international law scholar/practitioners have expended considerable effort mapping the differences among the banks' accountability mechanisms (Hunter 2008; McIntyre and Nanwani 2020), there is little on how they operate (Park 2020), and whether they change the banks (except Buntaine 2016). The argument propounded here is that the operations of the mechanisms and their strengthened powers is evidence that the MDBs have institutionalized the norm (Schimmelfennig 2000; Kelley 2004). Nevertheless, the norm remains a corrective rather than preemptive norm for ensuring justice in international development, with little impact on the banks' lending operations.

The Argument: The United States, Accountability as Justice, and the MDBs

How do collective expectations or norms for actors with a given identity like the MDBs emerge? Advocates of ideas are norm entrepreneurs that seek to gain acceptance for new understandings of what constitutes appropriate behavior. Norms are considered powerful when they are endorsed by most actors and become taken for granted (Finnemore and Sikkink 1998). The accountability as justice norm for the MDBs was created as a result of US norm entrepreneurship, providing further evidence that states are the "principle source of most decisions to open up international organizations" (Tallberg et al. 2013: 16). The United States, as a hegemon and predominant shareholder within all the banks, championed the idea that all the MDBs should be held to account by the people they affect. The United States proposed the accountability as justice norm in response to increasing evidence from transnational activist campaigns and public outcry alleging that the MDBs were harming the ostensible beneficiaries of international development. While most explanations of the creation of the Inspection

Panel correctly identify the role of transnational advocacy networks (Park 2010a; Clark et al. 2003) in demanding such accountability mechanisms, the book shows that this would not have been possible without the United States taking it up and advocating for it. The activist explanation also fails to explain how and why the United States continued to pursue the norm for all the banks even when activists' and other member states' interest in doing so was absent or muted. I argue that the norm emerged the way it did and not otherwise because other options for providing recourse for project-affected people were delimited by two factors: the nature of US engagement with the banks, and debates over MDB inefficiency and ineffectiveness. The United States has a long history of using accountability processes such as auditing, monitoring and evaluation, and oversight procedures to control the banks (Grigorescu 2008). These tools are routinely invoked as a means of ensuring the MDBs use their funds efficiently and effectively. In addressing the harm caused by the banks, the United States demanded that these tools be used to provide recourse for project affected people.[8] I draw on Melvin Dubnick's (2014) argument that accountability can be understood differently according to the purpose for which it is being used to explain how demands for the banks to be accountable for harming people and ecosystems resulted in the creation of formal sanctioning procedures. This is important because, as the book demonstrates, there are a variety of different ways that recourse for project-affected people could have been provided, but ultimately formal sanctioning process demanded by the United States won. Scholars recognize that there are multiple ways that states can adhere to norms (Winston 2018; Wiener 2009), and enacting accountability is no different. Although there is relative agreement on what constitutes accountability in global governance (Dowdle 2006; Ebrahim and Weisband 2007), there remains disagreement in the literature on how accountability ought to be applied (Kramarz and Park 2016). The purpose of holding (a collective) someone to account can vary significantly: for example, for financial, legal, public, and reputational reasons among others (Balboa 2015; Grant and Keohane 2005).

Most definitions of accountability recognize that an account is given to someone else, that it is based on social interactions and exchange, and implies rights and authority (Mulgan 2000: 555). Grant and Keohane define accountability as "when some actors have the right to hold other actors to a set of standards, to judge whether they have filled their responsibilities in light of those standards, and to impose sanctions if they determine that those responsibilities have not been met" (2005: 29; cf. Schedler 1999). This enables us to identify who is accountable, to whom, and for what. The normative purpose for which accountability is used matters because it shapes what standards, procedures, and sanctions are employed to hold those actors to account (Mashaw 2006). For IOs, accountability is generally used in response to widespread demands for more transparency, legitimacy, and democracy.[9] Much of the work on IOs is therefore situated within either the "delegated" or "participatory" models of accountability with the aim of increasing representation (Grant and Keohane 2005: 32). In short, this is whether IOs are accountable to member states (Woods 2001) or to a "public" (Held and Keonig-Archibugi 2005). Scholars have argued the World Bank should be accountable to both (Woods and Narlikar 2001). This is unsurprising: The World Bank has a significant economic impact on developing states through its loan conditionalities and programs, and environmentally and socially regarding the programs and projects it funds. Moreover, it has a highly unequal weighted system of member state representation and voting, based on the amount states contribute, which is replicated by the other banks (this described in chapter 2). This inequality means that "member governments (with the obvious exception of the United States) are too far removed from the workings of the representative body (the Executive Board), which in turn exerts too little control over the staff and management of the institutions" (Woods 2001: 84). In short, the MDBs have too much autonomy and member states and their publics too little control.

Yet the MDB accountability mechanisms examined here fit both the delegated and participatory categories of accountability, because most of the mechanisms to report to their member states on the banks' boards while being responsive to project affected people. In examining IOs, Woods (2001), Lombardi (2008), and Grigorescu (2008) further distinguish vertical from horizontal accountability. The former refers to a hierarchical relationship between those in authority to their subordinates, such as member states to IO management to staff. Horizontal accountability refers to units within the IO that seeks to hold the organization to account, for example, for reviewing performance or proper conduct. An example is the World Bank's Department of Institutional Integrity (INT), which investigates ethical misconduct and corruption. This is useful for identifying where the accountability "gaps" are; for example, between the banks and their shareholders or within specific operational units in the MDBs. Yet the accountability mechanisms instituted by the banks at the behest of the United States analyzed here are both vertical in responding to member states on the banks' boards and horizontal in assessing if bank policy noncompliance led to harm at the project site.

So how do we explain the creation of formal sanctioning procedures designed to identify MDB wrongdoing, with providing recourse to project affected people? Dubnick's (2014) four "narratives" are useful for explaining the normative purpose of invoking an accountability relationship, two of which are argued to be in existence in the United States' push for the norm: First, an accountability relationship is created in order to increase institutional accountability; second, an accountability relationship may be instantiated as a means of ensuring control; third, accountability may be used as a way to provide justice; and finally, accountability may be invoked to provide an incentive.[10] Each of the four is briefly outlined as a means of illuminating the central thrust of the book: While not using the language of justice, the United States nonetheless repurposed typical "control" procedures such as auditing and monitoring tools to provide recourse for communities and ecosystems harmed by MDB-financed projects. This constitutes using accountability procedures for justice, because the purpose of accountability in this case is to morally uphold the treatment of individuals considering the banks' own environmental and social protection policies (on the MDB's policies, see Humphrey 2016).[11] The structure of the original accountability mechanisms reflects this: while ostensibly providing recourse for project affected people to air their grievances, the mechanisms' main tools were investigations and audits of bank compliance with their own policies, which provided the United States and other member states more power to sanction bank management for their behavior.

Dubnick's first narrative is institutionalized accountability, which is linked to constitutional and electoral arrangements designed to render political authorities more answerable and responsive. Much of the literature on IO accountability described previously has this as its purpose: it examines delegated or representative frameworks either implicitly or explicitly drawn from democratic understandings of accountability.[12] The second narrative views accountability as a means to facilitate control, particularly for ensuring obedience and efficiency. Chapter 3 argues that this is how the United States traditionally engages with the MDBs and takes the form of evaluation, auditing, and monitoring tools to ensure the banks do what member states want (Dubnick 2014: 30). Since the 1960s the United States has demanded the establishment of auditing and reporting requirements to oversee and direct the operations of the MDBs. In the 1990s the United States created more monitoring and evaluation tools to better ensure the banks' efficiency and effectiveness. The principal agent (PA) model, exported from US domestic politics, is entirely based on how member states can maintain control over the IO (Hawkins et al. 2006; Vaubel 2006).[13]

Third, accountability may be understood within a justice narrative, where it "produces justice for those victimised by malicious or damaging behaviour."[14] This narrative has been incorporated into "both criminal and civil legal systems as well as formalised sanctioning processes within organizations" (Dubnick 2014: 29–30). In the 1990s activists demanded accountability mechanisms to help people hold the banks to account, which shaped US interactions with the banks (Park 2010a; Rich 1994). As chapter 3 shows, efforts to hold the MDBs to account for harm included demanding transparency; answers from the banks as to whether they did or did not comply with their social and environmental policies and whether that led to harm; and ensuring MDB compliance and monitoring if they had not. The fourth narrative, which is beyond the scope here, revolves around using accountability as an incentive, or accountability metrics and benchmarks through which "adjustments in performance . . . demonstrate that one has become more accountable" (Dubnick 2014: 29–30). The introduction of "new public management" within the World Bank fits this narrative (Lardone 2010).

As detailed throughout the book, the accountability as justice norm was advanced by the United States for all the banks beginning in 1993. While this did not take place in an ideational vacuum, the trigger here was increasing scrutiny of the banks' operations after reviews into their portfolios documented overinflated expectations and underperforming loans (Mistry 1995) at the same time as harm to communities was revealed in relation to large-scale World Bank–financed projects (Wade 1997; Rich 1994). Within the context of debates over MDB inefficiency and ineffectiveness, the United States sought to convince member states to add concerns of justice to the typical means it uses to control the banks. This was in contradistinction to alternative proposals floated by other member states and the World Bank itself, to create an internal post hoc review process to determine whether randomly selected projects had harmed people and local ecosystems. These proposals did not provide recourse for project-affected people. While transnational activists were central to getting the issue on the table (Park 2010a) and other donors initially brought their concerns to the World Bank's board, US norm entrepreneurship ultimately not only created the World Bank Inspection Panel but also enabled it to be independent from World Bank management *and* ensured that it had a mandate to provide due process for affected people seeking recourse. The United States would then make sure the other MDBs followed.

Why would the United States advocate such a norm?[15] The United States benefits from the MDBs, with a high volume of lending to its allies in the World Bank and the ADB (Kilby 2011; Vreeland and Dreher 2014). Thus US actions could be seen as upholding the reputation of the banks that it helped create, fund, and from which it benefits, and with no cost to the United States for pursuing such a norm. This fits power-based explanations of strategic material interests and rational action (Kaya 2015). However, this does not explain why the United States would choose to go beyond the World Bank and World Bank Group, the targets of significant opposition for their environmental and social impact, to advance the norm for all the MDBs. As argued throughout, understanding the social basis of US power through a relational and interpretivist approach can show how ideas help constitute states' interest, such that the United States continued to pursue the norm for all banks even when activists' and other member states' interest in doing so was absent or muted. This also explains why the United States went beyond advocating for their creation to ensure that they worked.

Like Babb (2009) and Lavelle (2011), I therefore argue that ideas drove the United States' demand for accountability mechanisms for all the MDBs. The initial locus for change came from the US Congress, where congressional members became concerned about the negative impact of MDB funding on people at development project sites. The US Congress is able to intervene in IOs owing to the United States' domestic political structure, which gives it the power to approve US financing for multilateral institutions. Concern for project-affected people stemmed from awareness of transnational advocacy campaigns revealing harm, demonstrating how nonstate actors can influence the relationship between member states and IOs (Johnson 2014). The United States then engaged in a concerted effort to support accountability as justice across all the banks for over 20 years.

The tools available to the United States to exert influence depend on the institutional structure of the IO (Kaya 2015) and its relations with other member states. All the banks except the AfDB were created with the US imprimatur.[16] The banks are similarly governed with similar development financing functions operating in the same policy space. The United States has influence in the MDBs which derives from its predominant shares in the banks, and which also translates into preeminent voting rights. Unequal voting systems linked to the amount of capital subscribed in the MDBs means that member states with large shares like the United States tend to shape the policy direction of the banks (Culpeper 1997), although research on the effect of such policies across the MDBs remains scarce (except Buntaine 2016). The United States can use its financial position in the banks to allocate resources and to promote certain ideas and practices, which influence other shareholders and the MDBs (Woods 2003: 95).

Strategies to advance ideas can be ideational or material (Schimmelfennig 2000; Kelley 2004). In this case, the United States used three strategies to advance the norm: its "power of the purse," its "vote" on the banks' boards, and its "voice." The "power of the purse" is where the United States links new ideas to commitments to replenish the banks' capital; its "vote" is where the United States has a greater number of votes on the banks' boards to support new ideas; and its "voice" is where the United States seeks to persuade other member states and the banks to accept the norm. As the book details, the power of the purse was an important lever for pressing for the accountability as justice norm for the MDBs except the EBRD (owing to a variation in its institutional design). The voice mechanism is invoked by the United States across all the banks to garner consensus for the norm to be taken up and defended, while the vote was used across all the MDBs bar the EBRD. Despite resistance from bank management, the United States was able to advance the accountability as justice norm across the MDBs through gaining multilateral support to do so.

Member states agreed to establish the norm of accountability as justice to constitute and regulate MDB behavior. As the largest contributor with the largest vote in all the banks except the AfDB, where it is second, the United States can influence their conduct. However, US power derived from material resources is not absolute. The United States does not always get its way (Strand and Zappile 2015), and member states will block US preferences that are viewed as overtly self-interested (Upton 2000). The United States was able to promote the accountability as justice norm because the idea the United States advocates matters. The United States was able to garner consensus from other large shareholder member states to create the norm because the idea being promulgated was accepted as a legitimate concern for the MDBs. This compares with previous US efforts for example, to introduce human rights, which was seen as going beyond the apolitical technical mandate of the banks (Braaten 2016).

The United States was able to garner consensus on the banks' boards in advocating for formal sanctioning procedures for communities and ecosystems harmed by damaging MDB behavior. Despite agreeing to establish the norm, some borrower member states were concerned with how accountability mechanism practices would affect their lending (specific instances of borrower resistance are detailed throughout the volume). Propounding accountability mechanisms put the United States at odds with increasingly powerful middle-income countries such as China, India, and Brazil (Wade 2009), although rising powers were just beginning to flex their multilateral muscles in the 1990s. Seen as a "hassle factor" by large borrowers (Humphrey 2016), "noneconomic" concerns of accountability, transparency, and environmental and social safeguards pushed by the United States and other member states constituting the Group of Seven (G7) are considered part of the reason, along with US resistance to IMF and World Bank governance reform, for the decision by China to create the AIIB and the New Development Bank with Brazil, India, Russia, and South Africa.[17] Nonetheless, even without the United States as a member, the AIIB has adhered to the accountability as justice norm, reinforcing that it constitutes appropriate MDB behavior (AIIB 2016).[18]

IO Change and Norm Resistance

The second aim of the book is to investigate how the banks responded to the emergence of the norm. The MDBs are relatively autonomous IOs with discretion for how they meet their articles of agreement or constitution. Nevertheless, the banks rely on member states for their financial security, which rests on members' capital subscriptions; for approving bank decisions through members' votes on their boards; and for normative support, which provides the MDBs with legitimacy (Chorev 2012; Weaver 2008). Given these constraints, the banks were forced to meet US demands to create accountability units despite fear that this would impact their lending practices. The norm was advanced by the MDBs' predominant shareholder to reign in the banks' "organizational hypocrisy" in continuing to espouse environmental and social protections while violating their own environmental and social policies (Weaver 2008: 19). Alternative explanations for the adoption of the norm, such that the MDBs tried to preempt US actions or began to see need to hold themselves accountable to beneficiaries are not supported by evidence. As documented throughout the book, the banks view the accountability mechanisms as time consuming, costly, and potentially damaging in revealing wrongdoing. The MDBs' engaged five resistance strategies to insulate themselves from the norm: compromise, acquiescence, avoidance, defiance, and manipulation; with avoidance being the most frequently invoked (Barnett and Coleman 2005; Oliver 1991).

Once the banks realized that an accountability as justice norm was emerging, they engaged in a strategy of compromise by bargaining with member states over what the mechanisms would look like (Oliver 1991; Johnson 2014). When the United States demanded the World Bank create its Inspection Panel it gave management little room to design a mechanism that better fit its organizational culture and mandate (Chorev 2012). The other MDBs were able bargain for a greater role for management in the investigation process (excluding the World Bank Group). The IDB and the ADB, for example, both argued they should be involved in processing claims from project-affected people to underscore the importance of accountability, which the EBRD and the AfDB followed (Filho and Rios 2007: 57; ADB 1995b: 6).

Two factors enabled the other banks to circumscribe the norm by restricting the independence of their accountability mechanisms. First, institutional dynamics within the MDBs' boards supported management having oversight of the accountability mechanisms. This enabled management to have the power to approve investigations into their own behavior. Moreover, even with the focus on identifying whether the banks had caused harm (via acts or omissions in meeting their environmental and social policies), the initial designs of most of the mechanisms did not give the accountability mechanisms the power to monitor or enforce management's development of remedies after findings of noncompliance (Naude Fourie 2009). This means that the norm was created to correct MDB behavior rather than as a means of instilling justice throughout bank operations. This constrained the ability of the mechanisms to enact accountability as justice, although this would change over time (as discussed later). Second, none of the other MDBs faced as much public scrutiny as the World Bank and World Bank Group for their negative environmental and social impact, sharpening the demand for independent investigation procedures for those banks.

The second resistance strategy used by MDBs was to passively acquiesce to US demands for the accountability mechanisms be reviewed every two to three years. Member states use a range of tools to control the design of IOs and their "progeny," including "financial domination, oversight meetings, veto power, and monopolisation of delegates" (Johnson 2014). The United States depended on oversight provisions to defend the norm. This succeeded. All the accountability mechanisms improved over time because of periodic reviews into their practices, including acquiring greater independence from management, which has enhanced their credibility. Beyond this, the United States would use the same power of the purse, vote, and voice mechanisms to overhaul the accountability mechanisms in egregious cases particularly in relation to the ADB.

The results of the reviews and US interventions is that the mechanisms now share similar features, demonstrating a form of mimicry or institutional isomorphism at work (DiMaggio and Powell 1983; Park 2015). This is theoretically interesting, as the book highlights how norms spread from one actor (the United States) to a class of IOs (the MDBs), but the norm has been strengthened, not only by US demands and oversight but also through the uptake of best practice and continual learning among the mechanisms. There is always a mechanism about to be, or being, reviewed. When they are reviewed, the banks look to the last MDB accountability mechanism updated to identify what member states and stakeholders (including accountability mechanism officers from other banks and accountability activist/consultants) will countenance as acceptable practice. As a result, as of September 2020 all the mechanisms included a problem-solving function to directly address people's grievances. The addition of problem solving takes the heat off determining whether it was bank compliance or noncompliance with its own social and environmental policies that led to harm, which potentially weakens the formal sanctioning process. To offset this, during the review process member states have given the mechanisms strengthened monitoring powers over bank management responses to findings of noncompliance leading to harm, which could precipitate transformational change within the MDBs in the future (Streek and Thelen 2005). In short, the United States remains committed to the accountability as justice norm, but it is not the only contributor to its increasing strength.

The third and most used strategy, is avoidance. The banks' management engaged in this strategy in three ways: first, by establishing accountability mechanisms that were hard to access. All the of accountability mechanisms had technical exclusion criteria that were beyond the capacity of many project-affected people and prevented their claims from being "registered" or eligible for assessment. Second, management often provided ceremonial information during accountability mechanism investigations into their activities to demonstrate compliance with the norm, without necessarily providing a full account of their actions. Finally, avoidance is evident in failures to respond to findings of MDB noncompliance with remedies to improve the plight of people negatively affected.

All the banks would also engage in a fourth strategy of defiance by dismissing and challenging the norm. Management consistently denied claims from affected people were legitimate and refuted any wrongdoing, with some seeking to undermine the investigation process. This included preempting and circumventing investigations by establishing their own actions, including remedial management action plans to eliminate the need for any investigation into their activities. Finally, bank resistance was evident with efforts to manipulate responses to the norm. In some cases, management would seek to influence the standards by which they would be evaluated. For example, the World Bank management sought to influence the definition of what constitutes a "project" that could be investigated. A more extreme form of manipulation is when the MDBs seek to control the investigation process. In some cases, this included management supporting staff that withheld evidence of wrongdoing, and staff that sought to persuade affected people not to make claims.

The final aim of the book is to evaluate the impact of the norm on the banks. Over time, the United States used its influence within the MDBs to institutionalize the accountability as justice norm within recalcitrant banks. Despite entrenched bank management resistance, the accountability as justice norm is now taken for granted in terms of the established practices of the accountability mechanisms and their growing caseloads. The book documents tensions and begrudging support by the MDBs as the United States continued its efforts to institutionalize accountability as justice. While opposition to the norm remained, it became accepted that if one had to have an accountability mechanism, then it should be able to operate according to its mandate. While they do not challenge the banks' operations and organizational culture, the accountability mechanisms have been incorporated into the institutional governance of the MDBs, with the most egregious cases of harm occasionally sparking policy change in the banks. Moreover, ongoing improvements in the operations of the accountability mechanisms generated by US efforts, the periodic reviews, and actions by the accountability mechanism officers, all contribute to making the mechanisms more accessible, transparent, and responsive to project affected people.

Although the norm has been institutionalized within the banks' governing structures, it is clear through perpetuating roadblocks for project-affected people that the banks do not see the importance of allowing people recourse in international development. Counterfactual reasoning is illustrative: if the banks persistently recognized the remit of the mechanisms, engaged in good faith with the accountability mechanisms, did not seek to intervene in the investigations, and accepted when they were proved to be wrong, then resistance is not evident. Categorizing this as institutionalization highlights that a norm exists as evidenced by its formal instantiation (Kelley 2004; Park and Vetterlein 2010), without weighing in as to whether this constitutes an identity change (Hug 2003). There is little evidence to suggest that the norm has changed the way the banks undertake their operations, and indeed the construction of the accountability mechanisms were always considered correctives to bank failures, rather than as integral to changing their culture and operations.

The Research Approach

A constructivist analysis enables the examination of how norms emerge, spread, and become institutionalized. This is important for examining how ideas shape member state decisions in IOs and for how IOs (management and staff) react to new ideas. Norm entrepreneurs use both material and ideational means to establish a norm and induce norm following (Kelley 2004; Park 2010a), and actors follow norms for both strategic and identity reasons. Rationalists and constructivists alike recognize that norm following covers a spectrum of practices that progress from calculated action to a change in beliefs and identity (Risse et al. 1999; Greenhill 2010). The accountability as justice norm has been institutionalized by the MDBs because the accountability mechanisms were created through formal resolutions, and the accountability mechanisms have established habitual practices for their problem-solving and compliance investigations. While bank management consistently espouses adherence to the norm, they nevertheless continue to deny wrongdoing despite evidence to the contrary, challenge due process in investigations, and repeatedly do not provide remedies where harm has occurred.

In examining the United States' efforts to generate the norm for the MDBs, an explaining outcome process-tracing method is used. This method is specific to the analysis of a single case study. Explaining outcome process tracing seeks to build a minimally sufficient explanation of the outcome in an individual case, such that all relevant facts have been accounted for (Beach and Pedersen 2013: 16–19). The book does not examine the six MDBs as separate cases, because US efforts began in 1993 targeting the World Bank in the first instance, while signaling its intension to follow through with all the banks. The cases are not separate but a sequence of events of the United States promulgating change in response to MDB activities leading to harm. To that effect, the creation and implementation of the norm by the banks is examined in chronological order throughout the volume: first by the World Bank, then the IDB and ADB, the World Bank Group, the EBRD, and the AfDB.[19] Process tracing is used to document how the United States took up the idea of accountability as justice in response to evidence of World Bank harm and began to pressure the MDBs to adopt it.

The research was undertaken via a process of abduction, which is a dialectic combination of deductive and inductive approaches (Pouliot 2007). The deductive path began with the initial literature review, detailed in the next chapter, which identified three strategies the United States uses to influence the World Bank: the "power of the purse," "voice and vote," and "American culture." After undertaking a first round of empirical investigation via interviews and document analysis between 2009 and 2012, no evidence was found to support idea that there is an American culture in the MDBs that could help propel the accountability as justice norm, and it was therefore dropped. As Beach and Pedersen highlight, most explaining outcome process tracing cannot explain an outcome without a second stage of analysis to build a better explanation (2013: 19–21). Further empirical data was collected between 2012 and 2014, which supported evidence of the "power of the purse," and the "voice and vote" strategies. These were then recategorized into three separate strategies to make clearer how the United States advanced the norm.

The methods used include semistructured interviews and analysis of primary documents including US Congressional records on MDB legislation, official MDB publications (both public and confidential), accountability mechanism reports, and documents from the private archives of accountability activists, backed by secondary sources. This captures norm entrepreneur–IO interactions through examining their discussions, correspondence, and meetings as evidence of how ideas and interactions shape practices in international politics (cf. Seabrooke 2014). In total 114 interviews were undertaken with key MDB staff including former and current accountability mechanism officers, executive directors of the MDBs, bank operations staff, former US officials, and accountability activists.

To identify how the banks institutionalized the norm I then reviewed the structure and practices of the accountability mechanisms. In documenting the ongoing iterative reviews of the mechanisms, US efforts to defend the norm from bank management and borrower reluctance become clear, as do the improved practices of the accountability mechanisms. I then documented all accountability mechanism investigations from publicly available data from their inception to the end of calendar year 2018, a total of approximately 1,055 known claims (published as a publicly available database, see Park 2019). I accessed the public case registry of investigation claims and the annual reports of the accountability mechanisms, as these are the best source of evidence for tracing how the accountability as justice norm has been institutionalized and how the accountability mechanisms have been strengthened over time.

I identified how many claims advanced through each stage of the accountability mechanisms process: first, whether they were accepted for registration, meaning that they were considered bono fide claims within the mechanisms' purview; second, whether they were accepted as viable for problem solving by the parties comprising the bank, the complainant, and the executing agency; third, whether an agreement was facilitated between the banks and claimants;[20] fourth, whether the claims were accepted for compliance investigation; fifth, whether the banks were found to be noncompliant; and sixth, whether this led to monitoring to ensure bank compliance. This shows how the accountability mechanisms operated in terms of seeking to broker solutions for project-affected people and to hold the banks accountable for their (non)compliance with their own policies leading to harm.

Through such an examination trends across the banks become clear, although confidentiality concerns and a lack of transparency of the MDBs means there are necessarily gaps within the data. The data highlights the MDBs attempts to minimize the impact of the investigations on their operations reinforcing the argument that the norm is not viewed as central to their operations. The case documents and bank publications reveal how the norm has been institutionalized within the MDBs, and that the accountability mechanisms have improved. They have become more transparent in terms of the documents available to the public and claimants; independent from bank management and the MDB boards in their decision-making; more responsive to affected people through the provision of problem solving; and more powerful in being given the capacity to provide recommendations and monitoring to ensure the banks improve their practices. These changes were instituted because of US pressure in egregious cases, the member state–driven periodic reviews, and the accountability mechanisms themselves. While it is not always clear that claims have led to improvements on the ground, the case documents demonstrate how the banks continue to resist by refuting claims, denying wrongdoing, and interfering in investigations.

Outline of the Book

The next chapter has two aims. First, it theoretically examines the basis for US and Bank behavior, and second, it identifies the strategies they undertook in their interactions over establishing the norm. The chapter identifies the United States as an entrepreneur seeking to generate new ways for the banks to think and act. It unpacks the social and relational nature of US power, and the ideational and material strategies it used to generate, spread, and defend the norm. Norm entrepreneurs have a range of strategies available to them to induce norm following, including the power of the purse to propel new ideas. To succeed in multilateral settings, states also need to use their voice to generate support among member states, especially when voting on the banks' boards is by consensus. Once states agree to establish a norm it is then enacted. It may affect states differently, leading to contestation in practice (Wiener 2009). Second, the chapter directly tackles the basis for IO intransigence. I argue that the MDBs resisted the norm because it impinged on their autonomy and organizational culture. It challenged the banks' apolitical technocratic lending culture, which contributes to lending large volumes quickly as evidence of success while minimizing underperformance including harm. Ideas therefore matter for understanding how and why IOs react to member state interventions. The chapter then outlines the strategies used by the banks as they resisted the norm: compromise, acquiescence, avoidance, defiance, and manipulation.

In chapter 3 I examine how providing recourse to people negatively affected by MDB financed projects was promulgated by donor shareholders, pivotally by the United States, which took up activists concerns about the impact of MDB-financed projects on people. It traces how the demand for greater MDB accountability resulted from member state dissatisfaction with MDB performance, which coincided with activist campaigns revealing large-scale harm to communities and ecosystems. The chapter articulates the US history of using accountability as control for the MDBs, to which concerns of justice were added in the 1990s. The design of the World Bank's Inspection Panel would reflect US demands for accountability as justice. The United States then used its power of the purse, vote, and voice, to press for the accountability as justice norm in the IDB in 1994, the ADB in 1995, and the World Bank Group in 1999. The EBRD and the AfDB would follow suit in 2003 and 2004. It also shows how the banks sought to compromise over the norm once they realized it was becoming a reality. MDB management were able to design accountability mechanisms that had limited independence, thus circumscribing the norm in practice outside the high-profile campaigns against the World Bank and World Bank Group.

Chapter 4 details how once the mechanisms were established, bank management engaged in strategies of acquiescence, avoidance, defiance, and manipulation in reaction to the norm. Norm acquiescence is evident when the banks accepted the periodic reviews into the accountability mechanisms structures and operations. Norm avoidance is evident because the banks designed highly technical accountability mechanisms that were difficult for project-affected people to access. They would also provide ceremonial information in response to investigation claims in order to demonstrate conformity with the norm. Frequently, they would fail to enact remedies once found noncompliant leading to harm. All the banks would defy the norm by denying that their operations led to environmental and social harm, despite evidence to the contrary. Defiance is also evident in seeking to challenge the process of enacting the norm through under-mining and circumventing the investigation process. In more extreme cases bank management would undertake manipulation by seeking to influence the evaluative criteria on which they are being investigated; controlling staff that withhold evidence of wrongdoing in investigations; and pressuring people not to make claims. The banks' boards exercised traditional oversight procedures to improve the mechanisms through periodic reviews. The contentiousness of these reviews would vary across the banks based on the level of opposition to creating such a mechanism in the first place and their initial experience with investigating harm. The chapter also documents US interventions to further in-stitutionalize accountability as justice in egregious cases again using its power of the purse, vote, and voice.

Chapter 5 analyzes how the accountability as justice norm has been enacted since the mechanisms were created. The first section of the chapter provides an overview of the operations of the mechanisms (up to end of 2018) to demonstrate the difficulties of achieving justice through problem-solving and compliance investigations. The mechanisms are part of the internal accountability processes of the banks to check their behavior and are "last resorts" for project-affected people. Yet projects generally continue during an investigation, and remedies such as stopping the harm and rectifying damage remain with bank manage-ment. The second section summarizes the banks' ongoing resistance to the norm that limits the mechanisms' provision of recourse, and the third section details how the norm has had a piecemeal effect on the banks' operations, policies, and procedures. This reveals how little the norm affects bank operations, given that it was created to provide recourse as a corrective to harm rather than to prevent it.

Chapter 6 concludes by outlining how the accountability mechanisms have improved in providing recourse over time: becoming more independent, ac-cessible, and transparent. It shows that accountability mechanism activities can sometimes impact on the banks' policies and practices but this is often a result of highly visible egregious cases rather than learning from the accountability mech-anism operations. The accountability as justice norm does not interfere with the banks' technical and apolitical lending culture. The conclusion explores how persistent strategies by the United States may be used shape the practices of other IOs but where ideas remain paramount to its likely success.

2

US Norm Entrepreneurship and the MDBs

Introduction

Between 1993 and 2004 the United States advanced the accountability as justice norm for all the multilateral development banks (MDBs), which they resisted. This chapter has two aims: first, to theoretically examine the basis for US and bank behavior, and second, to identify their strategies in promoting and resisting the norm. First, the chapter identifies the United States as an entrepreneur seeking to generate new ways for the banks to think and act. Using an interpretivist approach, it unpacks the social and relational nature of US power where ideational and material strategies are used to generate, spread, and defend the norm. Norm entrepreneurs have a range of strategies available to them to induce norm following, including financial resources to propel new ideas. To succeed in multilateral settings, states also need to use their voice to generate support among member states, especially when voting by consensus. Once states agreed to the norm it was then enacted, which affected states differently, leading to contestation in practice. Second, the chapter directly tackles the basis for international organization (IO) intransigence. I argue that the MDBs resisted the norm because it impinged on their autonomy and organizational culture. It challenged the banks' apolitical technocratic lending culture, which contributes to lending large volumes quickly as evidence of success while overlooking underperformance including harm. The chapter then outlines the banks' strategies for resisting the norm: compromise, acquiescence, avoidance, defiance, and manipulation. Despite this, the norm was institutionalized within the banks as a corrective to their operations.

The United States as a Norm Entrepreneur

A norm cascades when entrepreneurs persuade a critical mass to follow it, and it becomes stable when following it is no longer a matter of debate (Finnemore and Sikkink 1998). Norm entrepreneurs have projected new ways of thinking and doing across all aspects of international relations (Finnemore and Sikkink 2001; Keck and Sikkink 1998). A norm entrepreneur is willing to "devote considerable resources (material and/or ideational) in order to introduce, change, or replace

The Good Hegemon. Susan Park, Oxford University Press. © Oxford University Press 2022.
DOI: 10.1093/oso/9780197626481.003.0002

international norms in their areas of interest" (Orchard 2014: 37). To this end, the hegemon is ideally placed to be able to shape international norms given that US influence in the MDBs is tied to its role in the international system (Upton 2000: 69).[1] Indeed, the creators of the banks all lobbied hard to have the United States back their initiatives (Dell 1972; Matecki 1957; Menkveld 1991; Watanabe 1977).[2] The basis for doing so was to lend both financial credibility and political legitimacy to the MDBs, both of which are central to our understanding of US power. Despite most of the banks being regionally oriented, the United States invested substantial resources in the MDBs in exchange for the largest share of the vote in all the banks except the African Development Bank (see Table 2.1; Strand 2003).

The focus here is how and why the United States advocated for the accountability as justice norm within the MDBs even when pressure to address bank harm from activists was absent or muted. Arguably a constructivist understanding of power, interests, and rationality can explain the United States' engagement with the banks, by revealing the importance of a shared social purpose for the MDBs (and other IOs) underpinned by norms, rules, and conventions.

Power

International relations debates over the creation and operation of IOs focuses on power (Ben-Artzi 2016; Copelovitch 2010; Stone 2011). For realists, powerful states construct institutions to achieve their interests (Schweller and Priess 1997; Gruber 2001), which neoliberal institutionalists argue can help states overcome collective actions problems (Martin and Simmons 1998; Keohane 1984).[3] IOs are often designed to reflect the distribution of states; economic and military resources. For IOs to function, weak states may be accorded greater political status to ensure their participation (Stone 2011) and legitimize decisions (Thompson 2006). Analysts have therefore interrogated how institutional structures like voting rules can mediate power (Kaya 2015; Strand and Rapkin 2011) and curb the use of coercive diplomacy (Carnegie 2015). In contrast, constructivists emphasize how social norms help constitute power (Guzzini 2013: 6). Power is "any chance within a social relation to impose one's will also against the resistance of others, regardless of what gives rise to this chance" (Weber 1980 [1921–1922]: 28, cited in Guzzini 2013). A relational rather than relative approach to power recognizes that one cannot presume that material resources determine that one actor will adhere to another's wishes, without knowing what constitutes shared understandings in social relations, and the underlying values and preferences of the parties (Barach and Baratz 1970: 20–21; Wendt 1999).[4]

Table 2.1 Top Member States Voting Power as a Percent of Total Votes in the MDBs FY2018–2019.

Member States Voting Power	World Bank (IBRD)	IDA	IFC	MIGA	AfDB	ADB	EBRD	IDB
US	15.68	15.68	20.98	15.02	6.627	12.756	10.099	30.006
Japan	7.88	7.88	6.01	4.22	5.522	12.756	8.601	5.001
Germany	3.96	3.96	4.77	4.2	4.162	3.752	8.601	1.896
France	3.71	3.71	4.48	4.03	3.779	2.156	8.601	1.896
UK	3.71	3.71	4.48	4.03	1.811	1.929	8.601	0.964
Australia	1.32	1.32	1.77	1.49	0	4.917	1.010	0
Argentina	1.1	1.1	1.59	1.12	0.099	0	0	11.354
Brazil	2.21	2.21	2.08	1.3	0.342	0	0	11.354
China	4.37	4.37	2.3	2.64	1.191	5.442	0.098	0.004
Egypt	0.46	0.46	0.46	0.47	5.629	0	0.104	0
India	3.00	3.00	3.82	2.56	0.267	5.352	0.033	0
Mexico	1.66	1.66	1.15	0.65	0	0	0.151	7.299
Nigeria	0.69	0.69	1.05	0.78	9.334	0	0	0
Italy	2.61	2.61	3.02	2.38	2.446	1.741	8.601	1.965
Canada	2.90	2.90	3.02	2.5	3.863	4.474	3.433	4.001
G7 Total	40.45	40.45	46.76	36.38	28.21	39.56	56.54	45.73

Note: Figures are June 30, 2019, for World Bank/Group and December 31, 2018, for the rest.

Source: Data from:

http://pubdocs.worldbank.org/en/625641565356285634/IBRD-Financial-Statements-June-2019.pdf.

http://pubdocs.worldbank.org/en/625641565356285634/IBRD-Financial-Statements-June-2019.pdf.

https://www.ifc.org/wps/wcm/connect/ed91858c-7eac-4732-a945-5ce8870b682e/IFC+FY19+MDA+and+Financial+Statements+_FINAL.pdf?MOD=AJPERES&CVID=mNTeBV0.

https://www.miga.org/sites/default/files/2019-08/MIGA%20Financial%20Statements%20and%20Management%20Discussion%20%26%20Analysis%20-%20June%2030%202019.pdf.

https://2018.fr-ebrd.com/financial-statements/

https://www.afdb.org/en/documents/document/afdb-statement-of-voting-powers-as-at-31-december-2018-107971.

https://data.adb.org/dataset/adb-annual-report-2018-organizational-information.

https://publications.iadb.org/publications/english/document/Inter-American_Development_Bank_Annual_Report_2018_The_Year_in_Review_en_en.pdf.

The relative versus relational understanding of power is important for discussing the role of the United States in the MDBs. Overwhelmingly the literature on IOs focuses on relative, material power (Ben-Artzi 2016; Vreeland and Dreher 2014). It is indisputable that the United States has invested the most material resources in the MDBs (Table 2.1), and that member states remain concerned with their relative position within IOs (Kaya 2015). However, the United States continues to command significant sway in the MDBs despite an erosion of its subscriptions overtime, which in turn reduces its percentage of the vote (Andersen, Hansen, and Markussen 2006: 776).[5] This reduction of material resources has not affected the United States' position because all member states have reduced the amount of paid-in capital to the MDBs over the last two decades (Kapur 2002: 62). Instead of relying on member states' capital subscriptions, the banks' own equity generation became the means to ensure financial success, which gave the MDBs more financial autonomy from its member states (a point discussed further in what follows).

A relational approach to power is not incommensurate with current explanations of IO actions. For example, Kaya (2015) argues that three factors explain why changes in member states' material resources do not immediately translate into changes in their political power (such as voting shares) in the International Monetary Fund (IMF) and the World Bank. She argues that first, "the institutionally dominant states' core *interpretations* of the purposes and functions of multilateral institutions" shape if and how change is likely; second, how states choose to fund the IO and for what purpose affect whether burden sharing will be adjusted when the balance of material power changes; and third, there are institutional rules and conventions that limit what is and is not possible within the IO, including changing member states voting power (Kaya 2015: 7, emphasis added). A social understanding of power is fundamental to this account, given that ideas and values help construct states' interests in establishing multilateral institutions (her first and second explanatory factors), and change is mediated by abiding by norms, rules, and conventions (her third factor).[6]

Ideas are also commensurate with Ben-Arti's (2016) investigation of the role of hegemon(s) in determining whether the MDBs lend for "strategic" or development reasons. In her analysis of hegemon–MDB relations she identifies that the banks' internal norms, routines, and practices are important for determining lending (2016: 42–43). The MDBs, she argues, act strategically by providing loans that can be repaid, which accords with their status and culture as corporate-style banks that lend for profit for their own end but also endorse the political preference of donor member states to ensure their support. This account is underpinned by ideational arguments about the shared understandings between specific donors (which are characterized as regional hegemons) and member state borrowers of the MDBs. In short, borrowers that adhere to donor preferences get better bank loans. Donor preferences are identified in two ways, the affinity measure and polity scores indicating borrowers' ideological commensurability with the United States (as democracies). The affinity measure codes pairs of states in terms of their voting in the United Nations General Assembly (UNGA) (Ben-Artzi 2016: 121). This correlation is used as evidence that states are accorded MDB loans if they are willing to support hegemon(s) in the UNGA (2016: 121).

She shows evidence of a greater link between the United States and Inter-American Development Bank borrowers, while there is a more significant link between Japan and the Asian Development Bank, and Germany and the European Bank for Reconstruction and Development. There is no correlation between the United States and the African Development Bank (2016: 189–192). How and why borrowers have affinity with different donors in the MDBs could be explained through a relational approach to power by examining interactions between states in historical context.[7] Irrespective of the affinity between the United States and recipients, all the banks tend toward lending for "bankable" projects rather than to the neediest of borrowers within their region, which she argues evinces the organizational autonomy and banking culture of the MDBs. Ben-Artzi then assesses whether borrowers' polity scores (democracy) indicate ideological commensurability with the United States, especially during the Cold War. Her findings suggest that there is no strong overall preference of MDB loans going to democratic borrowers, with loans predicated more on their bankability, and thus according with the preferences of the MDBs.[8]

Interests

Beyond these studies there is extensive quantitative research showing alignment between how borrower member states vote in the UN and receiving increases in IMF arrangements and MDB loans. For example, states that vote in accordance with the G7 in the UN General Assembly and with the United States, United Kingdom, and France in the UN Security Council gain greater funding from the IMF, World Bank, Asian Development Bank, and the African Development Bank (Vreeland and Dreher 2014; Dreher and Sturm 2012; Dreher et al. 2009).[9] This raises the question: What constitutes interests? Both power-based and institutionalist accounts focus specifically on interests being equated with survival, competition, and utility maximization. This necessarily limits our understanding of interests, which are as much shaped by general principles of what constitutes accepted practice for states as they are of rationality (the latter is discussed further in what follows).[10] Constructivists have pointed out how states' interests result as much from social appropriateness as evinced by conventions, legitimacy, and public opinion as from presumptions of "logical or objective necessity" (Kratochwil 1982: 19).

Vreeland and Dreher (2014) argue that when materially weaker states sit on the UN Security Council they receive more favorable treatment by the IMF, World Bank, and Asian and African Development Banks.[11] While Vreeland and Dreher (2014) argue that this is an account of a rational trade of power for influence within the Security Council, an increase in aid to elected states is rarely consequential for influencing the outcome of a Security Council resolution (Kratochwil's objective necessity). This is commensurate with a relative approach to power and an interpretivist understanding of states' interests because it is premised on the importance that states place on the UN as a convention. Ideas matter because states recognize the symbolic importance of the UN and its resolutions for collectively legitimating states' actions (Hurd 2007).[12]

Powerful states work through IOs to serve their own interests (see also Andersen et al. 2006; Fleck and Kilby 2006).[13] The correlation between states gaining more favorable MDB loans and aligning their votes with the United States in the UN is predicated on the belief that the United States needs support in the UN to achieve its objectives. The United States' use of the UN could be considered rational in terms of using the UN for material burden-sharing. Dreher et al. (2009: 14) and Lim and Vreeland (2013: 49) do not know whether the increase in recipient aid is linked to rewards or bribes or which state took the initiative to increase aid in exchange for supporting powerful states in the Security Council. A relational approach to power would seek to trace this interaction. Vreeland and Dreher provide empirical evidence of US diplomats viewing such activities from both transactional and relational viewpoints (2014: 25–26).

Scholars also point out that public legitimacy for US interventions decline when the United States uses unilateralism and "coalitions of the willing" rather than working within a Security Council resolution (Vreeland and Dreher 2014). Gaining unanimity in the Security Council is "highly coveted" because elected members are the voice for the rest of the world and doing so bestows a high degree of legitimacy (Lim and Vreeland 2013: 39). The legitimacy of the Security Council is important because it can shape states' understanding of their interests as well as upholding the validity of the UN Security Council compliance system (Hurd 2007).[14] Legitimacy therefore figures prominently in seeking to explain the link between recipient states alignment with powerful states in the Security Council and gaining more favorable conditions in MDB funding (Vreeland and Dreher 2014). US actions in the UN and the MDBs does not make much sense unless we recognize the importance of the social construction of the US-led international order comprising multilateralism, economic liberalism, and the rule of law. Indeed, the United States used its power to construct an international order with a legitimate social purpose (Ruggie 1982). This reinforces the social in conceptions of how and what states seek to achieve, through upholding principles, norms, and rules. It should be unsurprising that the United States uses its material resources as a "globally motivated" donor in the IMF and World Bank to support borrowers with whom it has trade relations and is financially exposed (Stone 2011; Faini and Grilli 2004: 19).

The United States continues to support the MDBs not only to adhere to a common social purpose, but because it serves its national interest. Kratochwil maintains that national interest can only be understood through an interpretivist examination of a state's justifications. This recognizes not just a descriptive account of interests (for example what is "strategic" in any given situation), but one built on "reasons, excuses and justifications actors give for their actions" that are located within broader conventions of acceptable behavior for domestic and international audiences (1982: 27).[15] This holds for Vreeland and Dreher (2014), where desire to have support within the UN Security Council is based on an increase in domestic approval for US actions abroad when backed by a Security Council resolution (see also Thompson 2006).[16] The United States also defends its hold on its veto in the IMF and World Bank in order to maintain domestic support for them (Kaya 2015: 11). Although there is a low level of public understanding of multilateralism generally (Lyon 2016), and of foreign aid (Milner and Tingley 2013), and of the MDBs within the United States (Lavelle 2011), the hegemon nevertheless provides this reason for its decision to maintain its role in the banks.[17] In sum, both power and interests should not be reduced to material resources as power is social and relational in terms of how states seek to achieve their interests in a given historical context, while the national interest is as much based on justifying behavior as it is based on logical necessity.

Although most of the literature on the role of powerful states in the MDBs and the IMF focuses on their influence in IO operations, what makes this influence possible is the shared social purpose and underlying principles of IOs. The literature on powerful states in the MDBs reproduces extensive research on the IMF,[18] which reveals the influence of the United States and to a lesser extent France, Germany, Japan, and the United Kingdom (together constituting the G5) on the size of IMF loans, their conditions, and their enforcement (Stone 2011; Copelovitch 2010). For Copelovitch, the preferences of the G5 shape the IMF's lending decisions: whether they agree or not determine the size and conditionality of IMF loans. When the G5 have less interest in specific borrowers, loan conditions align with the preferences of IMF technocrats. Ideas in turn shape IMF staff preferences: When recipient states economic policy makers share the same neoliberal economic beliefs as the IMF loan conditions are more favorable, conditions less onerous, with less enforcement (Nelson 2014).

For Stone, lead states (hegemons) have structural power, or outside options compared with working within the IO, while operating within it generates externalities for other members (2011: 33).[19] The lead state balances its desire for control over the IO with the need for weak state participation, which gives the IO legitimacy and credibility.[20] Weak states are given formal influence beyond their material power through favorable voting and participation rules. This is offset by powerful states' informal influence that give them "special access to information" that "allows the leading state to override the common policy when its vital interests are affected" (Stone 2011: 33). While the distinction between formal and informal influence is compelling and discussed further later, these are not antithetical to a social and relational understanding of power for three reasons.

First, the relative autonomy of international financial institutions results from the "fundamental agreement of the shareholders on the general *principles* of financial stabilization, market openness, and liberal economic reform" (Stone 2011: 29, emphasis added). As Stone notes, there "must be sufficient agreement about common purposes that weaker states can expect to benefit from cooperation" (2011: 47). Again, this emphasizes how principles and rules bind states to multilateral endeavors. Second, US influence within an IO remains dependent on consensus among the major players toward upholding the IO's principles (2011: 52; Copelovitch 2010). This means that US power is relational to other member states that could challenge the basis for US action if it is not justified in terms of the principles and aims of the IO. Finally, Stone notes that US interventions in the IMF actually benefited recipient states that were unusually vulnerable to financial shocks rather than powerful creditors (2011: 209; Pop-Eleches 2009).[21] Thus, US interventions seek to ensure the maintenance of the international economic system to which major states adhere (constituting Ruggie's legitimate social purpose).

Not only do states project a social purpose for IOs but also they use conventions to justify their behavior within them. Scholars have found evidence that the United States has informal influence on MDB lending patterns. They show that borrowers' alignment with the United States in the UN General Assembly affects the speed of World Bank project disbursements (Kilby 2013), with disbursements of World Bank structural adjustment loans less conditional on recipients' macroeconomic performance (Kilby 2009).[22] That a donor such as the United States wants support for its position in the UNGA again points to the value it places on its position being considered legitimate in IOs. UNGA resolutions are nonbinding on members, but voting is viewed as an important means for the United States to gauge other states values (Thacker 1999: 53). As Kilby points out, UNGA votes are not close, and the United States often loses, but still rewards those that vote with it on important decisions.[23] This is evidence of US vote-buying, Kilby suggests, "if the US values support regardless of the outcome" (2013: 437).[24] More recently, Carter and Stone (2015) argue that the

United States tends to buy General Assembly votes of democratic states using bilateral aid because it is more popular in Congress than to give aid to authoritarian ones. Again, popular justification and legitimacy are vital to understanding what constitutes the United States' national interest.

Rationality

States act in accordance with their interests, which are as much determined by "logical necessity" as following conventions and providing acceptable reasoning and justifications for their actions. This is not necessarily based on rationality. Although more recent studies relax the rationality assumption (Ben-Artzi 2016; Kaya 2015; Johnson 2014), the quantitative literature discussed here presumes that it is optimally rational for powerful states to give more favorable loans to their allies through the MDBs to achieve its interests in the UN rather than (or in addition to) more direct means. For most IO scholars, the need to use IOs to bribe or reward allies for aligning with powerful states to achieve their "strategic" interests is obvious: states launder their dirty interests through legitimate, credible, relatively independent IOs (Abbott and Snidal 1998). Yet, the laundering argument only makes sense in examining the interactions of actors in historical context. It seems perfectly rational to work within a web of IOs to achieve states' national interest given the existing US-led international order comprising a plethora of multilateral institutions. While this speaks to actors operating strategically within a social framework (Hurd 2007; Johnston 2001), it also supports the role of ideas and values shaping actors' interests through the process of public legitimation (Kratochwil 1982).[25]

How the MDBs matter to the United States therefore goes beyond a purely rational cost-benefit analysis. Stephen Krasner (1981) argued that it was questionable whether the United States gained as much out of the MDBs as it has invested. Multilateralism, after all, dilutes states' ability to achieve their aims owing to the number of actors with divergent preferences in negotiations (Hawkins et al. 2006). Krasner surmised that the United States accepted the costs of maintaining MDB operations to support its Cold War interests.[26] This was articulated by the US government at the time, which "concluded unequivocally that the World Bank and other multilateral development banks had been effective instruments of US objectives" (Gwin 1994: 84; cf. McKeown 2009: 280). In this way, the Cold War rivalry was sustained through the beliefs and practices of actors that in turn constituted the norms and rules of the international system (Koslowski and Kratochwil 1994). The United States believed that it benefited from the banks in meeting its Cold War objectives (McKeown 2009) while believing in the desirability of the outcomes of MDB operations.[27]

The United States remains willing to support the banks, including advancing ideas that depart from the MDBs' traditional economic operations. A social understanding of power sheds light on how the United States advances new ideas in the MDBs. This is built on three components: first, the United States and other donor member states seek to instill specific principles and values in the multilateral development lending process as norms change. Over time donor member states have advocated new ideas including private sector financing, environmental and social safeguards, good governance, gender, poverty reduction, human rights, transparency, and accountability (Pasha 2000: 160). Donors "are more apt to get involved in with the banks' lending policies and priorities" (Culpeper 1997: 12). Second, to advance these new ideas in development lending, the donor states need to come to common agreement as to the values they want the banks to ascribe to in their lending practices. Often described as leading to "mission creep" (Einhorn 2001) or "antinomic delegation" (Gutner 2005a), the addition of these ideas points to member states coming to common agreement on the MDB boards (McKeown 2009: 280). Finally, donors can use their material resources to do so. Recognizably, "the largest shareholders within Part I (the members of the G7) typically launch new policy initiatives at the World Bank, the developing country members rarely do so" (Culpeper 1997: 29).[28] As chapter 3 details, ideas and values were pivotal to the US advocation of the accountability as justice norm during interactions with member states and the banks over their inefficiency and ineffectiveness, and with activists over their harm.

Three Strategies for Change

How the United States advances new ideas within the banks is inextricably linked to its position as the preeminent shareholder. While the early constructivist literature focused on when ideas matter absent material power, the asymmetry in material resources infuses almost all aspects of international relations. Indeed, scholars recognize that ideational and material factors are often used to induce others to take on new ways of thinking and acting (Risse et al. 1999). Norm entrepreneurs attempt to persuade others that following the norm is the right thing to do, while providing external inducements such as financial incentives to change actors' behavior and/or identity and create formal rules to bind actors to follow norms (Schimmelfennig 2000). The US position within the banks is detailed here before examining the ideational and material strategies the United States promotes to change the banks.

The MDBs provide development assistance for economic growth and cooperation through project and program loans to member states. Over time the MDBs' sectoral lending allocation has converged (Babb 2009: 137–143). The MDBs operate in the technical environment of multilateral development lending but are directed by cooperation among member states (Weber 1994: 37). Member states confer authority and therefore obligations on the MDBs because of member states' financial and political support (Grant and Keohane 2005). They establish the banks' articles of agreements, which determine the organizations' mandate, structure, and function (Woods and Narlikar 2001: 573). Member states are the governors of the banks, and are represented by states' ministers of finance or treasury. The governors meet only once or twice annually, delegating to their representatives on the MDBs' board of executive directors to oversee bank operations. The boards review MDB operations year-round. Projects and programs are presented to the bank's board for approval by management under the leadership of the bank president, who oversees the banks' daily operations. Beyond member state capital subscriptions, all the MDBs raise additional capital through interest and loan repayments and buying and selling on international capital markets. Both their decision-making structures and their ability to raise capital make them relatively autonomous IOs with discretion over enacting member states' demands.

Financially member states provide "paid-in" capital and "callable" subscriptions, with the latter held in reserve to cover lending risks (Mistry 1995: 5, 17).[29] Subscriptions were originally linked to states' "relative standing in the world economy" at the time the banks were founded and in the case of the World Bank were linked to states' quotas in the IMF.[30] Additionally, the regional banks allocated shares according to states' economic weight in their region and ensured a minimum subscription for regional members (Mistry 1995: 26–28). Membership dues determine states' voting shares in the banks, creating weighted voting systems (discussed later).[31] Over time the banks need injections of capital to offset their lending activities. This is done through member states' increasing their paid-in subscriptions through periodic general capital increases (GCIs), detailed further in what follows.

The structural similarity of the MDBs enables the United States to use the same strategies to influence the banks.[32] The MDBs are "a common family and share family traits" (Babb 2009: 23). The World Bank is the oldest of the MDBs, and the regional banks were modeled on it, adopting their "procedures and terms of lending" (Mistry 1995: 6).[33] As development banks, all of the MDBs have standard loans, designated as "hard loans" or ordinary capital resources (OCR), which are offered to borrowing member states at near market interest rates for extended loan periods (Culpeper 1997: 8, 32). All the banks except the European Bank for Reconstruction and Development also have "soft-loan" facilities, which provide subsidized loans and grants to borrowers that have difficulty accessing private capital markets, that is, the poorest member states (Tables 2.2, 2.3).[34]

Table 2.2 The Multilateral Development Banks and Their Concessional Loan Facilities.

Multilateral Development Bank, date founded	Concessional Loan Facilities, date founded
World Bank (International Bank for Reconstruction and Development, 1944)	International Development Association (IDA, 1960)
World Bank Group (International Finance Corporation, IFC 1956 and Multilateral Investment Guarantee Agency, MIGA 1988)	None, although as part of the World Bank Group, IFC and MIGA have overlapping shareholders with the IDA*
Asian Development Bank (ADB, 1966)	Asian Development Fund (ADF, 1973; wound up in January 2017)
African Development Bank (AfDB, 1964)	African Development Fund (AfDF, 1973)
Inter-American Development Bank (IDB, 1959)	Fund for Special Operations (FSO, 1959)
European Bank for Reconstruction and Development (EBRD, 1991)	None

*In 2007 IFC used its profits to provide funding for IDA-15 replenishment (Lowery 2013). IFC has now provided over $2.2 billion in funding for IDA through replenishments, while IDA has created new private sector financing vehicles for recipients (IFC n.d.).

The United States was able to advance the accountability as justice norm for the banks using three overlapping ideational and material strategies: the power of the purse, vote, and voice. The three strategies are invoked to garner support for the norm and their use highlights the dependence of the banks on member states for material resources, for approving decisions, and legitimizing their operations (Chorev 2012). The literature on the World Bank identified three strategies the United States used to achieve its aims: its "power of the purse," its "voice and vote," and the "spread of American culture" (Krasner 1981; Woods 2003). The latter refers to how the United States shaped the World Bank's organizational culture to respond to its aims (Ascher 1992). Scholars claimed that the World Bank's location in Washington, DC, with many US staff, and staff trained by US universities, shaped how it undertook its operations (Stern and Ferreira 1997; Kilby 2013). However, the first stage of research for this study, conducted between 2009 and 2012 and including 52 interviews at the MDBs and reviewing primary documents on creating the accountability mechanisms, revealed no indication that this shaped the World Bank or any other MDB's position on the accountability as justice norm. Indeed, all of the banks responded negatively to the norm despite having divergent locations, with only the World Bank/Group

Table 2.3 MDB Commitments and Disbursements 1998–2018.

Financial Year	World Bank Group							African Development Bank Group**				Asian Development Bank Group**						Inter-American Development Bank**						EBRD	
	IBRD		IDA		IFC*		MIGA	AfDB		ADF		ADB		ADF***		Other Grants		IDB		FSO		Other Funds		EBRD	
	Commitments	Disbursements	Commitments	Disbursements	Commitments	Disbursements	Gross issuance	Commitments	Disbursements	Commitments	Disbursements	Commitments	Disbursements	Commitments	Disbursements	Commitments	Disbursements	Commitments	Disbursements	Commitments	Disbursements	Commitments	Disbursements	Commitments	Disbursements
2018	23002	17389	24010	14383	11629	11149	5251	7128.0	4166.8	1513.5	1889.1	14108	12064	5,205	2121	6	2	14250	11,304	0	0	506	178	10937.0	8248.3
2017	22611	17861	19513	12718	11854	10355	4842	6411.7	5291.2	1366.4	2425.3	16707	9034	2267	2407	2	2	13003	10250	0	0	347	329	11625.3	7426.0
2016	29729	22532	16171	13191	11117	9953	4258	8516.8	4385.9	1704.5	1945.8	13964	9990	3071	2490	9	9	10803	9600	247	190	275	162	9908.3	8185.2
2015	23528	19012	18966	12905	10539	9264	2828	6261.0	2325.5	1811.6	1937.7	12731	9790	2869	2551	7	7	10404	9719	282	310	388	182	10183.6	7018.2
2014	18604	18761	22239	13432	9967	8904	3155	4638.1	2874.3	1938.8	1760.7	10334	7558	3091	2629	0	9	12652	9423	300	301	677	238	10713.0	7843.9
2013	15249	16030	16298	11228	11008	9971	2781	2820.8	2294.3	3179.9	2621.4	10192	6151	3850	2551	7	6	13290	10558	251	322	270	143	11709.4	8155.8
2012	20582	19777	14753	11061	15462	7981	2657	3197.0	3393.8	2725.1	1797.6	9400	6800	2300	1300			10799	6882	320	317	60	50	11761.9	7911.6
2011	26737	21897	16269	10282	12186	6715	2099	5664.3	2869.1	2529.6	1990.7	9100	6300	2000	1400			10400	7902	181	368	90	0	11741.9	8691.9
2010	44197	28855	14550	11460	12664	6793	1464	3975.0	2063.0	2072.9	1795.4	9249.7	5944.384	3179.76	1928.904			12136	10341	297	398	31	34	11954.0	7961.4
2009	32911	18565	14041	9219	10547	5640	1400	8785.4	3687.7	3232.8	2706.5	11019.88	7897.728	2210.31	2547.577			15278	11424	228	414	1	13	11266.4	7882.6
2008	13468	10490	11235	9160	11399	7539	2100	2783.3	1120.6	2510.3	1732.7	8704.71	6472	1789.56	2852			11085	7149	138	415	3	44	7098.7	6959.5
2007	12828.8	11055	11866.9	8579	8220	5841	1400	2639.1	1398.1	2183.5	1145.7	8212.75	5234	1892.84	2291			8812	6725	152	393	6	6	8177.7	5987.2

Year																									
2006	14135	11883	95056.2	8910	6703	4428	1300	1572.7	825.1	2323.7	1030.8	6116.9	4420	1279.39	1868			5774	6088	605	398	2	3	6466.5	5014.9
2005	13610.8	9722	8696.2	8950	5373	3456	1200	1241.6	850.9	2032.0	987.7	4421.23	4421	1375.58	2527			6738	4899	410	424	0	5	5092.1	2723.7
2004	11045.4	10109	9034.6	6936	4753	3152	1100	2359.9	978.8	1953.5	1056.8	4051.4	3997	1242.04	1242	196.6	104	5468	3768	552	463	0	1	5550.6	5009.1
2003	11230.7	11921	7282.5	7035	3856	2959	1400	1108.3	969.3	1482.9	546.9	4725.66	4706	1379.15	1379	176.5	454	6232	8416	578	486	0	0	4687.3	2645.4
2002	11451.8	11256	8067.6	6612	3092	4006	1200	1452.0	679.4	1306.1	741.0	4042.78	4008	1632.97	1650	179	178	4143	5522	406	313	0	2	4088.1	2464.0
2001	10487	11784	6764	5576	2732	3742	2000	1238.9	613.2	1733.4	463.5	3977.4	3977	1361.6	1362	146.4	146	7411	6037	443	422	0	0	3254.2	2180.7
2000	10919	13332	4358	6023	2337	3505	1600	1098.7	548.0	1472.4	366.2	4257.9	4060	1592.48	1592	171.99	172	4969	6683	297	386	0	0	2509.4	1361.3
1999	22182	18215	6813	5177	2842	6505	1310	1088.9	723.8	681.9	506.0	4000	3908	1000	1070	173	172	9061	7947	417	430	8	10	2177.1	1409.8
1998	21086	19200	7508	5600	2699	3412	830	940.5	625.1	810.5	623.0	4900	4995	987.1	987	163.2	148	9364	6085	686	535	13	15	2785.7	2406.5

*IFC figures are for its own accounts only.

** Data provided is approvals *** From 2017 concessional lending was delivered through the ADB, not the ADF. However, the 2017 figures in this table include concessional lending in the ADF for comparability. The ADF did not provide grants prior to 2005.

and the Inter-American Development Bank being situated in Washington, DC. Although the United States often has a de facto right to high-level managerial positions in the MDBs, in terms of overall staffing levels, the United States is outnumbered at the Asian, African, and Inter-American Development Banks. As a result, this strategy of US influence was then dropped from the analysis.

From 2013 the research focused on evidence that the United States uses its "power of the purse" and "voice and vote" to advocate for accountability as justice. Scholars identified the use of its "voice and vote" as a means through which the United States furthers its objectives (Woods 2003: 96; Krasner 1981; this is akin to informal versus formal influence see below, Stone 2011). The "voice and vote" strategy was parsed out to identify when the United States used its vote in favor of the accountability mechanisms and when it used its voice to promote the norm, because the United States did not always use them together. The studies fundamentally describe two separate ways through which the United States promotes new ideas: through articulating and conveying ideas to other shareholders and bank management and through formal voting. The United States may exert informal influence to shape policies and projects before they even get to the board for a vote, although the United States still needs to garner support to have them endorsed. A relational rather than relative approach to power is important, because the United States frequently does not get its way in formal voting in the MDBs, despite its material power (Strand and Zappile 2015). Each strategy is discussed next.

Power of the Purse

The United States can advance norms in the banks through using its financial clout. The United States can link new ideas to negotiations for replenishing the banks' "paid-in" capital as well as its voluntary funding of the banks' concessional financing facilities (Lavelle 2011: 21). Financially, the banks are underpinned by member states' capital. To gain the support of US capital markets, initial assessments of MDB financial soundness were rated on US contributions (Gwin 1994: 56–57). Scholars argue that the banks institutionalized US power early on because of this dependence on US resources (Woods 2003: 100). This excluded the African Development Bank because it had no input from the United States until 1982; it was a "borrower's bank" not linked to US capital or voting power (Gardiner and Pickett 1984: 29). The United States later became its second-largest shareholder after a major donor-driven restructure in the 1990s (Culpeper 1997: 16, 30). It also excludes the European Bank for Reconstruction and Development, which was established much later and with greater parity in US and European donor subscriptions. As discussed previously, the United

States and other member states have reduced their subscriptions over time, which has increased the autonomy of the banks. The MDBs now rely on a build-up of reserves from interest and loan repayments and capital market earnings to maintain their capital base (Woods 2003: 100). As a result, the MDBs are no longer as dependent on member states' capital contributions although it remains the organizational basis of the banks (Humphrey 2016).

The United States' shares give it "donor leverage" (Babb 2009: 109) in two ways: First, subscriptions are translated into voting power, with the United States garnering a greater share of the vote. This directly links the banks' resource reliance on member states to member states' voting power for approving MDB policies and operations (Chorev 2012). Second, the United States' predominant shares provide it with "go it alone power" (Gruber 2001).[35] The United States has the power to threaten to withhold funds or even walk away, which is enough to keep the banks in check (Babb 2009: 37).[36] The United States frequently withholds MDB contributions. Since 1972 the United States has chosen to provide only partial funds requested annually by the banks (Lavelle 2011: 16). Today it continues to have "a significant amount of unmet commitments at the MDBs" (US Treasury 2016: 9).[37]

Financial contributions are evidence of US influence because it can use negotiations for increasing the banks' capital resources through GCIs, to demand changes to the MDBs. GCI negotiations determine the amount of funding shareholders will commit to the banks to maintain or expand their lending operations. They vary in frequency across the banks (see Babb 2009: 41).[38] Evidence abounds of the United States using its financial contributions through GCI to direct the MDBs. Both the Inter-American Development Bank in the 1980s and the African Development Bank in the 1990s needed to increase their capital to remain viable; in exchange for an increase in US capital subscriptions the United States demanded organization-wide restructures (Culpeper 1997: 30). As chapter 3 documents, the United States used its contributions to demand accountability as justice in the Asian, African, and Inter-American Development Banks, as well as the World Bank Group.

A second aspect of MDB financial structures would become increasingly important for US influence in the 1990s: soft-loan financing. The United States and other donors began to indicate their policy preferences to the MDBs through soft-loan facility replenishments. The banks are not wholly dependent on member state subscriptions for their "hard" loans (OCR) because the banks borrow on international capital markets and can draw on interest and loan repayments from their borrowers. However, there are also subsidized "soft" or concessional loan windows that the banks use to provide grants and loans to low-income borrowers. Excepting recent changes to the International Development Association (IDA), these are entirely dependent on member state subscriptions.

The United States and other donors increasingly took advantage of the need to replenish these funds to demand changes.

The United States used the threat of withholding or reducing soft-loan funding to advance its interests, and it is here that US influence becomes readily apparent. In the 1970s the United States negotiated the fifth replenishment of the World Bank's IDA (known as IDA-5) to ensure that if the United States could not meet its IDA commitments, a pro rata provision would also give other donors the right to reduce their contributions (Woods 2003: 101). In other words, US contributions could signal other donors' commitments too. This would become the basis for future replenishments for IDA as well as for all the other MDB soft-loan windows (Mistry 1995: 95, fn 9). Therefore, the United States could wield a greater degree of influence over soft-loan fund negotiations by threatening or actually withholding its contributions, thus increasing MDB dependence on the United States (Gwin 1994: 60).[39]

In the 1990s the United States had the largest voluntary contribution in the World Bank's IDA, and it still retains a veto in the Inter-American Development Bank's Fund for Special Operations (FSO), the only fund where this is possible.[40] The FSO requires a two-thirds majority of the vote for decision-making in this concessional fund, which "provided an institutionalised vehicle of US national interest in the form of a veto over soft loans" (DeWitt 1977: 24). As the dominant contributor to the FSO, the United States has been able to introduce policies opposed by borrower member countries (BMCs; see Dell 1972: 41). Although Japan has lent vastly more in the Asian Development Fund, both Japan and the United States are the largest equal voting powers in the Asian Development Bank and Japan tends to vote in accordance with the United States.[41] Within the African Development Fund the United States is the second-largest donor after Japan (AfDF 2014). For both the African and the Inter-American Development Banks, resources generated by the soft-loan facilities have been used to cover MDB costs, thus providing another means through which the United States can direct these banks with its capital (Mistry 1995: 106–108; Wodie 1984: 94).[42]

US influence through the soft-loan windows cannot be overstated:

> The point has often been made, especially by MDB Executive Directors from developing countries which are usually not represented in MDF [multilateral development fund] Deputies Meetings, that a group of donor government officials who only represent a part of the ownership of any MDB, and who have no constitutional standing or formally legitimate role in the governance of the MDBs, have now usurped the roles of both the Board of Governors (as a whole) and the Board of Executive Directors (as a whole).

Negotiations for replenishing the funds now determine the "direction and content of MDB operational, financial and even internal administrative policies" (Mistry 1995: 118). The use of soft-loan facilities as a means of influencing the MDBs is pronounced in the IDA, which Ascher describes as the "most graphic symbol of the [World] Bank's dependence on member states, particularly the United States" (1992: 125). The United States has demanded changes to the International Development Association as well as pushing for broader World Bank policy changes unrelated to IDA through its replenishments (Babb 2009: 41; Lavelle 2011: 179); a process it enacted in the Asian Development Fund also (Wihtol 1988: 19, 24, 44). Chapters 3 and 4 demonstrate how soft financing negotiations would be used by the United States to advocate for the accountability as justice norm for the World Bank through IDA-10 negotiations, World Bank Group through IDA-11 replenishment round,[43] for the second time for the African Development Bank through the African Development Fund VII negotiations, and to modify the Asian Development Bank's accountability mechanism via Asian Development Fund VII replenishments.

In sum, US power of the purse is evident in the extent to which negotiations for GCIs and soft fund replenishments may determine MDB policy. Donor leverage allowed the United States to threaten the World Bank to establish an accountability mechanism (Woods 2006: 29), while providing strong incentives to the World Bank Group, African, Asian, and Inter-American Development Banks such that they followed suit. This was not the case for the European Bank for Reconstruction and Development, where there is greater capital subscription parity between the United States and European donors, and where there is no soft financing facility. In this case, the United States used its voice. For this reason, ideational strategies are just as important as material ones for how the United States spread the accountability as justice norm across the MDBs.

Vote

The United States can signal its preferences through its vote, but the ability of the United States to use its material resources are mediated by the banks' voting rules (Kaya 2015) and its relations with other shareholders. A relational approach to power is important for explaining how the United States interacts with other shareholders to achieve its aims. As the banks have overlapping member states and are dominated by the G7 (see Table 2.1), the United States can advance non-economic ideas across the banks with their collective agreement (such as environmental and social safeguards or accountability), which are seen as a hassle factor by less powerful borrowers (Humphrey 2016). This is so even though both the African and Inter-American Development Banks were "demand driven" banks originally dominated by borrowers (Culpeper 1997).

Within the banks, US use of material resources is constrained in three ways. First, soft-loan contributions do not count toward a member state's voting share, which means that "economic dominance as represented in contributions does not directly translate into political power exercised through voting" (Mingst 1990: 153). Second, voting rules mean that the United States can only single-handedly determine the outcome of "supermajority" voting decisions that require 85 percent of the vote, such as changes to membership, subscriptions, or the banks' articles of agreement in the World Bank, World Bank Group, and Inter-American Development Bank. The United States needs to vote in coalitions to realize its preferences in the African, Asian, and European Banks for supermajority votes on these issues.[44] Voting in coalitions is also required to determine lending levels, loan allocations, and bank policy that merely require simple majority voting and where the United States can be outvoted (Gwin 1994: 56). This is important because the majority of shareholders in the banks are borrowers not creditors. Therefore, "the number of votes held by a member is not always a reliable indicator of its ability to affect outcomes" (Strand 2003: 117).

Third, decision-making in the MDBs is generally by consensus. There is a norm of voting in favor of projects that come to the World Bank's board (Kaja and Werker 2012: 180). This does not mean that the weighted votes of member states are not important because voting tallies are often undertaken behind the scenes, and everyone knows which way the United States will vote (Woods 2003: 111). Gaining consensus is important across all the MDBs, with implications for how the United States seeks to introduce new ideas. Although the United States often proposes new initiatives within the banks (Kapur 2002: 64), these may be opposed by member states and bank management (Upton 2000: 65). Often the US position is on a "take it or leave it basis" (Upton 2000: 2), which may explain why the United States is not always able to achieve its interests. In other words, the United States needs support to achieve its objectives (Lavelle 2011: 99).

Capital subscriptions determine voting shares as well as how members are represented on the banks' boards of directors. Large voting states like the United States can appoint their own executive directors. Across the banks, smaller-weighted shareholders share a director in mixed constituencies (Woods and Lombardi 2006). Although constituencies vary on how they determine their representation, the weighted system marginalizes states that have too few shares to hold the director position. In 2015 the World Bank agreed to elect all executive directors rather than base it on subscriptions, but this has not affected the United States' grip on an executive director position (Kaya 2015). In the African Development Bank, the United States with its own executive director—it is the *only* member of this bank to have its own director, and the 1990s restructure increased its shares and voting power (Mingst 1990: 33; Shaw 1991: 546).[45] Although US influence is weaker in the African Development Bank compared to the other MDBs, the influence of other nonregional donors is even worse once one takes into account mixed constituency voting, which dilutes the votes of donors such as Germany, France, and Canada (Strand 2001: 216–217, 208).

Excepting the African Bank, the United States does have a substantial voting power in the MDBs and has a veto, or veto coalition capacity, for major changes. A distinction here must be made between US voting on project/program loans compared with bank policy, where the latter has ramifications for how the banks operate. The United States votes for projects and programs for "less developed countries trending toward greater democracy, [with] better human rights records, and openness to trade, favoring some of its longer term political and economic interests and arguably aligning with the mandates of the MDBs" (Strand and Zappile 2015: 234). While there is overwhelming evidence of US informal influence ensuring that loans are more favorable for borrowers supporting the United States in the UN, a formal US vote for an MDB project is not decisive for whether it is approved.[46] Between 2004 and 2011, 64 percent of projects were approved across the MDBs without US support (Strand and Zappile 2015: 227). This could be because these projects do not affect the US interests (Fleck and Kilby 2011; Anderson et al. 2006). Or it may be as a result of the United States opposing projects because the US Congress stipulates via domestic legislation to US executive directors to oppose loans on specific policy grounds (Gwin 1994: 18). The US government only provides justification for 15 percent of no and abstention votes based on US legislation (see Strand and Zappile 2015: 228), which means that further research is required to ascertain what drives the United States to oppose MDB project loans.

However, a member state's vote merely indicates a "preference-free measure of power" (Strand 2001: 208). For example, borrowing members of the Inter-American Development Bank can oppose the United States on lending and even sometimes on policy as they have over 50 percent of the voting share (Babb 2009: 28). Yet the United States has influence in formal voting in this bank if one takes coalition voting into account (Strand 2003: 20). This holds for the other MDBs also. Within the Asian Development Bank, the United States can indicate its preferences with Japan as the joint largest shareholder. As Japan has rarely challenged the United States on the ADB's policy direction, this has created an effective veto coalition (Wan 2001). Meanwhile, the United States has the largest share in the European Bank, but its voting share is below that required to give it a veto thus requiring it to garner agreement with other donors. This also allows the United States to effect a "blocking majority" in relation to most majority voting decisions if voting with another large donor (Bronstone 1999: 27). In contrast, the African Development Bank's financial turmoil in the 1990s forced major reforms, which allowed greater US voting shares, but not enough to give it a veto (Babb 2009: 31). The African Development Bank has a greater voting spread regarding its weightings: the United States has held generally held approximately 5–6 percent of the vote compared with Nigeria (10–13 percent), Japan (4–5 percent), and Germany, France, and Canada (3–4 percent). Even with the United States as the second-largest contributor, the relatively equal subscriptions among member states have muted US control over this bank, especially where coalitions among member states shift per issue based on regional versus nonregional status; geographical subregions in Africa; and linguistic and ethnic differences (Mingst 1990: 15–16, 157).[47] In sum, voting coalitions can give the United States "much greater control over outcomes than voting weights alone indicate" (Strand 2003: 20).

However, US voting in the MDBs is mixed. During the Cold War the United States was able to block some MDB projects, suggesting the United States was supported in its efforts.[48] Yet, US attempts to block World Bank loans because of human rights violations and Indian nuclear testing during the Cold War failed owing to their approval by the rest of the World Bank's board (Brown 1992: 25). In the 1970s attempts to link Inter-American Development Bank replenishments to specific policies including opposing the expropriation of US property and earmarking FSO funds also failed (Sanford 1982: 131).[49] Over time, many of the prescriptions pushed by special interest groups in the United States have failed to influence MDBs because they were seen to only advance their own interests (Lavelle 2011).

This has led critics to argue that the United States should not use its voting too openly because it uses up its multilateral "credit" (Tussie 1995: 31). Scholars have argued that the United States "needs the cooperation of the other countries if it is to make its influence felt" (Sanford 1982: 17). In order to do that the United States needs to "marshall support for its views to be decisive" on the MDB boards. During the late 1970s and again in the mid-1980s the United States made working with the other donors in the G7 a deliberate strategy to achieve its objectives (Gwin 1994: 56, 60). However, engagement with other member states over MDB policies through bilateral relations, the G7, and the US executive directors' networks "waxes and wanes according to the personal inclinations of key officials" (Upton 2000: 51, 85).

Not only does the United States need to build consensus in order to have its views taken up on the MDB boards but also the idea being floated must be seen to be legitimate. Ultimately Upton argues that if the United States wants something badly enough it will get it if it frames it the right way (2000: 68). This includes framing an issue in "economic technical language which is the normal parlance of the multilateral banks rather than when they use[d] more political terminology" (Mingst 1990: 168). This reinforces the relational understanding of US power: the "US has more influence within the World Bank than any other member state but that influence goes a lot further when it is used for a purpose which other members consider to be a legitimate concern for the Bank" (Brown 1992: 239). For example, the United States has been a strong proponent of advocating for human rights in the MDBs but has not been able to achieve change (Wilson 1987). This is in part because it used unilateral measures such as US legislation to determine the US executive director's vote on projects irrespective of other member states. It is also based on the appropriateness of making noneconomic demands, like human rights, of the MDBs, which are "apolitical" technocratic IOs (Darrow 2003). The United States was successful in building consensus on the need for providing recourse to people negatively affected by World Bank projects because it emerged in the context of improving the efficiency and efficacy of the banks, arguments other member states could view as legitimate. How ideas are taken up is therefore important for reconstituting what is appropriate practice for the banks (Finnemore and Sikkink 1998: 891).

The discussion of voting within the banks demonstrates that power is not just relative but relational and social. To advance new ideas they must be seen to be legitimate by other donors and agreed by consensus among all directors. This means that states must garner agreement to establish new norms. Researchers also highlight the importance of relations among member states and management on the board. They argue that states representing their constituency as directors on the World Bank and Inter-American Development Bank boards also receive larger and faster loan disbursements (Kaja and Werker 2010; Bland and Kilby 2015). Material explanations are ruled out on the basis that the relative voting share of the executive directors does not influence the increase in the loans they receive. Kaja and Werker attribute this to the "boardroom norms and informal rules and the relationship between board members and World Bank staff" (2010: 196). Understanding power as social and relational also helps understand how the United States also uses its voice to advance new ideas throughout the MDBs.

Voice

Sources of US influence "are multiple and sometimes subtle" (Upton 2000: 68). Advancing ideas, interests, and preferences through interactions with bank staff, management, and member states is linked to voting but separate from it. Scholars argue that US informal influence can "cast a long shadow," which may be hard to measure (Strand and Zappile 2015: 227). Voice incorporates formal processes such as US congressional legislation that restricts how the US executive director can vote, and informal channels through which the United States can articulate ideas (Sanford 1982: 16). It includes persuasion or when the heads of the IOs liaise with "finance ministers, foreign affairs ministries, and congressional leadership" above and beyond the level of the director (Lavelle 2011: 36). Daily interactions are possible with the World Bank, World Bank Group, and the Inter-American Development Bank, as they are all located in Washington, DC. It also includes how the United States undertakes detailed oversight of all the MDBs that goes beyond the activities of the other member states (Lavelle 2011). Informal discussions between powerful member states and MDB management on projects and policies proceeding board deliberations characterize all the MDBs, with the United States as a prominent player. Stone argues that this rests on the United States' structural power (in the IMF, which corresponds to the banks), which gives it "organizational advantages: superior information, better access to key agents, and greater cooperation with its requests" (2011: 13). However, this underplays US agency in actively seeking this information rather than relying on its predominant position.[50]

Research indicates that MDB management strives to reach a consensus among powerful members in order to gain agreement for a project before it goes to the board.[51] Woods argued that US informal processes mean that staff ensure that contentious projects gain US approval before they even get to the World Bank's board (2003: 107; Babb 2009: 40).[52] The United States could delay or have projects withdrawn or redrafted that it opposes from going to the Inter-American Development Bank's board for approval (Tussie 1995: 31). However, a US "yes" vote is not a requirement for projects to be approved in the MDBs (Strand and Zappile 2015). Scholars are unclear as to the relationship between formal US votes and informal influence or voice (Hernandez 2013; Bland and Kilby 2015). As previously discussed, there is a correlation between US influence via UN General Assembly voting alignment and the size and speed of loans being dispersed. This suggests that large shareholders like the United States exert informal influence over MDB lending patterns. Both decisions over the size of the loan tend to occur prior to a board vote, while the speed of disbursement occurs after. This means that voice is just as important as formal voting for understanding US influence in the banks.

Voice is important here because it matters for shaping the policy direction of the banks. In the World Bank this means that policy decisions are "often worked out between the United States and management before they ever get to the board, or among board members before they ever get to a vote" (Gwin 1994: 56). As a result, "management seeks approval only for policies or other decisions on which Part 1 [donor] support is known to be forthcoming" (Culpeper 1997: 29). The World Bank will even run a proposal past US Treasury while preparing it for a board meeting if they are unsure of US approval, creating what has been called an "early warning system" (Woods 2003: 107). Significantly, since the McNamara years, "all World Bank presidents have employed former members of Congress as special advisors, as a way of helping them manage congressional demands" (Babb 2009: 69).

Informal meetings prior to board approval also characterize Inter-American Development Bank relations (White 1970: 154). Within the Asian Development Bank, powerful states are consulted in depth prior to any policy or project coming to the board for approval. The United States is also consulted prior to major changes proposed by the European Bank for Reconstruction and Development. However, the United States has less informal means of influencing the African Development Bank (Shaw 1991). As chapters 3 and 4 document, the United States was influential in shaping the accountability mechanisms, reviewing templates before they went to the MDB boards for approval. As with the power of the purse, and vote, the voice of the United States within the banks is important. Having no recourse to its power of the purse, the United States used its voice in the European Bank to advocate for the accountability as justice norm, even though it ultimately chose *not* to vote in favor of the accountability mechanism that management devised in response. In sum, US power is social and relational. It uses ideational and material strategies in the form of its power of the purse, its formal vote, and its voice to establish new norms for the banks. How the banks respond is discussed next.

MDB Responses to Change

The United States' relationship with the World Bank is well known for driving change (Park 2010a; Babb 2009; Lavelle 2011). Yet scholars have noted that the United States has sometimes advanced its own agenda within the MDBs without assessing their ability to undertake it (Upton 2000: 49–50). It is therefore surprising how little has been written on how the MDBs mediate member state demands (for exceptions see Gutner 2002; Ben-Artzi 2016). The MDBs have some degree of autonomy in their actions and discretion over implementing member directives. All the MDB's organizational structures allow management substantial leeway to design programs, projects, and new units within the organization for member state approval; and board procedures can make it difficult for member states to oversee implementation (Lombardi 2008). This can insulate the banks from demands for change (Johnson 2014).

Both constructivism and the principal agent (PA) model recognize that IO's have autonomy that may constrain the ability of member states to achieve their interests. Attention has focused on how member states seek to control IOs including adjusting budgets, changing constitutions, and mandating new procedures that "stack the deck" in their interests (Weaver 2007: 497). The PA model assumes IOs seek to increase their autonomy and maintain or expand their budget and personnel, or their power (Hug 2003: 66). Oversight procedures are a primary means for member states to ensure the IO undertakes the activities to which it has been committed (Nielson and Tierney 2003). Constructivism is seen as a complement to the PA model because it focuses on the rule driven behavior of IOs as shaped by their organizational culture (Barnett and Finnemore 2004).[53] This establishes the rules, principles, and scripts as to how best to implement the mandate of the organization; it is sticky, and change tends to be incremental and path dependent (Weaver 2008). The culture of the organization locates, informs, and shapes its strategic action, including whether to accept or reject new norms (Barnett and Coleman 2005).[54]

The most extensive discussion of MDB change to date has focused on the World Bank, revolving around whether change came from inside or outside the organization and resulted from interests or ideas (Gutner 2005b; Nielson and Tierney 2003, 2005). One World Bank study argued that change was possible if shareholder reforms are "adjacent" to existing norms and fit within the existing culture (Nielson et al. 2006: 110). Member states should instruct management to align clearly identifiable and measurable internal incentive structures to ensure change will eventuate, but their efforts are likely to fail if these run counter to entrenched patterns of staff behavior. This is illuminating in relation to examining the accountability as justice norm. As shown in the next chapter, member states established formal sanctioning procedures to help people hold the banks to account. In doing so, members often delegated responsibility to bank management, raising questions as to the independence of the accountability mechanisms to investigate their own behavior. As the next chapter demonstrates, the MDBs resisted the norm, seeking to undermine the accountability mechanisms. This required the United States to spend considerable effort overseeing whether the accountability mechanisms worked as they were intended.

The rationale for the accountability as justice norm stemmed from the failure to ensure development projects did not contribute to harm (Park 2010a; Sud and Olmstead-Rumsey 2012). This has been attributed to its organizational culture (Weaver 2008; Gutner 2002). All the MDBs share a common culture, which reflects the fact that they are now dominated by development economists and financial experts (Sharma 2013). It is based on "neoliberal economic theory, a technocratic approach to problems, and apolitical norms that shape the way the bank staff collectively think about development" (Nielson et al. 2006: 109). The MDBs banking culture governs staff expectations and practices in implementing their mandate of lending for development projects and programs. It fosters decision-making based on economic modeling and financial prudence, and the banks all follow similar operational procedures in terms of the lending project cycle.

Operations' staff incentive structures influence how much and how fast they lend, which run counter to careful consideration of indicators of negative environmental and social impacts. The need to provide loans to developing states to spur economic growth and alleviate poverty may run counter to the banks technical, economic, financial, and legal criteria (Gutner 2002: 6). As apolitical financial institutions there is a tension between the banks determination of the creditworthiness of the borrower state compared with the project or program's development objectives, and technical, economic, and financial soundness (Ben-Artzi 2016; Gutner 2002). For Gutner (2002) the MDBs may be more bank-like in focusing on borrower needs with fewer internal incentives for staff to link broader MDB policy changes to loans. This is compared with MDBs that are more development oriented that incorporate more policy conditions to loans for borrowers to accord with member state demands (such as environmental and social conditions). Gutner argues that there is a sliding scale within the MDBs banking culture as to their development or financial preferences.

Yet all of the MDBs must grapple with this tension and their difficulty in incorporating environmental and social ideas is part of the reason for the United States' push for the accountability as justice norm across all of the banks. Over time, internal incentive structures have emerged that reward staff for lending volumes rather than supervising project performance including whether it contributes to harm. As Ben-Artzi notes, the

> trap multilateral financial institutions fall into is entirely counterproductive for achieving their goals: from the point of view of the Banks, loans were approved and disbursed after thorough investigation into their worthiness, expected value, and returns. The various country departments also compete for budgets and therefore must disburse their given budget during the year so as not to lose funds for the following year. Therefore, making the loan can sometimes be more important than the loan's substance. (2016: 106)

The lending imperative focuses on ensuring large loans that generate a revenue stream are made to borrowers within the banks' budget cycle (Gutner 2002: 107–108). Larger loans are equated with prestige and career advancement. Even when loan conditions are not being met, staff in the country departments feel pressure to disburse the loan anyway (Easterly 2001: 116). This is combined with a lack of staff incentives and resources allocated to mainstreaming environmental and social ideas (Park 2010a). The desire to get loans out the door is exacerbated by competition between the banks for financing development projects, which may undermine a "needs-based criteria for making loans" (Ben-Artzi 2016: 111–112). There are strong incentives for the MDBs to engage in "strategic lending" or loans that "serve the political and financial standing of the Banks—namely, the guarantee of the repayment of loans and the servicing of political interests of influential donors—rather than lending that follows the Banks stated goals of poverty alleviation" (Ben-Artzi 2016: 15, fn 18). This speaks to the MDBs' banking culture.

The banks have resisted any notion that they should be held directly accountable to the ostensible beneficiaries of development projects rather than to their member states as they are contractually obligated. MDB lending is bound by confidentiality and financial contracts with borrower governments and executing agencies (including companies), not individuals. The banks have been highly secretive in disclosing information (Blanton 2007). Indeed, it was not until the 1990s that increasing demands for transparency and accountability led the World Bank to provide information on its activities (Park 2010a). The other MDBs would follow suit with weaker versions of access to information and information disclosure policies (Humphrey 2016). While efforts have been undertaken to broaden consultation in borrowing states regarding MDB-financed projects, only the banks' articles of agreements and the lending contract between the banks and borrower member states identifies any form of binding obligation and therefore accountability.[55]

The accountability as justice norm is culturally incongruous to the banks, forcing them to be held to account by individuals rather than their member state representatives on the board of directors. World Bank management for example did not see how one poorly designed project like the Narmada dam that forcibly relocated 120,000 thousand people (discussed in chapter 3) should lead to the creation of oversight procedures for all projects which might affect people and ecosystems. Indeed, this challenged the banks' technical expertise and authority as development lenders. The MDBs argued that any additional accountability processes, if necessary, should remain internal and much of the opposition by the banks has focused on their time, effort, and cost that such oversight creates. Degrees of hostility from MDB management and staff denoted throughout the following chapters reveal the extent to which the banks viewed the norm as an unnecessary intrusion into their activities. Management opposition to the norm led to distinct strategies to undermine it, detailed next.

Resistance Strategies

Once member states approved resolutions establishing the accountability mechanisms, the banks were instructed to create them. IOs have a range of strategies that can invoke to ensure their autonomy and protect their culture while addressing member state concerns. The choice of strategy will depend on whether the norm is tied to their dependence on member states as well as the congruity of the norm to their organizational culture (Barnett and Coleman 2005). I argue that the banks resisted the norm because it was considered an unnecessary additional oversight that intruded on their lending practices. The banks could not reject the norm outright owing to their dependence on member states for resources, decision-making, and legitimacy. While dependent on their shareholders, the MDBs did not view their legitimacy or efficacy as linked to the creation of the norm, which meant that they were not interested in acquiescing to US demands (Oliver 1991: 162).

Other strategies were not possible. The banks were unable to alter member state expectations or engage in a strategy of strategic social construction (Barnett and Coleman 2005). This is where IOs seek to reframe the normative environment to fit the organization's aims (Chorev 2012). The debate over establishing the accountability as justice norm followed a decade of US and activist efforts to instill environmental and social concerns within the MDBs (Rich 1994). Given the high-profile activist campaigns of environmental and social harm from bank-financed projects in the 1980s and 1990s, there was little room to reframe the normative environment to better fit the MDBs autonomy and organizational culture. Instead, they fought a rear-guard action to oppose the accountability as justice norm and then to minimize its effects.

The banks challenged the accountability as justice norm in five different ways from passive to more active resistance strategies (Oliver 1991). All the MDBs engaged in compromise, acquiescence, avoidance, and defiance, with evidence of the banks using manipulation in some cases. Each is discussed in turn. First, once the MDBs realized that the accountability as justice norm was consolidating, they engaged in a strategy of *compromise* by seeking to bargain with member states over what the mechanisms would look like (Johnson 2014). The World Bank proposed an own internal oversight procedure that did not allow project-affected people recourse and was answerable to bank management not member states, which the United States rejected. Subsequent MDBs succumbed to US demands but sought concessions that gave greater management control over the accountability mechanisms. Second, *acquiescence* is a passive response to agree to habitual practices. All the banks accepted the inclusion of periodic reviews of the accountability mechanisms. This would enable the accountability mechanisms to be frequently reviewed, one after another, leading to similar improvements in all their structures and operations, thus strengthening the norm over time.

Third, once the resolutions establishing the accountability mechanisms were passed, the MDBs then engaged in a strategy of *avoidance*. This is where the IO is forced to change but is "unwilling or unable to conform because staff believe that to cave into such pressures would harm the organization's identity." This response seeks to protect the IO's identity and autonomy, while maintaining its resource base (Meyer and Rowan 1991: 50). This speaks to the banks' desire for autonomy and to protect their banking culture, compared with shareholder efforts to maintain control over the IO (Ben-Artzi 2016). The avoidance strategy indicates a willingness to change but without actually "attempt[ing] to bring form and function into conformity." Avoidance necessitates the appearance of conformity by IOs "adopting the myths and symbols of the international environment, but they continue business as usual" (Barnett and Coleman 2005: 601).

Norm avoidance is evident in bank management creating accountability mechanisms with a variety of technical exclusion criteria that prevented project-affected people's claims from being "registered" or eligible for assessment. This meant that although they created the very mechanisms shareholders wanted, they set a very high bar for people to be able to access it. Examples include requiring claims to be in English; requiring claimants to detail the exact policies they deem the banks to have breached; requiring that there is no legal claim by any of the parties to the development project subject to a claim; to demonstrate evidence of direct, material harm to affected people; and that the claim is submitted while the project's financing is still being disbursed. Many of these criteria were beyond the capacity of project-affected people to ascertain. Avoidance is further evident because the MDBs sought to conceal their nonconformity to the norm by providing ceremonial information that did not reveal the extent of the bank's practices leading to harm (Meyer and Rowan 1977). This ceremonial "buffering" strategy is an attempt by an IO to resist monitoring through the superficial reporting of its activities (Hawkins and Jacoby 2006: 210–212). Finally, bank avoidance is evident in management failures to adequately respond to findings of MDB noncompliance through the minimal provision of remedies. As documented throughout chapters 4 and 5, avoidance was rife among the banks.

The MDBs also engaged in a third more active strategy of *defiance* by dismissing and challenging the norm. Dismissing institutional rules occurs when the organization perceives enforcement of the rules to be low or when the rules dramatically conflict with the organization's values (Oliver 1991: 156; this is discussed further later). All of the MDBs' management consistently denied claims from affected people as legitimate, even when later found otherwise, and refuted any wrongdoing. In this way the banks sought to uphold the sanctity of lending as usual while challenging the norm as unnecessary. Some of the banks also engaged in challenging the accountability mechanism process. Challenging the rules occurs when the organization attaches less significance to the norm than to their own "insular and elevated vision of what is, or should be, appropriate, rational, or acceptable" (Oliver 1991: 156–157). Bank management would challenge the accountability mechanism process through limiting, preempting, and circumventing investigations; by challenging the scope of the investigations; and by establishing their own remedial management action plans. These alternatives were presented as a better way to address the harm, while eliminating the need for an investigation into their activities.

Finally, some of the MDBs further engage in a strategy of *manipulation* by attempting to influence and control the investigation process within the banks. In some cases, bank management would seek to influence the standards by which they would be evaluated. For example, the World Bank management sought to influence the definition of what constitutes a "project" that could be investigated. Furthermore, some of the banks would seek counter the accountability mechanism findings, based on their interpretations of the banks environmental and social standards. In this way bank management could seek to influence how the board would respond to the accountability mechanisms findings. A more extreme form of manipulation is when the banks seek to control the investigation process, including supporting staff that withheld evidence of wrongdoing in investigations, and staff that sought to persuade affected people not to make claims, as was evident in the World Bank, Asian, and Inter-American Development Banks.

The MDBs' responses are evidence of organizational hypocrisy, where there is a gap between the IO's talk, decisions, and actions (Weaver 2008: 19). Organizational hypocrisy is a necessary feature of IOs because they must respond to competing pressures within their environment, including shareholder demands for "strategic" lending that simultaneously does not have negative environmental and social impacts. Hypocrisy is evident in the MDBs violating their own environmental and social policies triggering harm leading to an accountability mechanism claim, and purportedly acting in accordance with accountability mechanism investigations. Organized hypocrisy is also evident through "mainstreaming gaps" or the failure of management to provide the resources to address ongoing problems until a claim is made (Weaver 2008: 20).

The accountability mechanisms, while ostensibly created to address organizational hypocrisy, were not actually designed to overcome it, and in some ways, reinforced it. Member states did not design the accountability mechanisms to fundamentally restructure the MDBs core lending practices. Rather they were created to provide recourse for project-affected people, meaning that accountability mechanism investigations generally do not stop projects from proceeding. As discussed in the next chapter, this is because the very discussion of how to be accountable to project affected people was delimited by the US relationship to the banks and debates over how to ensure the banks' efficiency and effectiveness. The accountability mechanisms are post hoc avenues for recourse only; they were not given the ability to stop projects, make binding recommendations, or monitor, or enforce the banks' activities. The banks' boards retained control over these activities, and they frequently chose not to invoke them (Naude Fourie 2009).

The frequent failure of the boards to do so may be because of the difficulties in ensuring control over the banks who conceal their activities (Lombardi 2008), or it may stem from an inability to come to consensus among different shareholders over how to address findings of harm. The procedural and the political are interlinked. Member state representatives on the boards change every two years, which affects how coalitions are forged and the stance member states will take on accountability mechanism findings.[56] This is underpinned by the significant amount of information board members must digest prior to meetings, which leads the board to rely heavily on the information provided to them by management. This allows management to insulate the banks from board oversight through the ceremonial provision of information on their practices. Perhaps recognizing this, over time member states on the boards have ceded more power to the accountability mechanisms to enforce the norm.

Foreshadowing the rest of the book, this means that there is little reason to expect the accountability as justice norm could change the banks' lending culture. Accountability as justice provides the means for recourse as a last resort for project affected people in the project cycle. Previously anecdotal evidence suggested that the banks have "panel-proofed" their portfolios, choosing less risky projects to limit accountability mechanism claims (Fox 2000). Research suggests that investigating accountability mechanism claims can have a positive effect on bank practices: lucrative projects that may have high environmental and social impacts are less likely to be funded in the five years after a borrower has faced a claim (Buntaine 2016: 140). As discussed in chapter 5, specific high-profile cases have triggered revisions to bank policy, with limited changes to improving MDB procedures. Overall, these changes do not budge the banks' organizational culture, which focuses on volume lent rather than the costs for project beneficiaries and their environment.

What does this mean for arguing that the banks have institutionalized the norm? Given the norm emerged as a corrective to specific instances of MDB actions leading to harm rather than as a means of changing all lending practices, the norm sits alongside rather than challenging the banks' culture of technocratic, apolitical, high volume lending. The norm is institutionalized within MDB resolutions establishing the accountability mechanisms, and the mechanisms are separate from the operations departments of the banks. As the later chapters demonstrate, the MDB's frequently invoke the accountability mechanisms as learning tools to improve bank lending, even though the accountability mechanisms were not invested with mandates to mainstream justice or given the power to intervene throughout the project cycle. They can only act once a claim is made by people in the project area that harm has been or is likely to occur as a result of the banks' acts or omissions. For the banks, evidence shown throughout the volume suggests that they are engaging with the norm through strategies of compromise, acquiescence, avoidance, defiance, and manipulation. Ultimately this means that the norm is currently enacted in practice (taken as given) by shareholders, the accountability mechanisms, and claimants, but sustained flouting of the norm by bank management could erode the norm over time (Wiener 2009). This recognizes that norms are not immutable structures: they may gain or lose strength according to the degree to which they are adhered to (Park and Vetterlein 2010). Ongoing bank management resistance may undermine the norm. Conversely, shareholders may yet transform the banks culture over time by giving the accountability mechanisms greater monitoring, enforcement powers, and mainstreaming mandates.

Conclusion

This chapter articulated a constructivist approach to understanding how and why the MDBs adopted the accountability as justice norm through theoretically examining the basis for US and bank behavior, and second, to identifying the strategies they undertook in their interactions over the norm. The United States is a norm entrepreneur seeking to generate new ways for the banks to think and act, which is based on understanding power as socially constituted and relational rather than based on rational material calculations. This provides a better means not only to understand how and why the United States uses IOs like the MDBs to advance its interests but also to identify how it constructs its national interest according to conventions, norms, and rules. Understanding power in this way enables us to view the ideational and material strategies the United States used to generate, spread, and defend the norm. Norm entrepreneurs have a range of strategies available to them to induce norm following, including the power of the purse, their voice to generate support among member states, and their vote. Second, I argue that the banks resisted the norm because it impinged on their autonomy and organizational culture. It challenged the banks apolitical technocratic lending culture, which contributes to lending large volumes quickly as evidence of success, while overlooking underperformance including harm.

The chapter outlined the strategies used by the banks to resist the norm: compromise, acquiescence, avoidance, defiance, and manipulation. The banks bargained to modify the design of the accountability mechanisms to limit their independence; passively accepted the need for routine reviews of the mechanisms; engaged in avoidance to seemingly conform to the norm while limiting its use; engaged in defiance by dismissing and challenging the accountability process; and tried to manipulate the norm by interpreting the standards against which they would be evaluated. They even tried to control staff and direct project-affected people not to make claims. Although the banks resist, the norm was designed as a corrective not preemptive justice norm that has become institutionalized as part of the banks' governance structures. While it cannot change behaviors that cause harm, and it does not challenge the banks technical operations and lending culture, it does provide recourse for project-affected people. The next chapter documents how the norm emerged as accountability as justice, and how the MDBs sought to resist it.

3

US Hegemony for What?

From Accountability as Control to Accountability as Justice for the MDBs

The United States is not a bad hegemon, as hegemons go.

—Kapur et al. (1997: 3)

Introduction

Given the relative autonomy and authority of the multilateral development banks (MDBs) in international development financing, it seems surprising that the idea that they should be accountable to their ostensible beneficiaries would become a norm. Yet, within a decade, it had. This chapter identifies how the United States took up the idea in response to activists documenting evidence of MDB-financed projects leading to environmental and social harm. It first examines the US relationship with the MDBs, and its history of using accountability tools to control them. Second, it traces how concerns for improving MDB performance in the 1990s merged with awareness of harm, leading to the invocation of traditional accountability as control tools being used for justice. Couched in terms of improving the banks' efficiency and effectiveness, the idea of providing recourse for project-affected people became acceptable to member states on the MDB boards. The subsequent sections trace how the United States use the power of the purse, its vote, and its voice with each MDB to spread the norm: In domino fashion, the United States threatened the World Bank using soft-loan financing negotiations to demand obedience; used financial carrots during general capital increase (GCI) negotiations for the Inter-American Development Bank (IDB) and the Asian Development Bank (ADB); and offered incentives during general capital increase and soft-loan replenishment negotiations for the World Bank Group and the African Development Bank (AfDB). By 2003, the norm was strong enough that the United States only needed to use its voice at the European Bank for Reconstruction and Development (EBRD). Once the banks realized that member states were intent on establishing the norm, the MDBs sought a compromise over the design of the accountability mechanisms (see Table 3.1)

The Good Hegemon. Susan Park, Oxford University Press. © Oxford University Press 2022.
DOI: 10.1093/oso/9780197626481.003.0003

Table 3.1 The Initial Accountability Mechanisms of the MDBs.

MDB	The Accountability Mechanism
World Bank	Inspection Panel 1994; clarified 1996 and 1999
Inter-American Development Bank	Independent Investigation Mechanism (IIM) 1994–2009
Asian Development Bank	Inspection Function 1995–2002
World Bank Group (IFC/MIGA)	Compliance Advisor/Ombudsman (CAO) 1999
European Bank for Reconstruction and Development	Independent Recourse Mechanism (IRM) 2003–2008
African Development Bank	Independent Review Mechanism (IRM) 2004

to give them greater control. Outside the highly visible campaigns against the World Bank and World Bank Group this strategy succeeded.

The United States in the MDBs

The US relationship with the MDBs is important for understanding how the accountability as justice norm emerged. This is because there are a variety of different institutional structures that could have been devised to provide accountability for people harmed by the banks. The demand came from US Congress in responding to evidence of World Bank harm. The accountability mechanisms look the way they do and not otherwise because the issue of justice was added to the United States' use of "accountability as control" that it had used in relation to the banks since the 1960s. The United States uses accountability as control not only because it invests substantial resources in the banks, but also because of its broader ambivalence about multilateralism (Karns and Mingst 2002: 278). Of course, there are differences within the US government: Congress is known to be more "suspicious of the impact of participation on US sovereignty and autonomy" than the executive (Foot et al. 2003: 9). Since the 1970s the executive or US president has designated exclusive authority to the Treasury department regarding US participation in the international financial institutions (IFIs; Nelson and Weiss 2013). However, the US Congress can direct that participation because it has the power to force international organizations (IOs) to meet its legislative requirements to secure funding (Babb 2009; Lavelle 2011).

Much of the literature on the United States and multilateralism focuses on how Congress constrains the executive and US foreign policy by threatening

IO funding (Karns and Mingst 1990; Patrick and Forman 2002). In this case
Congress used withholding funding to advance an idea. Congressional aims
for reforming the Mdbs began under a "changing of the guard from the Bush
to the Clinton administration" in 1993 (Babb 2009: 192). The push to advance
the norm then continued for the EBRD and AfDB under Republican President
George W. Bush from 2001. There is remarkable consistency within the executive on this issue during this period. Rathbun (2012) argues that the split between (anti) Republicans and (pro) Democrats over multilateralism is based on
a generalized dis/trust. While the push for the accountability as justice norm
did not occur in a period of heightened mistrust over multilateralism, it can
explain why key congressional Democrats seeking to reform the banks worked
with Republicans who aim to reduce MDB funding. Chapter 4 documents how
the US Treasury pressured the banks to adhere to the norm for ten years after
it was demanded by Congress. Bipartisan cooperation to establish the norm
took place irrespective of which party controlled the executive or the legislative branches. By May 1993 congressional members advancing the idea were
operating under Democratic president and House. Even after the Democrats
lost the House and Senate in 1995, the US Congress continued to advance accountability as justice for the MDBs (Babb 2009: 192-193). Under a Republican
president, the US Treasury continued to promote the norm to a Republican
House and a shifting Senate after 2001.[1] Before examining how the US Congress
demanded for accountability as justice, its history of using accountability as
control is detailed.

Accountability as Control

Driven by Congress, the United States has been a strong proponent of
establishing accountability processes such as auditing, monitoring, and evaluation to demand greater MDB obedience and efficiency. Grigorescu argues
that IOs are more like to have accountability processes covering internal audits,
inspections, investigations, and evaluations if they have "large budgets, large financing shares for the most important state, and where decisions are based on
weighted voting (and not on unanimity)" (2010: 872). From the 1950s, the US
Congress has used withholding payments, or the power of the purse, to demand the instantiation of accountability tools to control IOs. It began first in
the UN: "[W]hat had started as a trickle in the early 1950s with efforts to set the
ceiling on US payments unilaterally had by the 1970s become a favorite tool of
legislators seeking to shape American foreign policy choices" (Luck 1999: 238).
Demands for UN reform included substantive foreign policy issues as well as
managerial change to eliminate waste, corruption, and inefficiency. The United

States insisted on improvements to the UN's fiscal oversight, especially internal auditing and reporting. The United States has used "vague charges of the UN's lack of accountability" for not paying its dues, leading to a stalemate with the UN over whether the changes were sufficient to release funds (Karns and Mingst 2002: 290; Luck 1999).

The US use of accountability as control is entrenched in its relations with the MDBs. This is most prominent in the oldest MDBs, the IDB and the World Bank, where it has the largest shares. Despite the banks' interactions with the US Treasury on behalf of the executive, demands for accountability as control (and later justice) originated from Congress, which passes MDB funding. In 1968 the US Congress passed the Selden amendment, which directed the US executive director (US-ED) on the IDB's Board to create a post-project review evaluation unit (Mingst 1990: 141–142). In response, the Bank established a group of controllers for ongoing assessments of how it discharged its duties. This information was then used by the United States to examine the administration and implementation of Bank loans, which led to recommendations "for improving the scope of the audit and reporting standards" of the Bank (Dell 1972: 49). The power of the purse is a big stick the United States uses to control the MDBs. By the early 1970s, the IDB had reached the limits of its borrowing capacity. The US Congress used general capital increase (GCI-3) in 1970 to demand the Bank examine its use of resources and loan effectiveness before to agreeing to finance the fund for special operations (FSO). The US Congress then provided "only for the first-year authorisation of $100 million and made the second and third instalments contingent upon authorisation and appropriations to be considered later" (Dell 1972: 51, 71–74). Despite the IDB's dire financial situation, the US Congress authorized but failed to appropriate the first installment of the GCI-3. This signaled a distinct departure for Congress's relationship with the Bank and revealed the mercy of borrower member countries to the United States despite their majority voting. Further authorization of FSO replenishments were dependent on the IDB providing the United States with annual reports on each of its loans. The World Bank and the ADB were also asked to do so, demonstrating a common approach to accountability as control across the banks.

Demanding more accountability to control the IDB was fundamental to the acrimonious GCI-7 negotiations between 1985 and 1989. On the table was the United States' demand to allow the Bank to disburse program loans in response to the Latin American debt crisis. The United States wanted to change the Articles of Agreement to require 65 percent of the vote for policy change and project approvals, giving the United States a veto if voting in a coalition. The United States also wanted a Bank-wide reorganization in exchange for a $25 billion contribution. The Bank was seen as "moribund" with burdensome operational procedures, with a lack of direction, questionable efficiency, excessive loan delays, overcentralization, and allegations of nepotism (Griffith Jones et al. 1994: 101). The IDB's operational efficiency was called into question as deadlines for project completion were seen to be unrealistic; problems meeting contract conditions were evident prior to releasing funds; and because procurement guidelines were "more cumbersome that for any other MDB" (Tussie 1995: 134–135).

The negotiation revealed how far the United States would go to increase its control over the Bank. Borrowers rejected US demands. At one stage the US Treasury "withdrew from negotiations and cut to zero its budget request for the IDB from the Congress" to press the Bank to use its funds efficiently (Pierson 1987: 1). The negotiations took four years and "almost brought the bank to a standstill" (Tussie 1995: 31–32). The Bank's drastic decline in lending was a direct result of the delay in negotiating the 7th replenishment (Griffith-Jones et al. 1994) and led to the resignation of the president Antonio Ortiz Mena (Babb 2009: 143). A compromise was eventually reached, which allowed donors to delay approving loans if they objected to the proposals coming to the Board (Tussie 1995: 31–32). Some scholars interpreted the United States' demand for greater control over the IDB because of its declining hegemony (Culpeper 1990: 7). Although the US Congress might be more reluctant to lend to the MDBs during times of economic downturn, there is a long-standing focus on using auditing, monitoring, and evaluation processes to increase the banks' obedience and efficiency. Concern for controlling how the IDB uses its funds continued throughout the 1990s, with the United States demanding improvements in the internal evaluation units in GCI-8, which was approved in 1994.[2] As detailed in what follows, in the 1990s Congress also used general capital increases to advance accountability as justice in this Bank as well as the World Bank/Group and the ADB and AfDB.

The US effort to control the World Bank also has a long history. The United States has "persistently tried to strengthen Bank audit and evaluation procedures," with serious attention beginning in Congress in the late 1960s (Kapur et al. 1997: 267). Congress wanted evidence that World Bank projects were having their intended effects. In 1970, the US Congress recommended the US Government Accountability Office (GAO) undertake an audit of the World Bank as part of a bill authorizing funding for the International Development Association (IDA) replenishment round (IDA-3). In response, World Bank President McNamara established the post-project review unit, the Operations Evaluation Department (OED) in 1971 (renamed the Independent Evaluation Group, or IEG, in 2006). In the official history of the World Bank, Kapur et al. highlight how "for several years thereafter the United States urged independence from management of both the audit and evaluation operations" (1997: 267). It succeeded in 1973, when the US Congress proposed legislation requiring the United States to push for an independent evaluation unit in the World Bank. In response, the World Bank separated the OED from the auditing department, giving the OED its own vice president. The United States passed a law requiring the US executive director to "actively seek to establish an independent review and evaluation system under the World Bank's governing body." The United States then prepared auditing and reporting standards to help the World Bank's Board design an independent review system. World Bank President McNamara conceded that the OED report should go to member states on the Board independent from the executive, a process that remains in place today. This improved accountability procedures (Kapur et al. 1997: 269), and the United States continues to be a strong supporter of accountability for control to monitor the Bank's operations (Weaver 2008).

Strong donor support for evaluation led the AfDB to "establish evaluation machinery comparable in structures and purposes to the other Multilateral Development Banks" (Mingst 1990: 143, 150). The World Bank's evaluation procedures were emulated by the AfDB from 1977 and became formalized as an evaluation division in 1980. In the 1970s the US governor to the ADB stated that they had a questioning attitude toward its assistance, with US Congress criticizing the Bank's development efforts (McCawley 2017: 319). To appease Congress, the US executive director at the ADB advocated introducing better monitoring and evaluation systems for its projects (Wihtol 1988: 44). In 1978 the Bank made its postevaluation unit independent from the chief economist, reporting directly to the president (Wilson 1987: 104–105, 301).[3] By the time the EBRD was created in 1991 it was a given that MDBs should have a separate evaluation unit. Like the other banks, the EBRD was structured to have its own vice president of evaluation (Menkveld 1991: 83–84).

The US demand for accountability as control continues. In 2005 the US Congress passed legislation forcing the World Bank US executive director to "raise specific proposals for reform concerning loan oversight, audit functions and internal whistle-blower protections, and to push for the adoption of these new rules" (Weaver 2008: 65). In July 2017 the US House of Representatives Committee on Financial Services passed the World Bank Accountability Act to withhold IDA-18 replenishments. The bill aimed to increase accountability, combat corruption, and strengthen management effectiveness at the World Bank. This resulted from "management failures" that were revealed through an Inspection Panel investigation.[4] This demonstrates an ongoing US commitment to use accountability to control the Banks to ensure obedience and efficiency. The next section examines how the United States went beyond this in the 1990s to demand accountability as justice.

From Accountability as Control to Accountability as Justice

The United States has been essentially reactive to the banks, responding as new issues arise rather than presenting a strategic approach to their operations even when the banks request it (Upton 2000: 45–46). Concern over MDB lending leading to environmental and social harm was first raised by activists who demanded a response from the World Bank's shareholders. Activists took their concerns to key US Congress members who had oversight of US appropriations for the MDBs. In response, US Congressional members would work with NGOs to establish accountability procedures to provide justice for project-affected people (Rich 1994; Caufield 1996). This section sketches how key US Congressional members took up issues of harm resulting from bank operations, which occurred during discussions over improving MDB effectiveness at the board of executive directors. As detailed further in what follows, the United States went beyond standard accountability as control processes to advocate for formal sanctioning procedures for the banks for justice. The United States threatened to withhold IDA funding unless the World Bank created an Inspection Panel; and as subsequent sections will show, it would then use financial incentives for the IDB, ADB, the World Bank Group, and the AfDB to follow.

US congressional members took a principled position that the MDBs should address environmental and social harm. This challenges arguments that congressional members' positions on the banks derive from their economic ideology or voter preferences (Milner and Tingley 2011). Broz (2008) has argued that congressional members vote in favor of funding the MDBs because of their ideology but are also influenced by campaign donations from international banks that support the IFIs, and from having constituents that gain from economic globalization. As Lavelle points out, this does not accurately represent how legislation on the MDBs is made (2011). This is because many constituents are unaware of the impact of their Congress member's vote. Unlike the IMF, there is no direct link between domestic interest groups and support for funding the MDBs.

Indeed, Lavelle argues that congressional members' convictions determine why Congress takes up ideas like accountability. Owing to "the limited engagement of party and nearly non-existent mass geographic constituencies" on issues regarding the World Bank (and even less so for the other MDBs), the "private preference of the legislator influences his or her *choice* of the group to which he or she defers for information, advice and plan of action" (2011: 21). Put another way, rather than being captured by lobby groups "legislators tend to listen to lobbyists who tell them what they want to hear" (2011: 37). In this case, information provided by activists such as Lori Udall, David Hunter, and Bruce Rich to the chairman of the US House of Representatives authorizing committee Barney Frank (Democrat) highlighted how the banks were contributing to harm.

The World Bank's failure to respond to congressional concerns regarding these claims fed congressional views of the banks' lack of obedience and the need for greater US control.

Concerns of justice came to the forefront during debates over how to improve the banks' economic performance. By the mid-1980s the banks' project evaluations were demonstrating considerable deterioration because of the debt crisis and shift to structural adjustment lending (Culpeper 1997: 47). The US Treasury was concerned that the World Bank was an inefficient, overbloated bureaucracy, unable to acknowledge its impacts on the poor (Caufield 1996: 178–180). Member state dissatisfaction fit within a shifting normative environment focused on making IOs democratic, transparent, legitimate, and accountable.[5] This highlights the importance of changing conventions on what constitutes acceptable behaviour for IOs. In the early 1990s, member states requested an examination of all of the MDBs' portfolios through quasi-independent task forces: the Wapenhans report for the World Bank, the Tapoma (Qureshi) report for the IDB, the Shultz report for the ADB, and the Knox report for the AfDB.[6] The outcomes indicated significant weaknesses in the ability of the banks to deliver financially, economically, and developmentally sound projects on time.

According to Mistry (1995: 67–68),

> The major MDB shareholders, when instigated by their domestic political lobbies (such as for example, their environmental lobby or their gender lobby) usually become overenthusiastically exercised about the possible misjudgements that MDBs have made in their lending operations and decisions e.g., in financing dams or in financing unsuccessful adjustment. Shareholders have insisted on setting up elaborate and expensive, if not particularly effective and useful, Operations Evaluation Departments in the MDBs to evaluate these operations/decisions regularly. They have even occasionally insisted on augmenting such on-going internal investigations with periodic "quasi-external" probes of effectiveness (e.g., the Wapenhans Report in the World Bank, the Qureshi report for IDB and the Knox Report for the AfDB).

The portfolio reviews highlighted the "need to end the 'approval culture'" of the banks, and to reorient lending to enhance project quality. The reviews identified that this should be done by focusing on long-term development impacts on borrowers and by examining country-level indicators of development achievement (Culpeper 1997: 64).

For example, in 1991, World Bank President Preston requested an internal review of the Bank's project quality, which was undertaken by a task force on portfolio management led by Bank Vice President Willi Wapenhans. The Wapenhans report (1992) identified that over a third of World Bank projects completed in

1991 were "complete failures as judged by the Bank's own staff" with a "dramatic increase of 150 percent rise in failures over the previous ten years." This resulted in a 50 percent increase in cancellations of loan programs between 1989 and 1991 with staff claiming that 30 percent of projects in their fourth or fifth year of implementation had major problems. The cause of the deteriorating portfolio performance was identified as the Bank's internal procedures: overoptimistic expectations at the time of project approval; a culture of approving loans over realistic project performance; and prioritizing new commitments over continuing projects (Wapenhans 1992: 30–31).[7]

The US Congress increasingly scrutinized the banks' performance. In 1998 the Senate Committee on Foreign Relations under Chairman Jessie Helms (Republican) commissioned a group to examine the need for the IMF and the MDBs given their lending performance while vast private finances were flowing to developing countries (International Financial Institutions Advisory Commission 2000). The World Bank responded by developing a range of monitoring and evaluation tools to investigate project performance including a Quality Assurance Group and a dedicated Quality Assurance Compliance Unit (QACU) (see Park 2010a: 93–104).

Meanwhile, evidence began to mount over the social and environmental devastation of World Bank–funded projects (Fox and Brown 1998; Rich 1994). Campaigns to stop the harm included among others, the Polonoroeste project in Brazil, which aimed to open up the Amazon forest for farming, cattle ranching, and settlement through a roadbuilding and colonization program; and the biggest hydroelectric project in Indian history, the Narmada Sardar Sarovar dam (Wade 1997; Gutner 2002). Transnational advocacy networks challenged the World Bank by publicizing the negative impacts of projects to the international media, and lobbying donor member states to stop them (Park 2010a; Keck and Sikkink 1998). Activists targeted donor shareholders, and the issue was raised in the Japanese, Dutch, Finnish, German, and European Parliaments (Clark et al. 2003: 20, fn 8). Environmental groups lobbied the US Congress to address the negative impact of MDB financing through their role in authorizing and appropriating IDA replenishments (see Park 2010a).

Several congressional subcommittees hold hearings before voting on legislation to replenish IDA funds. Congress must legislate to release funds each year of a three-year replenishment round. These hearings would be a focal point of environmental and human rights campaigns. They convinced Jerry Patterson (Democrat), chairman of the House of Representatives Sub-Committee on International Development Institutions and Finance, to hold special hearings on the negative impacts of MDB funding; as well as Chairman of the House Appropriations Sub-Committee on Foreign Operations David Obey (Democrat); and Chairman of the Senate Appropriations Sub-Committee on Foreign Operations Robert Kasten (Republican) (Nielson and Tierney 2003: 258). In 1984, the House and Senate subcommittees issued a total of nineteen recommendations to the US Treasury and the US executive director of the World Bank for addressing environmental and social concerns. Known as the Patterson recommendations, many of them were passed into law in 1985. Operating under a Republican president, Congress was controlled by the Democrats until 1985. There was bipartisan congressional support for these changes (Rich 1994: 113–125). The next section traces how the US-led accountability as justice norm crystallized as harm resulting from the World Bank's Narmada Sardar Sarovar dam project in India became widely known.

Constituting Accountability as Justice for the World Bank

Accountability as justice for the World Bank began with Narmada.[8] This section details how the United States began to advance the idea of using accountability for justice in three ways: using its power of the purse over IDA replenishment negotiations; its voice through the US executive director on the Bank's board, and Congress's negotiations with Bank management over including justice in accountability templates; and finally, voting to create the Inspection Panel. Narmada was the "singularly defining reason for the necessity for the inspection mechanism within the Bank" which "underscored the Bank's prevailing culture of volume of lending at the expense of project execution" (Umana 1998: 2). The Narmada dam scheme involved two separate World Bank loans to India in 1985 and 1986 (Park 2010a: 72–73). The scheme involved the construction of 30 major dams and 135 medium-size dams and another 3,000 small dams over a 40- to 50-year period. Yet the project became one of the largest civil protests within India since its independence. Local and international NGOs "criticised both the environmental assessment and the resettlement/rehabilitation component of the Narmada projects" (Shihata 1994: 10).

Initially, the Narmada protests drew the attention of the World Bank executive director (ED) for the Netherlands, Paul Arlman, who arranged informal meetings of executive directors on the negative aspects of the project including with a prominent Indian activist Methar Patkar. In 1989 the project would be the subject of a special oversight hearing of the US House Sub-Committee on Natural Resources, Agricultural Research and Environment led by Congressman James Scheuer (Democrat) (Udall 1997: 7, 95). The subsequent Dutch executive director, Eveline Herfkins, along with the World Bank vice president Moeen Quereshi, recommended an independent review to World Bank President Baber Conable to ascertain facts about Narmada (Udall 1997: 8). Conable then commissioned the Bank's first ever independent review of a Bank project in

1991.[9] Led by Bradford Morse, a former US Congressman (Gutner 2002: 30), it was the first time that the World Bank had commissioned an independent project review.

The review was highly critical of the Bank's efforts (Park 2010a), discovering that there was no comprehensive resettlement plan, nor any data, to resettle villagers to be displaced by the project. These concerns had been detailed in earlier World Bank reports (Khagram 2004: 89). Deadlines for India set by the World Bank in 1985, 1988, and two in 1989 to provide resettlement plans were not met. The World Bank asked for partial plans from India in 1990 which were not forthcoming (Park 2010a: 73). In 1990 Japan, a co-financier, withdrew funding from the project. Released on June 18, 1992, the Morse report recommended the Bank review its approach (Morse and Berger 1992). The World Bank responded with a document titled *Narmada: Next Steps* ten weeks after the Morse report. The *Next Steps* document contains a statement by Bank management that "the interests of the Bank would be better served by the establishment of an independent inspection panel" (para 60, Shihata 1994: 8). Yet as Shihata notes, "none of the recommendations and action proposals made in this context mentioned the creation of a permanent inspection body. Attention at this stage was limited to existing internal mechanisms to monitor and control the quality of the Bank's operations which included . . . the possibility of establishing an ad hoc independent commission for this purpose" (1994: 13).

The *Next Steps* report claimed the Indian government was moving toward adherence to World Bank policies and that there was no need to halt the project. Bradford Morse and co-author Thomas Berger conveyed to the executive directors that Bank management had misrepresented the report.[10] In a meeting held by the executive directors on October 23, 1992, the executive directors from the United States, Canada, Japan, Germany, Australia, and Norway called for a suspension of Narmada loan disbursements, but the Board was split between industrial and developing member states (Khagram 2004: 130). The US executive director, Patrick Coady, argued for suspending the loan to India while articulating the need for the creation of a special independent commission to monitor the resettlement and rehabilitation of 120,000 dam oustees.

Coady recommended creating an independent panel,[11] a move backed by the Norwegian executive director.[12] Eveline Herfkins recommended that the Bank establish an independent unit that could arbitrate over controversial matters,[13] which was also supported by the German executive director. Ultimately, the Board voted to give India until April 1, 1993, to meet the terms of the loan. As the US executive director stated, the outcome of Narmada signaled that "no matter how egregious the situation, no matter how flawed the project, no matter how many policies have been violated, and no matter how clear the remedies prescribed, the Bank will go forward on its own terms."[14] Then, on March 31, 1993,

India asked the World Bank to cancel the rest of the Narmada Sardar Sarovar loan, which it would have had to do the next day due to noncompliance (Caufield 1996: 27–8). It was the first time a loan had stopped for environmental and social reasons.

On the day the Morse report was released, activists called for the World Bank to create a permanent "independent appeals commission" echoing the Morse Commission's recommendations that the World Bank should provide recourse to people harmed by the projects it funds (Udall 1997: 6).[15] The Morse report suggested, "[T]here should be a review of Bank procedures to ensure that the full reach of the Bank's policies is being implemented. The Bank should establish whether the problems we have found in the case of the Sardar Sarovar are at issue with projects in India and elsewhere. Our findings on this project may well indicate a need on the part of the Bank to strengthen quality control" (Morse and Berger 1992: 354).

Soon after the Morse report was made public the Wapenhans report was leaked, thus fueling public debates over how to hold the World Bank to account. Since 1990 activists had been circulating templates for mechanisms that would allow people to do just that (Christensen 1990; Wold and Zaelke 1992). The Natural Resources Defense Council (NRDC) promoted an independent adjudicatory panel such as an environmental commission of enquiry for the World Bank that would be authorized to hear complaints from member states, NGOs, or affected parties if the Bank had failed to uphold its environmental policies, or if the borrower had not met its loan conditions. The template they offered for all the MDBs was for an independent panel composed of non-Bank staff empowered to assess whether the loan conditions and Bank policies had been met (Christensen 1990: 1, 5). In early 1992 activists published another draft of a permanent independent review board for the newly created EBRD given the Bank's mandate includes advancing democracy and protecting the environment. According to this template, such a board would enable citizens to "challenge the EBRD-funded projects in their countries" (Wold and Zaelke 1992: 61–64). This drew on a template drawn up by the US Centre for International Environmental Law (CIEL) (Wold and Zaelke 1992). The judicial style template devised by CIEL allowed provisions to ensure public access to information, procedures for filing a claim, and gave power to the board to stop activities by the Bank that breach its own guidelines.

Lori Udall and Bruce Rich from the Environmental Defense Fund (EDF, now Environmental Defense) and David Hunter from CIEL lobbied the US executive, the US executive director, Treasury, and Congress to push for accountability for the World Bank.[16] They advocated for an independent appeals mechanism that reported to the Bank's board after investigating claims from individuals and NGOs (Udall 1997: 6; Shihata 1994: 25).[17] They presented their template to US

Treasury and Congress, the Bank's Board of Executive Directors, and Bank management. Despite Treasury's role in determining the direction of US policies toward the MDBs they did not support the initiative (van Putten 2008: 80).[18] It did however catch the attention of members of the US Congress. Over a three-month period, Lori Udall and David Hunter worked to create a formal appeals mechanism resolution with the Chairman of the US House of Representatives Subcommittee on International Development, Finance, Trade and Monetary Policy of the Committee on Banking, Finance and Urban Affairs, Barney Frank (Democrat) (van Putten 2008: 74). By May 1993 Frank was operating under Democratic President Bill Clinton and a Democratic House. Even after the Democrats lost Congress in 1995, congressional members supported the accountability as justice norm for the MDBs (Babb 2009: 192–193).

Meanwhile the World Bank's member states debated the need for a mechanism to investigate harm. Most borrowing executive directors opposed the idea of opening the Banks up to being held accountable to people harmed, as did mixed constituencies like Australia.[19] The Dutch executive director Eveline Herfkins was one of the strongest champions for an inspection unit for the World Bank, coordinating closely with Professor Bradlow in creating a proposal for such a mechanism. Herfkins's proposal was put forward in February 1993 with three other executive directors from Germany, Chile, and Malaysia.[20] It proposed an "in house evaluation unit that enabled Bank staff to review problem projects" and be responsible to the Board (Shihata 1994: 23).[21] The unit would be composed of between one and three inspectors to investigate complaints instigated by borrowers, the Board, or the unit itself with the capacity to review a random sample of projects.[22] The in-house mechanism advocated by the executive directors was neither independent nor allowed a role for project-affected people (Clark et al. 2003: 8). In reviewing the executive director proposal, Bank management concluded that there was "no apparent need for a permanent inspection unit. It suggested instead that an inspection function be established in the form of an ad hoc inspection capacity. . . . The President would also designate an 'operational ombudsman' through whom 'staff and others' could raise issues for review." Bank management sought a compromise that would give them control over an ad hoc review mechanism (Shihata 1994: 23).

Politics at the Board of Executive Directors was ultimately shaped by US congressional pressure.[23] As a result of the United States using its power of the purse, the proposal for an Inspection Function not only progressed but was modified to become accountability as justice in the form the United States propounded: being responsive to those affected by the Bank's operations and independent of management. The US Congress created a credible threat by linking the final year of IDA-10 replenishments to the establishment and operation of an accountability mechanism to provide recourse for project-affected people (Bowles and Kormos

1999: 220). Although the need for an accountability mechanism had been proposed by four executive directors earlier, "US approval of IDA funding and a proposed inspection panel became intertwined."[24]

Negotiations for the tenth replenishment covering IDA funds for July 1993–June 1996 (IDA-10) had concluded in December 1992. However, the amount that the US Treasury agreed to contribute had to be passed into law by US Congress for the money to be appropriated, as with all soft-loan replenishments to the MDBs (Lavelle 2011: 24). IDA replenishments require annual appropriations by US Congress in a three-year replenishment round and go through the normal congressional process. However, there is dispersed authority within Congress over matters pertaining to the MDBs which makes it complicated.[25] The House of Representatives and the Senate both have authorizing committees that consider IFI legislation, the former for Financial Services, the latter for Foreign Relations. Next, the IDA funds are included in the Foreign Operations Appropriations Bill that authorizes the expenditure. Appropriations bills "are 'must pass' legislation that originate in the House." Both the House and the Senate have appropriations committees for Foreign Operations that evaluate contributions to the MDBs. All four House and Senate committees follow the IFIs carefully including consulting with Bank staff, tracking IDA negotiations, and holding hearings to ascertain the main activities of the Banks.[26] Appropriations bills attract riders that attempt to change policy beyond approving financing where "appropriators can insert policy changes into bills that have a greater chance of passage because the bill must be passed." This is how Congress sought to demand accountability as justice for the World Bank.

Congress held hearings on appropriating funds for IDA-10. On May 5, 1993, activists testified to the US House of Representatives before the Subcommittee on International Development, Finance, Trade, and Monetary Policy of the Committee on Banking, Finance, and Urban Affairs, Chaired by Congressman Frank.[27] Frank opened the session by asking whether the United States should authorize the IDA replenishment. At the hearing NGOs advocated for an independent appeals commission for the Bank that would investigate complaints in developing countries from member states, NGOs, and individuals (Shihata 1994: 20).[28] This would be a three-person panel appointed by the World Bank's Board empowered to investigate claims in developing countries from individuals and NGOs regarding any violation of "World Bank policies, procedures, loan and credit agreements, World Bank Articles of Agreements and By-Laws, and international human rights and environmental law." Moreover, it would have the capacity to modify, suspend, or cancel a World Bank financed project (Shihata 1994: 20).[29] An alternative was also floated: Professor Daniel Bradlow at American University testified on the need for an ombudsman reportable to the Bank's Board.[30]

The Subcommittee under Chairman Frank made it clear that the United States would not allow IDA funds to be authorized unless the Bank established such an accountability mechanism.[31] Chairman Frank was deeply committed to alleviating poverty and wanted the MDBs to work effectively (Interview with US House of Representatives staffer, September 26, 2013). The Subcommittee drafted the International Development and Debt Relief Act on May 26, which linked US funding for IDA to establishing an inspection panel and disclosing information. Circulated internally, the draft would authorize the first two years of the three-year replenishment funds for IDA-10 with the third year's funding dependent on establishing an appeals mechanism.[32] The possibility of withholding the third year of funding was objected to by the Bank, but legal advice upheld Frank's capacity to do so (Lavelle 2011: 126–127).

The draft specifically advocated that the Bank establish an appeals commission that would be: appointed by the Board for fixed, staggered terms; staffed by people that had not worked for the IFIs for the previous decade; independent from Bank management with a separate budget; authorized to investigate complaints and make recommendations to the Board of Executive Directors "with respect to violations of the policies, procedures, and loan agreements of the Bank"; able to make its recommendations public and have access to Bank files; be open to people and organizations affected by Bank projects and activities. Lastly, the draft advocated giving the Board the power to vote on implementing the recommendations made by the mechanism.[33]

Ibrahim Shihata, the World Bank's General Legal Counsel at the time, noted

the formulation of these conditions for IDA 10 did not at the time progress beyond a house of representatives committee draft, and they eventually entered the US Appropriations legislation in October 1993 in a substantially modified form. However, the discussion gave a clear indication of an emerging trend in the US Congress to favour strongly the establishment of a commission or panel of inspectors in the World Bank and in other international financial institutions. This obviously influenced the US Administration in the Bank's Board discussions before the adoption of the Panel Resolution in September 1993. (Shihata 1994: 21)

Babb argues that the creation of the World Bank Inspection Panel was not linked to IDA replenishments. This argument may be based on two facts. First, the demand for an inspection panel did not come from US Treasury (2009: 192). This means that it was not therefore part of the negotiations for IDA funding among the IDA's member state representatives. Second, Babb may be arguing that there is no link between the Inspection Panel's creation and IDA funding because Congress did not cut IDA funding. Indeed, a legislative bill to drastically *cut* IDA-10 funds did not pass a Congressional vote. On June 17, 1993, Congressman John Kasich (Republican) sponsored an amendment (H. AMDT 115 to HR2295) to the International Financial Institutions Act to cut $55 million from the US capital contribution. The vote failed by six votes (Broz 2008: 353) in part because Congressman Frank argued that cutting funding would lose US leverage over the Bank.[34]

Instead, Congressman Frank's "main tactic was to *stall* the authorisation of the United States' $3.7 billion contribution until the Bank had concrete, adequate, written proposals on both [transparency and accountability] reforms" (van Putten 2008: 79; emphasis added). Congressman Frank advocated withholding the third installment of IDA-10 funding to coerce the Bank to establish an appeals mechanism. To be sure, "a great deal of congressional influence over IFIs derives from the institution's ability to threaten, refuse or fail to legislate" (Lavelle 2011: 29). As a result, the power of the purse was fundamental to the establishment of the World Bank's accountability mechanism.[35] Indeed, "[H]igh level Bank officials who worried that Frank would stall the funds indefinitely went directly to Capitol Hill to lobby Frank and others, often bypassing the US Treasury, the agency that normally lobbies the US Congress for US contributions to the Bank" (Udall 1997: 13). World Bank President Preston was being advised at the time by a former US congressman, Matthew McHugh, who purportedly stated that Congress "couldn't order us to do anything" to which Congressman Frank replied: "I agree, and you can't order me to pass the bill with the money" (cited in Lavelle 2011: 126).[36]

Senator Patrick Leahy (Democrat), Chairman of the Senate Foreign Relations Appropriations Subcommittee and Congressman David Obey (Democrat), Chairman of the House Foreign Relations Appropriations Subcommittee both backed Congressman Frank's initiative to hold the Bank to account for its actions. Leahy made it clear in a letter to World Bank President Preston that deficiencies at the Bank revealed by Narmada show the "lack of a formal mechanism for investigating and adjudicating public grievances about Bank-financed projects." He went on to argue that "serious consideration should be given to establishing a permanent independent commission for investigating public concerns about Bank-financed projects." Leahy would recommend the structure of such a commission as independent, accessible by the public and with its outcomes publicly available, be impartial and responsible to the Board of Executive Directors, and to make findings and recommendations on projects that they could investigate from their inception.[37] After much deliberation, the Senate Appropriations Subcommittee approved IDA funding in the Foreign Operations Appropriations Bill but shaved US funding to IDA by $200 million and to the International Bank for Reconstruction and Development (IBRD) by $15 million.[38]

Only then did Ibrahim Shihata, the World Bank's general legal counsel, begin working on the accountability mechanism proposal.[39] On June 10, 1993, Bank management released a draft paper presenting the executive directors' February proposal and an alternative management proposed for Board deliberation. This "options" paper stated, "an operations inspection function is appropriate and should be established immediately."[40] It was circulated on the same day that the US House of Representatives authorizing committee met to mark up the bill for IDA funding.[41] The Bank management option paper attempted to compromise on the accountability as justice idea by curtailing the new inspection mechanism. It advocated a three-person in-house inspection panel reporting to both the board and the Bank president. The panelists could be former Bank staff and would be appointed by the Board on the recommendation of the president.[42] It demonstrated that Bank management was seeking a compromise in order to gain control over the accountability function. It was also ready to support the ombudsman proposal that Professor Bradlow had presented to the Board of Executive Directors as an interim measure. Either way, management favored an in-house mechanism responsible to the president or located within preexisting departments (Shihata 1994: 25).[43] An updated Bank management proposal dated August 6, 1993, reiterated the need for an internal inspection unit but would give Bank staff the opportunity to make comments to the Board before the unit's recommendations were implemented (Bosshard et al. 1993: 11; Shihata 1994: 33). Many executive directors shared management's concerns with opening the Bank up to complaints against borrower activities as well as frivolous claims that would tie up the inspection panel. While some executive directors remained skeptical of creating an accountability mechanism it was by then agreed that such a body should be created.[44]

The inspection panel discussion broke down according to Part I (donor) versus Part II (borrower) lines. With the United Kingdom and Germany supporting the United States, it became clear that donors were in favor of creating such a mechanism. Owing to the weighted voting system, borrowers knew there was not much point voting against it and that it would be better to get consensus. According to former World Bank staff, "that's how things work" (Interview with former World Bank staff, October 10, 2013). In the discussion, one executive director made it clear that the proposal was "very much built on one shareholder's view [the United States] on what was needed to gain political support for IDA-10." This was reiterated by another executive director who added that the final result "had to be something that everyone was comfortable with." Another borrower executive director pointed out that they were only willing to go along with it because it had widespread support; they would not have supported it if it was only a minority position no matter how powerful they [the United States] were and no matter the consequences of IDA funding.[45]

The August 6 proposal was leaked to NGOs, which then met with the Bank's Board of Executive Directors to argue that the proposal was ineffective. There would then be some back and forth with one or two rounds of negotiations on the proposal among the executive directors, between the Board and management, and US Congress.[46] Tellingly, "[D]rafts of the Bank's revised information policy and a resolution creating an independent 'inspection function' were also sent directly to Rep. Frank's subcommittee for comments before they were presented formally to the Board" (Udall 1997: 13). The discussions would take some of the ideas from Bradlow's ombudsman idea and the principles of the independent appeals commission template to produce a single proposal. The combined proposal produced favored an independent permanent panel empowered to investigate complaints from the public. The independent appeals commission would be open to claims from individuals, NGOs, executive directors, and member states; it would be transparent; it would be granted full access to Bank files; and its findings and recommendations would be implemented by all Bank operational staff unless opposed by two-thirds of the Bank's executive directors (Bosshard et al. 1993: 5).

The importance of the US voice is revealing in how the Inspection Panel was finally approved by shareholders. While some executive directors feared the implications of creating a precedent in international law enabling IOs to be held to account by people, in the end it did not become a big debate because US Congress was pushing for it,[47] and ultimately the majority of what the United States wanted was accepted. The United States was able to play a "critical leadership role in the process and managed to induce consensus" (Fox 2000: 288). The Australian executive director stated, "[T]he Board was virtually unanimous in wanting it to come into existence."[48] The text was revised and resubmitted in a memo from the president to the Board on September 10 (Shihata 1994: 34). After two intense days of Board deliberation, on September 22, 1993, the Board adopted the resolution establishing the Inspection Panel (resolution number 93–10 IBRD, and resolution number 93–6 IDA).

US efforts to delay funding for IDA pending changes agreed to by the World Bank had succeeded. Yet the US Congress did not immediately authorize the full three years of IDA funding, which was dependent on ensuring the accountability mechanism's actual implementation (Clark et al. 2003: 9). On November 22, 1993, the US Congress announced that the Committee did not authorize the third annual contribution because the

resolutions [on information disclosure and the Inspections Panel] adopted by the World Bank are ambiguous in significant respects, and the way in which they will be implemented is not clear. The Committee intends to closely monitor the experience with the two reform measures and, if it finds the experience to be satisfactory, expects to recommend authorization of the third year of the replenishment. . . . As regards the Inspection Panel, the Committee believes that it is important to have a permanent independent review pane—building on the experience with the "Morse Commission"—to deal with complaints filed by both outsiders and executive directors about violations of World Bank policies, procedures, and loan agreements. . . . However, the Committee is extremely concerned that, under the resolution adopted by the World Bank, the panel might not have sufficient independence.[49]

Therefore, "the authorising lever would remain in place to ensure that the panels would be an effective accountability mechanism" (Lavelle 2011: 126).

In sum, the US Congress was critical to establishing the World Bank's accountability mechanism (Clark et al. 2003: 7; Kapur 2002: 72). Fox argues that "the Inspection Panel's creation was made possible by leverage politics based on conjunctural domestic state-society coalitions within the United States" (2000: 289). US efforts were crucial to holding the Bank directly accountable to people in addition to evaluating Bank compliance with its own policies and procedures (Udall 1997). This is evidence of accountability as justice being added to accountability as control processes. US House Subcommittee hearings on the World Bank's efforts were again held on June 21, 1994, when NGOs would again testify on the new Inspection Panel's processes with the aim of strengthening them. Indeed, Congress stated that its support was dependent on the Bank implementing new reforms (Udall 1997: 14). Congress authorized the final year of IDA-10 replenishment toward the end of 1994.[50]

The idea of justice was central to the design of the Inspection Panel rather than the creation of an in-house compliance mechanism to improve the Bank's project performance. The Bank was the first IO to "combin[e] the possibility of access of individuals and private groups to rights under international law, with the opportunity to question the activities of international organizations" (Bissell 1997: 741, Former Inspection Panel Member). It enabled communities to have their grievances heard by IOs (Clark et al. 2003; Umana 1998; Shihata 1994). In doing so, it redefined "paradigms for accountability and reform in international financial institutions" (Umana 1998: 2).

The Inspection Panel comprises three members appointed by the executive directors, after nomination by the Bank president. The Panel is independent from Bank management and has the capacity to investigate claims by affected parties (more than one individual) in the territory of the borrower. A claim can only be made if requestors have been inadequately dealt with by Bank management. The World Bank president may also trigger a claim. The panel investigates whether people have been or are likely to be affected "by an act or omission of the Bank as a result of a failure of the Bank to follow its operational policies and procedures regarding the design, appraisal, and/or implementation of a bank financed project where the failure has had or threatens to have a material adverse effect" (The World Bank Inspection Panel Resolution number 93–10 IBRD).

While chapter 4 discusses the structure and revision of the accountability mechanisms, of specific note is the design of the Inspection Panel as investigative (Grigorescu 2008: 289). In other words, the aim of the Inspection Panel is to provide recourse for harm (justice) from World Bank financed projects, while it investigates noncompliance to improve the effectiveness of the World Bank's projects (control). Although people trigger the process through making a grievance claim, the Panel uses traditional accountability tools to investigate Bank (non)compliance with its own policies, giving more power to member states to sanction the Bank. The remainder of this chapter documents how the United States used the same material and ideational strategies to spread the norm across the MDBs, and how the Banks compromised by pushing for a greater role for management in the process. Outside the World Bank Group, this weakened the accountability mechanisms' independence and ability to enact the norm.

Accountability as Justice for the Inter-American Development Bank

Immediately after the World Bank created its Inspection Panel the IDB formulated its Independent Investigation Mechanism (IIM). The United States again used three strategies to advance the norm: using the power of the purse through a general capital increase, using its voice on the Board and with management, and its vote to bring the accountability mechanism into existence. This took place within broader discussions over the Bank's economic performance, with the US push for justice building on its efforts to improve the IDB's operational efficiency and effectiveness. While the United States demanded the Bank establish an accountability mechanism, borrowers have greater weight on the Board. Although they agreed to establish the norm, there were concerns over what this might mean; they therefore favored Bank management's compromise strategy that gave them both greater control over the accountability mechanism.

Filho and Rios (2007) offer four reasons why the IIM was established: first, because agencies realized there was a need to examine criticism of their projects, although they do not give evidence of this. Second, because the G7 stated accountability was needed to uphold the credibility of lending institutions, although the G7 made this statement seven years after the creation of the IIM. Third, because there is increasing civil society activism and the IFIs would want to avoid negative publicity that could derail project operations. And fourth, because the World Bank has one, and "others felt that they should also do so in order not to be left behind and to avoid criticism" (Filho and Rios 2007: 26). Unlike the World Bank there was no immediate problem project campaign demonstrating harm with a strong activist campaign. While NGOs advocated for increased IDB accountability, Washington-based NGOs tend to defer to regional NGOs and "[C]onfrontations over projects with adverse social or environmental impacts have been less frequent and have had little impact at the IDB" compared with the World Bank (Nelson 2000: 411, 422). Filho and Rios's fourth point resonates only in the sense that the US Congress specifically highlighted the need for all the MDBs to establish a mechanism if they wanted Congress to approve their funding.

The United States signaled its position on the need for the IDB to create an accountability mechanism through the legislative process of appropriating concessional fund replenishments for the MDBs. In 1993 Congressman Frank's House of Representatives Appropriations Subcommittee stated that it "expects the regional multilateral banks, in the near future, to institute reforms with regard to disclosure of information and an independent review process similar to the reforms the committee is advocating for the World Bank."[51] Congress did not explicitly withhold funding for the other MDBs as they had with the World Bank over the Inspection Panel.[52] Nonetheless, Congressman Frank had a reform agenda and Treasury looked to where it could find success. According to former US Treasury staff, reforming the banks usually began with the World Bank's IDA before pressuring the other MDBs for policy change using its power of the purse. The United States would try to convince other member states to go along with its agenda. In reforming MDB policy reform, change is easier to initiate through the soft-financing replenishments than the ordinary capital resources but "what usually happens in the soft loans, happens for the hard loans" (Interview with former US Treasury staff, November 4, 2013).

Unlike the other banks, the IDB's ordinary capital resources and its soft-loan window, the FSO, are both part of the same organization. Ultimately this means that the FSO is replenished during general capital increases, which occur approximately every four years. General capital increases for the Bank have been described as "protracted and encompassing exercises" (Tussie 1995: 5). As discussed previously, despite being the largest contributor to IDB's ordinary capital resources and having the largest vote in the Bank, borrower member countries (BMCs) can outvote the United States except on issues requiring a supermajority. The BMCs also influence how the Bank's loans are allocated. Indeed, some argue that borrowers openly shop for loans in the IDB which they cannot do in the World Bank (Interview with accountability activist, August 20, 2013). This differs from the FSO, where the United States is the majority contributor and where it maintains a veto. This means that the United States can dictate how

FSO funds are spent but cannot with regard to the Bank's ordinary lending operations, thus limiting its control over the use of resources.

Nonetheless, the United States can control the timing of the general capital increases (Tussie 1995: 18). As the dominant, nonborrower shareholder, the United States "charts the direction of the Bank" (Interview with IDB executive director, October 17, 2013). Through the general capital increase the United States has been able to direct the policy agenda of the IDB, using its power of the purse to press for changes. This has been particularly effective during periods when the Bank has been desperate for capital, for example during financial crises in the early 1970s, during the mid-1980s debt crisis, and again during the 2008 global financial crisis. This provides the United States with considerable clout. While the United States "tries to consult and build consensus" (Interview with IDB executive director, October 17, 2013), the power imbalance can lead to policy gridlock with borrowers who collectively can oppose the United States. Stalemates have occurred in the past, as detailed earlier in relation to GCI-7 (Griffith Jones et al. 1994; Mingst 1990: 156).

Decision-making therefore takes place consensually among the Bank's Board of Governors regarding its policy direction, but where the majority borrowers are dependent on US funds.[53] The United States can take a strong policy stand via the Board of Governors but the Bank's Board of Executive Directors vote on projects according to their interests, which may override the United States in practice (Interviews with IDB staff and executive directors, August to October 2013). Nelson argues that "the IDB typically adopts new mandates and modalities by negotiating a regional agreement" after the World Bank has established a policy. This leads to a policy in the IDB that has "greater assent and ownership by the borrowing governments" (2000: 405). In comparison with the IDB, Nelson propounds that the World Bank's Inspection Panel is a "stronger institution on paper but encounter[s] strong resistance in practice" (2000: 406). As chapter 5 shows, however, Bank management was able to compromise with the United States and borrowers to design an accountability mechanism over which they had greater control compared with the World Bank Inspection Panel. This led to a mechanism that was weak on paper and resisted in practice.

The United States policy agenda was forced on the IDB (Interview with US House of Representatives staffer, September 26, 2013). The decision to increase accountability was one of the policy aims agreed on during the negotiations for the GCI-8. In the prelude to GCI-8 completed in 1994, the Bank president established a task force on portfolio management (the Tapoma report). Led by Moeen Qureshi, a former vice president of the World Bank, the six-person task force discovered that the problems the Bank faced were "to do with the culture and the environment of the Bank, its policies and procedures" (IDB1993: 1). The 1993 report identified the bureaucratic nature of the Bank's project cycle, which hampered portfolio management. It identified excessive layers of supervision: that there was no single department held responsible for the loan, nor a single loan interlocutor with borrowers. This meant that there was no single department accountable for a project (IDB 1993: 26). The report recommended a Bank restructure to take its recommendations into account (IDB 1993: 13–15). Unlike the Wapenhans report, Tapoma did not include an historical evaluation of Bank projects and therefore "was not able to document a decline in quality of the IDB's loan portfolio." The inadequate and duplicate operations monitoring systems in the Bank were revised in 1992 (Tussie 1995: 92–93). In 1999 the operations evaluation unit was restructured again as the Office of Evaluation and Oversight (OVE, Filho and Rios 2007: 52).

The IDB accepted $700 million in new money in exchange for accepting the US policy agenda. The then-largest general capital increase in the Bank's history, shareholders agreed to a $40 billion replenishment as well as a $1 billion increase in the FSO (IDB 1994: 10). Despite opposition from large borrowers such as Argentina and Brazil over introducing an accountability mechanism (Interview with accountability expert, October 21, 2013), the Board of Governors agreed to GCI-8 in April 1994 at the Bank's annual meeting in Guadalajara, Mexico. The aims of the GCI-8 included "that the Bank should lend directly to the private sector and increase transparency and accountability in Bank operations" (IDB 1994: 11; Nelson 2000: 424).[54] The United States used the incentive of vital resources as its negotiating strategy to further accountability as justice within the Bank.

The IIM was created under pressure from the United States during negotiations for the IDB's eighth replenishment (Nelson 2000: 424). The United States advocated strongly for an independent review mechanism to be adopted that would be analogous to the World Bank.[55] In response, the Board of Governors "asserted the desirability of further increasing transparency, accountability and effectiveness of the Bank's performance of its operations."[56] To this effect they directed the Bank's management to draft a proposal for an accountability mechanism. The Board deliberated over the proposal on March 28, 1994. The United States was backed by the Europeans in demanding an accountability mechanism while Borrowers wanted financing. According to one source, Borrowers did not know too much about what this meant; they thought accountability was "a principle that would not be applied too much" (Interview with former IDB staff, October 8, 2013).

In April, US Congressman Frank stated, "I am pleased to hear that the Inter-American Development Bank is moving in those two directions [an independent review mechanism as well as information disclosure]. Because while, as I said, it is not within our purview legally to condition anything on anything, facts are facts. . . . We do want to make it clear that, from our standpoint, it is very, very helpful for the Bank [IDB], for the regional multilateral banks, not simply to institute these policies but, in fact, to make sure that they are administered with the appropriate spirit. That is going to be a continuing concern of this subcommittee."[57]

On August 10, 1994, the Board of Executive Directors approved the introduction of an IIM to "investigate allegations by affected parties that the Bank failed to follow its own established operational policies" (McGill 2001: 194).[58] The proposal states that the "introduction of an Independent Investigation Mechanism would provide a 'safety net' to those groups of persons in the borrowing/recipient member countries who might be affected by Bank supported operations."[59] In 1995 US Treasury reported to Congress that there was considerable policy success in the replenishment with the agreement incorporating the creation of the independent Inspection Function.[60] US Congressional oversight aimed to keep pressure on the banks to follow through with their accountability mechanisms, while US Treasury pushed the banks to accept the norm.

It is clear that IDB management did not support the accountability mechanism (Interview with former IDB staff, October 22, 2013). The IIM has "substantially less independence and authority than the World Bank's independent Inspection Panel" (Nelson 2000: 420). Drafted by the Bank's Legal Department, the accountability mechanism was composed of a roster of ten investigators nominated by the president and confirmed by the executive directors, compared with the World Bank's permanent mechanism. The roster was designed "[P]artly for reasons of cost-saving, and partly for the purpose of assuring the continued independence and objectivity of the review panels" (Miller 2001: 210).[61] Claims went directly to the president of the Bank. The Board of Executive Directors then determined whether an inquiry was warranted before three investigators from the roster could analyze the claim. The findings of the investigation would then be submitted to the executive directors and the president, along with a response from Bank management. Based on the panel report and management's riposte, the Board had authority to determine whether corrective action should be undertaken.

In designing the IIM in this way, the hope for an "authoritative appeals panel has been almost completely frustrated at the IDB, where the independent investigation mechanism was granted virtually no independence from management" (Nelson 2000: 424). Nelson argues the design was the result of the power of borrowers to shape the Bank's decisions owing to the consensus decision-making (2000: 425). Despite determining that the investigation report and management's response would be made public (IDB 1994: 19), the mechanism "suffers from 'obscurity and a lack of independence from IDB control'" (CIEL, quoted in Nelson 2000: 424). In sum, the IDB was forced to establish its mechanism as part of a raft of policy changes determined by its largest shareholder in exchange for its then largest ever capital increase during GCI-8 (the power of the purse). The United States was then able to use its voice and vote on the Banks' Board to bring the accountability mechanism into existence. Yet borrowers and Bank management favored retaining control of the mechanism thus limiting its ability to enact accountability as justice. This would be repeated by the ADB soon after.

Accountability as Justice for the Asian Development Bank

On December 5, 1995, the ADB created its Inspection Function to provide redress for people "directly, materially and adversely affected" by an ADB-financed project (ADB 1995b: 9). The Inspection Function was created because of US entrepreneurship: the United States used a general capital increase negotiating round (Babb 2009: 192) and in preparation for an upcoming Asian Development Fund (ADF) replenishment to push for the norm, while using its voice on the Board and with management to devise the Inspection Function, before voting it into existence. Scholars state that the ADB adopted policies on confidentiality, information disclosure, and an accountability mechanism after the World Bank did without detailing the United States' role (Suzuki and Nanwani 2006: 177). Again, eliding the role of the United States, Bissell and Nanwani identify that external factors including the decision by the World Bank and the IDB influenced its decision (2009b: 7).

The US agenda for reforming the ADB to include accountability as justice emerged within the context of the 1993 Task Force on Improving Project Quality (the Shultz report), akin to the Wapenhans and Tapoma reports. This was again in response to member states' dissatisfaction with the performance of the Bank. The review stated that 10 percent of the projects evaluated were unsuccessful after evaluating 36 percent of projects completed since it began lending (ADB 1994: 2–3). As with the IDB, the ADB did not examine its overall history in terms of project quality, although it did recommend "spring cleaning" its portfolio to remove underperforming projects (McCawley 2017: 191). Like the World Bank, the ADB report identified an approval culture in how the ADB operates, recommending more time be spent on development impact than approving loans (ADB 1994: 5, 49).

While there was increased activism against the environmental and social impact of the Bank's lending activities in developing member countries (DMCs), this was not instrumental in the creation of its accountability mechanism. Campaigns against the environmental and social impact of the two hydroelectric projects, the Theun Hinboun dam and the Nam Theun 2 project in Laos, exemplified opposition to the ADB (Singh 2009). These campaigns occurred within the context of broader opposition to the Bank's neoliberal agenda (Oehlers 2006).

Civil society activists conducted a mass protest at the Bank's annual meeting in Chiang Mai in Thailand in 2000 (Tadem 2003), which took Bank management by surprise. While this led executive directors to push for new measures to monitor the organization's transparency and accountability in relation to civil society (McCawley 2017: 265), there was not the same concerted effort by activists to advocate for a recourse mechanism as had been the case with the World Bank.

According to one former executive director, if consensus cannot be reached at the level of ADB's Board, then donors may resort to the general capital increase and ADF financing to implement their policy preferences (Interview, November 15, 2013). The United States was the most vocal of the donor member states on the Board promoting accountability as justice, but it had the responsive ears of the other donors (Interview with accountability expert, November 27, 2013). There was increasing agreement between the Europeans and the United States on the need for accountability mechanisms among the Banks while DMCs saw the accountability mechanisms as a creature of the United States and a Western imposition.

The move to establish such a mechanism was not supported by Bank management. Establishing an accountability mechanism was difficult for the ADB, because

> in Asia it is somewhat different to disclose information. People shy away from direct confrontation. Inspection we are not accustomed to. . . . It requires a whole lot of internalisation for both staff and countries. But as a public institution, we have to move in that direction. Otherwise, we cannot satisfy all the donor countries that want to know how their taxpayer's money is spent. (Nanwani, cited in van Putten 2008: 123)

As with the other MDBs, the United States had plenty of opportunity to link funding to policy change in the ADB's five-yearly general capital increase and periodic Asian Development Fund replenishments. The United States had sent a clear signal to other MDBs about its intentions to flex its financial muscle when it threatened to withhold its replenishment to the World Bank's soft-loan facility in 1993 (Suzuki and Nanwani 2006: 176). Congressman Frank stated, "the adoption and implementation of satisfactory reform measures will affect the degree of support for future US contributions to the Asian Development Bank and Fund."[62] The Inspection Function was directly linked to the need for "commitments to the general capital increase for its ordinary operations and in relation to its Asian Development Fund (ADF) VII negotiations" (Bissell and Nanwani 2009a: 158).

In 1995, the US Treasury requested authorization of funding from Congress for $66.6 million for GCI-4. In requesting the amount, Undersecretary of the

Treasury for International Affairs Lawrence Summers pointed out that the ADB was meeting US objectives in establishing an independent Inspection Function.[63] GCI-4 led to the establishment of the Inspection Function in 1995 (Interview with accountability expert, June 7, 2013; Interview with accountability expert, November 27, 2013). As one interviewee stated, advocating for change is "most effective in the context of a replenishment" (Interview with a former ADB executive director, November 15, 2013). The US executive director advocated the need for such a mechanism and US Treasury reported to Congress that it had pushed for institutional reform leading to the establishment of an Inspection Function to ensure the Bank follow its own policies.[64] The United States was therefore willing to exercise its power of the purse to establish accountability mechanisms not only to stop harm but as part as part of a broader strategy to make all of the MDBs more effective.[65] In 1995 Treasury Undersecretary for International Affairs Lawrence Summer testified to US Congress, "we have been successful with the leverage the US support has provided in changing the practices of these institutions [MDBs]," and "progress has been made in the context of the Asian Development Bank and the other regional development banks."[66]

Once member states agreed to create the accountability mechanism, the Bank was very receptive to donors' policy agenda and the idea of an Inspection Function. Bank management was really involved with the alternate US executive director in pushing it forward. Representatives from the ADB visited Washington, DC, and the US Treasury was actively involved, commenting on several drafts (Interview with accountability expert, November 27, 2013). Despite this, US representatives argue that it is harder to get the ADB to meaningfully address US concerns compared with the other MDBs even when they agree to do so (Interview with former US Treasury staff, November 4, 2013). This is important for considering how the Inspection Function operated in practice, as discussed in chapters 4 and 5.

In short, the ADB devised an accountability mechanism because donors demanded it (Interview with ADB staff member, July 1, 2009). The push to create the Inspection Function emerged within the context of member states attempting to improve MDB effectiveness (ADB 1995a; Park 2010a), which the United States used to advocate for accountability as justice. It used the general capital increase and the ADF replenishments as a financial incentive. The ADB officially states, it "established the Inspection Function in the context of increased attention to accountability, transparency, and public participation by ADB and other multilateral development banks" (ADB 2003: 5). Within the Bank's Portfolio Task Review Report, accountability refers to internal decision-making procedures that affect Bank quality rather than for being held answerable for project operations to those outside the Bank (ADB 1994: 14). Nonetheless, Bissell and

Nanwani argued that the ADB's accountability mechanism would "complement the Bank's existing supervision, audit and evaluation systems" as part of its response to the Shultz report (2009a: 158).

Like the World Bank before it, ADB management suggested in a working paper proposal that the Bank's "experience did not suggest the need to establish a permanent . . . panel" (McGill 2001: 195). Instead, it recommended giving control of the Inspection Function to the Board. Bank management advised that a subcommittee of the Board be created to oversee a roster of experts as per the IDB's mechanism which would "reinforce the Board's responsibility to direct ADB's general operations" (McGill 2001: 195). The Board established a subcommittee called the Board Inspection Committee (BIC) composed of six executive directors (including three executive directors from DMCs) to oversee the Inspection Function. The Board Inspection Committee used a roster of independent experts nominated by the president to form a three-member Panel of Experts to investigate a claim like the IDB. Unlike the IDB where the president of the Bank would initially review inspection requests and then recommend an inspection to the Board, this would be done by the committee on behalf of the Board of Executive Directors.[67]

The Panel of Experts reported to the subcommittee, which in turn reported the findings to the Board (ADB 1995b). As with the IDB, people facing environmental and social harm needed their claim to be accepted by the Board, on which their own government sat. The Board had the power to approve an investigation and make the final decision about the investigation's outcome. This is like the World Bank, except that the World Bank's Board has, since 1999, accepted Panel recommendations on a "no objection basis" (Nanwani 2010: 121). From the beginning therefore, "the panel's lack of independence threatened the credibility and viability of the inspection process itself" (Suzuki and Nanwani 2006: 208, 217).[68] As with the IDB, the Bank management was able to successfully compromise the norm by recommending the DMC-dominated Board have greater control over the accountability mechanism, thus limiting its independence. Meanwhile, efforts to establish accountability in the rest of the World Bank *Group* composed of the International Finance Corporation (IFC), a private sector lender and investor, and the Multilateral Investment Guarantee Agency (MIGA), a political risk guarantor, again resulted from US demands for accountability as justice.

Accountability as Justice for the World Bank Group

The United States was the primary advocate for accountability as justice for the World Bank Group, again using its power of the purse, its voice on the Banks'

Boards and with management, and its vote to bring the Compliance Advisor/ Ombudsman (CAO) into existence. US Congressman Frank, when passing IDA-10 replenishment for the World Bank, stated that his subcommittee "expects the necessary resolutions to be adopted, as quickly as possible, to expand the jurisdiction of the of the World Bank's new inspection panel to include complaints about violations of IFC and MIGA policies, procedures, and loans or guarantee agreements. The committee intends to follow closely the progress of the IFC and MIGA in effecting such reforms." Frank made these comments about replenishing the capital stock of the IFC.[69]

The accountability debate within the World Bank Group was again the result of emerging evidence that the IFC contributed to environmental and social harm. US Treasury would be kept informed by activists uncovering how IFC-financed projects were negatively affecting communities and ecosystems. As with the large campaign against the World Bank's Narmada dam, the IFC's investment and funding of the Pangue dam in Chile (discussed later) became the focus of a large-scale activist campaign. The high-profile campaign against the IFC highlighted the importance of an adequate response to claims of harm, leading to a more independent accountability mechanism. This is despite previous arguments that the norm was not applicable to private sector financing. Owing to the structure of private sector lending, the debate over whether to have an accountability mechanism for the World Bank Group included not only shareholders but also the private sector and NGOs as to what such a mechanism should look like. In this context, the IFC management succeeded in having their preference for an ombudsman-style accountability mechanism that was designed less as a formal sanctioning process, compared with the other mechanisms.

Pangue remains controversial in IFC history because it was the first large project the IFC ever undertook, and its environmental and social repercussions would further shape the IFC's projects, policies, and institutions.[70] Pangue is discussed here as it galvanized the United States to demand accountability as justice for the World Bank Group. Empresa Nacional de Electricidad S.A (Endesa) a multinational corporation aimed to construct six hydroelectric dams, to meet Chile's increasing electricity demands along the Bio Bio, one of Chile's largest rivers. The first dam, Pangue, was designed to be the most efficient in the world "generating 450 megawatts of power while flooding 1, 250 acres, a much smaller amount than other large dams" and purportedly only requiring the resettlement of fifty-three nonindigenous individuals (IFC 1992; Nash 1992: 8). In April 1992 the IFC authorized $170 million in loans and approved an equity investment of $4.9 million in Pangue S.A., the Endesa subsidiary undertaking the project (IFC 1992). Despite the US executive director's abstention from voting for the project, the Pangue dam was constructed between 1993 and 1996 and began operating in 1997.

As with the Morse report for the World Bank on Narmada, the IFC was under intense pressure to respond to claims of harm. Bank management authorized the American anthropologist Dr. Theodore Downing to conduct an independent investigation of the impacts of the dam in 1995. The Downing report identified extensive deforestation, severe limitation of Pehuenche (indigenous people in the site area) land rights, and the general failure on the part of the Pehuen Foundation (established as part of its investment agreement with the IFC) to meet its objectives. Both IFC and Endesa were found to have "negotiated secret covenants on the future of the ethnic group without the knowledge or participation of the group or the government authorities responsible for Indigenous affairs. . . . They implemented a program of resettlement that failed to incorporate the rights of the indigenous peoples, and they failed to adequately compensate all affected peoples" (Johnston and Turner 1998: 2). The projects along the Bio Bio also led to unchecked in-migration to a previously isolated area, land speculation, and deforestation (Downing 1996: 5).

A local environmental and social umbrella network, Grupo de Accion por el Bibio (GABB), and close to 400 Chileans, including members of the Chilean Congress, filed a complaint with the World Bank Inspection Panel on November 17, 1995. It was rejected because the Inspection Panel does not cover IFC projects. As GABB argued in its claim, at that time the IFC had to meet the appropriate World Bank environmental guidelines and policies. They argued that because the IFC (and MIGA) share the same president and member states as the World Bank, they should be under the mandate of the Inspection Panel (GABB 1995: 4–5). The incident provided impetus for World Bank Group President Wolfensohn to commission an internal autonomous review of Pangue's environmental and social impacts like the Morse report for Narmada by Dr. Jay Hair.[71]

The Pangue Inspection Panel claim triggered discussions over the need to extend the Inspection Panel to cover the World Bank Group or establish a separate mechanism (Udall 1997: 52). In February 1996, the World Bank Group Board requested that IFC and MIGA management "formulate an inspection mechanism proposal designed to meet the needs of the private sector." They then created a working group that canvassed ideas from the World Bank, the Inspection Panel, NGOs, and the private sector. In June, IFC and MIGA management presented a draft paper to the World Bank Group Board of Executive Directors Committee on Development Effectiveness (CODE) which stated that they "support the establishment of an inspection mechanism that would review compliance [of IFC and MIGA] upon request by locally affected parties, while accommodating the special characteristics of the private sector."[72] The draft paper outlined three possible options: having the World Bank Inspection Panel cover the rest of the World Bank Group; create a roster of experts in the same vein as the IDB and ADB; or use the same structure and chairperson of the World Bank Inspection Panel but have two separate private sector experts to constitute a panel for investigations. The IFC favored the latter.

In July 1996, IFC and MIGA management deliberated with members of Committee of Development Effectiveness over the creation of such a mechanism. MIGA management stated that no bilateral political risk insurer was subject to an inspection mechanism but that as a multilateral institution, it was different and that "[S]ome kind of inspection mechanism was advisable."[73] Nonetheless, the MIGA's general counsel warned that an "ill-conceived inspection mechanism" could lead to "breaches of confidentiality which could subject the Agency to costly legal proceedings and potentially enormous losses." Other staff and executive directors present argued that any inspection mechanism for the World Bank Group "could have a negative impact on the ability of IFC and MIGA to carry out their mandate." The alternative argument was that such a mechanism may "have a positive effect by, among other things, enhancing the accountability of IFC and MIGA."[74] In September 1996 the IFC released a concept paper for external consultation. The paper reiterated the need to design a mechanism that would "accommodate the constraints and demands of the private sector marketplace. These include costs associated with project delays, the need for reliability and confidentiality, and the possibility that competitors might seek to misuse the process to achieve a business advantage for themselves."[75] The concept paper invited private sector clients and NGOs to comment on whether there was a need for an inspection mechanism and what it should look like.

Throughout 1996 the US executive director and Treasury worked with activists to advocate for the Inspection Panel to cover the rest of the World Bank Group, particularly in relation to draft operating guidelines and functions.[76] Much of the discussion around applying the Inspection Panel to the private sector were being discussed during the 1996 review of the operations of the World Bank Inspection Panel (as discussed in chapter 4). For some, reviewing the operations of the Inspection Panel was an opportunity to extend its structure and function to include private sector projects. The IFC stressed the differences in its operations to the World Bank based on intense private sector competition and the need for speed in investment decisions; that IFC and MIGA need to be flexible in responding to commercial pressures; and that "confidentiality of proprietary business plans and information must be preserved." For many, the operations of the IFC would be hampered by being under the Inspection Panel. IFC even argued that "[A]n inspection mechanism might be perceived as adding a new category of project risk in dealings with IFC and MIGA."[77]

Activists pushed for the inclusion of the World Bank Group under the Inspection Panel and opposed many of the restrictions and limitations that the IFC proposed to place on its mechanism, particularly with regard to the scope and time frame of any investigation.[78] Stakeholder meetings were convened to discuss how to incorporate IFC and MIGA loans and guarantees under the Inspection Panel mandate (Udall 1997: 52). In January 1997 NGOs argued that the IFC's response "has been disappointing" where IFC's preference for limiting the scope and timing of IFC/MIGA investigation "would negate the entire purpose of an inspection panel which is to provide an effective, independent forum for affected persons to request the Bank group to act in accordance with its own policies and procedures." They noted that "the IFC has never articulated why an inspection panel would be helpful for their operations. Instead, they have chosen to focus on how the panel needs to fit into their private sector operations and meet the needs of the private sector."[79] Negotiations between NGOs and the private sector came close to reaching agreement on extending the Inspection Panel to cover the rest of the World Bank Group, but one company and one NGO disagreed, and it fell apart (Interview with accountability expert, May 15, 2009). In August 1997 NGOs drafted a World Bank Group resolution for the inclusion of IFC/MIGA under the World Bank Inspection Panel, which they submitted to the Boards of the IFC and the MIGA.[80]

Meanwhile, the Hair report investigating the IFC's actions in relation to the Pangue project was completed. It concluded that IFC was unable to enforce its own environmental and social guidelines (Hair 1997: 35). The report argued that there "was no evidence in the record that comprehensive and systematic monitoring of requirements to determine compliance with relevant World Bank Group requirements were either a) identified within IFC or to the project sponsor [Endesa] or b) subsequently monitored" (1997: 38). One of the institutional recommendations the Hair report made to the World Bank Group was that "IFC projects *should be subjected to an Inspection Panel process such as the one currently in place at the World Bank Group's International Bank for Reconstruction and Development. Preferable, the IFC would be incorporated into the existing system*" (Hair 1997: Section B, p. 6, emphasis added).

After consulting extensively with the private sector, NGOs, and the Boards, in August 1997 the IFC and MIGA management presented their report to the Committee on Development Effectiveness. Management stated that "the majority of private clients and co-financiers told IFC and MIGA that they believed that the disadvantages of an inspection mechanism would outweigh any benefits. Many respondents suggested that an inspection mechanism would deter private companies from approaching IFC and MIGA to work together on projects in developing countries."[81] The basis for this stance was that an inspection mechanism would result in open-ended delays; that IFC and MIGA would be considered unreliable business partners; that inspections may investigate IFC and MIGA policies that were not clearly defined;[82] that NGOs could use the mechanism to block projects; and that retrospective investigations of projects would be "unfair and unreasonable." Nonetheless, as discussed further in what follows, the IFC and

MIGA concluded that some concerns of the private sector "could be mitigated by the appropriate design of an inspection mechanism."

The need for an accountability mechanism covering IFC and MIGA had long been supported by the US executive director Jan Piercy.[83] In October 1997, at a Committee on Development Effectiveness meeting regarding the establishment of an accountability mechanism Piercy stated that "the passive stance that IFC and MIGA have taken in exploring how to create an Inspection Function and in consultation with the private sector is unacceptable" and the "lack of progress since the last CODE meeting is troubling," although this was in part the result of "time spent dealing with the Pangue review." Piercy reaffirmed the United States' commitment to an accountability mechanism because the Pangue project "illustrates the need for having an inspection mechanism in place to avoid ad hoc approaches."[84] She further argued:

> The IFC/MIGA process for developing a proposal can proceed now. . . . The CIEL/Friends of the Earth proposal received by CODE members yesterday provides launching point [the August 15 draft resolution mentioned earlier]. We understand that the NGO proposal has been reviewed by the private sector and incorporates many of their concerns. This proposal can provide the basis for reconciling differences and to help focus the discussion and negotiations.

In a letter to US Treasury Deputy Assistant Secretary Bill Schuerch, Piercy outlined how there was little support at the meeting for her recommendation that IFC submit a specific proposal for a full Board discussion in February 1998.[85] It was clear that the United States was the strongest supporter for pressing ahead with the inspection mechanism. Borrower executive directors from Africa, Saudi Arabia, India, China, and Latin America "were united in their position that a decision on an inspection mechanism for IFC and MIGA should await the results of the Board's review of the Bank's inspection panel" and that they "felt that an IFC/MIGA inspection mechanism would inhibit investors from using IFC and MIGA and, in turn, reduce foreign investment in their countries." She further noted that "they were also pleased that IFC/MIGA had undertaken an extensive consultation process and had not made any specific proposals for an inspection mechanism in their paper." Some executive directors including the Nordics, France, and Germany wanted to "move cautiously and await results of the Boards review" while others such as Belgium, Korea, the Netherlands, and Italy "supported moving the process forward at the same time as the review." Significantly, "these countries did not take as strong a position as we did with regard to an Inspection Panel–like mechanism."

US power of the purse was instrumental in the creation of an accountability mechanism not only for the IFC, which invested in the company building the

Chilean dam but to ensure that any accountability mechanism would also in-clude the World Bank Group's political risk insurer, the MIGA. In 1997 member states agreed on the need for an $850 million general capital increase for MIGA, which the US treasury used to continue to push for both an independent inspec-tion mechanism and information disclosure.[86]

The power of the purse was necessary, as it was clear that IFC management was not in favor of creating such a mechanism. The IFC chairman and executive vice president, Peter Woicke, stated:

> When I joined the World Bank Group in 1998, to take the helm of IFC in 1999, our institution had come under tremendous pressure to accept a mech-anism which would allow people negatively affected by IFC projects to voice grievances. My future colleagues feared a World Bank–type Inspection Panel was likely to be forced on them and . . . yet it became quickly clear that IFC would not get away without providing such a platform, given [sic] project-af-fected communities the right to express their grievances. The Compliance Advisor/Ombudsman appeared to us as a more acceptable solution than the Inspection Panel and hence management stopped lobbying against an account-ability mechanism.[87]

Woicke's predecessor, Jannik Lindbaek, identified a range of alternatives for an accountability mechanism at the Committee on Development Effectiveness meeting in October 1997. In addition to the extended inspection panel or a new roster of experts, Lindbaek outlined options for "an independent office of envi-ronmental and social oversight reporting directly to President Wolfensohn; an ombudsman reporting directly to the president; and a strengthened internal re-view process." Meanwhile, MIGA's chairman and executive vice president Iida fa-vored extending the World Bank's Inspection Panel to IFC and MIGA. Ongoing discussions between NGOs and the private sector showed movement toward agreeing to an office that would accept complaints from affected peoples and re-port its investigations to the president of the World Bank Group.[88] A March 1998 paper by the World Bank Group fleshed out further two of these alternatives. The paper noted that no consensus had emerged but reiterated that most pri-vate sector clients and co-financiers "preferred a wholly separate private sector inspection mechanism in the event that any kind of inspection mechanism of any kind were established."[89] Here they outlined the disadvantages of using the World Bank Inspection Panel which would "establish a formal quasi-judicial process rather than focusing in the first instance on a problem-solving and ad-visory mechanism to assist IFC and MIGA in achieving better results; the more formalistic nature of this option could make the process more time consuming than necessary."[90]

The second option provided was the creation of a CAO, which is a well-known legal concept.[91] The ombudsman, which would be independent of IFC and MIGA "line operations, could be established to ensure compliance with environmental and social policies and procedures, while also facilitating constructive responses to external complaints."[92] Reporting directly to the World Bank president, the CAO would be a permanent position with a small staff and consultants to assist with compliance work. The CAO would also monitor World Bank Group policy compliance absent complaints and be able to initiate a review of projects for compliance. The report notes the positive response to the idea from NGOs and the private sector. The third, less-discussed option was an internal environmental advisory council, but it was recognized as not being able to address affected parties' complaints expeditiously. In a subsequent report from the World Bank Inspection Panel to the World Bank's Board of Executive Directors, the Panel stated that a "less judicialized approach focused on problem solving, as suggested by IFC and MIGA, could avoid some of the problems encountered by the Panel itself." With broad support it was decided to move ahead with the creation of a CAO for the World Bank Group.[93]

The US Treasury maintained pressure on the World Bank Group for creating an accountability mechanism using its full power of the purse:

> [T]he MDBs have established independent inspection mechanisms to provide recourse to local communities and individuals who believe they have been adversely affected by MDB projects. These inspection panels investigate alleged violations of institutional policies and procedures, and provide the analytical basis for remedial measures. The recent World Bank (IDA) replenishment negotiations produced an agreement to have management propose an inspection function for the Bank's private windows, IFC and MIGA.[94]

Here Treasury refers to IDA-11, which was negotiated in late 1998. The United States used the power of the purse to propel the creation of an accountability mechanism for the World Bank Group, thus using the two principal levers of soft-loan replenishments (IDA funding) and general capital increases for the IFC and MIGA. At IDA-12 negotiations, member states recommended that "Management should bring to the Executive Directors of IFC and MIGA a proposal aimed at instituting an appropriate and independent Inspection Function, suitable for the private sector."[95]

President Wolfensohn then announced to the IFC and MIGA Boards of Executive Directors that he had established the position of the CAO on September 30, 1998. Wolfensohn was committed to a multistakeholder approach to appoint a CAO agreeable to both the private sector and NGOs. Thus, unlike the IDB and ADB, both the private sector and activists were involved in the creation and initial operations of the World Bank Group's accountability mechanism.[96] Composed of IFC and MIGA staff, business groups and sector experts, and international and local NGOs, the committee selected Meg Taylor as the first CAO. A CAO Reference Group of the same members assisted in establishing its procedures through roundtable workshops between 1999 and 2001.

The CAO has vice presidential status within IFC and reports directly to the World Bank Group president (not the IFC's executive vice president, who manages the organization). It has three functions: compliance, advisor, and ombudsman. The first entails the evaluation of the IFC and MIGA's compliance with their environmental and social policies through a compliance audit. Compliance audits may be triggered by the World Bank Group president, IFC or MIGA management, the CAO, or from the ombudsman function (see what follows). The second role is as an advisor to World Bank Group staff, management, and president on policies triggered by a complaint, either informally or formally through regular reporting to the president and periodic reporting to the Boards. Third is the ombudsman role, which was established to respond and mediate problems regarding people adversely affected by World Bank Group projects.

The ombudsman is significantly different to the quasi-judicial accountability mechanisms established by the other Banks, although they were all established to enact accountability as justice. The CAO acts as an independent mediator compared with the World Bank's Inspection Panel, which determines whether people were harmed because of Bank noncompliance with its own policies. Like the other accountability mechanisms, the CAO becomes involved when it receives a complaint from peoples adversely or potentially affected. They all validate claims; after that they diverge. While the other mechanisms investigate Bank compliance, the CAO directly mediates between the affected community, IFC or MIGA, the project sponsor (corporation) and the host government. However, the ombudsman can only persuade parties to reconcile through conflict resolution and mediation. Consequently, the only leverage the CAO has is the cooperation of the World Bank Group in investing in or guaranteeing the project. This depends on the percent IFC has invested or at what time the complaint occurs and how much it has invested or recouped; or whether the corporation retains political risk coverage with MIGA. Under its compliance function the CAO operates like the other accountability mechanisms, which may require a change in Bank behavior if it has breached its own safeguards. The CAO was unique in directly attempting to influence companies (project sponsors) where they have breached IFC or MIGA policies. The other mechanisms can only achieve this indirectly through investigating the cause of Bank noncompliance. The second iteration of the other banks' mechanisms would include a problem-solving function not dissimilar to the ombudsman role.

The ombudsman function is crucial for providing recourse to affected people. It recommends practical remedial action while addressing "systemic issues that have contributed to the problems" (IFC 1999: Appendix). The process includes mediation, dialogue, and conciliation leading to a report to the president, notification to the parties and, hopefully, a settlement agreement. The complaint is closed, subject to continued monitoring and follow-up. Possible outcomes include: the successful settlement between the parties; an unsuccessful settlement of the parties with a report to the president outlining recommendations for a compliance investigation; or unsuccessful efforts to reach settlement with a report to the president outlining that no CAO action could resolve the problem. Under the CAO's 2007 revised operational guidelines, the second outcome automatically triggered the CAO's compliance function (CAO 2007b; discussed in chapter 4). A compliance audit may ascertain whether IFC and MIGA policies or a lack of monitoring failed to prevent environmental and social harm. The process incorporates a learning feedback loop, which was unique to the World Bank Group. While the creation of the CAO was driven primarily by the US power of the purse, voice, and vote, it was the United States' voice that mattered in creating the accountability mechanism for the EBRD.

Accountability as Justice for the European Bank for Reconstruction and Development

Unlike the other Banks, the United States did not use either its power of the purse or its vote to help bring the Independent Recourse Mechanism (IRM) into existence in 2003. The EBRD had resisted adopting such a mechanism since the World Bank had established its Inspection Panel ten years prior. EBRD management and staff were not in favor of having such a mechanism, and while there was NGO support for it (CEE Bankwatch Network 2001), it was not the main driver (Interview with EBRD staff, May 18, 2009). As with the other accountability mechanisms, the IRM was designed "to provide a venue for an independent review of complaints or grievances from groups who are, or are likely to be, directly and adversely affected by a Bank-financed project."[97] As argued in what follows, the United States would use its voice through the G7 and on the Board of Executive Directors to push for accountability as justice.

The EBRD is an outlier among the MDBs in the fact that the United States did not use its power of the purse to effect change, and it *abstained* in the vote establishing the mechanism proposed by management. Moreover, because the Bank had just been established, there was no task force to evaluate its performance and find it lacking. This is not to suggest that the United States was not concerned with its efficiency. From the beginning there were concerns over how the Bank was using its resources (Bronstone 1999). However, the United States did not use negotiations for concessional fund replenishments to push for accountability as justice because it is the only MDB not to have a soft-loan facility. Furthermore, the United States did not use its larger subscription at the Bank to push for changes during the Bank's first general capital increase in 1997 either. In requesting funds for GCI-I, the US Treasury identified a range of US policies that the Bank was undertaking including the creation of an information disclosure policy as it had consistently argued for across all the other MDBs. This generally precedes or has been implemented in tandem with the accountability mechanisms. Yet, no mention was made of efforts by the EBRD in creating an Inspection Function for people adversely affected by EBRD-financed projects at that stage.[98]

As with the IFC, there seemed little appetite with Bank management and other donors for the United States' push for accountability as justice. This is because both IFC and the EBRD lend primarily to the private sector. The EBRD is mandated to lend 60 percent of its loans to private sector operations. By 2003, it was lending 75 percent.[99] At that time, it was considered that the private sector operated differently than sovereign loans, which are most of the other MDBs' loans. For example, in establishing the World Bank's Inspection Panel, it was not considered vital that it incorporate the IFC. The reasons posited at the time were that private sector projects operate on shorter time horizons and were subject to commercial confidentiality and the sanctity of contracts, as well as host country laws covering the operations of the company and private sector project being financed. Additional concerns included ensuring certainty of access to MDB financing and that private sector clients have multiple co-financiers, thus complicating the limits of any accountability mechanism.[100] Moreover, the EBRD and the IFC have limited influence over companies undertaking projects in developing states because they invest small amounts. As a result, "IFC and the EBRD held out the longest" in terms of establishing accountability mechanisms but "once the IFC had done it the writing was on the wall" (Interview with EBRD staff member, June 9, 2009).

Advancing the accountability as justice norm was a concerted policy by the United States from the mid-1990s (Interview with former US Treasury staff, November 4, 2013). However, it was not until the failed World Bank Inspection Panel claim regarding the IFC-financed Bio Bio dam in 1995 that it became broadly apparent that the environmental and social harm produced by private sector projects were similar to sovereign loans and ought to be covered by an accountability mechanism. Unlike the IFC, there was no single "problem project" campaign against the EBRD that provided clear evidence of the need for redress for project affected people to provide momentum for a mechanism. Although NGOs like the CEE Bankwatch Network were pushing the Bank to improve its environmental and social impacts they were not the key driver of the European Bank establishing its accountability mechanism (Interview with former US Treasury staff, November 4, 2013; Interview with EBRD staff, June 9, 2009).

The US push for the accountability as justice norm gained traction after the World Bank Group created its CAO with donors increasingly agreeing on harmonization among the banks (Interview with former US Treasury staff, November 4, 2013; Interview with EBRD staff, October 14, 2013). This is important because donors dominate the EBRD's Board compared with much lower borrower shares. In 2000 in Fukuoka the G7 Finance Ministers Report expressly stated that "there is a clear need for additional progress in such crucial areas as information disclosure, public participation and accountability to the shareholders" of the MDBs and that "Independent inspection panels should be in place in an appropriate manner in all institutions" (G7 2000). In June 2000 the Parliamentary Assembly of the Council of Europe "passed a resolution that encourages the EBRD to 'consider the establishment of a body to hear appeals and grievances from the public'" (Hlobil 2002; Filho and Rios 2007: 41). In July 2001 the G7 reiterated their call for the MDBs to "strengthen or establish inspection mechanisms reporting directly to the Board" (G7 2001).

Both Bank management of the EBRD and the AfDB, discussed next, were asked to develop proposals for creating accountability mechanisms along the lines of the World Bank Panel.[101] As US Treasury noted to Congress, the

> G7 Finance Ministers report on Strengthening the International Financial Institutions and the MDBs recommends that all MDBs have an independent inspection mechanism to enhance internal governance, accountability and transparency. The EBRD does not have a mechanism and the US Executive Director and her G7 counterparts have requested that the EBRD establish such a mechanism.[102]

The EBRD's governors brought the policy issue of transparency and accountability to the Bank in 2001, and it was discussed for one year (Interview with EBRD staff, June 9, 2009). The United States strongly advocated for such a mechanism, while the European directors were concerned about the cost. In the end they agreed to establish a mechanism "without throwing money at it" (Interview with EBRD staff, June 9, 2009).

On May 14, 2002, the Board of Executive Directors held a closed executive session to agree on establishing an accountability mechanism for the Bank. As stated by President Lemierre, the session

> endorsed the principle of establishing a mechanism whereby local groups that may be directly and adversely affected by a Bank-financed project would be

able to raise their complaints or grievances with an arm of the Bank that would be independent from project operations. The desire to enhance the accountability and transparency of the IOs are the primary reasons for establishing such a mechanism.[103]

By this stage there was full Board support, and the session discussed what such a mechanism would look like. By then the Europeans wanted an accountability mechanism but were concerned with how it would affect the Bank's commercial confidentiality while the United States and Canada were more open (Interview with EBRD staff, June 9, 2009). President Lemierre then announced at the EBRD's annual meeting that such a mechanism would be created.

Recognizing that they had no choice, Bank management then sought to compromise over the accountability mechanisms design. A background paper was then prepared for the Board by the Bank's Office of the General Counsel. The paper set out the structure for an accountability mechanism, which was posted online from October 2002 to January 2003. Consultation periods were then undertaken by the Bank in cities including Moscow, Budapest, and London and in Azerbaijan along with experts from the Environment Department detailing the EBRD's new policies in this area. The US Treasury noted to Congress in 2003 that the EBRD was supporting US objectives because it had proposed an Inspection Function called the IRM, which had been circulated for public comment and was expected to be approved in 2003.[104] Another paper detailing a response to the public consultations was posted online.[105]

Owing to their lending to the private sector, the EBRD looked to the IFC and the ADB as to how to devise its mechanism instead of the World Bank Inspection Panel. The CAO was considered too expensive; it cost the same as the EBRD's entire environmental and social unit. Having a large Roster of Experts like the IDB and ADB was also considered immoderate. In the end the Bank chose to locate the IRM within the recently established Office of the Chief Compliance Officer (OCCO) composed of a single person charged with investigating staff conduct and corruption. According to one insider, this office was mere "window dressing" (Interview with EBRD staff, October 14, 2013). Activists argued that the EBRD designed its mechanism not to work, merely setting up the IRM to meet the requirement to have a mechanism (Interview with accountability activist, May 15, 2009). The chief compliance officer would receive claims that would then be assessed and investigated by a panel of three independent experts. The Office of the Chief Compliance Officer was chosen over the Office of the General Legal Counsel because locating an accountability mechanism there could taint the office where the budget for projects was prepared for Board approval.

As the Office of the Chief Compliance Officer reports to the president, the IRM was not independent of Bank management. Some argued that this ensured the IRM's budget and so that it could "be part of the institutional process" (Interview with EBRD staff member, May 18, 2009). For others this meant that the IRM was not independent at all and the smaller version of the IDB's and ADB's roster of experts was replicating structures that had proved unsuccessful for the other Banks (as detailed in chapter 4).[106] The initial idea for the IRM was to focus on problem solving with communities negatively affected by EBRD-financed projects but by 2003 this had flipped to focus more on compliance with EBRD policies.[107] President Lemierre argued in his recommendation of the IRM to the Bank's Board that "other IFIs have established permanent offices and/or panels to carry out the compliance review function and/or the problem solving function. Such independence may however be ensured through other means of a less bureaucratic and costly nature, more suited to the institutions specific mandate, organization and resources." He further argued that "the opening of ways of recourse to affected groups must be effected within the budgetary restraint that the Bank has imposed upon itself for many years."[108] The EBRD thus chose to have a limited accountability mechanism for enacting accountability as justice to demonstrate its efficiency.

In April 2003 the EBRD established its IRM, along with revised policies for information disclosure and the environment. The United States saw these as steps forward but argued that they "remain unsatisfactory. After advocating for the accountability as justice norm, the United States then voted against the PIP [public information policy] and abstained on the IRM." The US Treasury stated to Congress that "while pleased with the upcoming establishment of the IRM, Treasury believes that its independence and scope should be enhanced. At US insistence, there will be a review after two years of operation of the entire mechanism." It would then "push for more progressive positions on these policies when they are reviewed."[109] The US abstention focused on its lack of independence: the IRM is located within the Bank's management structure not independent of it; the president would determine whether to accept or reject the IRM Coordinator's recommendation of problem solving or a compliance audit; and the EBRD Board determines whether or not to accept the recommendations of an independent expert once an investigation has been undertaken.[110] As discussed in the next chapter, US efforts then focused on ensuring the mechanism could enact accountability as justice. While the EBRD was seen as a laggard in creating an accountability mechanism, it was not the last to do so.

Accountability as Justice at the African Development Bank

As with the other MDBs, the AfDB adopted the accountability as justice norm because of US power of the purse, its voice on the Board and with management, and its vote. Again, this was situated in debates over the economic performance of the Bank. While management acceded to US demands, they proffered a less independent accountability mechanism akin to the EBRD. There is no evidence of sustained pressure from activists in pushing for an accountability mechanism for this (Interview with accountability experts, May 15, 2009, and October 15, 2013) and the mechanism has been little used by NGOs since its creation (Interview with accountability expert, September 30, 2013). Compared with the World Bank/Group the AfDB is not "surrounded by an NGO network" (Interview with accountability officer, September 30, 2013). Local NGOs are more likely to work with official development agencies than to agitate against them (Interview with accountability expert, October 11, 2013), although the lack of NGO complaints may stem from a lack of opportunity (Independent Review Mechanism 2006: 3). Knowing that the regional development banks tend to follow the policy lead of the World Bank because the United States has the same policy objectives, means that Washington-based NGOs primarily focus on changing the World Bank.

The AfDB was the last MDB to establish a mechanism,[111] although management had "proposed the formation of an inspection panel to receive and investigate complaints from outside parties directly affected by a bank-financed project" in late 1994 (English and Mule 1996: 61 fn 44). The AfDB began to devise its independent review mechanism because of the US power of the purse during the concessional lending negotiations for the African Development Fund (ADF-VII). In 1994 the Board asked management to "develop proposals for an inspection panel along the lines of the World Bank"[112] as requested by its Western members (Hansungule 2009: 6, fn 3). The Bank sent a draft proposal in October 1994 for an accountability mechanism to the US Treasury for review.[113] The draft Inspection Function was similarly structured to the World Bank's Inspection Panel. Despite the US Treasury engaging with the draft between late 1994 to August 1996, the AfDB's accountability mechanism did not become a reality until a decade later.

The use of tying the norm to replenishments for the soft-loan facility is significant for the AfDB. Donor (extraregional) member states have less control of the Bank because regional member states control over 66 percent of the vote and because of the relatively equal weighting of members compared to most of the other MDBs. This was not the case for the soft-loan window where the donors are the major subscribers who can link replenishments to policy change. African Development Fund negotiations became increasingly important in the early 1990s because regional member states became dependent on their concessional loans. The African debt crisis meant that many regional members were uncreditworthy and unable to borrow ordinary capital resources from their own Bank. The Bank was in financial straits. Tensions reached a boiling point in 1994 between regional and nonregional member states during AfDF VII (English and Mule 1996: 1). Numerous issues were on the agenda, most tellingly how to ensure the Bank's financial viability when the AfDB had the capacity to lend but its borrowers had drastically reduced their borrowing and loan repayments. This in turn affected the Bank's bottom line and its future credit-rating, leading to a stand-off in negotiations at the Bank's Board over defining borrower creditworthiness.

This among other issues delayed the conclusion of the acrimonious AfDF VII round. It also led nonregional members to temporarily cease new concessional fund commitments until reforms were implemented (English and Mule 1996: 2–3). The United States led other nonregional members in suspending negotiations for a new replenishment for the Fund.[114] As a result, the Bank was near the brink of collapse. The Bank's "financial health was precarious, its administrative structure top heavy, its field offices ineffective and its future very much under threat" (AfDB 2004b: ii). In response to donor demands the Bank instituted a restructuring plan and a plan for African Development Fund replenishment.[115] The Bank's restructure was the most "far-reaching and comprehensive restructuring and reform ever undertaken by an MDB." As part of the reform agenda pushed by the United States through concessional replenishments during AfDB VII was an "inspection function with full participation from civil society organizations."[116] Both the restructuring plan and the replenishment plan made mention of creating an Inspection Function but it was decided that because of "limited restructuring resources . . . the Bank will only consider the inspection panel concept after restructuring is complete."[117]

Beyond the financial health of the Bank, nonregional members were also concerned with the quality of the AfDB's loan portfolio. As with the other MDBs the executive directors requested a task force to review the Bank's project quality to assess its effectiveness. As with the IDB, this was led by a former World Bank staff member, David Knox. Although the Bank had established evaluation procedures in 1977, and a unit for evaluation in 1980, evaluation procedures were slow to develop and executive directors did not receive critical post-project evaluations well (Mingst 1990: 143–147, 150). Dismissing the Bank's data as both incomplete and too small for generalization, the Knox report released in April 1994 nonetheless identified significant weaknesses in the overall quality of the Bank's project portfolio (AfDB 1994). A later review of the Bank by Phillip English and Harris Mule stated that good work undertaken by the AfDB was more an exception than the rule, despite the Bank judging its project lending as basically successful.

The Knox report identified that project monitoring "is not systematic and so does not allow management control and board oversight" and where problems were evident throughout the entire project cycle and across the lion's share of

Bank lending (AfDB 1994: 8). As with the IDB, no single department was seen to be responsible, and therefore accountable, for the management of a project. Hence, nobody was "responsible for identifying and resolving problems" leading to "buck-passing by Bank staff" (AfDB 1994: 21–22). Moreover, English and Mule argued that the AfDB tended to view projects as engineering challenges not as a means of aiding human initiatives, citing the neglect of borrower capacity as particularly egregious (1996: 4–5). The Bank underwent significant changes in terms of restructuring and reorienting its lending between 1995 and 2004, and the express wish of donors for an accountability mechanism remained on the table. The United States resumed lending to the African Development Fund in 1998 in the lead up to AfDF VIII negotiations and to the GCI-5 in 2000.[118] AfDF VIII negotiations included a specific requirement for the creation of an independent Inspection Function (AfDB 2004b: 158). It was not therefore until around 1999 that the Bank "seriously began thinking about the accountability mechanism" (Interview with accountability officer, October 28, 2013). By that stage, the Bank had established its revitalized vision and was about to embark on a second wave of organizational restructuring (AfDB 2004b: 3). It was increasingly recognized that international development financing institutions needed to have some form of accountability mechanism to address grievances to be taken seriously (Interview with accountability expert, October 11, 2013).

The Bank's decision was because the nonregional member states made it clear that it was nonnegotiable (Interview with accountability officer, October 28, 2013). The United States was a strong advocate for it, as were the Nordic member states (Interview with accountability expert, October 11, 2013). The US Treasury noted that it was not difficult to negotiate issues of transparency and the creation of an accountability mechanism within the AfDB once the other more significant policy changes had been agreed on by the mid-1990s (Interview with former US Treasury staff, November 4, 2013). The revitalization of the need for an accountability mechanism came from the United States: "As requested by the US, the AfDB is working to establish an independent Inspection Function by end 2002. An Inspection Function will provide recourse to local communities and individuals that believe that they have been adversely affected by AfDB projects."[119] Professor Daniel Bradlow, who had previously devised the ombudsman proposal for the World Bank, was hired to fashion a policy for the new mechanism between May 2002 and December 2003.

Despite this, President Kabaruka was not a supporter of the idea for creating an accountability mechanism. Nor were regional member states. Even some donor states were skeptical once difficulties began to emerge with other MDB accountability mechanisms (Interview with accountability officer, October 28, 2013). Nonetheless, "[A]t US urging, it [the AfBD] is continuing to . . . lay the groundwork for an Inspection Function." The Board would review Bradlow's report to determine the best mechanism for the Bank.[120] The AfDB's policy creating the Independent Review Mechanism came into effect on June 30, 2004 (AfDB 2004a: 13, 68; 2004c). Like the IDB's and ADB's accountability mechanisms, the Independent Review Mechanism was composed of a roster of experts (three) hired to undertake investigations of claims by groups of people "who demonstrate that their rights or interests have been or are likely to be directly affected by the failure of the relevant Bank Group entity to comply" with its environmental and social policies.[121] The IRM would be composed of a Compliance Review and Mediation Unit (CRMU) under the authority of a director who would in turn by appointed by the Bank president in consultation with the Board of Executive Directors and a Roster of Experts. Like the CAO and the EBRD's IRM (and based on the ADB's revised accountability mechanism, which is discussed in chapter four) the CRMU would undertake problem solving while two experts on the roster would undertake compliance investigations with the Compliance Review and Mediation Unit director. The last of the MDBs had adhered to the accountability as justice norm by creating an accountability mechanism under Bank management and Board control.

Conclusion

This chapter had two aims. First to trace how it became possible for the United States to take up the idea of justice leading to the creation of the accountability as justice norm. The United States traditionally engages with the MDBs through accountability as control and the debate in the early 1990s focused on improving the Banks' efficiency and effectiveness. However, increasing knowledge of the MDBs' negative environmental and social impacts on people would drive key members of the US Congress subcommittees, such as Congressman Frank, to demand recourse for project-affected people. The United States advanced the idea of accountability as justice through the power of the purse; through the US executive director's voice in garnering shareholder support on the Banks' Boards, and through the US executive director and Treasury reviewing Bank management drafts for the mechanisms; and through voting to pass policies creating the accountability mechanisms. All three strategies were evident across the Banks except the EBRD, where the United States was able to use its voice alone. In tracing how the United States championed the norm, two things become clear: high-profile campaigns revealing harm by the World Bank and World Bank Group led to accountability mechanisms with greater independence from Bank management. For the rest, management's compromise strategy succeeded in giving them and borrower-dominated Boards greater control over the accountability process. The next chapter examines how the norm became institutionalized in practice, and the different strategies Bank management used to avoid, defy, and manipulate the norm. In egregious cases this led the United States to revert to the same ideational and material mechanisms to ensure norm adherence.

4

Bank Resistance to Institutionalizing Accountability as Justice

Introduction

Once the accountability mechanisms were created, the banks engaged in a range of strategies to resist the accountability as justice norm. This chapter details the initial structures and functions of the six accountability mechanisms of the MDBs to demonstrate how borrowers interacted with the norm and how the banks used strategies of avoidance, defiance, and manipulation to resist it. It also reveals how much learning was taking place among the banks through the periodic reviews of the mechanisms, bringing them closer together in terms of how they operated. Borrowers played a prominent role in how the mechanisms operated because they feared the impacts of the accountability mechanisms on their lending. The chapter demonstrates how their agreement with the idea of providing recourse to project affected people had to be reconciled with enacting that through mechanisms designed to ensure compliance and greater oversight of lending practices in their territories. Over the course of a decade, borrowers and the banks would recognize that if the mechanisms had to exist, that they should be allowed to operate.

Meanwhile, the chapter shows how all the MDBs engaged in avoidance, including superficially conforming to the norm by designing highly technical accountability mechanisms that were difficult for project-affected people to access, concealing nonconformity by providing ceremonial information that did not reveal the extent of the banks' practices leading to harm, and failing to adequately respond to findings of bank noncompliance through the minimal provision of remedies. Defiance is also evident through dismissing claims that their operations may have led to environmental and social harm and challenging the accountability mechanism process. This included limiting, preempting, and circumventing investigations, challenging the scope of the investigations, and establishing their own remedial management action plans. There is also evidence that the World Bank, Inter-American Development Bank (IDB) and Asian Development Bank (ADB) tried to manipulate the norm by influencing how they would be evaluated in accountability mechanism investigations, while the

The Good Hegemon. Susan Park, Oxford University Press. © Oxford University Press 2022.
DOI: 10.1093/oso/9780197626481.003.0004

World Bank sought to control how staff and even claimants interacted with the investigation process. In egregious cases this led the United States to defend the norm by again reverting to power of the purse, voice, and vote. Periodic reviews advocated for by the United States attempted to limit bank resistance, leading to the mechanisms being reformulated (see Table 4.1).

Table 4.1 Chronology of the Establishment and Updates of the MDB's Accountability Mechanisms.

Year	MDB Accountability Mechanism Created, Replaced, or Updated
1994	World Bank Inspection Panel created
	IDB Independent Investigations Mechanism created
1995	ADB Inspection Function created
1996	World Bank Inspection Panel clarified
1999	World Bank Inspection Panel second clarification
	World Bank Group Compliance Advisor/Ombudsman (CAO) created
2003	EBRD Independent Recourse Mechanism created
	ADB Accountability Mechanism replaces the Inspection Function
	World Bank Group CAO updates its operating guidelines
2004	AfDB Independent Review Mechanism created
2007	World Bank Group CAO updates its operating guidelines
2009	EBRD Project Complaint Mechanism replaces the Independent Recourse Mechanism
2010	IDB Independent Consultation and Investigation Mechanism replaces Independent Investigation Mechanism
2012	ADB Accountability Mechanism updates its policy
2013	World Bank Group CAO updates its operating guidelines
2014	World Bank Inspection Panel updates its operating procedures
	IDB Independent Consultation and Investigation Mechanism updates its policy
	EBRD Project Complaint Mechanism updates its rules of procedure
2015	AfDB Independent Review Mechanism operating rules and procedures updated
2020	EBRD Independent Project Accountability Mechanism replaces the Project Complaint Mechanism
	World Bank Inspection Panel incorporates the Dispute Resolution Service

Rigid but Functioning: The World Bank's Inspection Panel

This section examines how the World Bank's Inspection Panel was undermined by borrower member states' suspicions that the norm punished them rather than improving the Bank's performance, while Bank management engaged in a variety of passive and active strategies to resist the norm. This resulted in two clarifications of the Inspection Panel Resolution in 1996 during a Board-mandated review, and in 1999 after Board members realized that the formal sanctioning process was not operating as intended. The United States staunchly defended the Panel using its power of the purse, its voice, and its vote. The clarifications would enable the Inspection Panel to enact accountability as justice.

Structurally, the Panel is composed of three people appointed by the executive directors and independent from Bank management. Project-affected people can submit a claim if they have taken their concerns to management, but the Bank has failed to address them in a reasonable time frame. Claimants have the right to seek redress where their rights or interests are directly affected by "an act or omission of the World Bank as a result of a failure of the Bank to follow its policies and procedures or loan/credit agreements." Any claim by project-affected people must relate to the design, appraisal, or implementation of a Bank-financed project (Shihata 1994: 41–42, 48). Such acts or omission must have "had or threaten to have a material adverse effect on the affected party."[1]

The first bank avoidance strategy is identifiable in terms of the highly technical criteria written by the Office of the General Legal Counsel for determining the eligibility of a claim. These established a high bar for claimants to jump. A claim to the Panel needed to include a written statement outlining the World Bank project and its adverse effects, the policies that the Bank has not complied with, a description of how the Bank's acts or omissions have led to a specific violation of a Bank policy, and what steps the claimant has taken in resolving these issues with Bank staff. While logical, they nonetheless require knowledge of the policies and practices of the World Bank beyond what might be expected of communities with often low levels of literacy and knowledge of the World Bank (Udall 1997; Inspection Panel 2009: 24, 48). Claimants have difficulties in overcoming significant barriers to lodge a claim, often at great personal risk (Clark et al. 2003: 257).[2]

Once claimants submitted a claim, project affected people have little role in the process. The original process meant that the Panel chair notified management and the Board when a claim was received. The Panel then had six weeks to determine whether it would recommend an investigation to the Board. During that period, Bank management had 21 days to respond to the Panel that it had or intended to comply with its policies. Based on management's response and the Panel's eligibility investigation, the Panel then made its recommendation to the Board. The Board determines whether an investigation should proceed based on a majority vote, before informing claimants. After an investigation, the Panel reports its findings to the Board and the Bank president. Bank management would then submit its response to the Board to the Panel's report. The final decision for determining how the Bank should respond to findings of noncompliance leading to harm rested with the Bank's Board (Bradlow and Schlemmer-Schulte 1994: 393). As noted in chapter 2, the Inspection Panel was designed not to be independent from member states in determining whether investigations were warranted. It was also not given the power to provide project affect people with remedies; only to provide redress, and only the ability to recommend to the Board an investigation into harm (Shihata 1994: 91–102). This constrained the Inspection Panel's ability to enact accountability as justice.

The Bank's defiance strategy became immediately apparent once the Panel began operating. Bank management denied all wrongdoing with the first panel request. Received in October 1994 the first claim concerned allegations of a failure of the Bank to comply with seven of its own policies in relation to the Arun III Hydroelectric Project in Nepal (loan 2029-NEP).[3] There was also internal Bank opposition to the project, with a high-ranking Bank staff member opposing the project and resigning on the basis that it would crowd out investment in Nepal (Fox and Brown 1998: 487). Nonetheless the project went to the Board for approval. As opposition intensified, the Panel accepted the claim by a Nepali NGO on behalf of two anonymous claimants in the project area. In November 1994 management submitted their response to the Board. It stated that they were compliant with the policies but "admitted some delays in releasing technical factual information" (Udall 1997: 18–19). The Panel recommended an investigation.

Bank management tried to dismiss the norm by attempting "to convince the Board and the Panel that there was no need for an investigation" (Udall 1997: 19). This would begin the highly adversarial nature of Panel investigations and management interventions that characterize this mechanism. In December, Bank management circulated a memo to staff that "implied that any policy violations were minor and could be resolved by merely supplying more information to the Inspection Panel, rather than justifying a comprehensive investigation."[4] On the same day, at a meeting of the Board of Executive Directors, Bank management stated that a full investigation was not needed, and that it could deal with the problems the Panel identified.[5] This was a concern, given that Bank management had previously misrepresented the findings of the Morse Commission report to the Board over the Narmada dam, which had led its author, Bradford Morse, to leave his hospital bed to refute (Park 2010a: 74).

In the end, the Board approved an Inspection Panel investigation of the Arun III project. However, it only allowed the Panel to investigate three of the seven alleged policy violations, despite opposition from the claimants. Bank management then tried to circumvent the Inspection Panel Resolution and procedures. While the Panel was undertaking its investigation Bank management challenged the norm by making preemptive recommendations for remedial measures to bring the project into compliance (Udall 1997: 20). This is despite denying any policy violations or the claimant's eligibility in requesting an investigation (World Bank 1994). The Panel later found the Bank to be in violation of the three investigated policies on environmental assessment, involuntary resettlement, and Indigenous peoples. The Panel stated that it was "doubtful that the project's mitigatory environmental and social measures" that Bank management identified in its remedial action plan could be implemented (Inspection Panel 1995: 36).

The Board then had to determine whether the loan could proceed. As the highly publicized first case, whatever decision made would be highly controversial (Clark et al. 2003). Before a decision could be made, the new Bank president James Wolfensohn overruled management and canceled the project (Gutner 2002: 30). Wolfensohn had walked into a Bank reeling from Narmada, and he had been advised that Arun III was a battle he did not need (Park 2010a: 78). From the beginning, Wolfensohn supported the Inspection Panel as part of changing the Bank. Indeed,

> [W]hen Wolfenson arrived at the Bank he invited the Panel to lunch. . . . He said I want to give you the ten most risky projects and you should tell me what the issues are. He took his idea to the Board, but the Board said no. The Board had gone through a painful process in creating the panel and they wanted control. (Ulvaro Umana, former panel member and chair, cited in Inspection Panel 2009: 5)

Indeed, many borrowing executive directors viewed the Panel's "creation as another example of US heavy handedness inside the Bank" (Udall 1997: 2).[6] The Panel was perceived as "an international court of justice . . . by some borrowers which has made it difficult to reach a consensus on whether an investigation should be conducted."[7] Borrowers opposed Panel investigations because they were concerned with the negative impact claims could have on their borrowing. According to Udall, this "politicization of the Panel process reduces the Panel's independence, because it has caused extensive delays in the process and has prevented valid claims from being investigated" (1997: 2).

To limit the Panel's operations, Bank management tried to manipulate the process by trying to interpret the Inspection Panel Resolution for the Board (Inspection Panel 2009: 96). Management argued that the second request received by the Panel in March 1995, regarding a program loan to Ethiopia, "falls completely outside the mandate of the Panel." This is because management interpreted the Resolution to exclude a country's overall lending program rather than a single "project." Management further tried to fix the meaning of what constitutes a project to exclude sectoral or structural adjustment programs for a Panel claim, even though this contravened how it was used in Bank practice. Management used this rationale to reject the Panel's sixth claim regarding a sectoral adjustment loan to Bangladesh (Shihata 2000: 37–41). management thus attempted to undermine the Panel through "back-door communications with the Board."[8] Efforts to do so failed, although management has repeatedly tried to limit what constitutes a project throughout the Panel's history (see chapter 5). In response, the 1996 clarification by the Board allowed for structural adjustment and sectoral loans to be investigated by the Panel and reaffirmed "that the authority to interpret the Resolution was vested with the Board."[9]

Borrower and Bank Resistance: Clarifying the Inspection Panel

The first two years of the Panel's operations were reviewed in 1996 as mandated by the Board in the Inspection Panel Resolution.[10] Rather than reopening the Resolution, the 1996 review led to the first clarification as to how the Resolution should be enacted. Donor members did not want to revisit the Resolution because they feared that this might weaken the Board's consensus and the Panel's mandate (Udall 1997: 2).[11] A Bank report stated that there was Board consensus "that the Panel had fulfilled its mandate and the experience had been generally positive."[12] The Panel had not been flooded with complaints as borrowers feared. Panel Chair Ernst-Gunter Broder stated that they had only received four claims in its first 15 months because it had established its impartiality, which in turn "enhanced its credibility as an open and fair complaint mechanism."[13] This included the Arun III and Ethiopian cases mentioned previously. The latter was rejected by the Panel because it had not exhausted local remedies or shown how an act or omission by the Bank caused harm. A third claim, a power project in Tanzania (Credit 2489-TA), was also rejected by the Panel for being unable to demonstrate harm. The Panel recommended an investigation for a fourth claim, regarding the Brazilian Rondonia Natural Resources management Project (Loan 3444-BR). However, the Board chose not to authorize an investigation; instead, it reviewed the loan with the Panel's assistance, pending changes made by management and the borrower.

The 1996 review focused on the Board's response to the Rondonia case. Rondonia was a highly controversial follow-up project to the Brazilian Polonoroeste project in the Amazon (discussed in chapter 2, Rodrigues 2003). The claim alleged ten policy violations most notable in relation to Indigenous peoples, environmental assessment, natural habitats, and forestry. The Board had asked for further substantiation of material harm and the connection to the Bank's acts or omissions.[14] NGOs argued this raised the burden of proof for claimants and for the Panel. For borrowers and management, Panel claims like Rondonia were contentious because they triggered sensitive discussions over whether borrowers were meeting their loan conditions and whether this should be addressed outside the Panel process. This is because the Panel was designed for inspection, where it sits in judgment and finds fault with the Bank. Moreover,

> the borrowing countries involved have typically seen it as an embarrassment to the government.... An attitude against full investigation whenever it could be avoided thus evolved among borrowing member countries and created a divisive climate every time the Board had to discuss Panel recommendations.[15]

The Panel process has been described as akin to World War III because of borrower hostility and "[M]anagement's adversarial and legalistic responses to Panel claims." Here the Bank's strategy of avoidance over technical criteria comes to the fore. By 1996 Bank management had argued that all four claims submitted to the Panel were inadmissible. NGOs argued that management "has chosen to treat the Panel like a court of law, and respond defensively by putting forward increasingly technical legal arguments against presumptively valid claims."[16] This means that "the procedure under which a Request is examined is so bound up with technical criteria that often legal counsel is sought in relation to a claim. Hence what began as a non-judicial procedure bears the hallmarks of what might be described as a 'quasi-judicial' process." This is because the burden of proof rests with the requestor in showing how harm is linked to detailed and technical policy noncompliance.[17]

The 1996 clarification gave the Panel up to eight weeks to assess a claim's eligibility (Shihata 2000: 164), because the Board sought more detailed information than the first stage of a claim could give. This preliminary investigation now took place after determining a claim's eligibility. While this was nearly as demanding as a full investigation, it enabled borrowers and the Bank to save face by assessing the extent of noncompliance without having a full investigation.[18] However, it "did not reduce the divisiveness in the Board's subsequent discussions on whether to authorize investigations" (Shihata 2000: 155–156). The Board then agreed in September 1997 to carry out a further review of the Inspection Panel as a result of Panel's recommendations for full investigation for two subsequent projects.[19] After a polemical decision by the Board to reject a Panel request for investigation of another Brazilian claim, this time in relation to a resettlement and irrigation project called Itaparica (Resettlement and Irrigation Project, Loan 2883-1-BR), it then authorized the Panel to conduct an investigation of an Indian power project (NTCP I Power Generation Project, Loan 3632-IN). Yet it chose to limit the investigation to a desk review, despite this case being the only one where the Bank admitted to violating some of its own policies (World Bank 1997; Inspection Panel 2003: 12). This is because the Indian executive director made it clear to the Inspection Panel that they might not welcome a Panel visit (Inspection Panel 2003: 35).

The limited independence of the Panel hampered its operations: By 1999, seven requests for inspection had been received, of which the Panel had recommended full investigations for five claims. Yet the Board only accepted the first claim, Arun III. Instead, the Board created "tailor-made" responses to each claim (Umana 1998: 317–318): In addition to the desk review for the Indian NTCP I project, the Board had requested a review of the Bank's practices in response to a claim regarding a hydroelectric project loan to Argentina (Yacyreta, IBRD Loans 2854-AR and 3520-AR). The Board had also asked the Panel to review the implementation of Bank management's remedial actions plans regarding the two Brazilian claims, for Rondonia and Itaparica.[20] For both Yacyreta and Rondonia the Board did not endorse or reject an investigation but determined other actions. For Itaparica, the Board explicitly rejected an investigation while asking for other measures (Umana 1998: 320–22).[21]

Clearly the process was not operating as envisaged by the United States in advocating its creation, by the Resolution, by the Panel's operating procedures, or by the 1996 Clarification. The Board informally debated background papers supplied by management and the Panel on how to mend the process during the second clarification. The discussions

> revealed a great deal of dissatisfaction on the part of Executive Directors representing borrowing countries. They saw that the remedial plans were always concerned with measures to be taken by the borrower, at the borrowers' own expense, and not with corrective actions to be taken by the Bank, thus implying that failures were only attributable to borrowers. (Shihata 2000: 176, 184)

Management presented an option to create yet another step in the Panel process: to allow the Board's Committee of Development Effectiveness (CODE) to review Inspection Panel recommendations to avoid "sharp divisions" in Board discussions. This was rejected.[22] The management paper also suggested that the Board's authorization of a full investigation should note that the purpose is to investigate the Bank not the borrower in order to reduce the negative view of borrowers to Panel investigations.[23]

In response, in March 1998 the Board created an Inspection Panel Working Group composed of executive directors representing Canada, India, the Philippines, the Netherlands, Saudi Arabia, and Switzerland.[24] The review assessed management's response to requests for inspection, the conduct and reporting of the Panel, the Panel's involvements in "action plans" of borrowing countries (which management negotiates with borrowers to bring a project into compliance separate from its own remedial action plans), and the borrower's response to a Panel investigation.[25] At that time, the Board also reviewed whether the World Bank Group should be incorporated under the Panel's jurisdiction resulting from the Panel's rejection of the 1995 Pangue claim regarding the hydroelectric project financed by the International Finance Corporation (IFC). Ultimately the decision was made by the boards of the IFC and the Multilateral Investment Guarantee Agency (MIGA) to create an independent mechanism for the World Bank Group owing to perceptions that private sector operations were different.

The second clarification was seen as an attempt to undermine the Panel.[26] The United States used its power of the purse to defend it. It pushed for a statement at IDA-12 negotiations in 1998 supporting the Inspection Panel to "head off current Board attempts to weaken the Panel."[27] In response, International Development Association deputies agreed to endorse

> the Executive Directors and managements support for an independent and effective Inspection Panel to provide a forum for private citizens affected by World Bank financed projects. They noted that it was imperative to ensure the Inspection Panels effectiveness and independence, as provided by the resolution establishing the Inspection Panel in 1993 and the clarifications issued in 1996. They recommended that the Inspection Panel's findings, management's Response and the Executive Directors' decision should be made public. (World Bank 1998: 27, para 77.)

The United States also used its voice: "[T]hree well-known members of the US Congress, one senator, one congressman and one congresswoman, also wrote a joint letter to the Bank president criticizing the Working Group's report and making specific suggestions" to uphold the Panel's process (Shihata 2000: 194). The US executive director reiterated three concerns at the April 20, 1999, Board meeting: the centrality of the Board for authorizing investigations, the threshhold for assessing harm, and the need to unbundle borrower versus Bank causes of project noncompliance. The United States indicated that they were prepared to accept the report and "urged the Board" to accept the Working Group's recommendations (Shihata 2000: 202). The Working Group report was approved by the Board and consensus was re-established over the aims of the Inspection Panel. Shihata notes that "[A]lthough the report presented a compromise among the members of the Working Group, it restored to a large extent the foundations on which the Resolution establishing the Panel was based" (2000: 184).

Of utmost importance to the future functioning of the Panel, the second clarification gave the Panel independence from the Board. It stated that the "Board will authorize an investigation without making a judgement on the merits of the claimants request" except in relation to the technical criteria for eligibility.[28] Thus borrowers agreed not to block Panel requests for investigations on a "no-objection basis."[29] Since the 1999 clarification, the Board has approved all investigations recommended by the Panel (Inspection Panel 2003: 32, 13). This has allowed the Panel to enact accountability as justice.

Management efforts to challenge the accountability mechanism rules were also countered. The second clarification stated that Bank management "will follow the Resolution" (emphasis added). It determined that management "will not communicate with the Board on matters associated with the request for inspection, except as provided for in the resolution." Management attempts to forestall Panel investigations by planning remedial action plans during a claim's eligibility phase were also forbidden (Inspection Panel 2003: 30). It stated that management must also clarify whether it was its own act or omission that led to noncompliance or that of the borrower, and management must consult with claimants.[30] Finally, the preliminary assessment of a claim that was added by the 1996 clarification was overruled. The Panel would resume its initial examination of the eligibility for an investigation before making a recommendation to the Board.

Bank Resistance: Institutionalizing Accountability as Justice

The Inspection Panel upholds three principles: independence, integrity, and impartiality (Inspection Panel 2009: 18).[31] According to Inspection Panel members, the Panel has "despite tremendous pressure, functioned as an independent structure, as it was intended, consistently providing the Board with an independent view of projects with potentially harmful impacts on local populations and the environment" (Umana 1998: 323). Some argue that the Panel was free from management interference in its operations because the first Panel chair, Ernst-Gunther Broder, demanded an independent secretariat with control over its own budget (Eduardo Abbott cited in Inspection Panel 2009: 95).

Although all World Bank presidents have supported the Panel (Umana 1998: 324; Inspection Panel 2009: xiii), management views the process as adversarial.[32] Management has, in some cases, tried to avoid the norm by not responding to requestor claims as they are required to do by the Inspection Panel Resolution (Naude Fourie 2009: 188; see World Bank 1997b). The Bank has continued to defy the norm through denying the validity of claims and undermining investigations. Management has even dismissed claims for investigation by the Panel but then chosen to suspend financing until changes were made to the project before presenting its response to the Board (World Bank 2004, 2007; Inspection Panel 2009: 42). This demonstrates management's resistance to Inspection Panel investigations even when policy violations are severe.

Management has "used every possible defense to avoid an investigation including questioning the eligibility of the claimants and preparing Action Plans outside the terms laid out in the Resolution." Management has challenged the accountability mechanism's rules by creating moving targets: presenting remedial action plans to the Board to address noncompliance when the Panel is due to present its investigation findings, giving the Panel no time to review the recommendations (Umana 1998: 324). This is reminiscent of what occurred in relation to the original Narmada dam case, but where the debate over facts on the ground regarding the harm caused by a project have been institutionalized within the World Bank between management and the Panel rather than management versus an international activist campaign. As an instrument of the Board, the Panel is also viewed this way by some executive directors, demonstrating the ongoing politicization of the process (Interview with World Bank executive director, October 17, 2013). Manipulation is also evident: Some operations staff claim a lack of knowledge or lie during Panel investigations (Inspection Panel 2009: 36–37; Interview with former World Bank staff, October 21, 2013). Worse, operations staff have even pressured communities not to submit requests for inspection, for example, in an investigation of the Bujagali hydroelectric project in Uganda and the Parana biodiversity project investigation in Brazil (Inspection Panel 2009: 49; Naude Fourie 2009: 210).

There have been calls to periodically review the Inspection Panel's operating procedures, but these did not eventuate until 2011. Draft procedures were circulated by the Panel for revising its procedures in 2001 but the issue became too controversial. The Panel feared Board and management interference, so it was dropped.[33] Relations at the Board of Executive Directors remain split between borrower and donors, although the Board has at times commended the Panel for the quality of its work (Naude Fourie 2009: 196). The degree of adversity at the Board waxes and wanes over which claims come before the Inspection Panel, and as executive directors on the Board change every two years. Although donors support the Panel, they are more fractured than the creation of borrower blocs that resist the Panel's efforts to investigate claims (Umana 1998: 324–325). In short, the "Panel experience has shown that the Board is far from a pliable instrument of a handful of donor governments, as is widely assumed" (Fox 2000: 288).

Although it has operated relatively unchanged since the 1999 clarification, Bank management remains defiant. One of the most contentious claims was a coastal project in Albania in 2007 (Albania Integrated Coastal Zone management and Clean Up Project, IDA Credit No. 4083-ALB). The Inspection Panel uncovered staff misconduct in the project. Bank President Robert Zoellick instigated an internal investigation by the Institutional Integrity Department (INT), which led to staff working on the project being fired, others sanctioned, and a vice president stepping down.[34] This was the first time that staff had directly been fired as a result of an internal investigation of staff misconduct brought to light during an Inspection Panel process. Later, the Inspection Panel discovered that management had willfully misled the Board by arguing that there was no link between the project and the harm caused to affected people in presenting management's case verbally to the Board of Executive Directors. This contrasted with their own written Board submission. The Panel brought this to the Board's attention, and management later recognized its "error" (Inspection Panel 2009: 27, 88–89). There is now a deep hostility by management and staff toward the Inspection Panel. The case was widely seen as reigniting staff "risk aversion" to putting forward innovative or risky projects that might trigger an Inspection Panel investigation that emerged after it was established in 1994.

During this period of heightened mistrust between management, staff, and the Panel, the precarious position of the Inspection Panel process became apparent. In 2012, Ethiopia again sought to overturn the "no-objection basis" at the Board by challenging a field visit by the Inspection Panel for two program loans (IDA Grant: 4578-ET and IDA Credit: H477-ET). The claims alleged that the loans helped facilitate the forcible expulsion of people including human rights abuses. The case returned attention to the hard-fought battle earlier in the Panel's history to ensure that Panel investigations proceed without Board interference. World Bank President Kim, the Panel, and several donor executive directors particularly the US executive director and members of US Congress defended the integrity of the Panel process and the investigation was allowed (Inspection Panel 2013b).[35]

The Board then demanded better working relations between management and the Panel as part of the overall World Bank restructure begun under President Jim Kim. Inspection Panel Chair Eime Watanabe was tasked with reconciling the Panel with Bank management including improving relations with the president while drafting new operating procedures.[36] The independent consultants tasked with canvassing staff and management views during the World Bank restructure in 2013 identified that staff "fear" the Panel and the Department of Institutional Integrity, which were lumped together. A management working group established to enact the change management plan included an aim to reduce "hysteria" over the Panel. The Panel's updated operating procedures identified that the Panel would work with management via an early solutions procedure to enable management to work directly with claimants to address problems (World Bank 2014). This aimed to allow a limited and separate form of problem solving compared with the other MDB accountability mechanisms, which is detailed further later.[37]

In sum, the Inspection Panel established itself as an independent credible accountability mechanism, yet its static structure is a result of the fraught relations between donor and borrowers at the Board, and between an adversarial management and an increasingly wary staff. Despite its difficulties, since 1999 the Panel has functioned effectively to provide recourse for project affected people. It has operated with integrity and independence in attempting to ascertain where harm has been caused by World Bank acts or omissions and to provide recourse through presenting its findings to the Board. The Board has also frequently chosen to ask the Panel to review the remedial actions plans proffered by Bank management after findings of noncompliance; even though the Panel was not invested with this power by its Resolution (see chapter 5). The Board's request for the Panel to review management's remedies of harm raises questions over the extent of the Bank's resistance to the norm and is examined in chapter 5.

Enacting Accountability as Justice: Inspection Panel Precedent Setting

The Panel adheres to its Resolution while finding ways to enact accountability as justice. For example, the Panel was designed to produce findings from its investigation, not recommendations for how to correct Bank noncompliance. However, the Panel's findings "may be suggestive of needed actions" (Inspection Panel 2009: 41). Since its creation the Panel has been able to create five precedents to better enact accountability as justice. First, the Panel in some instances facilitated discussions between claimants and management in order to mediate less contentious cases which has enabled "an earlier resolution of community concerns or policy compliance problems." This deviates from the Inspection Panel process as outlined in the Resolution but is now accepted customary practice by the Panel, management, and the Board. Since 2003 the Inspection Panel has diverged its Resolution by deferring recommendations for an investigation. This introduced flexibility into the inspection process to allow management to correct problems with project affected people. Deferrals have been used to sit on requests to see if management's response is adequate (Naude Fourie 2009: 224). This may provide communities with more immediate improvements to their condition, but it also means that the Panel may defer recommending eligible claims for investigation.

This may result in the Panel stating that an investigation is not warranted and that the Bank had addressed people's concerns (Inspection Panel 2013a). It may also subvert the Panel process in ways akin to the pre-1996 clarification where an investigation was never undertaken despite the request's eligibility for investigation. This gives the Panel more leverage over management, but the noninvestigation approach may also leave claimants vulnerable. Absent the protection that an Inspection Panel process could provide, project-affected people could fear there is no external party upholding their interests and providing implicit protection for their welfare. The Panel's departure from established practice thus raises questions about the predictability of the Panel process, an important provision of any justice mechanism.

The Panel has established several innovations to enact the norm. It accepts supplemental information from other parties including NGOs. The Inspection Panel has also instituted its own practice of returning to the project site after an investigation and Board decision to inform claimants of the outcome (Inspection Panel 2009: 31, xi). It has made it clear that the Board should consider human rights abuses in the context of specific investigations, despite the Bank's apolitical mandate. The Panel argued that human rights are "implicitly embedded in various policies of the Bank" and therefore within the boundaries of its investigation (Inspection Panel 2002: 61–63). Lastly, the Panel has further extended its mandate by commenting in its reports on the systemic issues it sees as a result of its experience with investigations on the causes of World Bank policy noncompliance (Inspection Panel 2009: xi, 13, 31, 50).

These modifications have been seen as setting precedents for how the Panel can operate and were hotly debated by the other banks when updating their mechanisms. Some argue that this indicates a broadening of the Panel's judicial discretion by "increasing its influence through interpretation of the Resolution" and specific operational policies and procedures, and through limiting the political discretion of management in the Inspection Panel process. The Panel set a precedent in international law for improving the accountability of IOs and further advances the rights of individuals internationally (Naude Fourie 2009: 213–214). Despite the various avoidance strategies employed by management, Bank watchers note that "on balance, it has been a remarkably autonomous body, permitting people negatively affected by Bank projects to gain some degree of diplomatic standing . . . and even the possibility of some tangible concessions" (Fox 2000: 279). This stands in contrast to the operations of the IDB's Independent Investigation Mechanism (IIM), discussed next.

Turbulent Non-Growth of the Inter-American Development Bank's Accountability Mechanism

Despite consensus over adopting the norm, the IDB's borrower-dominated Board and Bank management curtailed the independence of the accountability mechanism. The IDB's IIM was in a state of "turbulent non-growth" for its first seven years (Haas 1990), with repeated attempts to improve it but little evidence that it met its mandate. This section demonstrates how Bank resistance and borrower opposition contributed to its moribund state from 1994. In 2010 the United States reverted to its power of the purse, voice, and vote to demand its overhaul during the replenishment of the Bank's 2009 general capital increase (GCI-9). In 2013 it used its voice and vote to again improve its operations. While vastly improved, the mechanism remains limited in its capacity to provide recourse for project affected people.

Bank Resistance and Borrower Opposition to the Independent Investigation Mechanism

According to one commentator, the IDB took the accountability mechanism template from the World Bank and "made it worse" (Interview with accountability activist, May 15, 2009). It was intended to be independent of management through the creation of a permanent roster of ten investigators from different member countries to investigate environmental and social harm (Filho and Rios 2007: 49). Devised by the Bank's Legal Department, the mechanism's procedures from the beginning gave management and the Board control, limiting its ability to provide accountability as justice. The president and Board of Executive Directors were heavily involved in the process for determining the eligibility of a claim, for approving an investigation of allegations of harm caused by Bank actions, in choosing the Experts to undertake an investigation, in outlining the investigation terms of reference, and in whether to agree with the investigation findings. This meant that the mechanism could not function independently of management or the Board in assessing claims that the Bank had contributed to harm. This section demonstrates how management resisted the norm and how borrowing member countries opposed it, before showing how the United States defended the norm through the power of the purse, voice, and vote.

The Board of Executive Directors gave itself undue influence over the investigation process. While the World Bank's Board was heavily divided between donors and borrowers, leading to the introduction of the no objection basis for approving Inspection Panel recommendations, the borrower member countries on the IDB's Board are the majority. The IIM procedures gave the Board the power to appoint the Permanent Roster of Investigators, to authorize an investigation, to appoint the Panel to undertake the investigation, to accept or reject the findings of the Panel, and to determine whether the Bank should undertake corrective measures resulting from an investigation. This enabled executive directors to "try to use their power either to disqualify a complaint before an in depth analysis of its merits, or to narrow, as much as possible, the scope of the investigation through the approval of the terms of reference, even though there is no provision in the policy for Board participation in the matter" (Filho and Rios 2007: 54–55). It became clear that the Board was not interested in upholding the integrity of the process. The Board's power to choose experts to investigate claims enabled executive directors to refuse to accept experts who had previously "disagreed with them over certain issues," which "happened on more than one occasion." The Board thus restricted the IIM's ability to hold the Bank to account for its actions (Filho and Rios 2007: 56, 49).

The Bank's strategy of avoidance began with superficially adhering to the norm while doing little to enact it. The original procedure for submitting a claim by project-affected people was convoluted and unclear.[38] A complaint could be submitted to the "President, the Country office, the External Relations Office, the Office of the Secretary," but with "nobody knowing what to do with it" (Filho and Rios 2007: 57).[39] Many of the charges against the IDB as nontransparent and not taking accountability seriously stem from the lack of administrative procedures for a claim to be submitted and tracked (Miller 2001: 216). It was up to the president's office to ensure that the procedures were being followed for each claim, which did not seem to work. Although it was unclear to whom to submit a claim, once a claim was made known, it was meant to be passed on to the Bank's president, and then the Board and to management. Management would then respond to the president. The president would then pass the original request and management's response, with a recommendation for or against an investigation, to the Board.

That the president should be able to determine the validity of a complaint against their own staff was controversial and in no way constitutes an independent check on the Bank. Filho and Rios opine that it was most likely established this way in order to "underscore the importance" of the new mechanism (2007: 54). The Board determined whether an investigation should proceed and only then would claimants be informed. If the Board chose to approve an investigation, they would appoint three panelists from the Roster of Experts to investigate.[40] On submitting a request, claimants had no knowledge of where the claim went, how long the process would take, or what the possible outcomes might be. The three panelists would report their findings to the Board on whether the Bank had complied with its policies. The Board would then determine what actions the Bank should undertake if the investigation revealed noncompliance.[41]

The Bank's avoidance strategy was also apparent in terms of failing to inform people of the existence of the accountability mechanism and its detailed technical criteria for eligibility. Few were aware the IIM even existed. Accessing the mechanism was difficult because it was "not made public among potentially affected people in borrowing member countries," as intended by its Resolution (Filho and Rios 2007: 53). Indeed, the IIM did not begin producing and disseminating documents on its operations until 2008 (IIM 2009: 6–7). The design of the mechanism also limited access for people seeking recourse, because claimants had to show that the Bank had not followed its own operational policies or "formally adopted norms" and include how this had negatively affected them for their claim to be accepted.[42] While other mechanisms also requested that claimants indicate which policies the Bank had not followed, this was not a requirement.[43] Filho and Rios argue these requirements are nonsense given the lack of knowledge of the IDB in project areas that are often remote and rural and where projects often affect Indigenous peoples who may be illiterate (2007: 55). Advocates agree that Indigenous peoples in the region have no knowledge of the Bank (Interview with accountability activist, August 20, 2013; Interview with accountability activist, October 14, 2013), and NGOs advocating against the IDB spend most of their time explaining to communities what the Bank does.

The first complaint the IIM received was in September 1996, regarding a joint hydroelectric project across Argentina and Paraguay (the Yacyreta Hydroelectric project and the related Environment and Resettlement Project).[44] The project had large-scale impacts including: the potential displacement of up to 47,000 urban dwellers, their loss of titled land, a reduction in their employment prospects and income, and being forced to live in highly unsanitary and unhealthy conditions from untreated sewerage and waste (Filho and Rios 2007: 70). This was one of the largest projects undertaken by the IDB, and there is consensus now that Yacyreta was "an oversized undertaking with an inadequate feasibility study" (Tussie 1995: 71). Submitted by the Paraguayan NGO Sobrevivencia—Amigos de la Tierra (Friends of the Earth), the claim stated that communities suffered as a direct result of the project because the Bank did not follow its own policies. The IIM review panel highlighted that the project was "one of the most ambitious resettlement and environmental mitigation programs in the history of Latin America." However, no social and environmental planning and evaluation had been done prior to its commencement.[45]

When the Yacyreta claim was lodged, "no one within the Administration knew what to do with it, so the complaint wandered aimlessly around the Bank until it received proper attention" (Filho and Rios 2007: 77). Meanwhile, it was clear that the Board wanted a clean bill of health from its first investigation (Interview with accountability expert, October 21, 2013). After receiving the Panel report and management's response, the Board chose not to follow the procedures to authorize a full investigation as laid out in the IIM's Resolution. Instead, the Board authorized "an assessment of the issues raised in the complaint and the plans agreed between the banks [it was co-financed by the World Bank], the borrower and the countries involved." Much like the World Bank, after creating an accountability mechanism, the Board sought to avoid enacting the norm. A memo by the Board of Executive Directors stated that "at several meetings between November

10 and 24, 1997, the Board met with the three experts and reviewed the panel report and management's comments."[46] Management stated that the IIM's report investigating the claims of project-affected people was "important input which Bank staff look forward to discussing [with the project-implementing authority] and authorities from the two governments." Management also offered to discuss the IIM's report with the Board. Borrowers thus attempted to "limit the Panel's authority in daily operations by treating them as advisory bodies" not as independent investigators (Nelson 2000: 424).

The Panel report to the Board did not explicitly state whether the IDB had or had not followed its own policies and norms (Filho and Rios 2007: 57).[47] The Panel report only identifies problems that should be tackled, such as the lack of information provided to project-affected people about the project, the lack of participation, and a loss of trust and legitimacy stemming from the negative impacts facing local communities over the project's fourteen-year history. It identified the reactive stance of the executing agency in responding to community concerns in Argentina and Paraguay.[48] In the end, "the Board took note of the Panel report and management's comments, *without taking a final decision on the recommendations of the Panel.*"[49]

Management engaged in defiance in terms of denying wrongdoing and by not following through on providing remedies once problems were identified. A Legal Department staff member stated that, as a result of its first claim, "the IDB learned a great deal about the ability of the Mechanism policy to function in the Bank's culture" (Miller 2001: 216), which NGOs describe as a deeply embedded culture that is "adverse to evaluation" (BIC 2009: 45). Bank management concurred with the findings of the Panel without accepting any wrongdoing or responsibility and "proposed no solutions to any of those problems" (Filho and Rios 2007: 76). After some delay, the report of the Panel on the Yacyreta Project was released (Bradlow 2005: 424). The Board did not agree to provide any means to rectify the problems wrought by Yacyreta, and management did "little to follow up to ensure that the actions plans were implemented." In the immediate aftermath a Multi-Sectoral Forum was established to include all the banks involved, the executing agency and government, and project-affected people to discuss ways to resolve claimants' concerns (Clark et al. 2003: 84). Failure to mitigate and compensate for ongoing flooding and well contamination resulting from the dam led to a second claim in 2002.

The IIM was to be reviewed two years after its operations as mandated by its Resolution, but by that stage it had only received one claim. NGOs complained vigorously over the mechanism's "appalling lack of transparency and responsiveness" (Clark et al. 2003: 91, 274).[50] The fallout from Yacyreta led to modifications to the mechanism "to ensure greater transparency and to clarify miscellaneous provisions regarding its administrative and procedural aspects" (IDB 2000: 26).

After a year of internal deliberation, the IIM was amended mid-2000 (IIM 2001; van Putten 2008: 131). Changes to the procedures included that the president should not determine a claim's validity to make it more independent, that a co-ordinator be appointed to be responsible for processing the claims in consultation with the Legal Department and the advice of one member of the Roster of Investigators (to determine eligibility), that the Board appoint a chairperson for each panel once a claim has been accepted for investigation, and that a formal reply to claimants outlining the actions the Bank has undertaken in response to the request would be made once the Board was satisfied with management's response to an investigation (Filho and Rios 2007: 50–59). The changes sought to overcome the Bank's inexperience with accountability, the labyrinthine internal claim process, and NGO opposition to its handling of Yacyreta.

Between 1994 and 2010 the IIM received 17 requests for investigation, but it only investigated 5 (IDB 2012b: 9, fn 10; Appendix I). Here the Bank engaged in defiance by dismissing claims. NGOs argued that the small number of claims investigated supported their "profound lack of confidence that the process will deliver meaningful results to complainants" (BIC 2009: 31). This stems from not only a lack of awareness of the mechanism but also a distrust of its procedures by potential users.[51] The five claims accepted for investigation were hotly contested by management (Filho and Rios 2007). In 2000 the IIM received a claim from an affected community in Mexico that the Bank may have omitted assessing likely harm in approving an electricity project (the Gulfo Thermoelectric project, ME-0218). The request was denied on the basis that the community had not engaged with the Bank operations staff working on the project (IIM 2001: 1). In 2002 the Bank received three claims that were accepted: a subsequent claim regarding the Mexican electricity project (loan 1223/OC-ME), a second claim regarding Yacyreta (loan 760/OC-RG), and a claim regarding another electricity project in Brazil (the Cana Brava Thermoelectric project loan 1260/OC-BR). In 2004, the fifth claim was received in relation to a road project in Argentina (the Provincial Road 28 Project loan 1118/OC-AR).[52] Underscoring the importance of accountability as justice is the fact that when the IIM went to Brazil to investigate the Cana Brava case, the IDB's resident mission in Brasilia was occupied by 250 protesters demanding the immediate resolution of the problems arising from the project (IIM 2003: 3). The shock of the occupation drove home to the Bank that they had to take environmental and social claims by project-affected people seriously.

NGOs argued that the cases demonstrated that "IIM is not working, and the IDB's credibility among local communities, civil society, and Member Governments is at risk."[53] The IIM's lack of independence fundamentally weakened its ability to formally sanction the Bank for contributing to harm. The IIM's 2002 annual report discussed its difficulties in applying the policy to the claims submitted because of the lack of technical, administrative, and infrastructural support to conduct investigations; the challenge of attracting experts to serve on the roster of investigators; and time spent responding to NGOs complaints over a lack of publicly available information (IIM 2003: 4). By not providing resources for the mechanism the Bank could continue its usual operations while conforming to the norm of accountability as justice. As an internal Bank review would later state, "it was not independent of management and moved slowly and non-transparently on the few cases it handled" (IDB 2012b: i).

As detailed in chapter 5, the five cases investigated revealed that the IDB was not properly following its own policies, leading to harm, and the Panel reports still did not explicitly identify the Bank's policy violations.[54] This is because the process of investigating claims was highly politicized with executive directors from Argentina, Brazil, and Mexico fearing that any negative findings of the IIM would adversely affect their ability to attract capital to finance infrastructure projects. Opposition by borrower member countries grew with each investigation. Investigations were therefore being undermined by the Board and management. Filho and Rios argue that borrowers could not criticize the findings of the panel reports directly, as this would look politically incorrect as well as being "against the mandate of the Board of Governors" in establishing the mechanism in the first place. Attention therefore turned to the problems in the IIM Resolution (Filho and Rios 2007: 60–63).

In 2003, the Board of Governors agreed to completely revise the mechanism amid widespread agreement that the mechanism was not handling its cases (IIM 2004: 3–4). The Bank's deputy legal counsel, Ana-Mita Betancourt, was appointed to revise it. Draft proposals were floated in December 2003 with management proposing a "framework for an enhanced Independent Investigation Mechanism for problem projects." A restructured accountability mechanism proposal included both consultation and compliance review functions, staffed by a full-time secretariat.[55] Consultation refers to a process whereby the accountability mechanism would seek to resolve problems at the project level among stakeholders including the Bank, the executing agency (company or government agency), and project-affected people.[56] The Board reviewed the proposal in 2004 (IIM 2004: 3–4).

After public consultations on the proposal in 2005 in Brasilia; Mexico City; Washington, DC; and online, there was nothing but a "deafening silence" (van Putten 2008: 131). Board intransigence was evident. Betancourt was unable to gain Board approval for a revised mechanism. Lori Udall noted to US Congress in 2008 that "[S]ince 2005, the Inter-American Development Bank . . . has had a proposed revised policy for its independent investigation mechanism that has not yet been approved by the IDB Board."[57] This is despite pressure from activists for a more robust mechanism. Activists argue that engaging with the IDB is "like banging your head against a wall" (Interview with accountability activist, August 14, 2013). Nonetheless they tried to gain traction through another organization-wide "realignment" from 2006 by arguing that any restructure should include updating the IIM. However, the Bank reorganization and negotiations for a general capital increase (GCI-9, discussed next) were "exercises in Bank secrecy" (BIC 2009: 29).

US Pressure for Change: The Independent Consultation and Investigation Mechanism (MICI)

Between 2003 and 2008 the IIM was in limbo. Changes to the accountability mechanism were ultimately propelled by the United States through its power of the purse, voice, and vote, beginning with the ninth general capital increase (GCI-9).[58] Using GCI-9 funding, the US Congress outlined thirteen policy conditions it wanted the IDB to implement, including reformulating the accountability mechanism. The Bank needed the US vote to pass a general capital increase because of predominant voting share (30 percent). In preparation, management introduced its "Better Bank Agenda," which included improving its accountability (IDB 2010c: 1). Ana-Mita Betancourt was officially appointed as the IIM coordinator full-time in January 2008, and in May the Bank resumed the process of strengthening the IIM policy (IIM 2009: 8). Although the timing and size of the general capital increase resulted from the global financial crisis, the IDB had not had an increase since 1994 and the Bank knew that a new round of negotiations was coming.[59] In other words, the "IDB knows [sic] the US is watching" (Interview with senior congressional staffer, September 26, 2013). US Congressman Frank then met with Bank President Luis Moreno to convey US Congress Appropriations Committee interest in policy reform including revising the IIM.

After a public consultation period running from April to September 2008, a proposal was prepared by a working group headed by Betancourt and composed of twenty staff from across the Bank. This was under management consideration in November, for Board approval in 2009. While there is debate over the extent to which the large borrowers like Argentina opposed strengthening the accountability mechanism, it was widely agreed among the Bank's governors that the IIM was not functioning. In May 2009 the US Secretary of the Treasury Timothy Geithner used his voice to write to the Bank President Moreno to facilitate the strongest possible case for a capital increase that shareholders would support. He provided an attachment including "measures to improve on the Inter-American Development Bank's existing arrangements, including enhancements to an independent investigation mechanism."[60] The Bank hurried to comply. A first working paper on the reforms for GCI-9 including details for revising the IIM was discussed by the Board of Governors on June 18, 2009.[61] The Board of Executive Directors voted to approve the new accountability mechanism policy in February 2010 after reviewing the draft policy four times in three months. The Independent Consultation and Investigation Mechanism (known by its Spanish acronym, MICI) replaced the IIM.

The Bank's internal evaluation office later stated that the MICI "policy was the product of trade-offs agreed to on a compressed schedule within the Executive Board," which was because of GCI-9 (IDB 2012b: i, 9). In April 2010 the Bank identified what it needed to do to meet GCI-9 policy reform goals, including that the "Governors direct management to rapidly staff and implement the new Inspection Mechanism with phased-in coverage of all Bank policies" (IDB 2010a: 27, 21). In May 2010, the Board appointed Betancourt as MICI's first executive secretary. Two months later the Board of Governors approved GCI-9, which amounted to an increase of $70 billion for the Bank (IDB 2010a: 28). This was the largest increase in the Bank's history, enabling it to nearly double its pre-financial-crisis lending levels to $12 billion annually (GAP 2013; IDB 2010a: 3).

Coming into effect on May 19, 2010, the policy establishing MICI (IDB 2010b) differed substantially from the IIM. MICI would only report to the Board, not to management. In some ways MICI emulated the bifurcated system of accountability similar to how the ADB restructured its mechanism in 2003 (discussed next).[62] MICI involved a consultation process to resolve problems at the project level and a subsequent compliance review phase to assess whether Bank noncompliance had led to environmental and social harm. The consultation phase served to address claims of harm without attributing blame. However, a later evaluation of MICI stated that "the policy reflects ambivalence about the extent to which the Bank wants to receive complaints and learn from them, as well as confusion about the respective roles of problem-solving and compliance" (IDB 2012b: ii). Claimants would need to explicitly request the second phase of a compliance review after consultation, to ascertain whether the Bank's acts or omissions had contributed to harm.

Under MICI, requestors had to submit a claim to the executive secretary who would determine its initial eligibility. This is an executive level Bank role and is appointed by the Board. A claim's eligibility includes the standard requirements of a claim being brought to an MDB accountability mechanism: the claim must refer to the actions of the Bank; not be procurement, ethics, fraud, or corruption related; the project loan must not already have been disbursed (a claim is allowed up to two years after the final disbursement); and the claim must not be based on gaining a competitive business advantage. Additionally, requests are ineligible if they "raise issues under arbitral or judicial review by national, supranational or similar bodies" (IDB 2010b: 6, para 37 (i)). This final exclusion clause was included by management without activists' knowledge because of the rapidity with which the policy was constructed for GCI-9. The judicial review clause is an example of using technical criteria as a strategy of avoidance. It "has [been] or might have been a factor" in preventing five claims from being eligible for investigation and prevents MICI from being an effective vehicle for redress for project-affected people (IDB 2012b: 19–20). For example, if there is legal action between a company involved with the IDB-financed project and the government, then this automatically excludes the right of project-affected people to seek recourse through MICI. This has occurred in relation to at least one case (a Mexican wind project claim, loan ME-MICI002-2012).[63]

Once a claim has been deemed prima facie eligible, it is then forwarded to the project ombudsman for the consultation phase. For a claim to proceed, MICI had to obtain a written nonobjection from the executive director of the country where the project is being undertaken (IDB 2010b: 8, para. 49). This again undermined the independence of the mechanism to hold the Bank to account. If the borrower agreed to a site visit, the next step is for the relevant parties (the Bank, the executing agency of the project, and the claimants) to agree to a process of negotiation sponsored by the project ombudsman to attempt to resolve the problems affecting people. As a compliance-only accountability mechanism until recently, the World Bank's the Inspection Panel could not do this. The project ombudsman is appointed by the Board for a three- to five-year renewable term.

As with the other accountability mechanisms, the claimants must have first raised concerns with the Bank prior to lodging a claim and must "reasonably assert" that they have

> been or could be expected to be directly, materially adversely affected by an action or omission of the IDB in violation of a Relevant Operational Policy in a Bank-Financed Operation and has described in at least general terms the direct and material harm caused or likely to be caused by such action or omission. (IDB 2010b: 6, para. 40 (f))

If ineligible or not interested in consultation the requestor may proceed to the compliance review stage. As with the other accountability mechanisms filing a claim with MICI does not halt the project or disbursements by the Bank although the project ombudsman may recommend as such to the president and Board in light of serious irreparable harm (IDB 2010b: 8, para. 48). There is no record of the project ombudsman making such a recommendation. The consultation process seeks to gain agreement between the parties as to how to address the harm.

Should a request go on to the compliance review the claim is then passed on to the chair of the Compliance Review Panel (CRP). Two members are then appointed from a roster of five panelists to work with the chair on the investigation. The Panel prepares their own terms of reference for the investigation rather than the Board as was the case under the IIM, although both requestors and management have the right to comment. Once this is completed, the Panel submits a recommendation for investigation along with the terms of reference to the Board for approval. If a compliance review investigation is approved, the Panel must gain the written no objection from the host executive director for undertaking a site visit in the borrower member country (IDB 2010b: 12, para. 63).

If the Board rejects the request for inspection, the MICI flow chart states that the request and the terms of reference are to be "adjusted" and resubmitted to the Board for approval (IDB 2010b: Appendix II). Again, this gives borrowers the opportunities to limit investigations of Bank-financed activities. Once an investigation is completed, the Panel must submit a report on whether the Bank has violated its own policies and how noncompliance led to environmental and social harm. In presenting its findings, the Panel may also identify systemic issues that have contributed to policy violations leading to harm (akin to the World Bank Inspection Panel process) and provide recommendations. The panelists are appointed by the Board for nonrenewable five-year terms and may work for the Bank two years after serving on the panel.

MICI was a stark improvement over the IIM. MICI detailed clearer operational procedures that included being transparent to claimants and the public throughout (including the release of information directly from MICI rather than the Legal Department) and provided the possibility of consultation as well as requiring the compliance panel to detail policy violations and recommendations. Like the World Bank's Inspection Panel, at the Board's request MICI's compliance panel may be given the power to monitor any remedial measures required of management to bring the project into compliance (IDB 2010b). This has never happened. Arguably this is because there is a "weak demand for accountability" by management and borrowers (BIC 2009: 47). Moreover, the need for borrower consent for entering their territory provided borrowers with a means of shutting down an investigation from the very beginning, and the exclusion of any claim subject to legal proceedings also prevents claims from being investigated (Park 2019). The final decision as to whether to accept the findings of the investigation and any corrective measures required rests with the Board.

Reining-In Bank Resistance? The MICI Review

MICI received more claims in its first two years of operation than the IIM had in fifteen (ICIM 2011: 6–8). Between 2010 and mid-2019 it had received 151 cases: Despite improvements, the mechanism remained plagued by several problems undermining its operations. Early on, the Board recognized that MICI was having trouble functioning (Interview with IDB executive director, October 1, 2013). In 2012, the Board delegated the Office of Evaluation and Oversight to review MICI, which was required by MICI policy (IDB 2010a: 18, para. 99). The resultant report was damning despite conducting only three consultation cases and no completed compliance reviews (IDB 2012a: 2). MICI would be charged with being unable to function effectively owing to the policy's focus on procedures rather than principles (IDB 2012b: 11) as well as the office's tripartite structure and staff clashes. It also revealed the Bank's avoidance strategy in devising numerous, ambiguous, and overlapping eligibility criteria for project-affected people to access the mechanism.

The MICI structure was designed such that it had three principals who all led the accountability mechanism jointly: the executive secretary, who orchestrates the MICI office and receives the claims; the project ombudsman, who undertook consultation of project-level disputes; and the Compliance Panel chair, who investigates Bank policy compliance (ICIM 2011: 3). Each reported directly to the Board, with no overall coherence. The review stated that the three principals did not work as a team and that the project ombudsman and the Panel chair "invoke a misconstrued interpretation of MICI's independence to justify uncooperative behaviour." This "meant that routine issues around work planning, budget allocation, staff work assignments, and fiduciary control have become prolonged and recurring problems," with the executive secretary attempting to hold the two other principals to account through her "power of the purse." The project ombudsman and Panel chair did not accept the executive secretary's authority because it was not based in the MICI policy but in the later terms of reference of her appointment (IDB 2012b: i, 11).[64]

Board members raised concerns with the time that it took for MICI to undertake its investigations (Interview with IDB executive director, October 1, 2013). For example, rather than taking 5 business days to acknowledge the claim and pass it onto the project ombudsman, it took the executive secretary 21 business days. The project ombudsman also took approximately 61 days to declare two cases ineligible for consultation, despite requestors not wanting mediation from the outset. Another factor is the significant criterion for eligibility, and the fact that MICI did not determine whether claims were eligible through a site visit but through a prolonged desk review. This meant that "the average requestor waited almost three months (84 calendar days) before learning whether his or her case would proceed" (IDB 2012b: 14–15, 17–18).[65] The project ombudsman argued that the problems resulted from how the policy had been interpreted within the Bank and the "tendency to micromanage the mechanism and its functions" by management and the Board (IDB 2013a: Part II, p. 9).

The Office of Evaluation and Oversight report focused on the efficiency of the Compliance Review Panel chair in evaluating and investigating cases. While timeliness is important for addressing claimants' concerns, the chair had to grapple with ambiguity in the MICI policy guiding the investigations and the need to thoroughly investigate any judicial claims that would deem a claim ineligible at any time (IDB 2012b: 13).[66] The Panel chair also highlighted how the Board's request for further information at the initial eligibility stage for a compliance review slowed the process down, as had been the case with the World Bank Inspection Panel prior to 1999 (IDB 2013a: Part III, p. 7). By the end of 2013 the project ombudsman had resigned, and the Panel chair had concluded his term. Victoria Mees Marquez was reappointed as MICI's executive secretary.

Both Bank management and borrowers viewed complaints going to compliance as a worst-case scenario. Moreover, "some Board members and Bank management told MICI principals that they expected the consultation phase to serve as a 'gatekeeper' to limit—and, if possible, prevent—cases going to compliance review" (IDB 2012b: 10).[67] Even the MICI executive secretary characterized the MICI policy establishing the consultation phase as a means of "avoid[ing] the costs and inconvenience of an in-depth investigation by a Panel" (IDB 2013a: Part I, p. 3). The report identified frustration by management and staff over their lack of engagement with the process, while some country office staff viewed MICI as endorsing opposition to the Bank through the consultation process. Management and staff argued that the policy did not provide them with a right of reply as other accountability mechanisms did (IDB 2012b: 10), although management had the right to reply in the consultation phase (IDB 2013a: Part II, p. 4, fn 10). While only one-third of staff were aware that MICI even existed (IDB 2013a: Part II, p. 8), some operations staff felt that MICI was secretive in undertaking its investigations, which the Panel chair defended on the basis of confidentiality (IDB 2012b: 23, 28–29).

MICI was found not to "have addressed requestors' complaints promptly because it has spent too long assessing the numerous, ambiguous, and overlapping eligibility criteria provided under the policy." The result was that requestors have been denied meaningful recourse. Moreover, the report found that MICI had at times lacked transparency in its operations: It had not identified cases it rejected as eligible for investigation, had an outdated website, had not undertaken any outreach to project-affected people to inform them of its existence, or attempted to inform staff of its operations and lessons learned. In short, "MICI has provided *almost no meaningful recourse to individual complainants, nor has it generated systemic lessons to help the institution improve*" (IDB 2012b: ii; emphasis added).

Considering the report, the Board agreed to revise the MICI policy. The Board stated that there was "[U]nanimous support for the existence of an independent, transparent and cost-effective mechanism to ensure compliance of the Bank's operations with its policies" (IDB 2013b). The US Treasury supported an improved accountability mechanism (Interview with accountability activist, August 14, 2013), and the US executive director used their voice to demand that any revision to the accountability mechanism be conducted by an expert accountability consultant (Interview with senior congressional staffer, September 26, 2013). In May 2013 the Bank hired Lori Udall as the external consultant: She was one of the initial advisors to US Congressman Frank over creating the World Bank's Inspection Panel.[68] The review included two rounds of public consultations before presenting to the Board of Executive Directors the new MICI policy, which was approved in December 2014 (MI-47-3, ICIM 2014b).

During the review stakeholders argued that MICI was completely ineffectual and "designed to give the IDB the appearance of accountability when in fact there is none" (IDB 2012b: 25). Panamanian NGOs described MICI as "highly time-consuming and ineffective" with a "sense of obstruction permeating" MICI's response to their claim (IDB 2013d: 14). NGOs suggested making the mechanism more transparent and accessible for project-affected people, particularly in relation to the "seventeen separate exclusions and eligibility criteria, which place a heavy burden on affected communities trying to access the mechanism, both by making the complaint process more complicated and by screening out valid complaints that the ICIM [MICI] may be well-positioned to handle" (IDB 2013d: 41–42).[69]

Others pointed out that the office should be more independent from the Bank: the Board should not micromanage MICI through having the power to approve the terms of reference for a compliance review and allowing executive directors to object to site visits. Moreover, the Board should not appoint the executive secretary—the project ombudsman and Panel chair should (IDB 2013d: 20). A submission by the former accountability mechanism coordinator Mr. Angel Rene Rios made it clear that a Bank staff member (such as the MICI executive secretary) should not be given the capacity to determine a claim's eligibility, which has been the case for some but not all of the criterion, because a

> complaint will directly go against the interests of the . . . Bank, and because Board members, managers and technical staff . . . are not only "allergic" to have a complaint lodged against one of their projects, but will do their utmost to stop it, to discredit it, or seek ways to weaken the case. In this case, there are often attempts to pressure the complainants and/or those with the responsibility to make the decision about the validity of the complaint.[70]

In other words, stakeholders continued to question the capacity of MICI to hold the IDB to account. The updated MICI policy retained the tripartite governance structure but placed both the consultation phase "coordinator" and the compliance review phase "coordinator" (formerly ombudsman and chair) under the MICI director (formerly the executive secretary). This reaffirmed the power of the MICI executive secretary/director in reporting to the majority-borrower Board. Under the 2014 policy claimants can now choose whether they would prefer consultation or compliance review, providing greater flexibility into the mechanism (following the ADB, as discussed later). The number of exclusions on which MICI can deem claims ineligible was reduced from 17 to 6 (ICIM 2014b: 6). Under the new policy management now has a right of reply after a claim has been accepted at the consultation and again at the compliance review phase. The policy also provides management with the opportunity to ask MICI to suspend the eligibility determination process to enable management to fix project-affected people's concerns. In other words, management can ask MICI to defer its process, to give management more time to correct the problem. This is even though this is a last-resort process, where claimants need to have gone to Bank management with their concerns before seeking accountability as justice through MICI. The suspension process has been actively used by Bank management since 2014 (see chapter 5), which weakens MICI's ability to enact accountability as justice.

A major breakthrough was the introduction of the short procedure process for Board approval on a no-objection basis for aspects of the consultation and compliance investigation phases. Significantly any Compliance Review Panel recommendation for investigation will be submitted to the Board, or a donor-driven subcommittee of the Board, for short approval (ICIM 2014b: 14). This can override borrower opposition. The Compliance Review Panel then presents its findings of policy compliance or violation along with any observations of systemic concern to the Board for approval. The Board then has the power to determine any corrective action to be undertaken by management in consultation with MICI. Other routine parts of the process are also applicable for short approval (ICIM 2014b: 5–6, 12). Moreover, MICI was also given the power to monitor any corrective actions by the Bank after findings of noncompliance (ICIM 2014b: 16). The impact of these substantive changes on the Bank are discussed in chapter 5. Of note, is that pressure from the United States through the power of the purse, vote, and voice have institutionalized accountability as justice within the IDB despite borrowers seeking to block the norm in practice. Bank avoidance using technical criteria, undermining investigations, and defiance through denying claims and not providing remedies, remains. The next section examines how dramatic changes were affected at the ADB to improve its accountability mechanism, again through US power of the purse.

Ruptures and Change: The Asian Development Bank's Accountability Mechanism

As with the IDB's IIM, the ADB's Inspection Function initially failed to perform effectively owing to its lack of independence from the Board and Bank resistance. As with the other MDBs, the ADB instituted a requirement to review the Inspection Function after two years of operation. This section shows how the United States used its power of the purse as a financial incentive for the ADB to revise its accountability mechanism during a disastrous first attempt at inspection. Despite reformulating the mechanism in 2003, the same problems would plague the Accountability Mechanism in 2009, sharpening the need for a bureaucratically mandated review in 2012. The outcomes of the 2012 review reveal ongoing developing member country (DMC) reservation and Bank resistance.

Bank Resistance and Borrower Opposition: The Inspection Function

As mentioned previously the Inspection Function was similar to the IDB's accountability mechanism in being composed of a roster of experts; in this case of 17 individuals chosen by the Bank president, from whom 3 would be elected to undertake an investigation.[71] The Board Inspection Committee (BIC), a subcommittee of the Board comprised six executive directors (four regional, two nonregional, with three from developing member countries), would determine the eligibility of a claim from project-affected people.[72] The Board subcommittee could recommend to the Board if they felt an investigation was warranted, identify the three experts to undertake the investigation, and determine the investigation terms of reference (ADB 1995b: 13).[73] If approved by the Board, the Panel of Experts would investigate. The BIC would deliberate over the findings and then convey their view and the investigation report to the Board, which would then decide on a course of action for the Bank should it be found noncompliant with the Bank's operational policies and procedures.[74]

As with the other accountability mechanisms, once requestors submitted their claim (in this case to either the Bank's president or the BIC), they were no longer involved in the process except to be updated on the claim's progress (ADB 2002e: 6).[75] The ADB's legal office designed the Inspection Function to enable management to undertake remedial action during the eligibility phase of the claim if the claim was submitted to the president (ADB 1995b: 12). The Bank assumes a letter lodging a claim to the president is the first time a complaint has been received by management (rather than as a prior required step).[76] If the claim is submitted to the Board subcommittee, it decides whether to send it on to management to trigger the requirement to inform management of adverse effects *prior* to a claim as all accountability mechanisms demand, or whether to inform management that this is the beginning of the inspection process necessitating a response (ADB 1995b: 12).

The Inspection Function was not independent from the Board in determining a claim's eligibility and ultimately in deciding the outcome of an investigation. For the ADB, the "participation of the Directors in the entire inspection process, including the initial review of inspection requests, would contribute to the discharge of the Board of Directors' responsibility for directing the general operations of the Bank." As with the IDB, locating authority with the Board was intended to "emphasize the importance placed on the inspection function by the Bank and its Board of Directors" (ADB 1995b: 6). The role of the experts was therefore advisory, not adjudicative (ADB 1995b: 8). Ultimately this would pervert due process, with few claims being accepted by the Inspection Function. Indeed, the Inspection Function was unable to be reviewed in 1998 as mandated because so few claims had been submitted, and none had been accepted. By then, it had only received two claims regarding a Pakistan waste plant, the Korangi Wastewater Treatment Project (Loan number 1539-PAK), both of which were deemed ineligible because they did not cite the Bank's policy violations (ADB 1995b: 10).[77] Norm avoidance was evident in the Bank's technical criteria for accessing the mechanism, such as requesting claims be written in English (ADB 2002e: 29).

The United States and other donor member states on the Board of Executive Directors used the seventh replenishment negotiations of the Asian Development Fund in 2000 to advocate reforming the Inspection Function (ADB 2000: 36–37). Specifically, donors noted

with some concern, a paucity of requests for inspection and the absence of instances of the actual inspection approved by the Board of Directors since the establishment of ADB Inspection Function, apart from the Korangi Wastewater management Project in Pakistan, which was reviewed by the Board Inspection Committee. Although Donors noted that ADB's two projects co-financed by the World Bank had been subject to the latter's Inspection Panel's examination (the Jamuna Bridge Project in Bangladesh and the Arun III Hydroelectric Project in Nepal), they expressed concern about the need for the wider and more effective dissemination of information regarding the Inspection Function. Donors also felt that there is a need for review of procedures for making requests for inspection. In that regard, Donors noted and welcomed management plans, in full consultation with the Board of Directors, to strengthen the Inspection Function of ADB. *Donors recommended a strengthened and more independent Inspection Function*, and the Function should have oversight of private sector projects. (ADB 2000: 36–37; emphasis added)

Thus, even before the full extent of the problems with the Inspection Function became evident, donors including the United States forced the ADB to make the mechanism more accessible, transparent, and applicable to more Bank operations (Nanwani 2010: 121). As the review began, difficulties with the inspection process emerged: Developing member countries opposed the right of the Panel of Experts to investigate allegations of direct material and adverse effects at the project site; and developing member countries and management would defy the norm by challenging the Panel of Experts investigation findings.

During its history the Inspection Function received eight claims regarding four projects (ADB 2003: 5) and only accepted two for inspection: the first was a wastewater project in Thailand, the Samut Prakarn project discussed in what follows, which led to a frustrated investigation, the findings of which were rejected by management, and a stalemate at the Board of Executive Directors. The second request accepted for investigation regarded an irrigation project in Pakistan (the Chashma Right Bank Irrigation Project (Stage III) in Pakistan, Loan Number 1146-PAK SF), as formulations for the new accountability mechanism were nearing completion. Submitted in November 2002, the BIC narrowly approved its investigation in April 2003. The new mechanism later deemed that Chashma was not compliant with Bank policies, requiring remedial action and extensive monitoring (ADB 2012d).

The Inspection Function rejected two initial requests as ineligible for not citing policy violations regarding the Pakistan Korangi Wastewater project as noted earlier. The Inspection Function also rejected four separate claims by different local groups for a Sri Lankan road project (the Southern Transport Development Project (STDP), Loan number 1711-SRI). Significantly the BIC stated that there was an insufficient basis for deeming the first two requests for inspection eligible, while the third and fourth claims were clearly ineligible because they had not presented reasonable evidence of Bank noncompliance leading to harm (ADB 2002e: 12–13). After the Bank transitioned from the Inspection Function to its Accountability Mechanism[78] the BIC accepted a fifth claim regarding the STDP project from another group. This claim went to the new 2003 Accountability Mechanism's problem-solving function, although claimants were unhappy with the mediation process and felt that it had failed them. They proceeded to a compliance investigation through the revised Accountability Mechanism, which determined that the Bank had not met environmental and involuntary resettlement policies among others, and that further remedial action by Bank management was required (Nanwani 2010: 112).

The STDP investigation revealed confusion and inconsistency as to which operational policies and procedures were enforced and whether they were consistent with Board-approved policy (ADB 2003: 6–7). This contributed to the conversion of the ADB's environmental and social safeguard policies from 2006 to 2009. Ultimately, the investigation report stated that the "ADB should have inspected those policy violations [outlined in the four rejected STDP requests for inspection] but did not" and that the "failure of the inspection process to solve the problems of those affected by the project was one of the main reasons that ADB was forced to fully and properly review the Inspection process" (CRP 2004).

The only full investigation attempted by the Inspection Function demonstrates the full extent of Bank avoidance and borrower opposition.[79] The Samut Prakan Waste Water Project in Thailand (Loan number 1410-THA) claim was submitted to the Bank president in November 2000 by residents and the mayor of Klong Dam village, who had opposed the project since 1998 and had protested at the Bank's annual meeting in Chiang Mai in 2000 over toxic waste, effluent, and odor from the plant, and the need for analysis of the economic, health, and environmental impacts (Fukuda 2003: 33). A formal request for inspection was submitted to the BIC in April 2001. It was accepted as eligible by the Board in July 2001 in relation to nine alleged policy violations (ADB 2001). The investigation began in August 2001, but it had to be suspended in November. This is because Thailand refused to allow the Panel of Experts into its territory to investigate conditions without the Bank accepting liability or loss by the contractors working on the project from the investigation, which the Bank refused to do (van Putten 2008: 118).

NGOs criticized the Bank president for not intervening when the "Thai government objected to the Panel's site visit and Board opinion split between the South and the North" (Fukuda 2003: 37). Developing member countries such as Bangladesh, China, India, the Philippines, and Pakistan supported Thailand's right to determine whether an investigation in their territory would be allowed (Fukuda 2003: 35). Despite attempts by the BIC chair to negotiate with the Thai government, and efforts to clarify the liability issue with management, the Panel was unable to conduct the field visit (Park 2014). The Panel was thus forced to undertake a desk review, which "seriously disadvantaged [them] in making a fair assessment of the direct and material harm on the rights and interests of the requestors, due to the Panel's inability to have access to the requestors, the Project site and the experts in Thailand who have experience in this area" (ADB 2001: 2).

The Panel of Experts report on Samut Prakarn submitted to the Board subcommittee in December 2001 stated that Bank had violated six of its own policies in the project and partially complied with a seventh (ADB 2001). The BIC accepted the report, and it was sent to the Board. Bank management engaged in defiance: They rejected the findings and denied any wrongdoing (Bello 2002: 9). This precluded an agreement over what remedial steps needed to be undertaken to bring the project into compliance. According to the BIC, management "traversed almost every finding of the Panel, joined issue with it, at times severely criticizing the findings as well as its methodology" (ADB 2002a: 12). This the Committee felt, is not a correct approach for ADB's management to criticize findings of the panel on questions of fact, methodology or reasoning processes. However, if the panel makes a finding that is so demonstrably contrary to the weight of the evidence before it or so untenable that no reasonable panel could have reached the conclusion that it did, a case may be established for the intervention of the Committee. This is plainly not such a case. (ADB 2002a: 13)

The BIC's findings and management's response went to the Board for deliberation in March 2002 with developing member countries on the Board also rejecting the Panel's finding of noncompliance.

The Bank's Board was split over the BIC's endorsement, with China, Thailand, India, and Pakistan opposing the Panel report. The United States argued that Thailand's actions undermined the credibility of the process (van Putten 2008: 120), while the UK alternate director criticized the president and management for their defensiveness and for "rejecting the findings of an independent panel" (Bello 2002: 9). The Board ultimately approved the Inspection Function's recommendations for improving the process but it did not endorse the findings that the ADB had violated its own policies (ADB 2002b; Fukuda 2003: 33). The UK alternate executive director Frank Black resigned from the BIC in protest (ADB 2002c).

The Thai government suspended the project's construction one month after the report was released (Fukuda 2003: 33). In October 2003, with 95 percent of the project complete, the contracted loan between the ADB and the Government of Thailand was declared null and void (ADB 2004). The Samut Prakarn case revealed flaws in the investigation process and demonstrated the inability of the Board to ensure the Accountability Mechanism functioned. Despite the inability of the Inspection Function to complete its investigation, the Board nonetheless required management to submit semiannual reports on the efforts by the Bank to bring the project into compliance including a resettlement plan and ameliorating environmental damage (ADB 2002e: 10). After four reports, these activities ceased with "no further action or progress . . . on the compensation plan, monitoring activities, community involvement initiatives, or odor and effluent management" (ADB 2004). The failure to ensure remedies further speaks to the Bank's strategy of avoidance.

In sum, management used strategies of avoidance and defiance in relation to the norm: The Inspection Function was difficult for project-affected people to access, even when the Bank was later found to be noncompliant leading to harm in three of the four projects where claims were submitted (Samut Prakarn, Chashma, and the STDP). In all three cases deemed eligible for investigation, management denied any policy violation. In the one instance where the Inspection Function undertook an investigation (Samut Prakarn) the process was severely compromised. The ADB recognized problems arising out of Samut Prakarn, including "the role and mandate of BIC and the ADB Panel, lack of clarity in the Inspection Procedures and policy, the independence of BIC and the ADB Panel, potential conflict of interest issues, the responsiveness of the process to the concerns of the project affected people, and transparency of the process and communications issues" (ADB 2002e: 12). The BIC recommended amending the procedures, especially those relating to "access to [ADB] documentation, prohibition of visiting the project site, lack of transparency, and most of all the process's lack of independence" (van Putten 2008: 119).

The ADB noted that the Inspection Function had an "adverse impact on staff morale throughout ADB," leading project staff to feel under attack such that they may be afraid to take risks in the future (ADB 2002e: 35). After Samut Prakarn, operations staff working on the project were taken off their jobs and exiled, although they were later rehabilitated. Although it seemed as though the inspection process could adversely affect staff careers, the same staff went on to do well (Interview with ADB vice president, July 1, 2009). While the inspection process is adversarial by its very nature, the review of the Inspection Function identified that "a widespread consensus within ADB agrees that the Inspection Function should not resemble a court of law or become a litigious process, but that more energy be put into solving problems at least in the initial stages of a complaint" (ADB 2002e: 35). As a result, the Inspection Function was widely recognized as needing to be reformulated (ADB 2003: 7).

US Pressure for Change: The Accountability Mechanism

A review of the Inspection Function was begun in 2001 during the Samut Prakarn inspection. During 2000 and 2001 the G7 called for improving the MDB accountability mechanisms, which the ADB heeded (ADB 2002e: 3). In 2002 the US Treasury announced to Congress that they hoped to strengthen the ADB's inspection panel.[80] The subsequent review was considered the most "transparent and participatory policy making process in the ADB's history" (Fukuda 2003: 34). During 2002 input from NGOs and stakeholders was collected as roundtables and consultations were held in ten cities around the region and the world (ADB 2003: 6–8; van Putten 2008: 121–122). These fed into a 2002 working paper on revising the mechanism, which would be discussed by the Board in January 2003 before being sent out for public comment (ADB 2002d, 2003a).

At the Board meeting it became clear that there was strong support for an independent mechanism not under Board control from donor states such as the United States, United Kingdom, and Canada, backed by Korea. Both the United States and Canada recommended placing a requirement for accountability mechanism investigations into the loan agreement with developing member countries to ensure access should an investigation be warranted. India was opposed. Other developing member countries like Malaysia and Indonesia wanted to retain the ability of borrowers to place conditions on in-country investigations. India further wanted to restrict the role of any panel by limiting an investigation to ADB-financed projects where only 25 percent of the loan had been disbursed (as opposed to the Inspection Function's 95 percent). India also argued that environmental and social issues including resettlement are the primary responsibility of sovereign states, not the Bank. Developing member countries, including China, were concerned that any inspection process would delay projects and place additional burdens on borrowers, both of which would lose the Bank business; and they wanted to ensure that NGOs could not abuse the process. Yet they all agreed on establishing a consultation process for project-affected people to seek resolution with the Bank and to extend the accountability mechanism to private sector operations.[81]

In 2003, the US Treasury reported to Congress that a "review of the Bank's inspection procedures is currently underway . . . although we have been deeply concerned about lapses in professional conduct. Management has taken steps to correct the situation and we will continue to monitor this closely."[82] US oversight continued to place pressure on the ADB through its annual replenishments of the Asian Development Fund and through general capital increase negotiations. In May 2003 the ADB replaced the Inspection Function with its Accountability Mechanism. In 2004, the US Treasury highlighted the ADB's establishment, with strong US backing, of a new "inspection mechanism to reinforce accountability and address the concerns of persons affected by AsDB-assisted projects" as evidence of meeting the US reform agenda.[83]

The paper establishing the Accountability Mechanism clearly stated that during the Samut Prakarn inspection "it became evident that the current inspection process and procedures are lengthy, confusing, and complex for stakeholders inside and outside ADB. This reinforced the need for a further review of the current structure, and an evaluation of options for the future." It further noted that "first full inspection also raised concerns about independence, credibility, transparency and information dissemination, and effectiveness of the Inspection Function (ADB 2003: 1).

The option of retaining the basic structure of the Inspection Function in the review process carried the caveat that "the Samut Prakarn Investigation created such strong divisions and was so controversial within ADB that the . . . Inspection Function process may be tainted" (ADB 2002e: 42). A second option of creating a World Bank Inspection Panel structure was also floated, but the model "is by its very nature adversarial and this may only escalate the concerns of all ADB stakeholders." Moreover, it lacked a problem-solving function and had not been applied to private sector operations (ADB 2002e: 44). The third option suggested was the ombudsman model like the World Bank Group's Compliance Advisor/Ombudsman (CAO), which would be less divisive for the ADB and have no stigma of inspection. However, the mediation process could be indefinite or reach no agreement between parties, and it had not been applied to public sector lending (ADB 2002e: 47). A later proposition was to create two separate mechanisms akin to the Inspection Panel and the CAO, but there was not a sufficiently compelling reason to do so (ADB 2002d: 67).

In the end, the Bank adopted a fourth option. Based on extensive consultations in the region and Board support, the new mechanism established a bifurcated system. The first function was "consultation" between the Bank and project-affected people, and the second function was a "compliance review," where the ADB is investigated to assess where noncompliance with its own policies may have led to harm. Preceding the IDB's MICI, this two-step process was sequential, requiring project-affected people to first engage in problem solving before being allowed to submit a claim requesting investigation into Bank noncompliance. Despite following the CAO's separate but linked dispute resolution and compliance functions, the Accountability Mechanism was considered groundbreaking for being applicable to both public lending to sovereign states and to private sector operations (at that stage 10 percent of ADB's portfolio involved private sector operations, ADB 2002e: 23). This was a key US request.

The Accountability Mechanism is therefore composed of two separate offices: the Office of the Special Project Facilitator (OSPF), which offers consultation including mediation, dispute settlement, and dialogue, and the Office of the Compliance Review Panel (OCRP), which investigates noncompliance by the Bank with its policies that may have resulted in harm (ADB 2012d). The Special Project Facilitator reports to the president while the Compliance Review Panel reports to the Board of Executive Directors (Suzuki and Nanwani 2006: 221). The Office of the Special Project Facilitator is under management because facilitation is part of problem solving by the Bank during a project's execution. It is to address problems between project-affected people and the Bank because

> [M]any DMCs did not want the SPF to probe into their areas of responsibility. Thus, the 2003 policy clearly provided that "[t]he SPF will not interfere in the internal matters of any DMC and will not mediate between the complainant and local authorities." (Suzuki and Nanwani 2006: 221)

The Special Project Facilitator is now appointed from outside the ADB and is assisted by an expert and two administrative assistants hired from within the Bank (the first Special Project Facilitator was a career Bank staff member appointed at the level of a director general). The problem-solving function allows the Bank and requestors to attempt to fix a problem rather than finding fault. This avoids viewing management and operations staff directly and the borrower indirectly as violating Bank policies. Requestors may avail themselves of the second office of the Compliance Review Panel (CRP) if they choose to opt out of the consultation phase, or during or after the consultation process, or even after their request for consultation has been deemed ineligible for problem solving (ADB 2003: 19–20). Under the Accountability Mechanism the Office of the Special Project Facilitator received an increasing number of claims but only accepted approximately 30 percent as meeting its eligibility criteria (Park 2015: 461).

The Compliance Review Panel investigates allegations of Bank noncompliance with its own operational policies. The Compliance Review Panel departed from the Roster of Experts of the initial Inspection Function and the IDB's first accountability mechanism. It is composed of three Panel members appointed by the Board like the World Bank's Inspection Panel (ADB 2003: 8). However, it retained the process of reporting directly to the Board's subcommittee, which was renamed the Board Compliance Review Committee (BCRC). The Board Compliance Review Committee retains the capacity to establish the terms of reference for an investigation and to review the Compliance Review Panel's evaluation of its monitoring of the Bank's remedial actions as approved by the Board (ADB 2003: 10). This was despite the recognition that,

> Since the panel of experts reports to BIC, the relationship between the panel and BIC, on the one hand, and the relationship between BIC and the Board, on the other, have not only affected the independence of the panel, but also the functions of BIC and management's relations with the Board and BIC, resulting in delays, debates, and potential conflicts of interest in the application of the inspection policy. The perceived lack of the independence of the panel has threatened the credibility and viability of the inspection process. (ADB 2003: 6)

The Compliance Review Panel remains under the jurisdiction of the Board, which determines what actions are necessary to bring the ADB into compliance where it has found policy violations and made recommendations. The three Compliance Review Panel members are appointed by the Board on the recommendation of the president, and two must be from regional member countries and one from a developing member country (ADB 2003: 22). The Office of the Compliance Review Panel Secretary and administrative assistants are Bank staff. In the beginning the ADB even created a higher-paid executive secretary above the secretary; later this position was abolished, but both positions have been staffed by former Operations Department director generals. While senior operations staff therefore know exactly how projects are undertaken, they may also be less willing to challenge entrenched lending norms that overlook harm.

NGOs allege that Bank management has "at times attempted to exert undue influence on CRP processes," which are akin to a strategy of manipulation (Oxfam Australia 2011: 13). This has led some stakeholders to see the secretary as a representative of management (ADB 2012d: 10), meaning that "the panel is not given unfettered discretion in carrying out its work" (Suzuki and Nanwani 2006: 208).

Where the Accountability Mechanism was given real power to shape the Bank is the Compliance Review Panel's mandate to monitor management compliance with any remedial steps it recommended to the Board from its investigations. This was strongly supported in external consultations when revising the Inspection Function (ADB 2002d: 107). This substantial power provides with the Compliance Review Panel with greater influence than any of the other accountability mechanism except the World Bank Group's CAO (discussed next). This goes beyond the ad hoc requests for monitoring the World Bank's Board requests from the Inspection Panel, or the ability for the later iteration of MICI to be consulted as to the corrective actions to be undertaken by the IDB. It used this power in two cases: the Sri Lankan STDP case and the Pakistan Chashma case (ADB 2012d). Both would take five years of monitoring and lead to fundamental changes at the project site (Park 2015).

According to the policy establishing the Compliance Review Panel, the Board will approve recommendations for investigation on a no-objection basis (ADB 2003: 28). This explicitly sought to ensure that investigations would not be perverted as had been the case under the Inspection Function. Where the Accountability Mechanism has continuities with the Inspection Function is the requirement of the prior consent of the developing member countries to allow in-country investigations, which hampers its operations and remains a fundamental weakness (Park 2014). This clause was retained in procedures of the Accountability Mechanism even after the 2012 review during which another investigation was unable to proceed based on a failure to secure access to a project site.

Between 2004 and mid-2019 the Compliance Review Panel registered 19 cases, signaling that few of the 290 claims registered would go on to a compliance investigation (Park 2015: 459-61, 2019). Its second case in January 2009, a development project in China, was deemed eligible for compliance review regarding the forcible relocation of people (the Fuzhou Environmental Improvement Project, Loan number 2176-PRC). Again, the issue of developing member country sovereignty led to a stand-off with the Compliance Review Panel, with China denying a site visit for the investigation. The Compliance Review Panel wanted to corroborate the claims made by the requesting parties (ADB 2011: 62). As Suzuki and Nanwani state, "the policy assumes DMCs will routinely give consent as part of the good faith cooperation of all parties in the compliance review process" (2006: 215). China declined the site visit stating that the project met the

Bank's policies, that previous visits by the Office of the Special Project Facilitator should be sufficient for the Compliance Review Panel to work from (although they are separate offices with different mandates, staff, and functions), that those requesting a compliance review no longer lived at the site, and that the compliance review request was no longer necessary as the project had since been modified (ADB 2011: 62).

The Compliance Review Panel chose not to progress the investigation because it could not investigate without visiting the project site. The issue went to the Board, where donor executive directors stridently disagreed with China's reasons not to allow an investigation but did not call for a formal Board vote, thus letting the issue drop. Donor states such as the United States, Canada, and the Europeans indicated that limiting the Accountability Mechanism might affect future ADB funding, but this seemed an empty threat, as a substantial general capital increase was passed in 2009 and Asian Development Fund financing remained unchanged (Park 2014: 15–16).

Bank Resistance and Borrower Opposition: The Accountability Mechanism Review

According to the 2003 policy a review of the Accountability Mechanism was due three years after it had begun operating, but this was delayed because of the mechanism's limited experience. At that stage "only one complaint ha[d] gone through the full process of the consultation phase and one request ha[d] gone through the full process of the compliance review phase" (Bissell and Nanwani 2009b: 15). In May 2010 the ADB president announced that the Board and management would review the Accountability Mechanism together (ADB 2011). Bank management therefore oversaw the review of a mechanism that investigates whether management has complied with its own policies. A working group composed of four Board members and the managing director general established the review parameters and two external reviewers then conducted the review (ADB 2012c). As with the 2001–2003 review, the process included worldwide stakeholder roundtables to solicit input.

Most of the review's recommendations focused on overcoming the technical barriers for project-affected people to access the mechanism, including eliminating the two-step process to allow people to choose to file a complaint directly to the Compliance Review Panel (ADB 2012c: i). In addition, the ADB created a complaints receiving officer who would verify a claim's authenticity, register the case for assessment of its eligibility for the Office of the Special Project Facilitator or the Office of the Compliance Review Panel, and alert Bank management and operations departments to address ineligible but valid concerns.

The ADB therefore provided a focal point for requests, while claimants no longer had to go through the problem solving if they want to move directly to a compliance review (MICI would copy this in its 2014 policy). The review also improved the internal tracking of requests once they entered the Accountability Mechanism process, outlined aims to improve outreach and awareness of the mechanism, and aimed to enhance learning and improve the culture of the ADB (ADB 2012d).

Part of the reason for incorporating a consultation phase into the Accountability Mechanism was to overcome the adversarial nature of the Inspection Function (ADB 2003: 7), although tension remains (ADB 2012d: 13). The 2012 review reported that management, staff, and the Board view the Accountability Mechanism as a "tool to respond positively to public scrutiny and learn how the organization can do better" (ADB 2012d: 13). However, it is not clear that accountability is supported by the president or management (Park 2014: 16). The Compliance Review Panel continues to be heavily criticized by some in management and some executive directors, who view it as a nuisance (Interview with accountability expert, October 22, 2013). For management, it is considered a success if a complaint does not go to the Compliance Review Panel. Staff have a negative view of the Compliance Review Panel and do not want to be investigated. They are not in favor of the Accountability Mechanism because it interferes with the lending process and may draw attention to problems "caused by their funding" such that "staff consistently derail the inspection process" (Fukuda 2003: 34). The Bank engages in avoidance by being highly selective in providing the Compliance Review Panel with information during an investigation (Interview with ADB staff, July 1, 2009). However, differences do exist among the regional Departments in their interactions with the Panel and some staff have even been pleasantly surprised that investigations have not been as bad as they feared (Interview with ADB staff, July 1, 2009).

NGOs are highly critical of the Accountability Mechanism who see it as "image polishing" for the Bank because it remains relatively unknown by local groups, is difficult to access, hard to follow, time consuming, and with unclear outcomes (NGO Forum on the ADB n.d.). Activists argue that the ADB established more steps in the accountability process in order to retain control. Other practitioners see the Accountability Mechanism as one of the best mechanisms because of its bifurcated model and monitoring capacity (Interview with accountability expert, February 4, 2009). However, strong questions were asked over its independence given that the first Special Project Facilitator and the administrative staff were appointed by management with little regard for international legitimacy. NGOs viewed the Accountability Mechanism as being composed of ADB men or career Bank professionals, thus undermining its credibility (Fukuda 2003, 35–36). The lack of involvement of civil society in appointing the special project facilitator and the compliance review panelists continues to undermine its independence (Accountability Counsel n.d.).

Within the Accountability Mechanism itself, the implementation of dual offices in 2003 created "competition, non-collaboration and even separate annual reports" (Oxfam Australia 2011: 19). Although the separate offices worked together on outreach, they operate separately. The 2012 review mandated that they work together to produce a single website and annual reports. Staff in both offices think they contribute to improving the plight of project-affected people either through problem solving or through monitoring to bring the Bank into compliance (Interviews with ADB staff, September 3 and 10, 2013). Although former staff argue that accountability mechanisms "tend to have limited competence to review the internal law of their parent institution" (Nanwani 2010: 113), suggesting an inherent flaw in the Accountability Mechanism selection process.

Donors noted the improvement of the Accountability Mechanism (ADB 2012b) and the United States is relatively satisfied that the process operates effectively (Interview with senior US congressional staffer, September 26, 2013). A US Treasury report stated to Congress that the new Accountability Mechanism Policy increased Board oversight.[84] The Board Compliance Review Committee reviews the Compliance Review Panel's reports and overseeing its budget and personnel appraisals. From 2012 the Compliance Review Panel chair, who leads investigations into noncompliance, was given the administrative task of running the office rather than a secretary (generally a Bank staff member). The Board Compliance Review Committee can now control the office because they review Compliance Review Panel staff performance appraisals and the office budget (ADB 2012d: 16). Thus, the review increased the Panel's independence from management in terms of staffing but offset this with increased Board oversight that also threatens its capacity to act independently.

Meanwhile developing member countries continue to view the process as inspecting them, and they resisted stakeholder calls that Compliance Review Panel investigations be a condition of all loan agreements. They argued that "the ADB has no basis to mandate site visits through loan agreements because the compliance review is about ADB's compliance with its own policies not about a borrower's breach of any obligations." The review concluded that opinions on site visits are deeply divided (ADB 2012d: 10) and that giving the Panel responsibility for acquiring borrower consent does not always work (ADB 2011: 24). The review working papers posited options to overcome this problem including mandatory Compliance Review Panel site visits but notes that this has been "seen as infringing upon national sovereignty" (ADB 2011, 24). The final review report suggested that management try to use its good offices to help the Panel to obtain a site visit, but where developing member countries refuse, that the Compliance Review Panel should nonetheless complete their investigation (ADB 2012c:16,

39). The review was still underway when the Panel closed the Fuzhou investigation, claiming it could not make a recommendation to the Board. This fundamentally undermines the ability of the Accountability Mechanism to verify claims and ensure due process. China's determination not to allow in-country investigation also shows that the Board will acquiesce based on state sovereignty.[85]

A significant outcome of the review was to limit the power of the Compliance Review Panel to devise remedial actions that management should comply with when found to be noncompliant leading to harm (ADB 2012c, 16–17). This process was seen to cause confusion as remedial action plans must be agreed on between management and the borrower. Previously the Compliance Review Panel undertook lengthy monitoring processes in relation to the STDP and Chashma investigations to meet the Panel's remedial actions. These are the only two investigations that have been completed and they demonstrate that the Accountability Mechanism can hold the Bank to account leading to significant improvements in Bank actions (Park 2015). While the Compliance Review Panel can now only comment on the remedial action plan devised by management and the borrower, it has retained its ability to monitor the Bank's remedial actions (ADB 2012d: 26–27). However, this too has been circumscribed by limiting monitoring to two to three years. Although the Accountability Mechanism structure has substantially improved as a result of US pressure and the following 2012 review, Bank resistance and borrower reticence clearly remain. In sum, the ADB has engaged in strategies of avoidance including limiting the independence of its accountability mechanism, making unduly onerous technical criteria that hamper access to the mechanism, and defiance in denying the eligibility of claims and seeking to undermine investigations. In the two cases monitored the Accountability Mechanism took five years to ensure that remedies had been undertaken. The experience of the World Bank Group's mechanisms stands in stark contrast and is discussed next.

From Strength to Strength for the World Bank Group's Compliance Advisor/Ombudsman

This section details how the World Bank Group has institutionalized accountability as justice. The CAO is independent, and therefore relatively insulated, from the management and Boards of the IFC and the MIGA. This has allowed greater discretion for the CAO to undertake its operations compared with the other mechanisms, and therefore from requiring US interventions to overcome them. Meg Taylor was appointed as the CAO's vice president in 1999. Her terms of reference were negotiated with World Bank Group President Wolfensohn, with the president determining the budget, separate from management. The CAO vice president term was for three to five years, renewable by mutual consent. Taylor held the position of vice president for 14 years (stepping down mid-2014). Taylor provided stability and institutional memory, establishing the reputation and credibility of the CAO. Unlike other accountability mechanism officers, Taylor had not worked for the World Bank Group prior and would be banned from doing so after her term. The World Bank Group repeated the broad based and inclusive process in appointing her replacement. Except for the Inspection Panel, the CAO is the only accountability mechanism that has the capacity to hire its own permanent staff. The CAO office is now composed of approximately 16 staff and it hires independent mediators, compliance investigators, and environmental and social experts on an as-needed basis.

Board dynamics are also different in relation to this accountability mechanism as the IFC and the MIGA deal with private sector loans, investments, and guarantees. The private sector can choose not to borrow, invest, or buy political risk from the World Bank Group compared with the sovereign lending from the other MDBs, where Bank shareholders may depend on loans if they are unable to access capital from the private sector on reasonable rates. The IFC client surveys show that project sponsors choose the IFC as a financier based on its environmental, social, and governance expertise, and are more likely to remain as a result of their experience (IFC 2006a: 5). There is also a level of awareness of the CAO with IFC's project sponsors (companies). This does not mean that companies agree to engage with the CAO in mediating a dispute with project-affected people (Park 2019). Indeed, there is a high incidence of companies choosing not to engage in dispute resolution, although this is like other accountability mechanisms open to the private sector. Indeed, the company Endesa, which financed the Pangue dam that triggered the need for the CAO, withdrew from IFC financing (see chapter 3). The IFC also engaged in avoidance and defiance strategies in that case: denying the legitimacy of the claim, refusing to acknowledge wrongdoing, and failing to provide adequate remedies (Park 2010a).

This section focuses on CAO efforts to institutionalize the norm through its three reviews. World Bank Group resistance is less obvious here than for the other banks, because the CAO reports directly to the World Bank Group president, rather than the IFC or the MIGA Boards or management. The CAO may provide briefings to the Boards on request and regularly updates the Boards' Committee on Development Effectiveness (CODE).[86] IFC and MIGA executive vice presidents were mandated by their Boards to work with the CAO. Management had no say in devising the technical criteria for accountability mechanism claims, which meant that they could not devise highly technical restrictive barriers for accessing the mechanisms as the other banks had. Further, because the CAO operates independently, management could not interfere with, or undermine,

the investigation process. Two bank avoidance strategies are still evident in relation to denying claims as legitimate and failing to provide adequate remedies,
and these are more fully evident in the cases outlined in chapter 5.

First, its operations are detailed. The CAO aims to "assist IFC and MIGA address complaints of people affected by projects . . . and to enhance the social and
environmental outcomes of projects in which these institutions play a role" (CAO
2000: 4). Initially the CAO was the only accountability mechanism with a tripartite structure including its ombudsman role, advisory services, and compliance
investigation. The ombudsman role is to "deal with complaints from external
parties affected by IFC or MIGA projects" (CAO 1999). The addition of advisory
services ultimately means that the CAO provides advice to management in order
to improve the World Bank Group's policies, procedures, guidelines, and internal
systems. This complements its compliance function, which seeks to identify the
World Bank Group's environmental and social compliance. Initially none of the
other mechanisms had an advisory function, meaning that they struggled to
influence their banks in terms of the lessons learned from the claims filed by
project-affected people, which limited their ability to shape the banks' operations
and culture. The CAO was also the first mechanism given the capacity to monitor
projects to assess Bank compliance after investigation. This gave the CAO substantial muscle in enforcing Bank change, although it would take a while to build
this component.

From the very beginning, the CAO viewed its ombudsman function as
its "primary and its most important responsibility" (Bridgeman and Hunter
2008: 210; CAO 2000: 4). The CAO is well regarded, with one activist stating
that the other accountability mechanisms are so rudimentary that they cannot
be compared with the CAO (Interview with accountability activist, August 13,
2013). The CAO accepts complaints from any "individual, group, community or
entity or other party affected or likely to be affected by the social and or environmental impacts of an IFC or MIGA project" and can do so in any language. The
complainants may also be represented by another party and be confidential. The
CAO also provides guidance on how to lodge a complaint (CAO 2000: 11–12,
2013b).[87]

The CAO directly mediates between the affected community, the IFC or the
MIGA, the project sponsor (private sector entity or government agency), and the
host government. The "initial and primary emphasis is on the classic problem-
solving approaches such as facilitation, mediation and negotiation," leading to a
finding (CAO 2000: 14). The ombudsman seeks to establish a mutually acceptable solution through promoting dialogue and self-generated solutions. More
formal problem-solving processes such as conciliation proceedings and mediation may be needed to negotiate a settlement. The ombudsman can only persuade parties to reconcile through dispute resolution. Consequently, the only

leverage the CAO has is the cooperation of the World Bank Group in investing in or guaranteeing the project. This depends on the percent the IFC has invested or at what time the complaint occurs and how much IFC has invested or recouped. The CAO directly attempts to influence project sponsors where they have breached IFC or MIGA policies and attempts to improve the plight of affected people while the project is still in its design or implementation phase. Where these processes do not provide a solution, the CAO may investigate further in "promoting dialogue or arranging for conciliation or mediation, or for making recommendations to the president" (CAO 2000: 17). The CAO then reviews and monitors the agreement between the parties once concluded.

Complainants may raise concerns about a project's implementation or World Bank Group policies, the latter may be addressed by the CAO through its advisory function, its second role (CAO 2000: 12). The CAO is mandated "to provide independent advice to the President and senior management of the IFC/MIGA" (CAO 2000: 4). It may do so either informally or formally through regular reporting to the president and to the Boards as requested by the president, IFC and MIGA management, or of the ombudsman's own initiative. The advisory function created significant confusion in the first five years of the accountability mechanism's existence both inside and outside the World Bank Group. World Bank Group staff were unsure where advice on internal operations stops and the CAO independence begins, particularly as the mechanism may later become involved in an ombudsman process or compliance audit in relation to informal advice previously given. This was compounded by the early work of the CAO, which designated some of its work as an audit but viewed it as formal advice to management rather than under its compliance function (CAO 2003).

The mechanism's third function is the compliance investigation. The CAO may undertake "audits of IFC's and MIGA's social and environmental performance, both on systemic issues and in relation to sensitive projects" (CAO 2000: 4). A compliance audit may ascertain whether "staff and in some cases the sponsor, have complied with IFC and MIGA social and environmental policies, guidelines and procedures." The findings include recommendations for corrective actions that are submitted to the president which should then be integrated into management's monitoring of the project, which would be monitored by the CAO (CAO 2000: 20).[88] Compliance audits may be triggered by the World Bank Group president, management, the CAO, or after the 2007 review, automatically as a result of a failed ombudsman process. Based on Taylor's recommendation, the World Bank Group president eliminated the mechanism's right to trigger an audit pending an ombudsman mediation process. This was done in order not to compromise an ombudsman process and to ensure the impartiality of any audit conducted (Dysart et al. 2003: viii, 25). It also substantially reduced the power of the office to hold the World Bank Group to account.

The Compliance Advisor/Ombudsman Reviews

Throughout its history, the CAO has undertaken four reviews of its operations in 2003, 2006, 2010, and August 2020. The first and third were of its own accord, the second and fourth in response to World Bank Group Board requests. Possibly preempting a Board review request, the 2003 review was not dissimilar to the bureaucratically mandated reviews of the other mechanisms. However, the CAO 2007 operational procedure revisions were not Board-imposed changes following poorly handled cases as evident in the World Bank, the IDB, and ADB, but a course correction to improve its processes in response to Board engagement. Unlike any of the other accountability mechanisms, there was no need for the United States to pressure the World Bank Group to enforce the norm because the CAO was attuned to the need to improve its own practices.

In April 2003, the CAO commissioned three external environmental and social experts to independently review its operations (CAO 2003: 4). The report found that the CAO was successful in its ombudsman role but that it was overextended and needed to formalize its practices. In response, the office hired more staff and designated a life of the project mediator process in order to allow Taylor to supervise the office; this became vital for large multiparty dispute resolution processes for complex projects. The compliance audit function was seen as underdeveloped, with the review recommending that the CAO initiate its own compliance audits. In response, the office reinstated its right to trigger an audit, which the reviewers argued was a powerful tool that could wither if it was dependent on management for instigating a complaint or rely on local communities that might not have the capacity to do so (Dysart et al. 2003: 25–26).

However, triggering an audit during an ombudsman process created confusion in cases in the early 2000s, with uncertainty as to how the compliance process for evaluating claims and assessing fault worked amid the neutral ombudsman process (CAO 2010: 34). Tensions existed between resolving conflicts through the ombudsman process and finding fault with the IFC for policy non-compliance that may impact negatively on the project sponsor's reputation (and undermine their willingness to be part of mediation efforts) (CAO 2010: 37). For example, in a large multisited complex dispute over land in a palm oil project in Indonesia, the project sponsor, Wilmar, felt "betrayed after having made a good faith effort to resolve issues through problem-solving" when the case proceeded to a compliance audit simultaneously (Fairman et al. 2010: 14; this is discussed further in what follows and in chapter 5).

Regarding its advisory role, more was also needed to be done to overcome the confusion as to what the CAO does both outside and within the World Bank Group. The World Bank Group president stated that "formal advice would stem from complaints to the ombudsman and from compliance audits and would address process and policy issues in a broader context [rather] than an individual project" separating the level at which the office engages in providing advice (CAO 2003: 11). In sum, no project specific advice would henceforth be given to staff by the office. The review also recommended that the accountability mechanism provide the World Bank Group with broader strategic advice on how to avoid and address project-level conflict and systematic lessons learned (including sectoral based recommendations) that emerge from its case work. The Office's operating procedures were updated in 2004.

The review highlighted that "IFC and MIGA senior management has clearly affirmed publicly the importance of the CAO as a credible and independent environmental and social 'accountability' mechanism." World Bank Group staff hold the Office in high esteem and there is "respect for its staff and, in general, for the fairness and independence with which it operates" (Dysart et al. 2003: 4–5). According to the review, the "CAO seems to genuinely strive to be respected by and be comfortable with both senior management inside the institutions and the affected communities on the ground" (Dysart et al. 2003: iv). Yet in the early days the CAO's advice to management on controversial issues was "sometimes attacked openly" although its value was later privately acknowledged, leading to CAO recommendations being implemented. For the CAO, the World Bank Group was "a sometimes hostile, antagonistic, reluctant environment that has difficulty learning and changing in the newer areas of accountability, openness, and trust vis-à-vis environmental and social development results" (Dysart et al. 2003: 12). Indeed, after the CAO informed the World Bank Group that all formal advice provided to management would also be made public, MIGA management indicated that it would not solicit advice from the CAO (Dysart et al. 2003: 20).

After experiencing a deterioration of relations between parties in mediating three separate projects (CAO 2006a: 21), the Office was increasingly aware that it needed to identify when to conclude mediations "where the parties involved are not cooperating voluntarily or where we cannot play a constructive role." The World Bank Group Board subcommittee on development effectiveness (CODE) then asked the accountability mechanism to review common triggers for requests for mediation, and to comment on the effectiveness of each of its three roles. The CAO hired three consultants to undertake the review in 2006. The *Trends Report* discovered that the Office was involved in 1 percent of World Bank Group projects but that it was receiving an increasing number of complaints (CAO 2006a: 7). The increase in complaints most likely stem from the CAO's outreach efforts, and the fact that the IFC invested in the world's largest cross-border infrastructure construction project, the Baku–Tbilisi–Ceyhan (BTC) pipeline running through Azerbaijan, Georgia, and Turkey. This project generated 33 ombudsman claims (Park 2019).

The CAO revised operational guidelines in May 2007 (CAO 2007a).[89] Changed practices include complete neutrality in the ombudsman process "rather than assessing policy violations or conducting fact-finding or recommending a specific course of action independent of the stakeholders" (CAO 2007b: 2). It also began monitoring during the ombudsman and compliance processes to ensure that parties meet agreed-on practices; and it opened a window for the World Bank Group and project sponsors to evaluate compliance after completing a compliance audit (CAO 2007b: 3, 8). Furthermore, an unsuccessful mediation would now also automatically trigger the compliance function (CAO 2007a). The 2007 Operational Guidelines also clarified the relationship between the CAO and the Boards, where the former provides information at the request of the latter (CAO 2006b: 9). Since the 2006 review the compliance function has been increasingly utilized, the majority of which are triggered by the Ombudsman process (CAO 2007b: 12; 2006a: 7, 13). Indeed 51 cases would be investigated under the compliance audit function between 2000 and mid-2019.

These activities all fed into the Office's third review of its operational procedures beginning in 2010, leading to the update of its operational guidelines in 2013 (CAO 2012b: 22–24). Again, the mechanism hired three consultants to undertake the review (Fairman et al. 2010), with public consultation from June to August 2012. The review aimed to continue the CAO's best practice in dispute resolution and compliance (CAO 2011: 4–5, 2012a: 13).[90] The most significant change was the option given to claimants to choose mediation or proceed directly to compliance, which NGOs had long pushed for (Interview with accountability activist, May 15, 2009; CAO 2012b).[91] Again such revisions were instigated by the Office, not by the Board or the World Bank Group president, or by powerful shareholders such as the United States. This reinforces the view that the accountability as justice has been institutionalized within the World Bank Group.

All of the World Bank Group presidents have supported the Office: Wolfensohn in creating it in 1999 after the Chilean Pangue dam claim (see chapter 3), Wolfowitz in using it by triggering a compliance audit in 2005, and Zoellick in dramatically enacting a World Bank Group–wide moratorium on palm oil lending in response to the CAO's findings of the Wilmar project in Indonesia soon after.[92] In 2009 President Zoellick stated that the "dispute resolution work of the CAO has proven critical in finding satisfactory solutions and delivering results on the ground" and that the Office "is a crucial part of our development work" (CAO 2009: 1). Two of the last three IFC executive vice presidents have backed the CAO's work, Peter Woicke (1999–2005) and Jin Yong-Cai (2012–2016) (Interview with CAO staff, February 20, 2009). Yet it was not until 2009 that the World Bank Group "made a concerted effort to institutionalise processes" for responding to its operations (CAO 2009: 3).

The 2010 review uncovered cases of IFC avoidance where staff have been un-helpful in the ombudsman process. Although "interviews suggest that manage-ment sees the Ombuds function as a net positive for IFC and wishes to support it, but the Risk management Committee has not always ensured a constructive or usefully neutral IFC role in Ombuds cases" (Fairman et al. 2010: 27). Activists question the extent to which the CAO can hold the IFC to account, when medi-ation aims to solve the problem without finding fault (Interview with accounta-bility activist, August 13, 2013). Feedback during the 2010 review argued that the Office was cleaning up the mess made by the IFC (CAO 2012b: 9). The CAO also notes that management responses to its compliance audits remain dismissive (CAO 2013a: 4). As with the other banks, investment officers fear the CAO, feel that they are trying their best, and do not want to be investigated for compliance. IFC staff are overwhelmed in trying to ensure that the organization is policy compliant with regard to monitoring and supervision. Interviews by the review team noted that staff were not familiar with the CAO's advisory notes that seek to help organizational learning (Fairman et al. 2010: 30; CAO 2012b: 17–18).

In short, the CAO has not needed presidential or Board intervention even though it is clear that the World Bank Group Board's Committee on Development Effectiveness keeps an eye on the work of the CAO and management's response. This demonstrates that accountability as justice has been institutionalized within the World Bank Group. As chapter 5 demonstrates, this does not mean that IFC and MIGA do not engage in resistance strategies in relation to claims, or that the CAO has impacted on the lending imperative culture of the World Bank Group. Indeed, the most recent review of the CAO's operations, led by former IFC executive director Peter Woicke, was prompted by increasing polarization between IFC, MIGA, and the CAO over insufficient IFC responses to its findings of noncompliance (Woicke 2020). However, the independence of the Office from management and the Boards does mean that it has not faced the same avoid-ance, defiance, and manipulation strategies in relation to technical criteria for accessing the mechanisms and interference in its investigations.[93] The next sec-tion examines Bank resistance to accountability as justice at the European Bank for Reconstruction and Development (EBRD).

Making Accountability as Justice Work at the European Bank for Reconstruction and Development

The EBRD created the Independent Recourse Mechanism in 2003 to be part of Bank management rather than be independent, resulting in the United States abstaining from voting for it. The Independent Recourse Mechanism was designed to be part of the Bank's decision-making structure, to ensure its budget, and to keep costs down. As this is a donor-heavy Bank, there is less borrower opposition to the accountability mechanism at the Board and many of the projects funded by the Bank are carried out by private companies. However, companies can and do oppose problem solving (Park 2019). This section documents the Bank's avoidance strategy in designing an internal mechanism for accountability as justice that made access difficult for project-affected people. This was a powerful means of restricting submissions to the Independent Recourse Mechanism, fundamentally undermining its ability to operate. The United States pushed to ensure that the policy establishing the Independent Recourse Mechanism included a review of its operations after two years. US influence led to its restructure as the more independent Project Compliant Mechanism (PCM) in 2009. Subsequent improvements in 2013 were again backed by the United States, and in 2020 it was restructured as the Independent Project Accountability Mechanism (IPAM).

Bank Resistance: The Independent Recourse Mechanism

Designed by the Legal Department with input from Bank operations staff, the Independent Recourse Mechanism was positioned within the Office of the Chief Compliance Officer (Interview with EBRD staff, October 14, 2013). The Office of the Chief Compliance Officer was charged with ensuring the Bank's highest standard of integrity covering Bank codes of conduct for personnel and the Board, including investigating allegations of fraud, corruption, and misconduct (EBRD 2014a). Independent of Bank operations, the Office of the Chief Compliance Officer reports to the president. Within the Office, the Independent Recourse Mechanism is "designed to provide . . . the independent review of complaints from local groups on whose common interest a bank-financed project has, or is likely to have, a direct adverse and material effect" (EBRD 2004: 1). The operations of the Independent Recourse Mechanism are separate from the other functions of the Office despite the chief compliance officer overseeing everything. The Independent Recourse Mechanism provides recourse for those outside the Bank, but the mechanism reports to management or the Board depending on the status of the loan subject to a complaint.

Following the ADB's 2003 Accountability Mechanism, the EBRD chose to establish a unit that could assess whether the Bank could rectify people's grievances through problem solving and/or whether harm had occurred as a result of Bank actions through a compliance review. The Independent Recourse Mechanism process differed markedly from the dual functioning sequencing processes of the later mechanisms by allowing simultaneous problem-solving and compliance review.[94] Despite debates over the extent to which other policies could be invoked by the Inspection Panel, the ADB's 2003 Accountability Mechanism, and the African Development Bank's (AfDB) 2004 Independent Review Mechanism are not limited to assessing the environmental and social safeguard policies and information disclosure.[95] While the IDB's first mechanism was limited in this way the second, MICI, now covers all Bank policies, although it identifies which ones may be the most applicable.

In contrast, the EBRD engaged in an avoidance strategy to limit the Independent Recourse Mechanism's applicability to whether the Bank is following its 2003 Environment Policy and project specific provisions of its Public Information Policy. As such, the EBRD from the very beginning excluded any other policies that local groups could challenge in calling the Bank to account, such as any economic evaluation of the project or financial management that could lead to harm. Moreover, the policy makes clear that the accountability mechanism cannot be used to invoke the Bank's first article of its Articles of Agreement: where the "purpose of the Bank shall be to foster the transition towards open market-oriented economies and to promote private entrepreneurial initiative in the Central and Eastern European countries committed to and applying the principles of multi-party democracy, pluralism and market economics" (EBRD 2006: 5). In other words, the Independent Recourse Mechanism cannot be used as a tool to further the European Bank's support for democratic processes at the project level.

The 2003 Independent Recourse Mechanism policy was explicit that investigations or problem solving at the project level to address people's grievances would be done "as expeditiously as possible and to minimize any disruption that they may cause to the daily operations of the Bank, project sponsors and Bank clients" (EBRD 2004: 1). Activists commonly denounce the MDBs for continuing to ignore the social and environmental costs of the financial decisions they make as they continue their business as usual, something clearly signaled here. As with all of the other mechanisms, a claim to the Independent Recourse Mechanism does not stop a project from continuing to be financed and built, although an Independent Recourse Mechanism officer could recommend the halting of disbursements to the president or Board if "serious irreparable harm shall be caused" (EBRD 2004: 6). There is no evidence that this has over occurred.

The mechanism's procedures made submitting a complaint difficult, with complainants needing to address nine components in their submission. Oddly enough, this included why "there is no reasonable prospect of resolving the issue through an effective dialogue with the Bank," which undermines the need for a problem-solving function (EBRD 2004: 6). Much of the policy reflects the other mechanisms in terms of what is considered eligible for investigation and the time frames for the Independent Recourse Mechanism to respond to requests. The mechanism emulated the idea of a roster of ten experts on which the Independent Recourse Mechanism can call for assistance (as per the initial IDB and ADB mechanisms).

The Independent Recourse Mechanism proceeds by evaluating whether a complaint is eligible and warrants an investigation through an initial Eligibility Assessment Report. Eligibility assessment experts are hired by the chief compliance officer. Irrespective of whether the claim warrants a compliance review, the chief compliance officer may determine that the claim may be suitable for problem solving (EBRD 2004: 11–12). The recommendation is then submitted to the Bank's president. The president is charged with responding to the recommendation if the project has not yet been approved by the Board for financing, or for projects that do not need Board approval.[96]

Under certain conditions the president therefore has the power to block an investigation of his own staff, as was the case with the IDB's original mechanism. If the project has been approved by the Board, then the president must pass the recommendation for a compliance review to them for approval. As with the IDB's first mechanism, the Board "*may choose to send the recommendation back to the Assessors for revision*" (EBRD 2004: 14; emphasis added). Again, this gives the Board the power to delimit the nature of the compliance review or to accept or reject the Independent Recourse Mechanism's recommendation for investigation. Despite being established nearly a decade after the IDB's first mechanism and being aware of the difficulties and lack of legitimacy of the IIM, the EBRD emulated similar processes for its accountability mechanism. The lack of independence from Bank management and the Board undermined its capacity to hold the Bank to account.

The chief compliance officer determines whether a problem-solving process may benefit affected communities and has a likelihood of success irrespective of whether a compliance review is ongoing. A recommendation to proceed with a problem-solving initiative is then submitted to the president by the chief compliance officer along with a recommendation for appointing a problem-solving facilitator (EBRD 2004: 18). If a compliance review has been requested this is approved by the president or Board (for the same reasons as previously discussed). The compliance review is undertaken by a compliance review expert chosen from the roster. Upon completion, they submit the findings and recommendations to either the president or the Board. The Compliance Review Report may identify remedial actions to be undertaken by management to bring the project back into compliance. Importantly the Independent Recourse Mechanism was given the capacity to indicate recommendations for Bank management including "any remedial changes to systems or procedures within the EBRD to avoid a recurrence of such or similar violations" as well as at the project level. Significantly the chief compliance officer was also given the capacity to monitor Bank management's implementation of its recommendations and report on it at least annually (EBRD 2004: 15–16). In sum, this means that the Bank restricted what claims could be made for, had a high level of technical criteria for claimants to meet in submitting claims, and enabled the president to reject claims or enabled the Board to modify the accountability mechanism's recommendation for investigation. If a claim passed all these hurdles, the mechanism would be able to force policy compliance if an investigation found the Bank noncompliant leading to harm and requiring remedial action to bring it into compliance.

Even before it had begun operating, the Independent Recourse Mechanism was criticized for not being independent of management, for not being transparent, and for only covering the Bank's environmental and information disclosure policies (EBRD 2003). NGOs argued that "the weaknesses in the proposed IRM undermine the independence, credibility and effectiveness of the IRM for the affected people it is meant to serve."[97] It was also pointed out that the roster of experts had not proven to work in other cases and that adding accountability to a staff member, with multiple other duties does a "disservice . . . to both the claimants and to the Bank."[98] NGOs recommended separating the functions of the Independent Recourse Mechanism rather than attempting to do both simultaneously, just as the CAO was struggling to separate its functions (2003; CEE Bankwatch 2007).

The Independent Recourse Mechanism began functioning in July 2004. Its first annual report was delayed due to the mechanism's relative inactivity. Some argue that the mechanism "made an effort not to be known" (Interview with Accountability Officer, October 4, 2013). By that stage, the Independent Recourse Mechanism had received seven complaints, but only two met the eligibility criteria leading them to be evaluated to determine whether problem solving or a compliance review was warranted (IRM 2004–2005: 1–2). Throughout its existence the Independent Recourse Mechanism would register 5 out of 13 claims in order to assess their eligibility for a compliance review or problem solving.[99] In 2006 the chief compliance officer reported that she was having difficulties in applying some of the mechanism's rules of procedures but that a review of the Independent Recourse Mechanism policy was precipitous due to its relative operating inexperience (IRM 2006: 5).

Of the five cases that were accepted during the Independent Recourse Mechanism's existence (2004–2009), three went through problem solving, two of which were halted by the project sponsor. Recall that 60 percent of the Bank's loans must go to the private sector and many of the projects investigable by the Independent Recourse Mechanism are executed by private companies that may not want to engage in problem solving. Only one claim to the Independent Recourse Mechanism would then go on to a compliance review, a thermal power project in Albania (the Vlore Thermal Power Generation Project, number 33833) regarding the impact of the power plant on tourism, fishing, and biodiversity in Vlore Bay (IRM 2007: 3). The findings of the Vlore compliance review were that the Bank did not meet the public consultation and information disclosure requirements of the Bank's Environment Policy but that this was a minor technical violation not requiring changes to the project (EBRD 2009b; CEE Bankwatch 2008: 9). As with all the other IRM recommendations, this was approved by the Bank's Board and president (IRM 2008). The Independent Recourse Mechanism did undertake a post hoc compliance review that showed where the Bank could have improved its procedures. The reviewers argued that its findings could feed into the Bank's update of its Environment and Social Policy, which took place in May 2008.

While the Board and president approved all the recommendations of the Independent Recourse Mechanism during this period, there was little in the way of protracted problem solving or compliance reviews being undertaken that challenged the Bank's operations or culture. Both the Board and management accepted the mechanism's findings of minor technical policy violation of the Vlore case (Interview with two EBRD staff, September 27, 2013). This led one NGO to state that the "IRM does not pass judgement on ineffective EBRD policies and strategies, it does not encourage active engagement with all parts of civil society . . . and it does not have power over the actions of the EBRD's clients" (IRM 2007: 2). For that reason, the Independent Recourse Mechanism was not a significant challenge to the Bank as had been the case for the other MDBs.

Nevertheless, a shareholder-mandated review was required. Unlike the other Bank reviews, this was an internal process for restructuring an in-house mechanism. In 2007 it was agreed that the Independent Recourse Mechanism be comprehensively reviewed to improve its ability to meet the timelines laid out in its Rules of Procedure and address the limited scope for problem-solving initiatives (IRM 2007: 6). The Independent Recourse Mechanism recognized that its "Rules of Procedures are considered by many to be less than 'user friendly' and not well known (either internally or externally to the Bank)" (IRM 2008: 4) and that its process was overly technical and cumbersome (Interview with EBRD staff, September 27, 2013). NGOs argued that the mechanism was "effective in preventing requests to look into the compliance of certain projects with EBRD's policies" because of its excessively legalistic language (CEE Bankwatch 2007: 1, 3). The limited policies that were investigable under the mechanism and technical criteria and language made it difficult for project-affected people to make claims.

Natalie Bridgeman of the NGO Accountability Counsel was hired to benchmark the Independent Recourse Mechanism to the other accountability mechanisms, conduct internal Bank surveys, and to provide a revised draft policy for the Bank's consideration.[100] An internal working group was set up to recommend changes involving the Office of the Chief Compliance Officer, the Legal Department, and the Environment and Social Department. As with the previous process establishing the mechanism, the Bank responded to stakeholder submissions and included some of their recommendations (EBRD 2009b). Yet it was clear that there was no possibility that the accountability mechanism would be given independence by being moved out of the Office of the Chief Compliance Officer (Interview with accountability expert, May 18, 2009). This was seen as problematic because it could not ensure confidentiality requested by complainants, withstand pressure from management, or ensure the integrity and functioning of the unit separate from budgetary pressures.[101]

The revised draft of the Independent Recourse Mechanism's Rules of Procedure was opened for public comment between December 2008 and February 2009. Revisions that were taken up from stakeholders included: changing the name to a Project Complaint Mechanism to make it clear what the unit was for, establishing a specific position for a Project Compliant Mechanism officer to administer the mechanism, streamlining the process for eligibility, dropping the need for president/Board approval for compliance reviews, giving management a formal right of reply to a complaint, allowing NGOs to submit claims, providing clear language and time frames for the mechanism's operations, and appointing at least three experts to serve on the roster (IRM 2008: 4–5).

Enacting Accountability as Justice: The Project Complaint Mechanism

During the review, the US executive director used their vote and voice to advocate for ensuring its independence. On May 6, 2009, the Board voted to replace the Independent Recourse Mechanism with the Project Complaint Mechanism The reformulation enabled the Project Complaint Mechanism to determine whether a claim is eligible independent of the president or the Board (EBRD 2009a: 10). The Project Complaint Mechanism undertakes a problem-solving initiative pending the president's approval, but if the Project Complaint Mechanism believes a compliance review is warranted, it will notify the Bank president or the Board as required. Once it has conducted the review, the mechanism submits its report to Bank management and the president or Board as appropriate. If noncompliance has been detected, management must formally respond in the form of a management Action Plan. Both management and claimants then can respond to the Compliance Review Report. The Project Complaint Mechanism then revises the recommendations (but not the findings) of the report for submission to the Bank's president or Board for acceptance (EBRD 2009a: 13). Thus, the mechanism is notably free of interference from the Bank's president or

Board, whereby the Project Complaint Mechanism now informs them of their deliberations rather than seeking approval to continue to investigate allegations of harm by project-affected people. A newly created PCM officer was placed in charge of the mechanism. The first officer, Anoush Begoyan, was "fierce" in protecting the office from management involvement (Interview with accountability officer, October 4, 2013). The Project Complaint Mechanism retained the Independent Recourse Mechanism's power to monitor any remedial actions that arise from a compliance review where the Bank has been found noncompliant.

Most of the changes to the Project Complaint Mechanism were pushed through because they had the backing of the US executive director (Interview with accountability expert, May 18, 2009). The Board generally supports the work of the mechanism, but by early 2013 there had not been any significant findings of Bank policy noncompliance from any investigations. Nonetheless the Board does not want projects stopped or to be held hostage for financing operations (Interview with EBRD staff, October 14, 2013). Under the revised rules the Board now plays very little role compared with the Independent Recourse Mechanism (in stark contrast to the IDB and ADB). The Board is informed about the president's determination to approve problem-solving initiatives and they are informed by the mechanism should a compliance review be recommended. They are then informed as to what the findings are, and management's responsive actions to the accountability mechanism's findings. In short, the Board cannot kill it (Interview with EBRD staff, November 5, 2012).

There has been no problem with the Bank president signing off on problem-solving initiatives by the accountability mechanism. Under President Sir Suma Chakrabarti this was a formality (Interview with two EBRD staff, September 27, 2013). Arguably it is not within the president's interest to oppose improving dialogue between project-affected people and project sponsors. The president and management support the Project Complaint Mechanism (Interview with accountability expert, October 11, 2013). The Project Complaint Mechanism states that there is a good relationship between the panel, management, and the Environment and Social Department allowing for frank discussions even when it is leaning toward a finding of noncompliance (Interview with two EBRD staff, September 27, 2013).

In reformulating the accountability mechanism, the complaint process was streamlined in terms of the number of criteria to be included in a submission, although it retained its overly technical structure or legalese (Interview with accountability expert, February 27, 2009). The US executive director, the external consultants conducting the review, and Independent Recourse Mechanism experts pushed for the right of individuals and NGOs to make claims, not just two or more project-affected people, which the Bank accepted (Interview with Accountability Officer, September 27, 2013; Interview with accountability expert,

May 18, 2009). This substantially altered the number of claims being accepted for investigation (PCM 2011, 2012: 3) with 34 claims being accepted (registered) between 2010 and mid-2019 (compared with five under the Independent Recourse Mechanism between 2005 and 2009). The second major improvement was the decision to allow affected people to choose whether they wanted problem solving or a compliance review or both rather than having that be determined by the accountability mechanism (as per the other revised mechanisms).

In 2013 the Project Complaint Mechanism detailed three findings of Bank noncompliance—the first since the establishment of the mechanism in 2003 (PCM 2013: 4, 7–9). All three were hydro power plants. All were found noncompliant in relation to the Bank's policies on biodiversity and sustainable natural resource management. After three findings in a row of noncompliance the Bank was reeling, with the Legal Department advising the Board and backing up staff (Interview with Accountability Officer, October 4, 2013). There is now greater awareness of the Project Complaint Mechanism by operations staff at headquarters (more so than in the resident offices in the regions) but claims make staff nervous, and they do not know how to proceed (Interviews with EBRD staff, November 5, 2012). Staff know about the Project Complaint Mechanism, especially those have been complained about such as the extractives and energy sectors. Unlike in the early days of the Independent Recourse Mechanism, bankers now "accept it but [they] don't necessarily like it." By including staff input into the 2013 review they were able to engage with the process without being able to scuttle it (Interview with EBRD staff, October 14, 2013).

The former chief compliance officer viewed the Project Complaint Mechanism as a definite improvement over the Independent Recourse Mechanism (Interview with EBRD staff, October 14, 2013). Noncompliance findings emerging from investigations concluding in 2013 reveal that the mechanism can show where the Bank has failed. The PCM officer has the power to monitor the implementation of the Bank's management Action Plan devised in response to its recommendations. Monitoring may take place biannually or until "the PCM Officer determines that monitoring is no longer needed" (EBRD 2014b: 8). These robust provisions provide the Project Complaint Mechanism with the ability to better enact accountability as justice.

The then–PCM officer, Anoush Begoyan, stated that the number of claims submitted shows that it "has gained the trust of project-affected communities and civil society groups and is viewed as a credible recourse mechanism" (PCM 2011: 2). The Project Complaint Mechanism accepted 32 cases for either problem-solving or compliance investigation between 2010 and mid-2019. The Project Complaint Mechanism noted that civil society was "largely approving, but also constructively critical and incisive" (PCM 2013: 2). Unlike the CAO, there is no publicly available evidence of the Bank's private sector client's position on the mechanism. Project Complaint Mechanism staff and experts do state that the project sponsors improve their behavior when the mechanism is around (Interview with two EBRD staff, September 27, 2013). In 32 cases eligible for problem solving between 2010 and mid-2019, nine of those were rejected for consultation by the project sponsor.

As with the 2009 review, a 2013 review of the mechanism was conducted internally with the assistance of an accountability expert, this time by Mr. Richard Bissell, former World Bank Inspection Panel and AfDB Independent Review Mechanism chair. The main focus was to improve the Project Complaint Mechanism's timeliness in responding to claims and undertaking investigations, making the process more efficient when shifting from the eligibility assessment to the compliance review, and hiring more staff to undertake outreach and in-reach.[102] Stakeholders recommended the mechanism cover more than just the Bank's Environment and Social Policy and Public Information Policy, both of which the Bank was reviewing in 2013 (PCM 2013: 19). The Project Complaint Mechanism fed its findings back into the Bank's review of its environmental and social policies, which led to its revised Environmental and Social Policy in 2014. The 2013 update of the PCM was shareholder mandated with minor technical changes to its Rules of Procedure (EBRD 2014b). A subsequent review in 2018 led to the revision of the mechanism, now called the Independent Project Accountability Mechanism (which came into effect in 2020). The revised version of the mechanism is now completely independent of Bank management, reporting to the Board via its Audit Committee (EBRD 2020). The head of the mechanism is now a senior leadership position answerable to the Board and hired through a multistakeholder process. This gives the accountability mechanism the independence the United States has pushed for from the beginning. The AfDB, discussed next, established a mechanism that looked very similar to the EBRD's initial mechanism in enacting accountability as justice.

The Slow Emergence of the African Development Bank's Accountability Mechanism

This section outlines the structure, operations, and reviews of the Independent Review Mechanism while documenting AfDB management's strategy of avoidance. Although it was initially floated in 1994, the AfDB's accountability mechanism did not come into effect until 2004. Many regional member states (RMS) and management were not in favor of having a mechanism, but the Bank nonetheless adopted the norm once the United States demanded it, and the G7 statement made it clear that it was needed. Even though there is greater opportunity for the regional member states to control the Board, there has been less obvious

Board opposition to the Independent Review Mechanism compared with the other banks. This may be the result of two factors: First there is a high degree of churn at the Board, meaning that executive directors change over quite rapidly for many constituencies (Interview with accountability expert, October 28, 2013). Executive directors might be unfamiliar rather than hostile toward the accountability mechanism. In response, the Independent Review Mechanism has conducted a lot of outreach to the Board over time to explain what it does.

Second, despite the Bank's heavy focus on infrastructure lending, which often triggers accountability mechanism claims, the Independent Review Mechanism has a much smaller caseload. The Independent Review Mechanism has the shortest track record of the mechanisms examined here, receiving 37 cases between 2007 and mid-2019, and accepting 14 for problem solving or compliance. This may stem from the fact that there is little known about the mechanism. It may also result from the fact that there is not a support network for claimants, or that there is a less antagonistic relationship between civil society actors and the Bank, meaning that it is not a beleaguered institution like the World Bank (Interview with accountability expert, September 30, 2013). Some note that the larger banks that co-finance projects with the AfDB attract claimants (Interview with accountability expert, September 30, 2013). For example, requestors may choose to lodge claims with the better-known Inspection Panel or the CAO if the project is being co-financed. However, the Independent Review Mechanism's first case, regarding the Ugandan Bujagali Hydropower Project, was the focus of both an Independent Review Mechanism and an Inspection Panel claim. Bujugali showed the AfDB that a compliance review request was not fatal for the Bank, considering how the World Bank weathered it (Interview with accountability expert, September 30, 2013).

The structure of the accountability mechanism is detailed to demonstrate its lack of independence and the Bank's avoidance and defiance strategies: The Bank adopted restrictive technical criteria for accessing the mechanism, denied any wrongdoing even when found noncompliant leading to harm, and failed to respond to the mechanism's findings. Recall that the AfDB began formulating the mechanism in 1999, when the World Bank was undertaking its second clarification of the Inspection Panel resolution. The Panel was considered a hostile presence in the World Bank. Such views may have led the AfDB's Legal Department to aggressively protect the Bank by being actively unhelpful during Independent Review Mechanism investigation processes, particularly by undercutting the Panel in Board meetings (Interview with accountability expert, October 28, 2013).

There was a lot of tension with management in its first five years, leading the Independent Review Mechanism to conduct internal outreach to management (Interview with accountability expert, September 30, 2013). The then Bank president Donald Kabaruka (2005–2015) was "formally supportive, not substantive" of the mechanism, but relations deteriorated over time (Interview with accountability expert, October 28, 2013). Nonetheless the first Compliance Review and Mediation Unit (CRMU) director did a good job of building relationships in the Bank and they never had difficulty accessing information for investigations or interviewing staff, as was the case with some of the other mechanisms (Interview with accountability expert, October 28, 2013).

As with the revised mechanisms, the Independent Review Mechanism featured a bifurcated problem-solving and compliance review process (Resolution B/BD/2004/9—F/BD/2004/7). Some argue that despite being the latest mechanism it did not learn from the weaknesses of the others (Interview with accountability expert, February 4, 2009). As with the ADB's revised mechanism and the European Bank's accountability mechanism, the Independent Review Mechanism was given the power to go beyond detailing the findings from an investigation to make recommendations for how management should undertake remedial action, and the power to monitor any changes implemented. This gives the mechanism the capacity to enforce the accountability as justice norm (AfDB 2006). The Bank's mechanism has already gone through two reviews of its operations, which were undertaken as mandated by its Enabling Resolution. This led to improvements advocated for by external stakeholders being incorporated in 2010 and 2015.

The Independent Review Mechanism

It is clear from the Enabling Resolution establishing the Independent Review Mechanism that Bank management looked to the previous accountability mechanisms to base much of its design: Control of the mechanism was overseen by a single individual answerable to management—the CRMU director—in the same way that the chief compliance officer did for the EBRD's Independent Recourse Mechanism. Like the European Bank, the policies investigable were limited. Although all policies are investigable for public sector projects, the policy limits any Independent Review Mechanism action to assessing the effect of environmental and social policies for private sector operations (AfDB 2004c: 3, para. 11). In this way, the AfDB's avoidance strategy was to emulate the MDBs that preceded it. As with the 2003 Accountability Mechanism for the ADB and the EBRD's mechanism, project-affected people could seek recourse for both public and private sector operations funded by the AfDB.

The Board was also given the power to determine the terms of reference for any investigation (see AfDB 2006). The Independent Review Mechanism policy contains much the same information relating to the eligibility of claimants to make a request as the other mechanisms: that claims should not be frivolous, should be related to Bank actions and policies, should not regard corruption or procurement, and should not be made for competitive business advantage. Like the IDB, the AfDB policy declares that it excludes complaints that are before other judicial review or similar bodies (AfDB 2004c: 4, para. 14 (vi)).[103] The Independent Review Mechanism's operating procedures signaling the power of the Compliance Review and Mediation Unit to advise the president or Board to suspend a project if serious irreparable harm is likely to stem from a project. Again, this has never happened.

As with the other mechanisms, a registration process is enacted once a claim has been received to determine whether it is bona fide. The operating procedures also determined that lessons learned from the cases would be identified in the Independent Review Mechanism's annual reports, although whether and if they are taken up by the Bank remains questionable. Both problem-solving and compliance reviews are undertaken by the Compliance Review and Mediation Unit, with the compliance review being conducted by the CRMU director along with two of three independent experts on a roster. The Bank president appoints the director, while the Board appoints the Independent Review Mechanism experts. The CRMU director is appointed for five years with one renewable term; the roster of experts is appointed for one nonrenewable five-year term and cannot work for the Bank for two years afterward. The CRMU director chooses whether problem solving or compliance review or both are appropriate per request (Independent Review Mechanism 2006: 9). They also choose whether a request to keep a claimant's identity confidential is warranted (AfDB 2006: 7, para. 7). The CRMU director may also trigger a compliance review if a problem-solving initiative is not concluded within three months. The outcome of a problem-solving initiative is then submitted to the president or Board; if they reject the outcome of such a mediation, they will have to notify the parties to the problem-solving process (AfDB 2006: 26).

For a compliance review, the CRMU director establishes the terms of reference and chooses two of the three experts on the roster to constitute a compliance panel with the director. The director will make a recommendation for a compliance review to the president (if the project has not yet been approved) or to the Board for approval. If the CRMU director does not recommend a compliance review (and the claim has not been through mediation), or if it is unclear whether the request is eligible, it goes to an expert on the roster to determine whether it should proceed to a compliance review (AfDB 2004c: 5, para. 23, 2006: 11, para. 27; Independent Review Mechanism 2006: 9). After this, management then has the right to comment on the claim.

The policy states that the Board will accept the Independent Review Mechanism's recommendation for an investigation on a no objection basis but as was the case with the EBRD and the IDB, the Board still has the power to *send the recommendation back to the IRM to have the terms of reference or the experts chosen reassessed* (AfDB 2004c: 5, para. 24). The Board invoked this to limit the compliance investigation of its second compliance claim regarding a power project in South Africa (the Medupi Power Project, RQ2010/02) with reference to the governance, climate change, and corruption charges made by claimants. It is up to the president (prior to a project being approved) or the Board to accept the findings and the recommendations of an IRM investigation, so the final decision rests with the president or Board. As with the other banks, the AfDB has underscored the importance of the accountability mechanism process by requiring Board and management intervention, thus undermining the independence of the mechanism. However, the Compliance Review and Mediation Unit was given the power to make recommendations for remedial action it deems warranted from its findings, and it was also given the capacity to monitor any remedial action by the Bank agreed to by the president or Board from those recommendations.

Again, like the EBRD's accountability mechanism, the AfDB restricted what claims could be made for, had a high level of technical criteria for claimants to meet in submitting claims, and enabled the Bank president to reject claims or enabled the Board to modify the accountability mechanism's recommendation for investigation. If a claim passed all these hurdles, the mechanism would be able to force policy compliance if an investigation found the Bank noncompliant leading to harm. Moreover, the Independent Review Mechanism policy enables the accountability mechanism to make recommendations and monitor changes to the AfDB's policies and systems as well, again following the EBRD (AfDB 2006: 13; EBRD 2004: 15). This gives the Independent Review Mechanism substantive power to shape the Bank *if* an investigation finds the Bank noncompliant with its own policies leading to harm.

The Compliance Review and Mediation Unit began functioning in April 2006, but it took a while for the Office to be staffed (Independent Review Mechanism 2006: 3, 7; 2007a). On May 16, 2007, the Compliance Review and Mediation Unit received its first request for a compliance review regarding a hydropower project in Uganda, the Bujagali Hydropower Project and Interconnection Project (Independent Review Mechanism 2007a: 8). After a preliminary assessment the director recommended to the Bank's Board that a compliance review be undertaken. This was approved in September 2007. The findings and recommendations of the compliance review were submitted to the Board in July 2008, they found some policy noncompliance but also discovered "gaps or lack of clarity in the Bank's policies and procedures" and was therefore "unable to make clear findings of either compliance or non-compliance" (Independent Review Mechanism 2008: 11).

The Bank engaged in a strategy of avoidance. The Board requested management prepare an action plan to respond to the panel's recommendations regarding specific policy and procedural issues for early 2009. The first case highlighted the need to clarify the Bank's policy framework; to make policies publicly available; and to improve project collaboration of staff across the Bank (Independent Review Mechanism 2008: 11). It took close to 10 months for management to present their action plan, which was only done after the Independent Review Mechanism complained to the Board. The delay was excused on the basis that there is no time frame for management's response to be completed and the Bank was awaiting the outcome of the findings of the World Bank Inspection Panel's investigation of the Bujagali claim (Hansungule 2009: 21; the World Bank co-financed the project).

Having only just become fully operational, the Compliance Review and Mediation Unit was already preparing for a review of its operations at the end of 2008 (Independent Review Mechanism 2007a: 14, 2008: 4). The review was begun in 2009 with the intention of submitting the results to the Board in early 2010. An independent consultant, Professor Michelo Hansungule, was appointed to undertake interviews in and outside the Bank before meeting with the Board and then publicly releasing the draft for comment (Independent Review Mechanism 2009: 5, 8).

As with the other mechanisms, stakeholders argued that the Independent Review Mechanism was overly technical and legalistic requiring simpler language for affected people and easier means to submit claims (by email for example). They also argued that project-affected people should be able to choose whether they want problem-solving or a compliance review and this, as well as the issue of confidentiality, should not be left up to the CRMU director. In addition, both public and private sector operations, NGOs and accountability officers from other mechanisms argued, should be fully investigable with the latter not limited to environmental and social policies (AfDB 2009: 2). All commentators, including accountability officers from other mechanisms recommended that Bank management should formally reply to an Independent Review Mechanism investigation within a short time frame (AfDB 2009: 4).

As the mechanism was still in its infancy, the draft report did not recommend major changes. Three alterations suggested throughout the review process were taken up by the Bank: first, that the CRMU director be approved for appointment by the president of the Bank with the concurrence of the Board (AfDB 2010a: 2, para. 3). The director is also not to sit on the compliance panel but to allow the three experts to undertake a compliance review separate from the Compliance Review and Mediation Unit to allow them greater independence (AfDB 2010a: 6, para. 22). Second, the Board was given the power to submit a request for compliance review or problem solving, which stakeholders had also recommended (AfDB 2010b: 4). Finally, management now must formally respond to the Compliance Panel's findings and recommendations to the Board (AfDB 2010b: 18, para. 57). The Independent Review Mechanism's revised operating procedures were approved by the Bank's Board on June 16, 2010 (Independent Review Mechanism 2010: 5; AfDB 2010b).

The Independent Review Mechanism has accepted 37 requests since its inception. While requests were evenly divided between those seeking problem solving versus compliance review in its first three years, most cases have requested problem solving. Recall that choosing problem solving does not preclude a later compliance review. Prior to the review beginning in late 2009 the Compliance Review and Mediation Unit had received three more requests, two in relation to a hydropower plant in Ethiopia (the Gibe III hydroelectric power plant, Request 2009/01 and 2009/01b)—one requesting mediation the second requesting a compliance review, and a power plant in Egypt (the Nuweiba Combined Cycle Power Plant, Request 2009/02). Both the Gibe III claims were not investigated as the borrower chose not to continue with the project; the Nuweiba claim was also discontinued as claimants believed the Egyptian government planned to move the project. Further research is needed to identify the role of the claims in influencing borrower behavior. Since then, most problem-solving initiatives have been successfully concluded (Independent Review Mechanism 2010, 2011a, 2012).

To date, the Independent Review Mechanism has designated eight claims for compliance review.[104] The Gibe III requests were dropped as just described. For the third claim, a road project in Morocco (Marrakesh-Agadir Motorway RQ2010/01), the director rejected a compliance review based on the fact that the problem did not result from a Bank act or omission per se and the requestors were satisfied with the outcome of mediation (IRM 2010: 20).[105] The Bank came off badly in terms of the only two compliance reviews it has undertaken, the Ugandan Bujugali hydro project, and the 2010 claim regarding the South African Medupi Power project (RQ2010/02).[106] Bank defiance is evident because management denied any wrongdoing in both cases. The Bank was found noncompliant with its policies in both investigations. Bank avoidance was also evident: During the 2009 Independent Review Mechanism review, the compliance panel began monitoring whether the Bank had implemented its action plan in relation to the Bujagali project. It found that the Bank continued not to be compliant in relation to resettlement, its sustainable management plan, and consultation processes with project-affected people (Independent Review Mechanism 2009: 17). The IRM would undertake four years of monitoring the Bank in relation to Bujagali for these issues to be addressed (Independent Review Mechanism 2012: 5). The compliance panel also found evidence of Bank noncompliance in the Medupi case requiring a management Action Plan and monitoring (Independent Review Mechanism 2012: 5).[107] The compliance reviews revealed the hodge-podge of statements and purposes that constituted the Bank's environmental and social policies, contributing to their replacement with an Integrated Safeguard Strategy in 2014 (Interview with accountability expert, October 11, 2013).

The small number of cases and high turnover of senior management and Board members means that there is still not a great deal of awareness of the accountability mechanism (Interview with accountability expert, October 11, 2013). The current Bank's Board and management support the Independent Review Mechanism (Interview with accountability expert, October 11, 2013). The Board is always available to the mechanism and has not blocked any investigation. There were disagreements with the Independent Review Mechanism's findings in relation to Medupi, but this was not based on bad faith. Indeed, some EDs became more appreciative as a result of learning from the Independent Review Mechanism's investigation. As a result, there is not a sense of hostility or fear that is engendered within the other banks from their accountability operations, although management still views the process as antagonistic where compliance investigations have revealed Bank wrongdoing. The Independent Review Mechanism's experts therefore spend a "great deal of time building bridges with management . . . there is a lot of tension" (Interview with accountability expert, September 30, 2013). Resources are stretched and staff become defensive during an investigation. Yet the process may also "empower staff" to ensure they find the best way of undertaking a project contra management, where other factors such as the cost and expediency may influence project design and implementation. Experts argue that there is some panel proofing at the Bank although it is hard to establish the degree of risk aversion from having an accountability mechanism. The compliance investigations have positively influenced the Bank to better document following the safeguard policies (Interview with accountability expert, October 28, 2013).

The 2013 review was shareholder mandated and examined increasing the mechanism's staff and resources to better inform project affected people (Interview with AfDB staff, October 13, 2013). The revised 2015 policy now gives claimants the opportunity to choose problem solving or compliance review as per the other mechanisms. It also gives the mechanism some independence for undertaking a compliance review but not its scope: The policy reinforces the Board's acceptance of the Independent Review Mechanism's recommendation for compliance review on a no-objection basis (AfDB 2015: 3), but the president and the Board still retain the power to delimit the terms of reference for an investigation and may choose whether to accept the mechanism's findings and recommendations. Thus, the management and the Board retain control over the process (AfDB 2015: 6).

The Independent Review Mechanism was given the ability to provide advice to the Board and Bank management like the CAO. Despite the systemic recommendations made in the mechanism's annual reports, previously there was no mandated role for the Independent Review Mechanism to advise staff, management, or the Board on how to improve its governance, even though it is increasingly being asked to do so (Interview with accountability expert, September 30, 2013). This gives the Independent Review Mechanism the ability to influence the practices of the Bank before claimants come to the mechanism as a last resort. This can contribute to changing the culture of the Bank. For example, the Compliance Review and Mediation Unit is now also able to identify not more than two high environmental and social risk projects for its Independent Review Mechanism experts to spot check for their policy compliance under an advisory review (AfDB 2015: 6). This practice is unusual for the MDBs: many of the other banks have environmental and social staff able to track compliance during a project's execution, and independent evaluation units to conduct random evaluations once projects are complete. Given the small caseload of the Independent Review Mechanism, this may be a way to take advantage of the expertise of the roster of experts. Although, yet again, the Board retains control over the terms of reference for the spot-check. While the Bank's president and Board still retain control over the accountability mechanism, it has institutionalized accountability as justice at the AfDB and has been given broader powers over time.

Conclusion

This chapter examined how the norm of accountability as justice was resisted by the banks and some borrowers, resulting in accountability mechanism operations being stymied. Nonetheless, borrowers generally agree with the accountability as justice norm, they continue to contest specific provisions. The banks engaged in three strategies of avoidance, defiance, and manipulation. Avoidance was evident by foot-dragging in responding to claims of noncompliance leading to harm, through only providing ceremonial information for investigations, and by not providing remedies once found noncompliant. Defiance is also evident across all the banks, with management denying any wrongdoing even in the face of evidence to the contrary. They further challenged the rules of the investigations, seeking ways to preempt or interfere with investigations, and in some cases engaged in manipulation to influence evaluative criteria and control how staffs respond to the process. The blatant mishandling and obvious inability of the IDB and ADB to allow people to hold the banks to account would lead the United States to use its power of the purse, voice, and vote to demand improvements.

Member states required periodic reviews of the mechanisms to ensure they functioned. The reviews have improved the ability of project-affected people to access the mechanisms and they have made the mechanisms more independent. For example, for the Inspection Panel this took place through quasi-judicial precedent setting within the confines of a rigid resolution determining its operations, while the CAO instigated its own reviews to improve its practices. All the mechanisms are now able to independently determine whether a claim is valid and whether an investigation should ensue. Greater independence enables the mechanisms to better enact accountability as justice. Over time, the mechanisms have shifted to bifurcated processes of mediation between project-affected people and the banks and separate investigations into Bank noncompliance (and even the rigid Inspection Panel has now accepted dispute resolution). The banks and borrowers and hope that problem solving efforts address the problem while reducing the likelihood of investigating bank compliance. The next chapter documents the improvements in the mechanisms over time, while showing how this sits alongside the banks' operational practices and culture. Infrequently egregious harm leading to an accountability mechanism claim sparks policy change in the banks.

5

Accountability as Justice in Practice

Challenging the Banks?

Introduction

The last two chapters demonstrated the strategies the United States used to generate a norm of accountability as justice and how the banks and some borrowers continue to resist it. This chapter examines how the accountability as justice norm has been enacted since the mechanisms were created. It shows how the accountability mechanisms became accepted as part of the banks' governance structures through routinizing their operations and their growing caseloads. The mechanisms are part of the internal accountability processes of the banks to check their behavior and are "last resorts" for project-affected people. Yet projects generally continue during an investigation, and remedies such as stopping the harm and rectifying damage remain with bank management. The chapter provides an overview of the operations of each of the mechanisms up to the middle of 2019 to demonstrate the difficulties of achieving justice through problem-solving and compliance investigations. It also demonstrates when and how bank management has engaged in passive and active strategies to resist the norm, and when this has been supported by the banks' boards. The chapter reveals differences between the multilateral development banks (MDBs), with more independent decision-making, monitoring, and advisory powers enabling the provision of justice through accountability emerging over time.

The Accountability as Justice Norm in Practice

The accountability mechanisms are formal sanctioning processes that now have two components: the direct provision of recourse to project-affected people through problem solving and evaluating bank behavior to determine whether bank noncompliance caused harm.[1] Both are examined here. As discussed previously, bank management favored the introduction of problem solving, hoping this would reduce investigations into their culpability for contributing to harm. However, problem solving can only work if it is in the interests of claimants, the government, and/or the project sponsor (for nonsovereign loans), and if

The Good Hegemon. Susan Park, Oxford University Press. © Oxford University Press 2022.
DOI: 10.1093/oso/9780197626481.003.0005

project-affected people's concerns can be integrated into the project. In many cases, improvements are evident for complainants after problem solving compared with conditions prior to the process, but not necessarily compared with conditions prior to the project. While these acts may not improve the conditions of project-affected people to preproject levels, they can make a difference to vulnerable communities (Park 2015). In some instances, particularly for the European Bank, the bank has not gone ahead with financing the project after a claim, in some cases stopping the project altogether.

The following sections outline each accountability mechanism's engagement with problem solving before examining their ability to undertake compliance investigations. The problem-solving process begins with a claim being accepted as bona fide and registered as meeting the mechanism's procedural criteria (the eligibility phase). The mechanism then assesses the claim for its veracity and willingness of the parties to engage in problem solving (the assessment phase). If willing, problem solving is undertaken through a dialogue facilitated by the accountability mechanism. If successful, this will lead to an agreement among the parties (the facilitating settlement phase). This is followed by monitoring to ensure the agreement has been reached (monitoring and close out phase). Through problem solving the accountability mechanisms are in some cases able to resolve issues leading to an agreement of the parties (see Table 5.1).

Claimants first need to pass the registration process and then the assessment phase as to whether problem solving is possible. More information is needed as to why some claims are not accepted for problem solving across the banks, although they have become more transparent over time. In some cases, procedural criteria may impede the possibility of problem solving. For example, if the bank has finished disbursing its loan this determines whether claimants'

Table 5.1 Percentage of Claims Registered for Problem Solving Leading to the Monitoring of an Agreement among the Parties, 1994–2018.

Bank	Monitoring/ Close-out
AfDB's IRM	2.9%
ADB's Accountability Mechanism	4.6%
EBRD's IRM and PCM	4.1%
IDB's IIM/MICI	13.8%
World Bank Group Compliance Advisor Ombudsman	19.1%
World Bank Inspection Panel	NA

Source: Data from Park 2019.

concerns will be considered. Problem solving relies on the willingness of the parties to be involved. This is the overriding factor for determining whether access to recourse is possible. Fundamental to the process, however, is whether the claimant's concerns fit within the project design. In other words, claimants may want options that are not possible through problem solving, such as fundamentally restructuring the project or scrapping it altogether. Each accountability mechanism's efforts to enact accountability as justice through problem solving is detailed in what follows.

Often considered the strongest tool in the arsenal of those seeking to hold the banks to account, compliance investigations also may be of limited use for enacting the norm. If the aim is to provide a formal sanctioning process for evaluating whether the banks' acts or omissions have led to harm, and then establishing sanctions to prevent reoccurrences, then the original design of the mechanisms left much to be desired. The earlier versions of the mechanisms did not include functions that would enable the accountability mechanisms to provide recommendations on how to address claimants' concerns and become policy compliant, or the capacity to monitor the bank's responses to findings of noncompliance. Such designations were left to bank management and the board, meaning that the opportunity for project-affected people to air their grievances was frequently not followed up with remedies for harm.

After the Inspection Panel, the other accountability mechanisms established bifurcated sequential processes that required claimants to go through problem solving even if this is not what they wanted. This frequently delayed identifying and rectifying bank noncompliance causing harm (especially for cases where the financing is disbursed, and the project completed). The sections document when compliance investigations deemed the banks were not compliant with their environmental and social policies, and when the mechanisms were given the capacity to make recommendations on how bank management should rectify policy noncompliance, and to monitor bank responses thereafter. All of the mechanisms have now also been given advisory powers to better feedback lessons learned from their case histories. The compliance investigations reveal the tendency, most evident in the two most recent accountability mechanisms, those of the African Development Bank (AfDB) and the European Bank for Reconstruction and Development (EBRD), to use the claims to identify gaps and weaknesses in banks' actual policies, which may contribute to improving the banks' operations (as discussed later). This can be traced through the accountability mechanisms' recommendations, the banks' response via their management action plans (MAPs) to rectify the damage, and the accountability mechanisms' monitoring reports evaluating bank actions. While all of the compliance investigations reveal lessons the banks can learn to lessen their negative impact on people and their environments, it is clear that the norm was established to be a corrective of the banks' behavior rather than as a means of mainstreaming justice throughout the banks' operations and organizational culture.

The World Bank Inspection Panel

The Panel operates indirectly to address harm resulting from bank acts or omissions by investigating whether the bank is compliant with its policies. Since its inception it has received 133 claims (to mid-2019), registering 99 of those as bona fide and within its purview. Of those, 41 would be investigated for compliance, with 38 leading to findings of noncompliance leading to harm and 27 requiring a response from management as to how they would bring the project into compliance (see Figure 5.1).[2] This demonstrates that the Inspection Panel is able to hold the bank to account for not complying with its policies, with the following section detailing when the World Bank's Board or management have attempted to intervene.

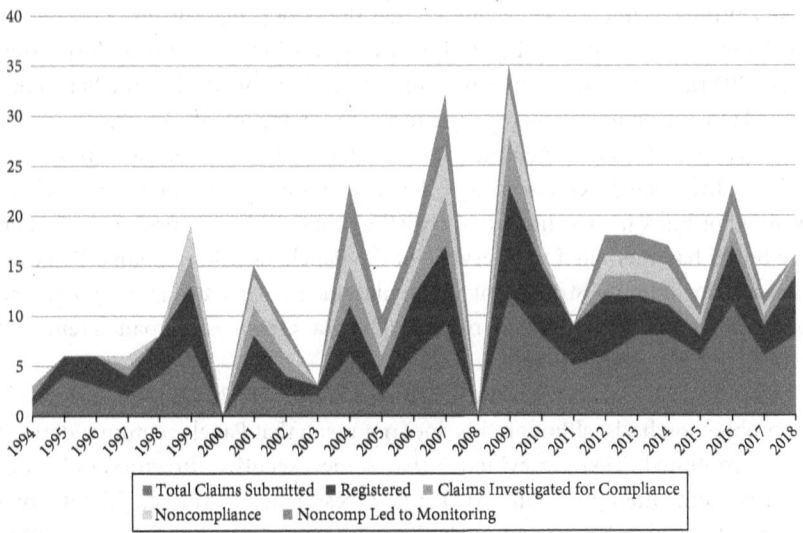

Figure 5.1 World Bank Inspection Panel Claims Accepted for Compliance Investigation and Their Outcome, 1994–2018.

Note: This is a stacked area graph that denotes the total sum of claims to the accountability mechanisms over time, broken down into the categories of which claims made it to which stage in the process. Investigations underway are excluded from the noncompliance or noncompliance led to monitoring categories. As the World Bank does not have official monitoring powers, this graph shows when the board asked the panel to monitor bank management's implementation of its management progress reviews.

Over time the oldest accountability mechanism would be increasingly viewed as inflexible because it did not have a problem-solving capacity for addressing grievances. In response, the Board amended the Inspection Panel Resolution to approve an early solution "pilot process" (World Bank 2014). This would allow the Panel the opportunity to negotiate between the parties prior to registering a claim for investigation, but only if the claim raises issues that are "clearly defined, focused, limited in scope, and appear to be amenable to early resolution in the interests of the Requestors." A pilot case would also need to be within the ability of management to address and be acceptable to project-affected people (World Bank 2014). The pilot could thus attempt to speedily address issues without a full investigation, while the World Bank also established an internal unit in 2012, the Grievance Redress Service (GRS), to address project level grievances before they escalated to an Inspection Panel request (World Bank 2010, 2017). The Grievance Redress Service operates under Bank management to work with the project teams to address complaints rather than as an independent facilitator (World Bank 2016b). Reflecting the will of the Board, two cases were deferred by the Panel under the early solution pilot in 2013 and 2014. Nongovernmental organizations (NGOs) were critical of how the Panel addressed the second case, arguing that its approach to mediation set a dangerous precedent for future Panel deliberations. While the Panel argued that the pilot process is not a process of mediation and would only be used for exceptional circumstances (Inspection Panel 2014), interest in using early solutions quickly waned while the Bank continued to work on how to incorporate problem solving into its activities.

This section looks at when the Panel has deviated from established practices, such as increasingly choosing to defer a recommendation or sit on a claim waiting for Bank management to rectify the problem. This compares with when the Board has attempted to intervene in the Panel's decision-making. Bank resistance, including a strategy of manipulation, remains strong, although the Board has, more often than not, requested the Panel oversee the bank's remedial actions to rectify harm (Figure 5.1).

After the 1999 clarification, the Board accepted all Panel recommendations on a no-objection basis, although this does not mean that Panel recommendations are uncontested. There is evidence that some executive directors and Bank management attempt to thwart Panel investigations. This highlights two factors: First, despite the entrenched nature of the accountability as justice norm, borrowers subject to a claim will still seek to challenge a Panel recommendation for investigation. Such efforts have not succeeded because the Panel is an entrenched part of the World Bank's governance structure and there is no strong anti-Panel coalition on the Board (Nelson 2000). Second, bank management often uses Board discussions over the Panel to avoid adhering to the norm, including instances of staff seeking to manipulate project-affected people during Panel investigations.

At different times, World Bank executive directors have challenged Panel claims by seeking to have World Bank programs excluded from investigation.[3] For example, in 2009 the Board pressed the Panel to reverse its recommendation for an investigation into a program loan in Yemen (in Panel case 57).[4] This was another attempt to challenge the accountability as justice norm regarding what constituted a "project" and was therefore "investigable."[5] This was an attempt to limit what the Panel could investigate, an issue that had been settled in the clarifications of the Panel in its early years. Bank management used the opportunity to attempt to avoid the investigation. They approached the Panel "to discuss additional actions and ways forward," backed by a follow up document outlining how management was addressing claimants' concerns. Member states rallied to defend the Panel, with the chair of the Inspection Panel noting "the written statements submitted by Executive Directors in advance of this Board meeting. We appreciate their indications of support." The Panel chair stated, "It would be a pity and also a reputational risk for the Bank if opportunities for listening and for recourse would be unduly restricted for an increasing percentage of the Bank's portfolio" (Inspection Panel 2009b). Nonetheless, the politicization worked. The Panel changed its recommendation to a deferral pending further action by management after being satisfied that requestors had "indicated their interest in exploring opportunities for additional actions to address their concerns." This allowed bank management to settle the problem outside the Panel process.

In 2010 a Lebanese water project (Panel case 71) again evinced Board interference. Here the Board "invited" the Panel to again defer its recommendation for a compliance investigation to give management time to undertake further analysis of the project's impacts. This is after the claim had been lodged and despite the Panel arguing that management's actions did not address claimants' concerns (Inspection Panel and the World Bank 2011). The Board then requested the Panel review three further management-commissioned technical studies, which is not in the Panel's mandate. The Panel had to square the circle of the Board's demands with its resolution:

> [T]he Panel cannot provide its independent assessment of issues of compliance and related harm unless through a formal investigation. The Panel is mindful that the level of technical assessment, undertaken as a basis for this Report in reporting back to the Board, is greater in depth than is normal outside a formal investigation. This was necessitated by the Board's request to revert "after considering and taking into account the analysis of the study commissioned by Management on the water quality, availability, and cost." However, this report

has carefully avoided any pre-judgment of policy compliance and simply
addresses the question of whether there are outstanding issues of risk raised in
the Request for Inspection that remain to be addressed. (Inspection Panel 2011)

The Panel identified further outstanding issues, which management agreed to
address. In 2013 the Panel made a final determination that a full compliance investigation was not warranted because it was satisfied that the Bank had complied, or had evidence of its intention to comply, with its policies.

As the Panel does not have a mandate to monitor Bank management's activities, the use of deferrals became a tool to provide impetus for both Bank compliance and stopping or ameliorating harm. The Panel has increasingly chosen to
defer investigating cases to allow management to resolve grievances. From 2004
the Panel increasingly began to defer recommendations for investigation, withholding decisions pending further information for 13 cases, 11 of which were
then rejected for a compliance investigation. However, the Panel prevaricates
between deferring judgment to facilitate the amelioration of harm and making
recommendations to investigate noncompliance. It is unclear why the Panel has
used this tool in some cases and not others. For example, the Panel rejected registering two claims in 2006 where project-affected people did not go to management first (Panel cases 42 and 43) but deferred another case in 2007 for the same
reason (Panel case 45).

For claimants, this has led to mixed results: Project-affected people were satisfied with the outcome for three cases where the Panel deferred registration to
allow management time to address a problem.[6] However, there are also instances
where the deferral process enabled Bank manipulation, and where project-affected people's concerns remained unfulfilled. In the Brazilian Parana biodiversity claim in 2006 (Panel case 41), the Inspection Panel deferred recommending
a full investigation because there was "constructive and potentially fruitful dialogue between government authorities, the Requestors and Bank staff regarding
possible steps to change the direction of Project implementation in a manner
that addresses the issues and concerns raised by the Request" and that "adequate
steps had and were now being taken to comply with Bank Policies." Yet there is
evidence of Bank manipulation in this case, where operations staff attempted to
stop project-affected people from complaining. As the Inspection Panel noted,

> [T]he Requestors felt unduly pressured by Bank staff and others not to file a
> Request for Inspection and then to withdraw the Request. The Requestors have
> cited various arguments as having been used to exert pressures. The Panel finds
> that this practice threatens the integrity of the Panel process and may have a
> chilling effect on local people who genuinely feel harmed or potentially harmed
> by Bank projects. The Panel wants to call the attention of the Board of Executive

Directors and Bank Senior Management to this matter, and trusts that these kinds of practices will not recur. (Inspection Panel 2006)

The Final Eligibility Assessment Report (EAR) then determined that a full compliance investigation was not warranted. This is despite project-affected people believing that changes to the project would not achieve the project's objectives (Inspection Panel 2007). The case was then closed.

A second claim, regarding the Quilleco hydro project in Chile in 2010 (Panel case 67), revealed that Bank management had not taken project-affected peoples' concerns seriously until the claim, after which action was immediately undertaken. The Panel then chose to defer a decision pending a review of management's efforts. In assessing whether management had addressed complainants' concerns, the Panel agreed with management that much of the damage in the area and on claimants' lives was not the direct result of the bank-financed hydro project but stemmed from previous hydro projects in the area. This included the Pangue dam that was rejected by the Inspection Panel for being financed by the International Finance Corporation (IFC) in 1995 (Panel case 5) that had led to the creation of the Compliance Advisor/Ombudsman (CAO) in 1999 (see chapter 2). The Panel recognized that the harm had been done and was irreversible. It identified the

cumulative impacts of a series of relatively small run-of-river hydropower plants, each of which could be potentially beneficial to the global environment, can have a significant impact on the local environment and the lives of people living in and from the areas affected by such projects, and that these cumulative impacts need to be appropriately evaluated in the social and environmental impact assessments of such projects. (Inspection Panel 2011b)

As the harm could not be rectified, the Panel's only recommendation was compensation and continued dialogue between the project sponsors and the bank. The Panel therefore chose not to recommend a compliance investigation despite identifying weaknesses in the social and environmental assessment of the project, thus undermining its own process.

Deferrals can be helpful if used judiciously, but they can also undermine the transparency, predictability, and the credibility of the Panel process. This undermines the provision of justice. As can be seen, the Inspection Panel's rulings are not as clear-cut as it would seem, despite being the most transparent of the accountability mechanisms (discussed in what follows). If the Panel has directed its attention to being able to provide justice through accountability, this does not explain why the Panel has chosen to reject cases whether there is prima facie evidence of noncompliance leading to harm;[7] or where the Panel has decided that investigating noncompliance would not serve a purpose (as occurred in the 1996 claim regarding a sectoral adjustment loan to Bangladesh, Panel claim 6); or when it decided not to investigate on the basis that the damage had already been done (in relation to the Chilean Quilleco hydro project discussed previously, Panel claim 67).

Outside highly politicized debates over how to react to the Panel's findings, particularly in its early years, the Panel's compliance investigations have revealed partial or full bank noncompliance with one or more bank policies leading to harm (see Figure 5.1; Park 2019).[8] The most frequent policies triggered include: Project Appraisal (OMS 2.20), Disclosure of Information, Economic Evaluation of Investment Operations (OP 10.04), Environmental Assessment (OP/BP 4.01), Physical Cultural Resources (OP/BP 4.11), Project Supervision (OP13.05), Indigenous People (OP/BP 4.10), Natural Habitats (OP/BP 4.04), Investment in Project Financing (OP 10.00), Involuntary Resettlement (OP/BP4.12), and Poverty Reduction (OP 1.00).

Partial compliance is possible for two reasons. First, because the World Bank's operational policies and procedures allow for a significant degree of discretion, invoking clauses such as "whenever feasible," that make determinations of compliance difficult (Naude Fourie 2009: 245). In some instances, the Panel merely identifies the policy without stating in the final investigation report whether the Bank was policy compliant or not. This may stem from the second reason: Some of the World Bank's operational directives (ODs) or policies contain both binding and nonbinding provisions, which had to be clarified during the late 1990s and early 2000s so the Inspection Panel could determine whether they had been breached (Naude Fourie 2009: 170). This is because it is the overall umbrella policy for all environmental assessments and incorporates multiple subcomponents, allowing for partial compliance. For example, in half of the investigations the Bank was "partially compliant" with its Environmental Assessment policy (OP/BP 4.01). As stated previously, the Panel was not given the power to monitor whether the bank has become policy compliant or whether it has developed remedies for project-affected people after an investigation. It lacks the tools either to enforce remedies or to ensure that the remedy is effective (Naude Fourie 2009: 274). As a result, even after identifying noncompliance, an investigation may not necessarily translate into positive improvements on the ground.[9] Researchers identified early in the Panel's history that only "ten of the twenty-eight claims filed had (in some case limited) positive project-level impacts" (Clark et al. 2003: 258; Inspection Panel 2009: 107). One full-length examination of the Polonoreste and subsequent Rondonia Panel investigations regarding World Bank financed projects in the Amazon in Brazil revealed that little had changed on the ground after both investigations (Rodrigues 2003).

After the Inspection Panel details its investigation findings the process ends unless the Board requests management address outstanding issues of non-compliance through a management progress review. Nonetheless, the Board can and does use the Panel to hold the Bank to account. The Board has asked the Panel to monitor Bank efforts in nearly all cases where investigations have uncovered noncompliance leading to harm. To this end, the Inspection Panel identifies whether it has monitored and followed up on the Bank actions where management was required to submit a management progress review report. In some cases, the Board has demanded more than one review. For example, in a 2004 transport project in India that included the forcible movement of people (the Mumbai Urban Transport Project, Panel case 32) the Board suspended the loan based on the Panel's findings and requested the Bank provide six management progress reports on its remedial action plans. The Board gave the Panel the power to oversee Bank management's progress.[10] Only in 2016 did Bank management begin to provide a tracking document of its responses to Inspection Panel eligibility and investigation reports (World Bank 2016e). Although the Panel can only produce findings from its investigations not recommendations, it does produce "lessons learned" summaries to the Bank on what it needs to correct to enact accountability as justice. In 2018 the Board gave the Panel the power to formally provide advice to the Bank on how to improve its practices. In short, despite its limitations the Panel is often asked to monitor the Bank's activities to ensure accountability as justice and is increasingly recognized as having case history knowledge that could be used to preempt harm. This compares quite starkly to the limited capacity of the accountability mechanism of the Inter-American Development Bank (IDB).

Inter-American Development Bank's Accountability Mechanism

The initial mechanism of the IDB, the Independent Investigation Mechanism (IIM), was unsure in its initial guise whether it was there to address people's concerns or correct IDB practices (Filho and Rios 2007: 51). Its revision in 2010 clearly pronounced that it would undertake consultation with communities and undertake a compliance investigation into IDB acts or omissions if required. While the number of claims increased, the number of those investigated remained low. Of the 168 claims submitted to the IDB, only 69 of those would be considered bona fide and within the accountability mechanism's purview (41 percent; see Figure 5.2). Only 26 would then progress to the consultation phase between the parties to try to resolve project-affected peoples' grievances. Of those, 14 would continue with the consultation process and nine would lead

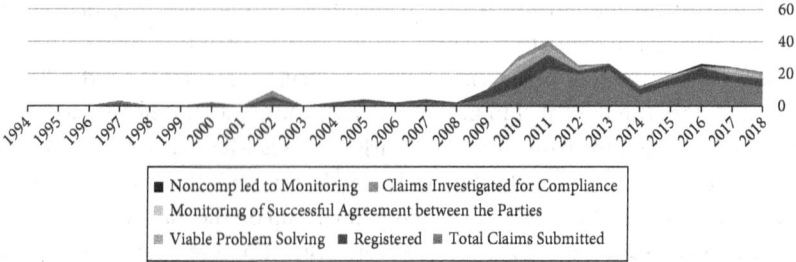

Figure 5.2 IDB's Accountability Mechanism Claims Accepted for Mediation and/or Compliance Investigation and Their Outcome, 1994–2018.
Source: Data from Park 2019.

to a settlement between the parties. In comparison, only 15 claims (21 percent) would be accepted as bona fide by the Compliance Review Panel (after 2016 claimants could proceed directly to a compliance investigation). Recall that the IDB had a high number of exclusion criteria for registering claims until 2014, while the IDB Board viewed a claim's going to a compliance investigation as a worst-case scenario.

Hence, the Independent Consultation and Investigation Mechanism of the IDB (known by its acronym MICI in Spanish) has been more fully utilized in relation to consultation than compliance. After the MICI executive secretary (now director) registers a claim as bona fide, the ombudsman (now the consultation coordinator) then reassesses the claim as meeting the procedural criteria for consultation. Most of the claims were rejected for consultation because they had first not taken their claims to management and/or because the claim fell outside the time frame for disbursing a project loan (see Figure 5.2). Yet one-third of claims (33 percent) were rejected for consultation with no documents publicly released as to why this was determined (see Park 2019). Given the lack of transparency (discussed in chapter 6) it is difficult to ascertain the basis for such a high rate of rejection for registering claims. After passing the initial registration stage, the ombudsman evaluates the viability of a claim for consultation (the assessment stage, or whether the parties to the project are willing to engage in problem solving). Of the 26 cases that went to assessment, 4 were underway by the middle of 2019 while 14 had moved into the facilitating an agreement phase (53 percent of "viable" consultations). Seven claims accepted for consultation closed without addressing claimants' grievances. In these cases, mediation was no longer possible because of a deterioration of relations between stakeholders.[11] These cases then went to a compliance audit.

Ten of the remaining 14 claims that made it to the facilitating agreement stage led to an agreement between the parties. The consultation coordinator then monitored adherence of the parties to nine of those agreements. The four other claims broke down, with stakeholders withdrawing or the ombudsman determining that nothing further could be done to address the issues. Brokering an agreement between the parties demonstrates that consultation can achieve accountability as justice for project-affected people, with some cases being resolved in full or in part. The consultation process has become more transparent and credible over time but remains dependent on the parties' willingness to cooperate as well as the timeliness of a claim (i.e., before relations break down and harm becomes irreparable as the project progresses). By the middle of 2019 five consultations had successfully concluded.

The IDB's accountability mechanism has faced strong Board and Bank resistance throughout its history. Considering this, when MICI replaced the IIM in 2010, it was given the capacity for monitoring Bank compliance with remedial action plans after a finding of noncompliance. This was a substantial boost to the power of the mechanism. This section unpacks the claims received by the IDB's accountability mechanisms in terms of whether they were accepted for compliance investigation, to show where and when the Board and management have intervened in its decision-making, and when the accountability mechanism has chosen not to use its powers. It highlights the power the Board to limit accountability as justice by rejecting the Compliance Review Panel's recommendations for a compliance investigation or rejecting the findings of their investigations.

Of the 70 cases registered by the IDB's accountability mechanism, 38 would go to the compliance component for appraisal (54 percent of registered claims). Five cases went directly to the compliance phase under the IIM because it did not have a consultation phase. Of the 38 claims that went to the compliance, 16 claims were assessed as eligible for an investigation (42 percent going to compliance). The rest were rejected for a variety of reasons. Four cases were closed because the Board rejected the recommendation for an investigation by the Compliance Review Panel (see Park 2019). This evinces the unwillingness of the Board, composed primarily of borrowers, to hold the IDB to account.

One of those cases took place under the IIM. During the initial accountability mechanism five cases went to compliance audit, leading to four investigations (between 1994 and 2009).[12] Any form of redress through the IIM was undermined by its lack of independence from the Board. In all five cases, the Board and management defied the norm by rejecting the findings and refusing to accept the need to improve project-affected peoples' situation (Filho and Rios 2007). The IDB engaged in a strategy of defiance by rejecting the findings of the first three investigations and intervening in due process in the remaining two. As outlined in chapter 4, the first claim, the Yacyreta hydroelectric dam claim in 1997, led to little substantial changes to the project and IDB practices despite a full investigation. A subsequent second claim about worsening conditions from Yacyreta was lodged with the accountability mechanism in 2002. The investigation revealed that IDB avoidance as management had not addressed the previous investigation recommendations and was noncompliant with the IDB's policies on involuntary resettlement, supervision, and environmental impacts. Management rejected the findings, and the Board ultimately determined that the IDB had complied with its procedures. The Board publicly announced that it concurred with the findings of the Panel, which the investigators rejected (Filho and Rios 2007: 103, 112–113).

In 2000 the mechanism received a claim from a project-affected community in Mexico regarding an electricity project (ME-0218), but the request was denied because claimants had not engaged with operations staff (IIM 2001: 1). The claim was resubmitted in 2002 (loan 1223/OC-ME). In this case a Panel, drawn from the Roster of Experts, concluded that the IDB had "(i) failed to comply in the application of most of the operational policies raised in the complaint, and (ii) failed to comply with even some of the contractual clauses." Management again rejected the Panel's findings and issued only general recommendations about how they could improve their practices. It took three years from the submission of the claim to the final decision of the Board (Filho and Rios 2007: 60, 93, 88), but there is no evidence that the recommendations were followed.

In 2002 the mechanism received a claim regarding a hydroelectric project in Brazil (Cana Brava, loan 1260/OC-BR). After the complaint was lodged, management attempted to address complainants' concerns by performing a social audit of the effects of the project on people in the area (Filho and Rios 2007: 146). The IIM hired a consultant to determine whether a full compliance investigation was warranted. Engaging in a strategy of defiance, management challenged the process by asking the consultant on three occasions to delay their report to the Board until the social audit was complete. The consultant eventually recommended a full investigation, which the Board accepted (Filho and Rios 2007: 133). A panel of experts determined that the IDB was not in compliance with Involuntary Resettlement (OP-710) and parts of Environmental Impact (OP-703), and they discovered "errors of judgement" regarding Supervision (OP-304) (Filho and Rios 2007: 60). However, the final Panel report was delivered two months after the project sponsor prepaid the loan for the project, thus undermining the IDB's leverage to improve the practices of the company. Management contested the Panel's findings and rejected the need for any additional action (Filho and Rios 2007: 123, 125–126).

In 2004, the IIM received a claim regarding a project in Argentina (the Reconditioning of Water and Infrastructure for the Provincial Route 28 project, loan 1118/OC-AR). The IIM coordinator recommended a consultant determine whether an investigation was warranted. The Board again challenged the process by rejecting the consultant's recommendation for a compliance investigation.

Instead, they instructed management to respond to the consultant's report directly, again contravening due process. Management then sent the consultant evidence of efforts to rectify the problem. Meanwhile, there had been no formal Board decision on the case for 18 months. After analyzing the management report, the consultant belatedly determined that a full investigation was not required (IIM 2006: 1). As with the Cana Brava case, the Board and management subverted the process to avoid an investigation. A follow-up complaint by project-affected people on the completion of the project was deemed a misunderstanding by the IIM, and the case was closed (IIM 2007: 2).

According to Filho and Rios, the Board was gridlocked between borrowers and donors over whether to agree to compliance investigations and over their findings (2007: 145–147). The IIM chose not to accept any more claims as registrable until it was reformulated in 2010, despite receiving another ten claims in that period. Two cases are of note: In 2006 the IIM responded to a claim regarding the environmental impact of a Brazilian water plant (the PRODETUR II–Northeast Region [1392/OC-BR]—Tamandaré Water Treatment Plant) with a public meeting between affected people and claimants—again not in accordance with the accountability mechanism's resolution. The IIM then determined the case inactive and closed it. In 2008 a local Argentine court requested to know the outcome of the investigation, but the IDB responded that it had immunity under international law, that its documents were protected except those already in the public domain, and that the case was closed (IIM 2009: 3). The IDB continued to defy the accountability as justice norm.

Finally, a 2008 case reinforces how the IIM was not operating according to its resolutions. Regarding a claim in relation to involuntary resettlement following a social and environmental project in Brazil (the PROSAMIM II project), the IIM coordinator signaled to the complainant what they needed for a complaint to be lodged correctly, informed management about issues they could address, and sent a consultant to verify whether the concerns were valid. The IIM signaled that the case was "pre-eligible" for an investigation based on the consultant's initial findings. Management then commissioned another resettlement consultant to examine the issue, who found the IDB policy-compliant. The IIM accepted this without investigation, with the IIM coordinator highlighting how engagement with various units of the IDB could address issues cooperatively (IIM 2008: 3–4). Clearly the accountability mechanism was not being used as an independent check on IDB behavior.

As discussed in subsequent sections, the IDB's mechanism is becoming more transparent and more accessible. However, it remains difficult for project-affected people to hold the IDB to account. Under MICI, 33 cases went to compliance but only 12 cases were deemed eligible for a compliance investigation (36 percent). The hurdle requirement of having to first go through mediation before going to compliance, even if this is not what requestors want, substantially delayed any efforts to address claimants' grievances (this was changed in 2014; ICIM 2014b). Overall, there is no clear trend for MICI to reject a claim, which is compounded by MICI listing more than one reason for a rejection (see Park 2019). Once deemed eligible by the chair of the Compliance Review Panel (now compliance coordinator), they might still be rejected for investigation by the Board.

The Board remains disinterested in using accountability for justice, either for correcting the damage wrought by projects financed by the IDB or for interrogating the practices of bank management. For example, three claims were rejected by the Board despite the Compliance Review Panel deeming them eligible for compliance investigation. In one case, the Board engaged in a process of avoidance by taking a very narrow understanding of project lending. Despite providing loans for a bridge in Bolivia (the Santa Barbara-Rurrenabaque Northern Corridor Highway Improvement Program, MICI-BO-2011-013) the Board argued that Bolivia's determination not to use the loan for the contested bridge obviated the need for a compliance investigation despite harm occurring because of the project. Another two claims regarding the impacts of a road in Brazil were accepted, rolled into a single investigation, and then rejected (the Mario Covas Rodoanel Project—Northern Section 1 and Mário Covas Rodoanel-Northern Sections 1 and 2 MICI-BR-2011-015 and MICI-BR-2011-022). The Board rejected the Panel's request for an investigation of both complaints as a single review despite the Panel finding merit regarding the broad environmental, social, and health impacts of the project.[13] No documents were made public and no justification was given on the MICI case registry or in its annual reports (ICIM 2014a: 28). As a project with several subsequent claims, it is unclear whether MICI has been able to provide accountability as justice for project-affected people.

By mid-2019 three investigations were underway and eight had been completed.[14] All eight were found noncompliant with IDB's policies leading to harm, all in relation to the IDB's environmental and social policies including involuntary resettlement, breaches in information disclosure, indigenous people's policy, disaster risk management, and the IDB's operational lending procedures. The first case under MICI, a hydro project in Panama (the Pando Monte-Lirio Hydroelectric Project, MICI-PN-2010-002), went through a full investigation and was found noncompliant. Yet MICI did not monitor management to bring the project into compliance. As with the first case of the IIM, there seemed to be a willingness by the IDB and Board to test the process. An association of 16 Panamanian NGOs questioned the environmental and social impact of a series of hydroelectric projects. A consultation was undertaken, but the project sponsor withdrew in March 2011 and mediation ended. The MICI ombudsman submitted the case to its Compliance Review Panel and the IDB's

Board approved the investigation. The Panel found the IDB noncompliant with three policies—Environment, Disaster Risk Management Policy, and Operation Administration—and made recommendations to bring the project into compliance.[15] The Board accepted the findings and recommendations of the Panel, and requested that management establish a management action plan.[16] Management sent their action plan to MICI in January 2013 with ongoing targets to make the project compliant.[17] This was accepted by the Board in February 2013, but there is no evidence that the IDB implemented its action plan or that MICI monitored its actions.

In another case, a Brazilian urban planning program (São José dos Campos Urban Structuring Program, MICI-BR-2011-020) the IDB was found noncompliant in relation to its Involuntary Resettlement (OP-710), the Environment and Safeguards Compliance (OP-703), and the Access to Information (OP-102) policies. The Board approved the seven recommendations MICI provided to bring the project into compliance. Despite having the power to do so, the Board chose not to ask MICI to monitor management's actions. Management did, however, submit two reports to Board on how it had met MICI's recommendations. This demonstrates unwillingness on behalf of the Board to use MICI to oversee management's response to findings of noncompliance. Cases where the IDB had been found noncompliant but did not go to monitoring include cases where the project was already completed and the loan fully disbursed (the Colombian El Dorado International Airport, MICI-CO-2011-023). Avoidance is evident in this case, because management requested *six times* to delay the Compliance Review Panel's evaluation of whether the claim for eligible for an investigation. Once it was accepted as eligible, the Board then determined the terms of reference of the compliance review, which was not made public. The investigation then closed in November 2018. Avoidance on the part of both management and the Board highlight how they engage with the norm without following it.

The Board has also engaged in a strategy of defiance to dismiss MICI findings and challenge the process. For example, in a Paraguay road project (Program to Improve Highway Corridors in Paraguay MICI-PR-2010-008), the Compliance Review Panel stated the Bank was not compliant in following its Environment policy contributing to the harm of the Indigenous Ache people. However, the Board rejected the findings of the report, stating that the "panel report does not provide compelling findings that would serve as evidence of Management's noncompliance." The Board ultimately stated that there were "doubts about the usefulness of the report," especially considering that the investigation should never have been undertaken, owing to an administrative error in the loan disbursement date (the loan was considered 98 percent disbursed when the claim was lodged).[18] Thus the Board effectively closed off any further effort to use accountability as justice to correct damage wrought by an IDB-financed project.[19]

Another case demonstrates how the Board sought to limit the efforts of the Compliance Review Panel to enact accountability as justice. In the case of the Panama Canal Expansion Program (MICI-PN-2011-031) the Compliance Review Panel determined that an investigation was warranted in relation to the potential loss of livelihood and increase in risk of exposure from the project. The Panel was instructed by the Board to clarify its terms of reference for the investigation twice between February and September 2013 before approving a limited review of the project's risk to seismic activity and water availability. The Panel was only allowed to assess technical requirements for being policy-compliant, not whether the Bank was compliant with policies relevant to project-affected people. Foreclosing the outcome, the Panel was instructed that "no new technical studies or additional technical due diligence were to be undertaken by outside experts" in assessing compliance (ICIM 2015b). The final report of the Compliance Review Panel stated that the IDB was not policy compliant with its Environment and Safeguards Compliance policy or its Disaster Risk Management policy, which Bank management rejected. The MICI public case registry makes available management's presentation to the Board stating that they were compliant with all the policies except a procedural reporting requirement. The Board concurred and instructed management to correct this minor oversight. Case closed.

Only one of the cases where the Bank was found noncompliant has resulted in the Compliance Review Panel monitoring of management remedial actions. This refers to a 2016 claim in relation to the Paraguay Downtown Redevelopment project (MICI-BID-PR-2016-0101). In this case, the Board asked management to prepare an action plan in response to seven findings of noncompliance, and for the MICI to create a monitoring plan in 2018. A September 2020 document details what management agreed to improve to bring the project into compliance (IDB 2020). Thus, even where full compliance investigations have been undertaken, it remains unclear whether MICI can address damage wrought by an IDB-financed project or influence the practices and culture of the IDB. The Board of the IDB does not seek to uphold the norm, while management engages in both avoidance and defiance. This compares with the robust monitoring actions of the accountability mechanism of the Asian Development Bank (ADB), discussed next.

Asian Development Bank's Inspection Function and Accountability Mechanism

Like the World Bank and the IDB, the ADB's original Inspection Function did not have a problem-solving function. The Inspection Function received eight claims that were assessed for Bank compliance (see chapter 4). Problem-solving was introduced when the Inspection Function was rebooted in 2003 as the Accountability Mechanism. Between 2003 and end of 2012 when the policy changed, all claims had to first go through problem solving with the Office of the Special Project Facilitator before being eligible for a compliance investigation by the Compliance Review Panel. The 2012 review allowed people to choose to file a complaint directly to the rather than be forced to go through problem-solving. Overwhelmingly, project-affected people have chosen problem solving (88 percent).

The Bank received 298 claims up until the middle of 2019. Of those, 159 would be accepted as bona fide and meeting the mechanism's criteria (54 percent). As with the other mechanisms, there are a range of reasons for rejecting claims, but a vast majority (99 or 71 percent) of those rejected were because the claims fell outside the purview of the mechanism (for example in relation to corruption, fraud, or ethical violations). Two trends stand out in the accountability mechanism's rejection of claims for problem-solving: Of the eligible 141 cases designated for problem solving 26 were rejected with no information provided (18 percent), and another 21 because claimants had not first gone to management with their complaint (14 percent) (Figure 5.3).

Showing an increase in its use, 80 of the 141 would be accepted for problem solving (56 percent), with 55 assessments ongoing by mid-2019. Twenty-five claims would move into the problem-solving phase, with only three claims ending at that stage. This demonstrates that there is stakeholder commitment to the process, particularly when compared with other accountability mechanisms (see further in what follows). Seventeen of those problem-solving processes moved into the facilitating a settlement among the parties phase (12 percent of viable problem-solving claims). Six then entered into the monitoring and close out phase of the process. Of the 17, 10 ended at the facilitating settlement

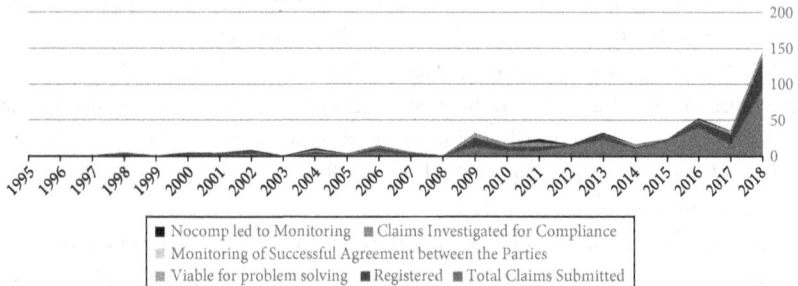

Figure 5.3 ADB's Accountability Mechanism Claims Accepted for Mediation and/or Compliance Investigation and Their Outcome, 1995–2018.

Note: Claims underway are not included in the outcome categories.

phase: Four of the 17 cases reached an agreement of the parties, in two cases claimants withdrew, in three cases there are no public documents available, one case is ongoing, and one complaint exhausted the process without resolution. Six of the 17 would continue to the monitoring and close out phase: three would successfully close, two are ongoing, and in one case claimants withdrew from standing by the agreement. In sum, there is evidence of resolution to the satisfaction of the complainants in seven cases, with an eighth being concluded and a ninth resulting in a partial agreement (ADB 2012d: 7).

There are reasons for caution however, as a successful case may belie the differences between stakeholders in seeking recourse. For example, a successful case shows how only some project-affected people may benefit from problem solving. In the case of the Cambodian Rehabilitation of the Railway Project (Request 2011/06), 116 project-affected people signed the claim to the Office of the Special Project Facilitator. This is the largest relocation project in Cambodia, with people being moved to make way for the railway (Accountability Mechanism 2013: 2). Project-affected people sought compensation for resettlement, indebtedness, and a lack of access to a livelihood resulting from relocation, as well as seeking improved basic services at the resettlement site. The Special Project Facilitator was able to improve *some* complainants' concerns particularly in addressing discrepancies in compensation entitlements and helping establish structures for further improvements to social services financed by Bank. The problem-solving process closed in February 2014.

In isolation this looks like a successful resolution to the claim. Yet this project led to four separate claims to the Special Project Facilitator and two separate claims to the Compliance Review Panel (discussed later). Only the first of the four requests regarding this project were accepted. The 2012/01 claim was rejected for not first approaching the Operations Department, the 2013/01 claim was rejected because there was no new evidence, and there was no reason given on the public case registry for rejecting the fourth claim, 2013/02.[20] The project had wildly uneven effects on project-affected people: Some villages were adequately relocated to levels akin to that prior to the project and others, like those in the Accountability Mechanism claims, placed in conditions of hardship at a level much worse than prior to the project (Connell 2015). Although the Special Project Facilitator has contributed to improving people's lives, like the other accountability mechanisms, it is limited in its ability to influence the Bank's operations once relocation has occurred.

There are four claims where claimant's concerns were not addressed through problem solving and claimants withdrew from the process to lodge claims with the Compliance Review Panel. Reasons for dissatisfaction with mediation included a bias favoring the Bank by the Special Project Facilitator; the inability to provide claimants with the remedy they sought; and the time taken for mediation without any indication of an outcome (Park 2015: 462).[21] Dissatisfaction was evident particularly in the early years, especially in the Sri Lankan Southern Transport Development Project claim (request 2004/02) where problem solving was canceled because no resolution was deemed possible (OSPF 2005). In the first claim, the Nepal Melamchi Water Supply Project (request 2004/01), the complainant withdrew from the mediation process in order to be able to lodge a complaint with the Compliance Review Panel. Complainants also withdrew from problem solving nine months after submitting their claim with regard to the Indonesia Integrated Citarum Water Resources Management Investment Program (request 2011/01), because they had not received compensation for being evicted from their houses (Accountability Mechanism 2012: 7; OSPF 2012). In the Philippines Visayas Base-Load Power Project claim (request 2011/ 03), project-affected people withdrew the request for mediation because they "decided that consultative meetings and discussions were not appropriate. They did not see how the proposed course of action could help achieve their desired outcomes and remedies; some were concerned about compromising their request for confidentiality; and they did not accept OSPF's consultants" (OSPF 2012: 9).

These patterns highlight how the problem-solving process is limited to providing project-affected people with the ability to air their grievances, although sometimes remedies are possible. While communities may be stuck with a project, attempting problem solving may make the situation less bad (Accountability Mechanism 2008; Park 2015). In many cases the Special Project Facilitator has been able to ensure that project-affected people are adequately compensated and their conditions improved (OSPF 2009). Improvements are evident for complainants after problem solving compared with conditions prior to the process but not necessarily compared with conditions prior to the project (see for example, Accountability Mechanism 2012: 3).

Both the Inspection Function and the Accountability Mechanism undertake compliance investigations. From 2003 the Compliance Review Panel was given the ability to provide recommendations arising from findings of noncompliance as well as monitoring powers to ensure the Bank became policy compliant. The Panel has been able to use these powers to hold the Bank to account. However, from 2012 the Board restricted the Panel's ability to conduct compliance investigations and limited monitoring to two years.

The Inspection Function was designed only to undertake compliance investigations. The Inspection Function only accepted two of eight requests for inspection. Two were rejected for the Korangi Wastewater Treatment Project in Pakistan for not outlining ADB policy violations; four were rejected regarding the Southern Transport Development Project (STDP) in Sri Lanka; one was accepted for investigation regarding the Samut Prakarn Waste Treatment Plant in Thailand; and another was accepted for the Chashma Right Bank Irrigation Project in Pakistan. Indeed, claims to the Inspection Function were rejected even though the Bank was later to be discovered to be noncompliant leading to harm into three of the four projects where claims were submitted: the wastewater plant in Thailand (Samut Prakarn), an irrigation project in Pakistan (Chashma), and a Sri Lankan road (STDP). In all cases bank management engaged in defiance by denying any policy violations leading to harm. The Inspection Function's only attempt at a full inspection (Samut Prakarn) failed to mitigate environmental and social problems stemming from the project (see chapter 4). The Chashma Right Bank Irrigation Project in Pakistan claim was approved just before the reconfiguration to the Accountability Mechanism in 2003. The Compliance Review Panel documented policy violations leading to harm in the Chashma case (Compliance Review Panel [CRP] 2004b). Ensuring full compliance with 24 and partial compliance of 4 of 29 Panel recommendations took five years of monitoring because of Bank management's slow response. The Inspection Function process was also not transparent: the Board Inspection Committee stated that two of the STDP claims were rejected because of "insufficient basis," and the third and fourth STDP claims were rejected because they were clearly ineligible for not having "presented reasonable evidence" of ADB noncompliance leading to harm (ADB 2002e: 12–13). This is despite the Compliance Review Panel later recognizing STDP's substantial negative impacts on project-affected people. In the STDP case Bank policy violations contributing to harm were documented (request 2004/01, Park 2015). After 5 years of monitoring, 18 of the 19 recommendations made by the Compliance Review Panel were met (the 19th could no longer be met). The Sri Lankan government and project-affected people recognized that the process led to positive results, including "the creation of new legislation and procedures for land acquisition and compensation, and the institution of local grievance and conflict resolution mechanisms" at the project site (OCRP 2011: 5–6). This demonstrates that the compliance process can be used to ensure the Bank addresses project-affected people's grievances.

Up to the middle of 2019 the Compliance Review Panel received 19 claims (excluding Chashma but including the final successful STDP claim), 8 of which would be accepted for compliance investigation (42 percent acceptance).[22] There are relatively few cases assessed by the Panel: indeed, there were no claims submitted for compliance investigation between 2004 and 2009. The 2012 ADB review of the Accountability Mechanism noted that the low number of claims was in keeping with the other MDBs' mechanisms, although this gap was concerning (ADB 2012d: 13; Park 2014). The publicly available claims registry does not include enquiries from project-affected people that did not meet the procedural criteria (see OCRP 2008: 6), but analysis of all the Compliance Review Panel documents reveal that the Melamchi Water Supply Project in Nepal (request

2004/02) was the only claim rejected as a result of unsubstantiated claims. Of the cases rejected for compliance investigation there is no clear trend (Park 2019).

The Compliance Review Panel has documented policy violations leading to harm in all eight of the cases it investigated. In seven cases the Bank was found noncompliant in relation to the ADB's environmental policies. In five cases the Bank was found noncompliant in relation to its policy on involuntary re- settlement. In four cases the Bank was found noncompliant with its public communications policy. The Compliance Review Panel would undertake mon- itoring to ensure Bank compliance with its recommendations resulting from its investigations in seven of the eight cases (for the CAREC Transport Corridor 1 [Bishkek-Torugart Road] Project 1, 2011/2 claim Bank management corrected its omissions immediately). Monitoring is complete for two claims: the Sri Lankan road project (STDP) claim, discussed earlier, and the Indonesian Integrated Citarum Water Resources Management Investment Program (claim 2012/1). For the latter, the Compliance Review Panel was able to report that Bank management were partially compliant with two of its three recommendations and fully compliant with the third. The first two could not be fully complied with because the program was discontinued, and the Bank was not financing fur- ther components of the project. The Compliance Review Panel demonstrates its ability to provide accountability as justice through compliance investigations, recommendations, and monitoring.

Despite the ability of the Panel to make findings of noncompliance, provide recommendations for Bank management to become compliant, and then mon- itor their activities, Bank resistance and borrower opposition remain. In a repeat of the Inspection Function's only attempted investigation, borrower opposition again perverted due process for the Compliance Review Panel regarding the Fuzhou Environmental Improvement Project in China in 2010 (request 2009/ 01; see also chapter 4). The case was deemed eligible for a compliance review, but China refused to allow an in-country investigation (OCRP 2009: 8). China declared that the Special Project Facilitator had already undertaken mediation and the Compliance Review Panel could use their notes (at that stage, the two offices operated completely separately). They also stated that the project had al- ready been changed thus undermining the need for an investigation. The issue went to the Board, where donor executive directors stridently disagreed with China's reasons not to allow an investigation but did not call for a formal Board vote, thus letting the issue drop (Park 2014: 14–16). This took place during the Accountability Mechanism review where it was determined by the Board and management that where a developing member country refused entry for an in- vestigation and the Bank's good offices had failed to produce a solution, that the Compliance Review Panel should complete a desk review of the complaint. The Panel rejected this on the basis that this would legitimate a deviation from due process (Interview with accountability officer, October 1, 2013). As with Samut Prakarn under the Inspection Function, the issue of developing member country sovereignty prevented the mechanism from fully functioning (Park 2014). The 2012 review did not resolve this issue.

Further attempts by Bank management and the Board to limit the Panel is evident in relation to its monitoring. In the Cambodia railway project mentioned earlier (Greater Mekong Subregion: Rehabilitation of the Railway in Cambodia Project claim, request 2012/02) project-affected people sought an investigation into the Bank's failure to properly implement its involuntary resettlement, leading to forced eviction and a lack of adequate compensation, a loss of livelihoods, and a lack of access to basic services. Despite claimants' finding recourse through the Special Project Facilitator, particularly in relation to addressing discrepancies in compensation payments and conditions at the resettlement sites, many other affected people remained outside the process. While the process was underway the Bank hired an involuntary resettlement expert to review the project (Dr. Michael Cernea, who wrote the World Bank's policy on Involuntary Resettlement). The Bank chose not to release the report. His recommendations (not the full report) were made public only after concerted NGO pressure. The Board approved Terms of Reference for an investigation in October 2012, but a site visit was not conducted until October 2013 because Cambodia requested that the Panel investigation be delayed for domestic reasons. The final investigation report was submitted to the Board in January 2014.

The Compliance Review Panel final report upheld requestors' claims that the project was not policy-compliant regarding involuntary resettlement, the social dimensions of Bank operations, and the Bank's communications policy leading to harm. The Panel made seven major recommendations for restitution (CRP 2014). However, the Board accepted only three of the Panel's recommendations and modified the remaining three, a significant departure from established practice. The Board accepted that the Bank should improve the facilities at the resettlement sites, improve the functioning of the grievance redress mechanism, and improve the capacity of the government's resettlement body. It modified the three remaining recommendations, including dropping a key recommendation from Dr. Cernia, because "the government does not favour a resettlement audit" (CRP 2014b). The Board curtailed the specifics of three of the recommendations regarding addressing the damage caused by policy noncompliance.

Bank management also used a strategy of avoidance with implementing changes required for the project to become policy compliant. The Compliance Review Panel highlights that the April 2014 Management Action Plan to bring the railway project into compliance "fall[s] short of the Board-approved recommendations" in several aspects. The Panel stated that even if the monitoring plan is implemented fully, it may not be policy-compliant. The most recent monitoring report in June 2016 notes compliance with only one of six recommendations and partial compliance with the other five (CRP 2016). A subsequent request for another investigation regarding the case was denied, owing to the ongoing monitoring of the policy violations from the first claim (request 2015/01). There are clearly significant adverse impacts on project-affected people that are still to be addressed by management.

However, the 2012 Accountability Mechanism review concluded that Compliance Review Panel monitoring should be limited to two to three rather than five years, despite recognizing the remarkable progress in remedial actions undertaken because of the investigation and monitoring of the STDP and Chashma cases (ADB 2012d: 5, 8–9, 26–27). As a result, the monitoring process can improve conditions for project-affected people in some cases but Bank avoidance and interventions by the Board may undermine the Accountability Mechanism's capacity to change the Bank's operations. For example, Bank avoidance is also evident in the Philippines' Visayas Base-Load Power Development Project claim (request 2011/01). The requestors had already withdrawn dissatisfied from problem solving, believing the Special Project Facilitator to be biased in favor of the Bank. The Panel documented that the Bank had violated its Environment, Public Communications, and Social Dimensions into ADB Operations policies, and that it was only partially compliant with its Energy Policy. To that effect it made four recommendations, and after three years of monitoring the Bank was partially compliant in meeting the recommendations. The Panel made it clear that it had been waiting for management action on some recommendations for over two years (CRP 2012, 2015).

The 2012 Accountability Mechanism policy restricted the Compliance Review Panel's powers, giving the power to management, not the Panel, to determine the Remedial Action Plan after a finding of noncompliance (Park 2015: 463; ADB 2012e: 17). This is evident in the Indian Mundra Ultra Mega Power Project claim (request 2013/01). The Panel found that the Bank was not compliant in relation to its Environment Policy, Involuntary Resettlement, Incorporation of Social Dimensions into ADB Operations policy, and Public Communications policy as well as standards outlined in the World Bank's Pollution Prevention and Abatement Handbook, to which the Bank adheres. Although the Compliance Review Panel could not provide recommendations about how to make the project compliant, it did provide a section on lessons learned from the complaint. The Panel can nonetheless comment on the Remedial Action Plan, stating that Bank management's report "does not bring the project into compliance." It notes that this is not an "'action plan' but a 'studies plan' where actions will be specified only later; dependent on the outcome of the studies." Calling management out for their avoidance strategy, the Compliance Review Panel thus cautioned:

> It is important for the Board to note, that the RAP is largely a preliminary program where actions which would address the noncompliance area and harm incurred, would only be defined in a subsequent plan. Given the tentative and preliminary nature of the proposed RAP, the CRP is of the view that (i) all studies conducted should be submitted to the CRP for review and comments, and, (ii) the CRP be directly engaged in the review of the action plans formulated in response to the studies conducted. (ADB 2015)

The Board approved the remedial action plan in June 2015 and the Panel has begun to monitor its implementation, although it is unclear as to whether the Compliance Review Panel will be granted its wish. Changes to the Accountability Mechanism policy thus limit the Compliance Review Panel's ability to force management's compliance. In sum, the Compliance Review Panel has been able to help people hold the Bank to account, although post-2012 changes weaken its capacity to do so. The role of the Board in limiting its own Accountability Mechanism is taken up in the book's conclusion. This compares with the strength of the CAO to enact accountability as justice, discussed next.

The World Bank Group's Compliance Advisor/Ombudsman

As mentioned previously, the CAO has by far the largest caseload, registering 207 claims as bona fide of 301 known claims submitted. When claims go to the CAO they are assessed as to whether the claim is valid. Claims are rejected if they do not deal with a project, investment, or guarantee by the World Bank Group, or do not pertain to their environmental and social impacts. Given that many of its cases are confidential, there is no indication of why some claims are rejected for registration. Those that are detailed identify a small number of cases where the World Bank Group is no longer or not financing the project, or because the claims do not raise substantial or systemic concerns regarding environmental and/or social outcomes that would warrant an investigation (Park 2019). This determination was explicitly included in the revised 2013 operational procedures of the CAO (2013b). This speaks to the management of the CAO's increasing caseload, where they limit investigations of cases that may address substantial harm or harm resulting from systematic World Bank Group practices. Importantly this caveat determines not that harm has not occurred but that it does not raise systemic concerns regarding the World Bank Group's actions. The EBRD has similar provisions (discussed later) regarding substantive rather than technical violations of the Bank's environmental and social policies. The remaining claims were not eligible for assorted procedural reasons (Park 2019).

Of the cases registered, 183 claims were assessed for mediation (60 percent of claims submitted) and nine for immediate compliance investigation (2.9 percent of claims submitted).[23] From the beginning, the emphasis of the Office has been mediating disputes at the project level to address complainants' concerns. Of all the mechanisms the CAO stands out for its long-term commitment to sustainable community-based solutions and for helping to train local mediators to continue to assist communities once the formal mediation has concluded (CAO 2014: 12). The CAO has a history of long-term engagement in dispute resolution, and its caseload has both expanded and intensified as it deals with increasingly complex mediations over prolonged periods (CAO 2015: 72). Even if claims are eligible for mediation, it is still dependent on the desire of all parties to engage in facilitated discussion as to how to resolve a conflict. Frequently there is not a willingness on behalf of claimants to engage in dispute resolution with the company undertaking the project, and they may ask to be transferred to the compliance process. Companies may also decline to be involved in dispute resolution, opting for their own processes or to go through judicial procedures. The CAO nonetheless has a strong track record in negotiating disputes. It has also become more adept at identifying when there is no prospect of resolution through mediation. These cases are then sent to compliance for appraisal.

Overwhelmingly cases that did not go beyond the assessment phase for mediation did not do so because of opposition by one of the parties (35 percent of cases registered for mediation; Figure 5.4). Other reasons for mediation not proceeding included that there was insufficient evidence of harm, or the harm was not caused by the project, or the harm not caused by violation of policies (3.8 percent). Or that the World Bank Group is not yet or no longer financing the project (3.2 percent). Or because the CAO determined it could not play any

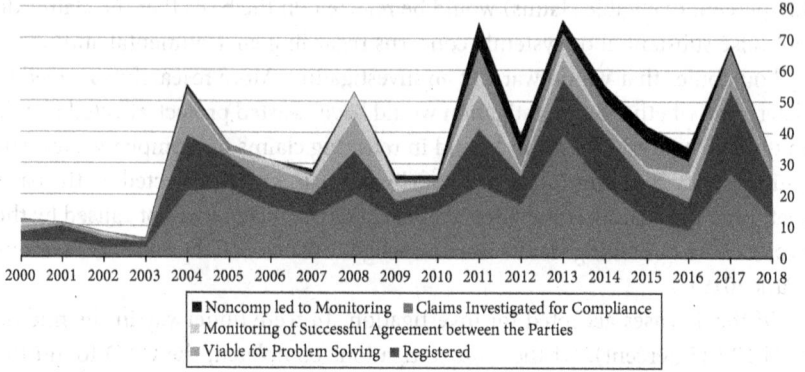

Figure 5.4 CAO Accountability Mechanism Claims Accepted for Mediation and/or Compliance Investigation and Their Outcome, 1999–2018.

further useful role or help the parties reach full agreement (this includes cases where partial agreement was reached by the parties, 3.2 percent).

Of the 183 claims assessed for mediation, 88 cases were considered viable for mediation (48 percent of cases registered for mediation) between 2000 and the middle of 2019.[24] Of these, 83 would lead to a facilitated settlement of the parties (45 percent of viable problem solving). Of those settlements facilitated, 13 would end after exhausting efforts to reach a settlement (15 percent), and 12 would end after stakeholders withdrew from the process (the company and the claimants equally, 14 percent). This highlights how the ombudsman process may be scuttled at any time, as large-scale multiparty negotiations may not appease all parties; there must be enough agreement for the parties to work together to achieve common goals. Where this is absent, there is no agreement and no monitoring. The remaining claims would not progress for different reasons (see Park 2019).

Forty-seven cases would go to the monitoring stage of mediation, 27 cases would be closed after reaching an agreement and being monitored for implementation of the agreement, and another seven cases were in the process of being closed. As with the previous stages, cases may end for a range of reasons without an implemented agreement. In some cases, the mediation process continued but was transferred from the CAO to local mediators (Park 2019). In sum, in 32 percent of cases where parties agreed to, and the CAO accepted, mediation, an agreement was reached and implemented. This is a testament to the willingness of the ombudsman to stay engaged and to assist in transferring long-term development agreements among the parties onto local mediators.

Of the 207 registered claims, 110 would be assessed for eligibility for a compliance audit (53 percent). Of these 47 would be accepted for investigation (42 percent of eligible claims) with another seven being assessed. Two trends stand out in terms of cases rejected for compliance investigation. Twenty-five claims (22 percent of eligible claims) would be rejected on the basis that the claims do not raise substantial or systemic concerns regarding environmental and/or social outcomes that would warrant an investigation. More research is needed to determine whether an investigation would have assisted project-affected people in these instances. The second trend in rejecting claims for compliance investigation is that 20 claims (18 percent of eligible claims) were rejected on the basis that there was insufficient evidence of harm or that harm was not caused by the project. The remaining claims were not eligible for assorted procedural reasons (Park 2019).

Of the 51 cases accepted for investigation, 14 were underway in the middle of 2019 (27 percent). Of the 36 investigations completed, the CAO found the World Bank Group compliant in only three cases, while not explicitly identifying findings of (non)compliance in one more. In other words, 88 percent of investigations revealed World Bank Group noncompliance. In 22 cases (61 percent of cases investigated) this was in violation of its environmental assessment or policy on environmental and social sustainability. It was also found to have breached its information disclosure policy, its involuntary resettlement policy, natural habitats, and community health, safety, and security policies (Park 2019).

The CAO is significantly different compared with the other accountability mechanisms because it has the power to trigger a compliance audit. Initially, the Office had discretion to trigger a compliance audit if mediation failed. For example, in 2000 the CAO triggered its first compliance review for a mine in Peru (the Compania Minera Antamina S.A.-01/Huarmey 732 case). The CAO would also instigate compliance audits not linked to claims. Recall that the CAO had asked the World Bank Group president to remove this power in 2003 but it was reinstated in 2006. The compliance process can also be triggered by the World Bank Group president or executive vice presidents of the IFC or the Multilateral Investment Guarantee Agency (MIGA; CAO 2010: 34). These powers have been used for eight cases (7.2 percent of eligible claims), with the CAO initiating six investigations (excluding the Peru Compania Minera Antamina S.A.-01/Huarmey [732] case noted earlier). The CAO may begin a compliance audit resulting from allegations surfacing in the media regarding the activities of companies financed by the IFC. The World Bank Group president has triggered one compliance audit, as has the executive vice president of the IFC. Both were responses to high-profile campaigns against World Bank Group investments and guarantees. This is an incredibly powerful tool to hold the World Bank Group to account for justice because it does not depend on the most vulnerable, project-affected people, lodging applications.

In 2004 the IFC executive vice president triggered a compliance audit of its investment in soya bean production in terms of its environmental impact (the Brazil/Amaggi Expansion-01 case). The CAO found the investment to be noncompliant with its own environmental policies. The CAO noted that the audit "reveals a considerable institutional discomfort with the exacting nature of the compliance role" (CAO 2005: 2, 9). The finding of noncompliance was upheld by the World Bank Group's Independent Evaluation Group (IEG) in 2007, which concluded that the project sponsor's corrective action plan for the plantation had not been supervised and that pollution levels exceeded the IFC's limits (World Bank 2008: 52).

In 2005 the World Bank Group President Paul Wolfowitz also instigated a compliance audit, this time over claims of human rights abuses the Dikilushi Copper-Silver Mine in the Democratic Republic of Congo. MIGA provided a political risk guarantee for the mine (Anvil Mining Congo, SARL-01/World Bank President Request (5054). The CAO found that MIGA had "weaknesses in following" due diligence in relation to its environmental and social review procedures (ESRPs) and "and on conflict and security issues specifically, [which] echo a number of concerns that were the subject of our recommendations in our 2002 review of MIGA's ESRPs" (CAO 2006b: 8). The CAO would keep a compliance audit open until the World Bank Group had adequately addressed its noncompliance.

The IFC's response to the CAO investigations has varied from passive to active resistance. In one of the first cases to be found noncompliant requiring monitoring, an oil and gas project in Kazakhstan (Lukoil Overseas-01/Berezovka, 9953), management denied the allegations of wrongdoing, rejected the CAO's findings, challenged their processes, and demanded explanations for their recommendations (World Bank Group 2005). Subsequent management responses in relation to the same claim have been more moderate for example, arguing that management believes that they are compliant but they "recognize the difficulties the CAO team may have faced in confirming IFC's assurances and decisions based on the information available" (World Bank Group 2008). Later management statements have become much more solicitous in either omitting any discussion of wrongdoing or in defending staff actions in response to findings of noncompliance.[25] While CAO staff have not had any difficulty accessing information from the IFC to undertake their investigations, many of the issues of noncompliance remain unaddressed. This is because the IFC clients often choose to repay investments thus ending the relationship between the company and the World Bank Group. This ends the CAO's ability to monitor the project.

There is evidence of IFC norm avoidance. Specifically, the IFC sold its equity in the company that built the Pangue dam in Chile. Recall that it was opposition to the harm caused by this dam that led to a failed claim to the World Bank Inspection Panel and the creation of the CAO (see chapter 4). The company repaid the loan and therefore the IFC was unable to address the problems. Yet project-affected people submitted another claim to the CAO in 2002 over outstanding issues from another claim in 2000. Unbeknownst to the CAO, who was engaged in a process of mediation, the IFC exited the project soon after the 2002 claim, without informing the CAO. Together the CAO and the World Bank Group president then committed to respond to the claim even though the IFC had walked away. The CAO remained engaged with the community until 2008 (CAO 2006c, 2010). The IFC's actions reflect that Pangue remains an open sore for the Bank (Interview with IFC staff, February 23, 2009), triggering the need for accountability as justice for private sector investments.

Three further claims lodged against IFC investments in the Wilmar corporation in Indonesia reveal borrower attempts at norm avoidance: Wilmar Group-01/West Kalimantan (25532 & 26271), Wilmar Group-02/Sumatra (25532 & 26271), and Wilmar Group-03/Jambi (25532 & 26271). In these instances, the complaints were mediated at the project level with attempts to negotiate agreement between the parties over land rights. A negotiated settlement was reached in relation to the Sumatra claim. In the Jambi case the CAO was engaged in mediation with stakeholders between 2008 and 2013. However, in 2013 the Wilmar Corporation sold the subsidiary engaged in mediation. The mediation ended, and project-affected people were evicted from their land (CAO 2013c). The Jambi claim would then go onto to be assessed for IFC compliance and the CAO would identify policy breaches requiring monitoring. In the third claim, the Office responded to a complaint against the IFC for investing in the Wilmar Group palm oil project in West Kalimantan in 2007. In May 2008 parties to the mediation agreed to a code of conduct to resolve the land dispute. Meanwhile, the CAO determined in March 2008 that the IFC's due diligence prior to project approval and its project supervision "were not amenable to resolution" leading it to transfer this to a compliance audit. This took place alongside mediation (CAO 2008: 26). The company felt betrayed when the CAO triggered the compliance audit function simultaneously to the dispute resolution (Fairman et al. 2010: 14).

The compliance audit would later find the IFC noncompliant with its environmental and social policies, and avoidance was evident in its weak response to the audit (World Bank Group 2009). Public outcry "combined with the direct intervention of the World Bank Group president forced IFC to respond diligently" (CAO 2010: 36). In response, World Bank Group President Zoellick then suspended all IFC palm oil investment lending in August 2009, and then all World Bank Group palm oil investment lending in November until all palm oil lending had been reviewed and a revised strategy was established. In 2010 the IFC conducted a multistakeholder consultation process to create new sectoral guidelines, which it launched in March 2011 (CAO 2010: 41, 2011: 3).[26] To reiterate, mediation is complex but reliant on the willingness of the parties to engage and agree on steps to resolve community grievances. In a quarter of cases, the CAO was able to bring meaningful recourse to project-affected people, although IFC avoidance is evident in some cases. Over time the Office has ramped up its compliance investigations, thus providing the World Bank Group with recommendations to bring projects into compliance and monitor those activities.

The CAO has undertaken monitoring in 34 of the 36 cases with completed investigations. In 2008, at the request of the World Bank Group's Committee on Development Effectiveness (CODE), the CAO established a Management Action Tracking Record to review the World Bank Group's responses to its findings in 2008 (CAO 2008: 2, 2011: 59). By 2009 the CAO noted that the World Bank Group's unsatisfactory responses to audit findings were changing with the increasing robustness of its auditing tools (CAO 2009: 2). The IFC's central Corporate Risk Committee, chaired by the executive vice president and the chief operating officer, now review all the CAO's recommendations quarterly (CAO 2011: 59). In sum, the Office has ramped up its compliance investigations since 2000. It has found that the World Bank Group violates its policies, requiring remedial action to the satisfaction of the CAO. This points to a robust compliance system of finding the World Bank Group noncompliant leading to monitoring.

Also distinct from the other accountability mechanisms is the CAO's use of sectoral compliance investigations. In April 2011, the CAO vice president, Meg Taylor, triggered a sectoral rather than a project compliance audit of IFC's Financial Intermediaries portfolio. This was done to gauge whether lending to third parties for project financing in developing countries was obscuring the ability of project-affected people to hold the World Bank Group to account (CAO 2011: 55). The audit examined 188 Financial Intermediary investments, releasing the findings in February 2013. It noted that the IFC does follow its policies but that it cannot track whether the projects contribute to its overarching Sustainability Framework. Recognizing the importance of evaluating World Bank Group practices across more than one project, the revised CAO's 2013 operational guidelines now formalize the Office's ability to conduct multiproject compliance audits (CAO 2013a: 17, 77). The idea behind doing so was to assess "systemic concerns raised by complainants" in high-risk sectors (Fairman et al. 2010: 23). Through this, the CAO is attempting to address the World Bank Group's overall portfolio and organizational culture.

European Bank for Reconstruction and Development's Accountability Mechanism

The EBRD's accountability mechanism did not do much problem solving in its early years, and from the beginning has had a strong focus on compliance. While the latter is a strong tool to hold the Bank to account, it has also been criticized for not taking project-affected people's interests as primary. It also has a high rate of rejecting claims: only 36 of the known 170 claims submitted to mechanism were registered (21 percent). Two of the main reasons for rejecting claims were first, that claims were not registered because the grievance was outside the scope of the mechanism (such as for fraud or corruption, 69 claims or 40 percent). More of a concern is the second trend, that 47 claims were not registered without any justification as to why (27 percent, see Figure 5.5).

Of those registered, only 13 (36 percent of registered claims) would be assessed for problem-solving. This is primarily because stakeholders have opposed the problem-solving process (13 cases in the eligibility phase or 36 percent). In comparison, 39 claims were assessed for compliance investigation leading to 29 compliance investigations (74 percent of eligible claims). Other reasons for rejecting

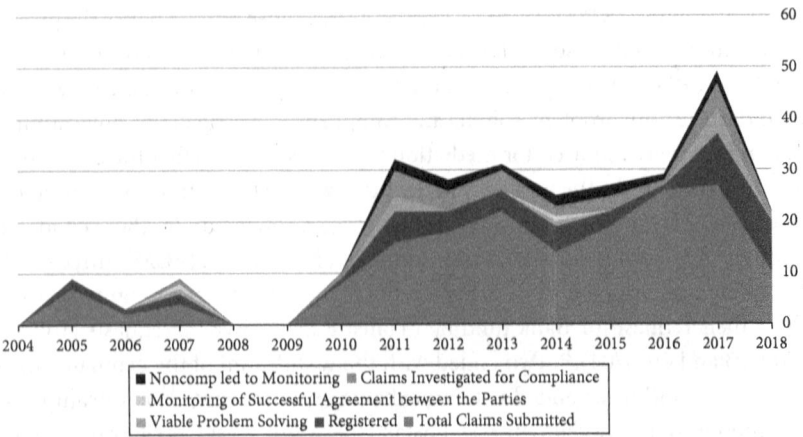

Figure 5.5 EBRD Accountability Mechanism Claims Accepted for Mediation and/or Compliance Investigation and Their Outcome, 2003–2018.

Note: Investigations underway are not included in the outcome figures. The mechanism was not operational until 2004.

problem-solving include because the Bank was no longer choosing to finance the project or because the claim was past the final disbursement threshold. In one instance problem solving was rejected by the Independent Recourse Mechanism because it was satisfied that the actions being undertaken by management were sufficient (Park 2019).

Between 2004 and 2009 the Independent Recourse Mechanism only undertook problem solving in one if its five registered cases, regarding the impact of the world's largest oil pipeline the Baku–Tbilisi–Ceyhan (BTC) pipeline on the Atskuri village in Georgia (request 2007/02; IRM 2007: 3–4). The Board accepted the chief compliance officer's recommendation for problem solving. The initiative was considered successful because most complainants' concerns about compensation for housing affected by the construction of the pipeline were addressed (IRM 2008: 3).[27] Another case would be accepted for problem solving, a claim regarding the impact of a thermal power project in Albania on local biodiversity (the Vlore Thermal Power Generation Project, request 2007/01, IRM 2007: 3) but only a compliance review was undertaken.[28]

Two other claims were rejected because the project sponsor was not willing (requests 2005/02 and 2006/01, IRM 2006: 3). In another claim neither problem-solving nor the actual loan took place because the project (Russian Federation Sakhalin II Phase 2, request 2005/01) had not been approved by the Board. Meanwhile, the complainants and the company were engaged in negotiation, prompting the Independent Recourse Mechanism to choose not to undertake problem solving (IRM 2006: 2–3). The Bank later chose not to finance the project for environmental reasons; the claim may have influenced this decision (IRM 2007: 5; EBRD 2009b). In sum, the Independent Recourse Mechanism was able to undertake both problem-solving and compliance investigations, but a number of conditions are required for mediation to succeed, no less that the company is willing to undertake the process and the Bank willing to continue with the loan.

Of the 12 claims accepted as viable for problem solving under the second iteration of the mechanism, the Project Complaint Mechanism (PCM), three would be rejected regarding a railway bypass in Georgia, because the company withdrew their request for Bank funding (Tbilisi Railway Bypass requests 2011/02, 2011/03 and 2011/04).[29] Two ended with the withdrawal of the claimants from the process and three ended with an exhaustion of recourse.[30] For example, in the another roadway claim in Kazakhstan (the South West Corridor project, request 2014/04), the PCM was unable to help the parties reach full agreement and the case was closed. In short, after operating for 10 years there are 6 examples of the Bank's accountability mechanism undertaking problem solving and limited evidence of it addressing project-affected people's grievances. This points to the limited conditions under which problem solving can provide accountability as justice.

In terms of compliance investigations, the Project Compliance Mechanism has become more confident in identifying findings of noncompliance over time, and it has the power to provide recommendations to the Bank and monitor its actions. Here again Bank avoidance and borrower opposition are evident, with the latter withdrawing from loans. Only one claim was accepted for compliance review under the Independent Recourse Mechanism, the previously mentioned Vlorë Thermal Power Generation Plant (2007). The Independent Recourse Mechanism found that the Bank did not meet the public consultation and information disclosure requirements of its Environment and Social Policy (ESP) but that this was a minor technical violation not requiring changes to the project. Instead changes to the Bank's procedures could feed into revisions to its Environment and Social Policy, which the Bank approved in May 2008.[31] As with all of the other Independent Recourse Mechanism recommendations, this was approved by the Board and president (IRM 2008) but rejected by NGOs (EBRD 2009b; CEE Bankwatch 2008: 9). The finding did not constitute a significant challenge to the Bank, as had been the case for the other MDB accountability mechanisms.

Under the PCM there is a strong trend of undertaking compliance investigations. The PCM can undertake problem solving and compliance reviews simultaneously, and the complainants can determine whether they would like one or both. Of the 39 cases assessed for compliance investigation between 2010 and mid-2019, 28 would be investigated, with another in progress

(71 percent). Of the 10 rejected claims, 4 were rejected for insufficient evidence of harm, another 4 were not investigated because the mechanism thought that it would yield limited information to warrant an investigation. One more was rejected because the Bank was already addressing claimants' concerns, and another because the Bank was no longer financing the project. Of the 28 investigated by the PCM, 9 were found policy-compliant and not leading to harm (with one investigation underway). Of the remaining 18 cases, 13 would find evidence of noncompliance with the Bank's environmental and social policy, 5 with the Bank's involuntary resettlement and information disclosure policies, 3 breaching natural habitats policy, 2 in relation to labor standards, and another 2 breaching the Bank's resource efficiency and pollution prevention policy. Of the 13 found noncompliant, only 1 would be considered to have been adequately addressed by management. The rest would be monitored by the accountability mechanism to bring the projects into compliance, most requiring multiple monitoring reports.

The first few complaints to go through a compliance review revealed both PCM leniency and borrower opposition. The first case, a motorway in Slovakia in 2010 was found compliant (request 2010/01). However, in a later compliance review report, the PCM expert noted that they had been flexible in their interpretation of whether the Bank had met its Environmental and Social Policy requirement, which they would not permit again (PCM 2014b). 2011 was a turning point for the PCM. It made its first findings of noncompliance, which the Board and management had to accept. Like the Albanian power project under the Independent Recourse Mechanism, the PCM was dealing with possible noncompliance in relation to multiple claims regarding the railway bypass in Georgia in 2011 but the company withdrew its request for Bank funding (Tiblisi Railway Bypass project requests 2011/01, 2011/02, 2011/03). Despite finding that the Bank had violated its Performance Requirement 1 (PR1) Assessment and Management of Environmental and Social Impacts and Issues, and PR10 Information Disclosure and Stakeholder Engagement, the PCM could not require the Bank to become policy-compliant because the Bank was no longer involved in the project.

Bank defiance is also evident in its response to a claim regarding a dam's impact on the critically endangered Balkan Lynx within the Mavrovo National Park in North Macedonia (the Boskov Most Hydro Power Project, request 2011/05).[32] The PCM determined that the Bank was not "sufficiently comprehensive and conclusive to satisfy the requirements of Performance Requirement 6" of the Environmental and Social Policy on biodiversity assessment (PCM 2011b). Management disagreed with the findings, but nonetheless was required to establish a Management Action Plan. The mechanism has undertaken biannual monitoring to ensure that the Bank has implemented the required changes.

The Bank also withdrew financing for an underwater hydro project in Croatia in an area being considered for EU biodiversity protection (the Ombla Hydro

Power Project, request 2011/06).[33] The Bank had already withdrawn funding for the project in May 2013, prior to the completion of the compliance review. The Bank was found noncompliant for its biodiversity assessment of the underground hydropower plant, which the Board accepted. Although management again rejected the PCM's findings, they nonetheless were required to devise a Management Action Plan. The action plan was generic on how to improve its internal processes for devising environmental impact assessments including biodiversity. As determined by its Rules of Procedure, the PCM has been monitoring the implementation of the Bank's revised Environmental and Social Policy as part of its mandate to monitor Bank compliance with policy violations arising from claims. After five monitoring reports the mechanism continues to assess whether the Bank has met the conditions of its Management Action Plan. Thus, despite the Bank's decision to withdraw funding for the project, the PCM has been used to improve the internal processes of the Bank.

Despite management denying wrongdoing, the PCM's recommendations after findings of noncompliance are informing broader Bank policy change. The outcomes of two more cases are noteworthy: In another hydro project, this time in Georgia (the Paravani Hydro Power Project, the 2012/01 claim) the Bank was again found noncompliant with regard to three of the six alleged breaches: regarding Performance Requirement 1 on environmental and social assessment, Performance Requirement 6 on biodiversity, and Performance Requirement 10 on information disclosure and stakeholder engagement. However, the PCM made no specific project-level recommendations to bring the project into compliance. Rather they argued that the Bank was noncompliant because of weaknesses in the environmental and social policy itself, which revisions to the policy could address. As a result, while management refuted the Paravani findings, they nonetheless had to prepare a Management Action Plan in accordance with updating the Environmental and Social Policy for 2014 (PCM 2014c). In another claim, this time in relation to harm induced by a lignite mining operation in a basin in Serbia (the EPS Kolubara Environmental Improvement Project, the 2012/04 claim), the Bank was again found noncompliant. Of central concern here was the limited understanding of the extent of the impacts of the project on resettlement and greenhouse gas emissions, with a lack of stakeholder engagement and consultation. The investigation noted that the Bank did not take the company's environmental and social performance history into account despite investing in its operations since 2001 (PCM 2015b). Recommendations from the investigation again fed into the environmental and social policy review with little in the way of project changes. This is because the events leading to harm had already taken place. In response, the complainants argued that there is little in the way of recommendations for improvement for the people adversely affected in the project area. Claimants were critical of the PCM because its purpose is to provide recourse for people "instead of dealing with just inner bank regulations without addressing the reality of outer world" (Center for Ecology and Sustainable Development 2015). The Bank did include an audit of the impacts of the project on mining communities in the area, closing the claim in 2016.[34]

The PCM demonstrates that it is undertaking due process and increasingly that it has the independence and integrity to determine whether the Bank is in breach of its policies. This is a testament to the Board's willingness to accept the findings of the experts. Moreover, the PCM has the capacity to provide recommendations and undertake monitoring to ensure the Bank becomes compliant. The cases demonstrate the mechanism has tended to make recommendations on getting the policies right, rather than be able to make project-level changes. This highlights how the Bank and the company must provide justification and reasoning for their behavior but not necessarily pressing the Bank to provide project level remedies. In 2020 the PCM was replaced with the Independent Project Accountability Mechanism, with direct reporting to the Bank's Board outside the operations of management. While the EBRD's accountability mechanism is strong on compliance, the PCM's record on problem-solving stands in contrast to the AfDB's mechanism.

African Development Bank's Accountability Mechanism

Of the 37 cases registered up to the middle of 2019, the Compliance Review and Mediation Unit (CRMU) director registered 17 cases, 11 cases were designated as viable for problem solving (64 percent of registered cases), and 8 were assessed for a compliance investigation (47 percent of registered cases, see Figure 5.6).

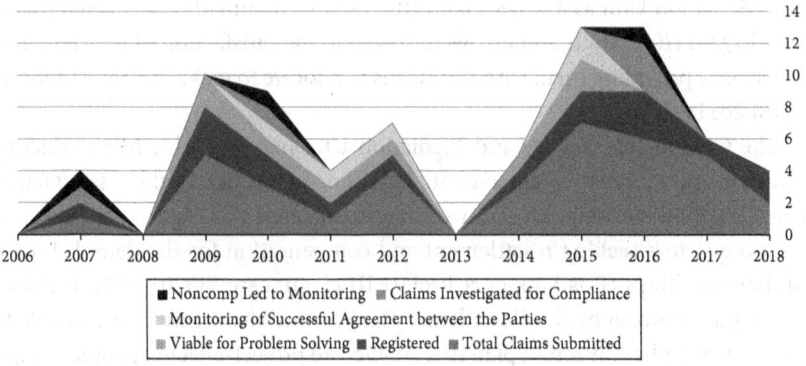

Figure 5.6 AfDB Accountability Mechanism Claims Accepted for Mediation and/ or Compliance Investigation and Their Outcome, 2004–2018.

Claims were rejected for registration for a variety of reasons, foremost because claims were outside the mandate of the mechanism (Park 2019). The Compliance Review and Mediation Unit undertakes fact-finding, including on potential policy violations, while negotiating with communities as to whether they would like to undertake problem solving, with the potential for compliance review subject to Independent Review Mechanism expert approval thereafter.[35] Of the 11 cases for problem solving, three assessments were underway in the middle of 2019. Two of the early problem-solving cases were accepted but discontinued because the borrower withdrew its funding request or reconsidered the project location (see chapter 4; the Gibe III Hydroelectric Power Project case RQ2009/01; and the Nuweiba Combined Cycle Power Project RQ2009/02).[36] The remaining six would go through the problem-solving process and enter the facilitating a settlement phase (54 percent of viable problem-solving claims). This demonstrates a high degree of stakeholder engagement in the problem-solving process.

Two claims led to problem-solving resulting in efforts by management to address the concerns. The first was a claim submitted in July 2010 regarding relocating people for a motorway in Morocco (the Marrakech-Agadir Motorway, case RQ2010/01). The mediation process led to an agreement between the requestors, the Bank, and the company undertaking the project regarding six of the eight issues of concern to claimants (IRM 2011a: 12). The Compliance Review and Mediation Unit continued to follow up on the implementations of the action plan agreed to by the parties in 2011. The problem-solving case was expected to be closed in early 2015 once all issues had been resolved to the requestor's satisfaction (IRM 2014: 25–26). However, the case seems to have been closed without information on the final status of claimant's concerns. The second case of management addressing the concerns raised by the problem-solving initiative related to two claims submitted within a week of each other regarding another motorway in Senegal were registered by the Compliance Review and Mediation Unit as a single claim (the Dakar-Diamniadio Highway Project, case RQ2011/01). Both requests were solved to the satisfaction of the claimants in terms of providing them with the means to relocate to make way for a highway (IRM 2011a: 10).

The Compliance Review and Mediation Unit has been able to successfully monitor and close three agreements between the parties to their satisfaction (Park 2019). For example, a claim again was triggered by a highway in Tanzania with requestors seeking resettlement and compensation for the demolishment of their dwellings (Road Support Project III claim, case RQ2012/01). Problem solving undertaken by the Compliance Review and Mediation Unit was able to establish a mediation action plan that enabled all project-affected people to have access to land valuation, compensation, and resettlement in accordance with the Bank's resettlement action plan. This also included the establishment of a working project-level grievance mechanism to address project-affected people's concerns. The Compliance Review and Mediation Unit was also able to trace funding for compensation and it expected all compensation to be paid by the first quarter of 2015 (IRM 2014: 25). The matter was not eligible for a compliance investigation to resolve the issue because the problem did not result from a Bank act or omission, combined with the fact that the requestors were satisfied with the outcome of mediation (IRM 2010: 20).[37] To date, the AfDB's accountability mechanism has demonstrated that it can provide accountability as justice through problem solving, although some cases remain open. In sum, the Compliance Review and Mediation Unit has been active in attempting to resolve requestors' claims to their satisfaction in a transparent and effective way, which gives the mechanism both legitimacy and credibility.

Yet, no reference to a compliance review was articulated in the more recent problem-solving report for the Tanzania Road case (RQ2012/01), and it is unclear why, considering the case involves the involuntary resettlement of people (IRM 2014b). This may stem from capacity. Elsewhere the Compliance Review and Mediation Unit has noted that a compliance review might be unwarranted in cases where problem-solving reports have revealed inadequacies in Bank implementation of overlapping policies, which a compliance review would only duplicate (IRM 2012b). This is overlaid by the review of the Bank's environmental and social safeguard policy framework and the review of the mechanism's operational policies throughout 2013. Both policy updates not only took up considerable Bank staff time but also underscored the need for policy clarity for any compliance review to be meaningful.

In terms of compliance investigation, Bank defiance and Board efforts to limit the Independent Review Mechanism are evident, as is borrower opposition by withdrawing from projects facing a claim. Of its 17 registered claims, 8 were designated for compliance review and 5 were undertaken (29 percent of registered claims).[38] Two early claims deemed eligible for compliance review did not proceed because the government discontinued the loan (the Ethiopian Gibe III Hydroelectric Power Plant project, RQ2009/01 and RQ2009/01b). The third case not to go to investigation was the motorway in Morocco for reasons mentioned earlier (Marrakesh-Agadir Motorway in Morocco, RQ2010/01). Of the five investigated, one investigation is still underway. Four completed investigations revealed significant breaches in the Bank's compliance with its environmental and social policies. Bank defiance is clear, with management opposing the findings of completed investigations where policy violations were found.

The Bank's very first claim was designated for compliance review, leading to a full investigation. The Bujugali Hydropower Project and Interconnection Project in Uganda (RQ2007/01) was the subject of a claim by local NGOs, which submitted that the AfDB had not met 11 of its environmental and social policies.

They argued that the AfDB's project analysis was based on flawed hydrological and climate models, an underestimation of the "project's ability to generate electricity or review alternative energy sources, an overestimation of the project's economic benefits, and a failure to adequately recognize the Indigenous Basoga peoples in the area, or provide land titles and suitable dwellings for those moved for the project.[39] Management rejected this, stating that they were fully compliant with relevant AfDB policies, which were undertaken to "high professional standards" (AfDB 2007). The Compliance Review and Mediation Unit determined that there was evidence that harm could be linked to the project, particularly regarding resettlement and thus determined that a compliance review was required. The Board approved the investigation on a no-objection basis. As a claim had already been accepted by the World Bank Inspection Panel (in 2001, see chapter 4) the compliance review was undertaken collaboratively.

The Independent Review Mechanism found evidence of both compliance and noncompliance of Bank policies leading to harm, although this was clouded by "gaps or lack of clarity in the Bank's policies and procedures," which ultimately meant that the Independent Review Mechanism was unable to make a finding of either compliance or noncompliance (IRM 2008: 10–11). Despite this, a Management Action Plan to accord with the Independent Review Mechanism's recommendations was required by the Board and the Independent Review Mechanism was charged with monitoring its implementation. Monitoring has taken over seven years and including four monitoring reports, which demonstrate that the Bank has moved toward compliance. The closure of the case to requestors' satisfaction was expected in 2013 but final resettlement and compensation was delayed.

The next full compliance review undertaken was the Medupi Power Project in South Africa (RQ2007/01). Borrower opposition may have led the Board to circumscribe the investigation through limiting the Independent Review Mechanism's investigation. Requestors sought a compliance review on September 28, 2010, regarding multiple concerns about the coal-fired power plant. The claim was accepted by the Independent Review Mechanism over concern of harm or likely harm. However, when the recommendation was submitted to the Board for approval, they sent it back to the IRM for reassessment. The Board upheld management's concerns that neither procurement nor economic benefit were within the purview of the Independent Review Mechanism and that the Bank had met its policy on good governance. The Independent Review Mechanism pushed back against the Board with revised terms of reference for the investigation, outlining that four of the six complainant's concerns were valid, again requesting approval to investigate the claims of environmental harm, negative health impacts, failure to comply with the clean energy policy, and failure of community consultation and participation. The Board approved an investigation into the project on the July 15, 2011, on clean energy/climate change, and environmental and social impacts. A completed Independent Review Mechanism investigation report, submitted to the Board on January 24, 2012, highlights that the Bank was noncompliant regarding eight policies including environmental and energy policies including a failure to address climate change; additionally, it failed to meet its participation and consultation policies, and its involuntary resettlement policy. The report did find that the Bank was compliant with the environmental assessment for air emissions from the plant, but findings could not be made on land and water degradation (IRM 2011b). In December, the Board stated that management needed to provide an updated plan and work with the Compliance Review and Mediation Unit to address factual discrepancies arising between the Bank and the Independent Review Mechanism's reports. Both the updated action plan and the IRM's monitoring plan were approved in February 2013, but the Management Action Plan, the Board's decision, and the Independent Review Mechanism monitoring terms of reference are not publicly available (IRM 2012c).

Third completed investigation found noncompliance in relation to the Bank's environmental and social policy and poverty reduction policy. The claim asserted human rights abuses and land grabbing in an agricultural diversification project in Mali (Diversification of the Activities of "Moulins Modernes du Mali (M3)" Project in Mali, RQ 2016/1). In response, management rejected the claims being made and dismissed the authority of the requestors (IRM 2016b). The investigation found that the operations staff had not engaged in full due diligence on the environmental and social impact of the project and that management's assurances to the Board were inaccurate. The project is now being monitored to bring it into compliance.[40]

In sum, four full investigations have been undertaken. There has only been one instance where a claim was rejected by the Independent Review Mechanism for review (on the basis that the lessons learned would duplicate that of the problem-solving exercise). All investigations revealed noncompliance of the Bank with its own policies leading to a Management Action Plan and ongoing Independent Review Mechanism monitoring. In all cases management denied wrongdoing. In all cases the Board approved the investigation although returning the request for investigation to the IRM in the Medupi case before approving a more limited investigation. It is clear that the process is working, and that the Independent Review Mechanism can push the Bank to become compliant in ways that address harm to project-affected people. This demonstrates that the Independent Review Mechanism is following due process, and that it has integrity and credibility in providing accountability as justice to project-affected people. As the following section demonstrates, one of the major impacts of the Independent Review Mechanism investigations has been the revision of the Bank's environmental and social safeguard system to provide greater clarity to Bank policies, thus helping people hold the banks to account.

Conclusion

This chapter documented how the accountability mechanisms work to enact justice through the provision of recourse for project-affected people. They engage in both problem-solving and compliance investigations that report either to the banks' management or their boards. Yet there are obstacles for providing accountability as justice through these means, leading to small numbers of successful mediations, and claims resulting in bank management being monitored to rectify the harm (see Figure 5.7).

Although the accountability mechanisms are entrenched parts of the banks' governance, there is evidence of both management and board interference in their activities. Management resistance is evident across the banks, but is most acute in the early days of the mechanisms' instantiation. This resistance ranges from norm avoidance to defiance and manipulation. Avoidance was evident through two practices: first, where management concealed their nonconformity with the norm by providing ceremonial information that did not reveal the extent of their Bank's practices leading to harm; and second, failures to adequately respond to findings of Bank noncompliance through the minimal provision of remedies. All the banks also engaged in defiance by dismissing and challenging the norm. Dismissing institutional rules occurs when the organization perceives enforcement of the rules to be low or when the rules dramatically conflict with the organization's values (Oliver 1991: 156). Management consistently denied claims from project-affected people as legitimate, even when later found otherwise, and

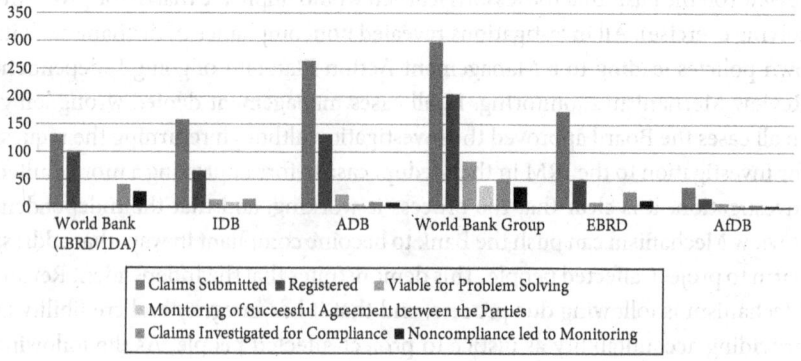

Figure 5.7 Progress of Claims Submitted to the MDB Accountability Mechanisms up to December 31, 2018.

refuted any wrongdoing. In this way the banks sought to uphold the sanctity of lending as usual while challenging the accountability as justice norm as unnecessary. Some of the banks, like the World Bank, ADB, and IDB also engaged in challenging the accountability mechanism process. Challenging the rules occurs when the organization attaches less significance to the norm than to their own "insular and elevated vision of what is, or should be, appropriate, rational, or acceptable" (Oliver 1991: 156–157).

Finally, there is also evidence of manipulation or attempts to influence and control the investigation process within some of the banks. Bank management would seek to influence the standards by which they would be evaluated. For example, the World Bank management sought to influence the definition of what constitutes a project that could be investigated. Some of the banks would seek to counter the accountability mechanism findings based on their interpretations of the environmental and social standards (such as World Bank, ADB, and EBRD responses to the findings). In this way management could seek to influence how the Board would respond to investigation findings. A more extreme form of manipulation is when the banks seek to control the investigation process, including supporting staff that withheld evidence of wrongdoing in investigations (the World Bank and ADB), and staff that sought to persuade affected people not to make claims (the World Bank).

The banks do not operate in a vacuum and the actions of their Boards contribute to enforcing or undermining the norm. The World Bank Inspection Panel is routinely given monitoring powers by the Board, even though some borrowers seek to limit Panel investigations. The IDB's Board routinely attempts to block compliance investigations, seeing them as a worst-case scenario. The ADB's Board has taken more control over its Accountability Mechanism and limited its monitoring powers. The Boards of IFC and MIGA play less of a role than the other banks because the CAO reports to the World Bank Group president. The president has been supportive of the CAO's ability to undertake mediation, and both the president and the IFC's executive vice president have triggered compliance investigations into management's activities. For the other banks, while borrowers may not like investigations, these have become routinized and therefore less controversial. Nonetheless, the EBRD, AfDB, ADB, and IDB boards can limit the terms of reference for a compliance investigation, which raises questions as to what role the board should play in the process. The combination of bank management resistance and board behavior are examined in the book's conclusion, but first, how the norm has strengthened over time, and its impacts on the MDBs' overall operations and culture are examined.

6

Changing the Banks and Strengthening Accountability as Justice?

The last chapter demonstrated how the multilateral development banks (MBDs) continue to resist the norm through a range of strategies even though their boards have increasingly given the accountability mechanisms more monitoring and advisory powers. This chapter has two aims. First, it outlines how the norm has improved over time: The accountability mechanisms' have become more independent, transparent, and accessible, which enhances their legitimacy and credibility in providing justice. Combined with their increasing responsiveness to project-affected people covered in chapter 4, and their ability to monitor and advise their banks in chapter 5, there is a greater potential for the norm to shape the MBDs' practices and culture. However, the second part of this chapter reiterates how the norm is a corrective to bank actions rather than a preemptive norm for ensuring justice in international development. It documents how little the norm impacts the MDBs' lending operations, policies, and procedures.

Strengthening the Accountability as Justice Norm

Thus far the focus of the book has been how the norm emerged and how bank management and their boards engaged with it. Beyond the accountability mechanism resolutions and the reviews, there was no clear direction from member states as to how to enact the norm. This led accountability officers to devise their own procedures, including meeting annually to share their experiences in the Independent Accountability Mechanism Network from 2004. In 2007 the chair of the Inspection Panel, Professor Edith Brown Weiss, presented the four criteria the mechanisms could use to evaluate themselves: access, credibility, efficiency, and effectiveness (Inspection Panel 2009: Annex B, 109–112). In 2012 the accountability officers reframed the criteria as principles: accessible, transparent, independent, impartial, to act with integrity and professionalism, and to be responsive (Lewis 2012).[1] The principles comprise both the means to achieve justice and the reality of responding to people affected by MDB lending. These criteria underpin their operations and are increasingly referenced during board-mandated reviews (ADB 2002e: 19; PCM 2014: 2). The following sections

The Good Hegemon. Susan Park, Oxford University Press. © Oxford University Press 2022.
DOI: 10.1093/oso/9780197626481.003.0006

document how the accountability mechanisms are meeting these principles through becoming more independent, accessible, and transparent.

Independent

As highlighted in chapter 3, the banks' avoidance strategy meant limiting the independence and operations of the accountability mechanisms. From the beginning the mechanisms had to fight to be independent from bank management and the board. To enable accountability as justice, the mechanisms and the complaint process should be credible in terms of being independent from bank management and operations. Through iterative processes of board-mandated reviews and US interventions, the mechanisms are now able to determine the eligibility of claims from project-affected people without interference. The mechanisms all now have the power to make recommendations to their presidents or boards as to whether they should engage in problem solving or a compliance investigation, and these are generally accepted on a no-objection basis. This makes the accountability mechanisms credible and legitimate in terms of providing recourse for the banks' damaging behavior.

Although the mechanisms are claim-driven, the interactions between the banks and the accountability mechanisms focus on accepting responsibility for causing harm to affected people. All the banks continue to defy the norm by denying wrongdoing and all engage in avoidance by attempt to limit actions to bring the projects back into compliance. In some cases, the banks' boards have continued to interfere with the ability of the mechanisms to undertake investigations or accept their findings (this is most evident in the Inter-American Development Bank, as per chapter 5). In a few cases projects have been halted as a result of an accountability mechanism investigation, but this tends to be when the project is in its appraisal stage (which is most evident in the European Bank for Reconstruction and Development's Project Complaint Mechanism). The further advanced the project, the less likely a claim to rectify damage is possible. Moreover, as all the banks now lend to nonsovereign entities (except the World Bank), the process is then contingent on companies' willingness to allow investigators to assess bank compliance, with ramifications on how they too should address noncompliance.

Accessible

For a recourse mechanism to be of use, people need to be aware of the mechanism and have the capacity to file a claim (Lewis 2012). The accountability mechanisms resolutions were devised by the banks for member state approval, as detailed in chapter 3. This gave the banks the capacity to delimit the actions of the mechanisms, with far-reaching implications for their capacity to enact accountability as justice. The banks and many member states feared that they would be flooded with frivolous or malicious claims or claimants seeking economic advantage. This meant that most of the initial mechanisms were written by the banks' legal departments as complex, highly proscribed, technical documents. As shown in chapter 5 and in what follows, most of the accountability mechanisms receive few claims and even fewer that meet the eligibility criteria to be registered. The World Bank and the World Bank Group have the highest rates of receiving and registering claims, which befits their global reach. For all the banks, registered claims reflect between 0.45 and 1.8 percent of their annual number of projects (see Table 6.1).

The banks' accountability mechanisms are detailed here in terms of registering claims.[2] Claims were considered bona fide if they met the eligibility criteria as set out in the accountability mechanisms' resolutions or rules of procedure. The accountability mechanisms all created their own initial procedure to "register" a claim if it seemed worthy of a preliminary assessment based on the eligibility criteria. Claims could be rejected for registration for procedural reasons or where the claims fall outside the accountability mechanisms' mandate, including claims regarding ethics, procurement, fraud, or corruption; claims against projects where the loans had already met a specified disbursement threshold; claims against projects not (yet) implemented; claims where a prior complaint is already addressing complainants' concerns; claims where a case is subject to legal action, even if this is unrelated to the claim (for the Inspection Panel, African, Inter-American, and European banks); claims where complainants have not first taken their concerns to bank management; claims

Table 6.1 Registration Figures for Claims Submitted to the MDB Accountability Mechanisms, 1994–2018.

Multilateral Development Bank	WB	IDB	ADB	WBG	EBRD	AfDB
Percentage of submitted claims that have been registered	74.4%	41.4%	49.4%	68.5%	28.3%	45.9%
Average number claims registered per year	3.9	2.6	5.4	10.7	3.3	1.3
Registered claims as an approx. percent of the MDB's annual projects	0.71%	0.94%	1.83%	1.10%	1.03%	0.45%

that demonstrate insufficient evidence of harm; or claims where the complaint could not be verified (Park 2019).

The accountability mechanisms of the banks are similar in terms of the procedural criteria that determine whether a claim can be registered as eligible for assessment for problem solving or a compliance investigation. However, they differ with regard to which criteria exclude claims from being registered: For example, the Inter-American Development Bank's 2010 Independent Consultation and Investigation Mechanism (MICI in Spanish) included 17 procedural criteria and exclusion clauses that were a significant hindrance to requestors' claims being registered (IDB 2012b:17). This compares to 10 eligibility criteria for the African Development Bank, 8 for the Asian and European Banks, and 6 for the World Bank Inspection Panel, while the Compliance Advisor/Ombudsman (CAO) for the World Bank Group has only three criteria.[3] In 2014, the Inter-American Development Bank's MICI policy identified only six criteria that requestors must meet, bringing it closer to the other mechanisms (ICIM 2014b).

The procedural criteria thus identify what project-affected people can make a claim about, as well as how they must do so. The specifications on who could submit a claim included: determining that a claim had to be from more than two people, and from the project-affected area, with specific identification of the banks' noncompliance with regard to the limited number of relevant operational policies directly leading to harm or potential harm. It also excluded NGOs, unless these were verified designated representatives of project-affected people (the European Bank would later allow NGOs to submit claims independent of project-affected people). Each of the banks is discussed in turn.

The Inspection Panel acknowledged that it receives a low number of claims (Inspection Panel 2009: 90, 24), compared with over 650 active World Bank projects per year with committed annual Bank lending averaging $19.6 billion dollars per year for the last 20 years (World Bank 2016d; Table 2.3 in chapter 2). Yet the World Bank has the highest percent of claims registered of those submitted. By the end of 2018, the World Bank's Inspection Panel had received 130 claims but it had registered 98 (75.4 percent of claims submitted) or an average of 3.9 claims per year; claims registered therefore represent less than 0.71 percent of projects annually. Clearly the Inspection Panel is not being overrun with claims, despite being the oldest, largest, most global, and most well-known of the accountability mechanisms. Staff are aware of more "problem" projects that do not result in Inspection Panel claims, but there has not been any attempt to determine why so few project-affected people lodge claims (Interview with former World Bank staff, November 2, 2013).

The dominant cause for not registering a claim is because the Inspection Panel deemed that there was insufficient evidence of harm or that the harm was not caused by the project, or that the harm was not caused by violation of policies.

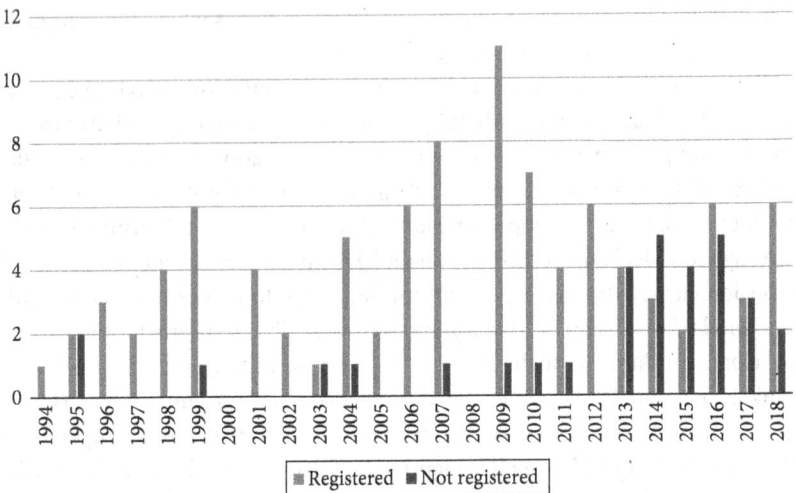

Figure 6.1   Claims Registered versus Not Registered for the World Bank's
Accountability Mechanism, 1994–2018.

Once accepted for registration, a claim is then reviewed through an Eligibility
Assessment Report. Of the 98 claims registered, 56 were determined not to be
eligible for investigation through the Eligibility Assessment Report (57 percent).
The dominant reason for rejecting a claim for investigation (in 31 cases or 55 percent) was because the Panel was satisfied that actions were already underway,
or had already been completed, by Bank management to address requestor
concerns. The Panel would increasingly invoke this from 2009: 23 of the 31
claims (74 percent) rejected for this reason were in the last nine years of the
Panel's operations. While Panel satisfaction is a basis for the Panel to choose not
to undertake an investigation, this is a significant shift in Panel determinations.
It suggests that the Panel is now more willing to accept management's statements
that the problems can be rectified. Moreover, from 2013 the number of cases
rejected for registration increased (see Figure 6.1). Both the increased rejection
rate for registration and the rejection for compliance investigation occurred as
the Panel was being pressured to be more conciliatory toward management.

The likelihood of a claim progressing within the Inter-American Development
Bank's accountability mechanism is much worse. Since its inception up to the end
of 2018, the accountability mechanism received 145 (known) claims. However,
it registered only 53 claims (36 percent) or an average of 2.6 per year. This is
within the context of approximately 300 active projects per year or 0.94 percent of projects annually and committed annual lending levels of approximately
$9.6 billion over the last 20 years (see Table 6.1).[4] Of the 92 claims that were not

registered, the vast majority (56 claims or 60 percent) were deemed ineligible, but no public information was provided for the determination. After MICI was created in 2010, a greater emphasis was placed on public awareness, leading to a dramatic increase in claims from 2011 onward, but a high portion of these were not registered (see Figure 6.2). In the 2012 MICI review, the Bank's Office of Evaluation and Oversight was satisfied that MICI had appropriately rejected claims, most of which either sought information about the project or MICI operations or did not meet the procedural requirements (IDB 2012c: Annex 3). The Office of Evaluation and Oversight did however recommend that MICI be more consistent and transparent in rejecting claims (IDB 2012b: 16–17). The number of claims not registered remains high, signaling that MICI's efforts at outreach are working to inform project-affected people of their existence while not clearly conveying its registration criteria (ICIM 2015: Annex 2, 47–51; ICIM 2014a: 47). The reduction of exclusion criteria for registration after 2014 does not seem to have affected the number of claims being registered.

Figures for the Asian Development Bank's mechanism show that it has become more transparent (discussed further in what follows). By the end of 2018 the Accountability Mechanism had received 263 known claims. However, it only registered 131 of those (49 percent), an average of 5.4 claims per year. This is compared with over 300 active projects annually and a total committed annual lending on average of $8.2 billion over the last 20 years (see Table 2.3 in chapter 2); thus, constituting less than 1.8 percent of active projects (Table 6.1). The original Inspection Function proved difficult for project-affected people to

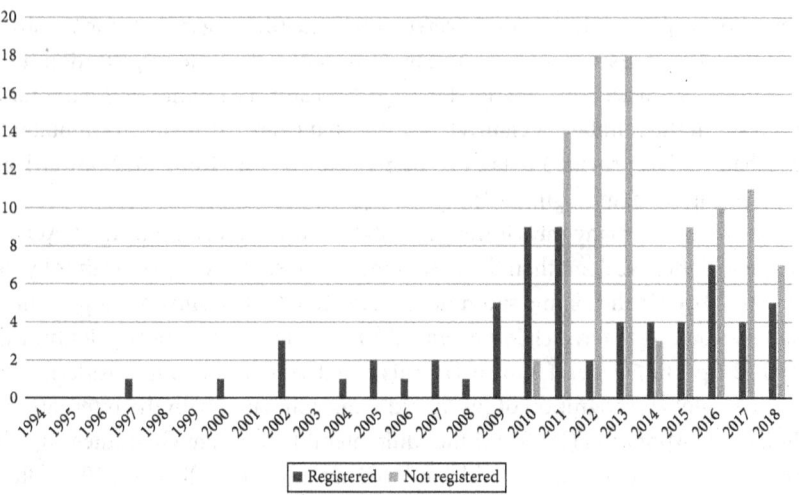

Figure 6.2 Claims Registered versus Not Registered for the IDB's Accountability Mechanism, 1994–2018.

access, for example, requesting claims be written in English (ADB 2002e: 29). Of the 132 cases that were not registered, the vast majority of cases, 94 (71 percent), were rejected because the claims were not within the mandate of the mechanism because they related to fraud, ethics, corruption, personnel matters, or procurement. Importantly, there is no record of the actual number of claims fielded by the Office of the Special Project Facilitator (OSPF) from 2004 to 2011, access to this data may increase the number of claims submitted but rejected.

Unlike the other mechanisms, the Accountability Mechanism was "registering" cases that did not meet its procedural criteria; it assessed claims for eligibility once placed on the public case registry. However, according to the first Special Project Facilitator,

> the OSPF found it desirable to prescreen requests even if they do not meet the stipulated requirements for filing of complaints, to stay engaged with the affected persons, and to work behind the scenes with the operations departments to resolve problems before they grow into full-blown complaints. A significant amount of time was also spent trying to anticipate and avert complaints. And, there were a few successes. Even ineligible complaints must be dealt with thoughtfully and convincingly, which requires significant effort. The complainants have to be treated with respect and have to be convinced that their complaints are ineligible and that they have to endeavour to resolve the issues with the assistance of the borrower and ADB's operations departments. (OSPF, 2006, p. 5)

There was no articulation of how and why some claims were registered but later rejected on procedural grounds versus those neither registered nor recorded (OSPF 2006: 5). As a result, the increase in rejecting claims for registration from 2012 reveals a lack of information between 2004 and 2011 rather than a dramatic increase in the number of claims being rejected from 2012. The Accountability Mechanism has provided data of its nonregistered cases from 2012 onward, although gaps remain (Figure 6.3).

The outlier in many ways is the CAO of the World Bank Group. The CAO has a much higher caseload than the other mechanisms, receiving 298 claims by the end of 2018. Of the claims submitted, it registered 204 claims or 68 percent of submissions. Registered claims averaged 10.7 claims per year, nearly double that of the Inspection Panel (Figure 6.4).[5] This might seem surprising considering the size and global recognition of the World Bank compared with the International Finance Corporation (IFC) and the Multilateral Investment Guarantee Agency (MIGA). On average, the World Bank has an annual lending of $19.6 billion while the IFC invests approximately $8.1 billion for over 500 projects annually, and MIGA guarantees of $2.3 billion (see Table 2.3, chapter 2). Despite its high

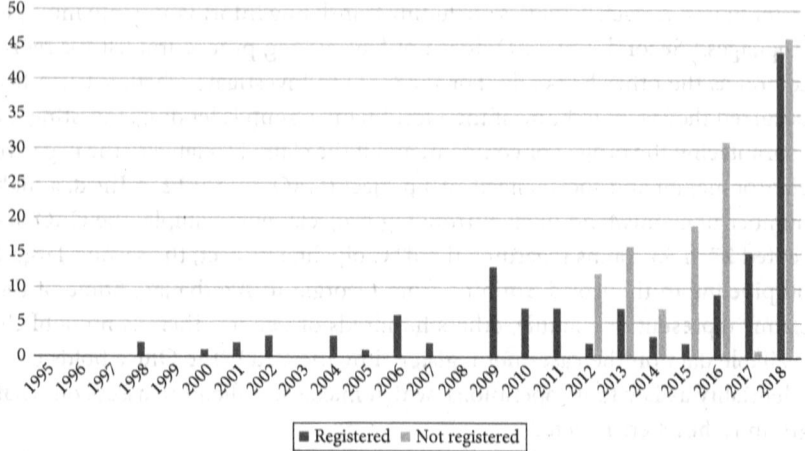

Figure 6.3 Claims Registered versus Not Registered for the ADB's Accountability Mechanism, 1995–2018.

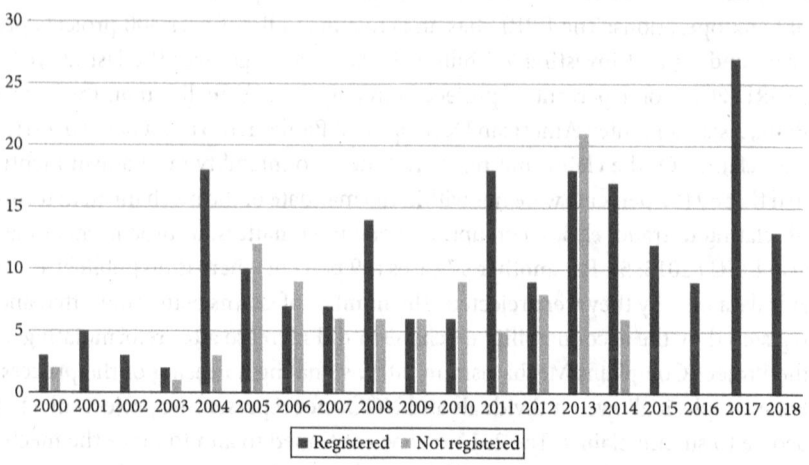

Figure 6.4 Claims Registered versus Not Registered for the World Bank Group's Accountability Mechanism, 1999–2018.

load, the number of cases the CAO deals with still represents only 1.1 percent of their combined portfolios (CAO 2015: 6).[6]

There are three possible explanations as to why the CAO has a higher case-load and registrations. First, the CAO attributes the increasing number of claims to its efforts at outreach and its success in helping to mediate disputes with companies and communities. Notably, the CAO was more focused and faster in its outreach activities, including translating information into multiple languages.[7] Second, the CAO does not have a long procedural list for registration as the other banks do. For the CAO to investigate whether harm has occurred they want to know if the World Bank Group is lending, investing, or guaranteeing the project or company, and if the claim is related to the negative environmental and social effects of a project (CAO 2013b: 12).[8] Third, a high number of claims tend to stem from big projects. For example, the CAO accepted 27 of 33 claims regarding the BTC pipeline project, the second-largest oil pipeline in the world, running from Georgia to Azerbaijan. Some of the claims represent one family, others hundreds of people. There is no publicly available data on the cases not registered by the CAO. The Office holds confidentiality as key to its operations, which makes it difficult to assess on what grounds they were rejected.

The accountability mechanism with one of the lowest rates of registering claims is the European Bank for Reconstruction and Development. It has received 169 claims since it began operating in 2004. However, it only registered 49 of those claims (28 percent) up to the end of 2018, or 3.3 registerable claims per year. The number of registrable claims must be placed within the context of bank operations: The EBRD has an active portfolio of over 300 projects per year, lending and investing 7.7 billion Euro on average over the last 20 years (EBRD 2015) or 1 percent of projects annually. While smaller than the World Bank, Asian and Inter-American Development Banks, it too is not being overrun with claims. Of the claims not registered the accountability mechanism identified that 69 (57 percent) were not within the mandate of the mechanism in terms of relating to fraud, ethics, corruption, personnel matters, or procurement (see also EBRD 2015: 5). For another 47 cases (39 percent) there is no publicly available data on why they were rejected. The number of claims being submitted and registered by the accountability mechanism did increase after reformulating as the Project Complaint Mechanism in 2010, signaling an easing of the process. For example, it allowed individuals and NGOs not representing project-affected people to submit claims. The 2013 review continued to aim to make the mechanism more accessible, but overall, the mechanism has one of the lowest registration rates among the MDBs (EBRD 2015b: 1; see Figure 6.5 and Figure 5.7 in chapter 5).

The smallest mechanism is the African Development Bank's. It has received 37 claims since it began operating in 2006. Of those however it has only registered 17 claims (45 percent) or 1.3 per year. The AfDB is also small, with committed lending accounting for $3.5 billion on average for the last 20 years, with 240 projects initiated in 2015, but registered claims only representing 0.45 percent of projects annually.[9] Of the claims not registerable, eight were outside the scope of the mechanism's procedural criteria (40 percent), and the remaining claims

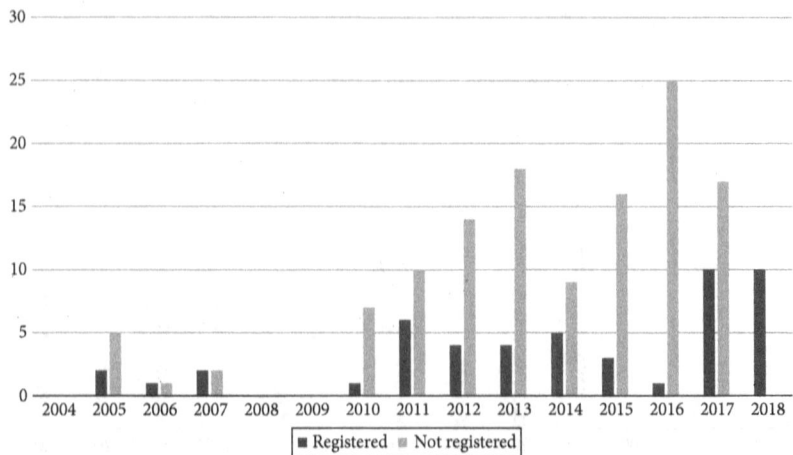

Figure 6.5 Claims Registered versus Not Registered for the EBRD's Accountability Mechanism, 2003–2018.

did not meet different basic procedural requirements (IRM 2016a). Like the CAO, the CRMU did undertake one mediation despite not registering the claim; assisting in the settlement of a contract despite this falling outside its mandate (IRM 2014: 21). Like the other mechanisms the CRMU has also chosen to defer registering a case for problem solving (RQ2009/01b) where a similar complaint was raised by other parties already undertaking mediation (IRM 2009: 5).[10] The Independent Review Mechanism is transparent in determining what is registered and why (see Figure 6.6).

As the MDB accountability mechanisms have become more transparent they have increased the number of claims submitted to them but not necessarily increased the number of claims they register. The Inspection Panel and the CAO remain the most accessible and the Panel the most transparent, although the CAO has the highest caseload. Most claims submitted to the accountability mechanisms are rejected for procedural reasons such as being related to concerns of procurement, fraud, and corruption, although there are some decisions for rejecting claims (such as being satisfied that management is adequately dealing with the problem) or deferring registering claims that raise questions of due process (see also Park 2015, 2019). Both the Inter-American Development Bank and the European Bank for Reconstruction and Development have low rates of registering cases, revealing hindrances for project affected people to have their grievances heard. Subsequently each and every review of the accountability mechanisms has prioritized improving awareness of, and access to, the mechanisms.

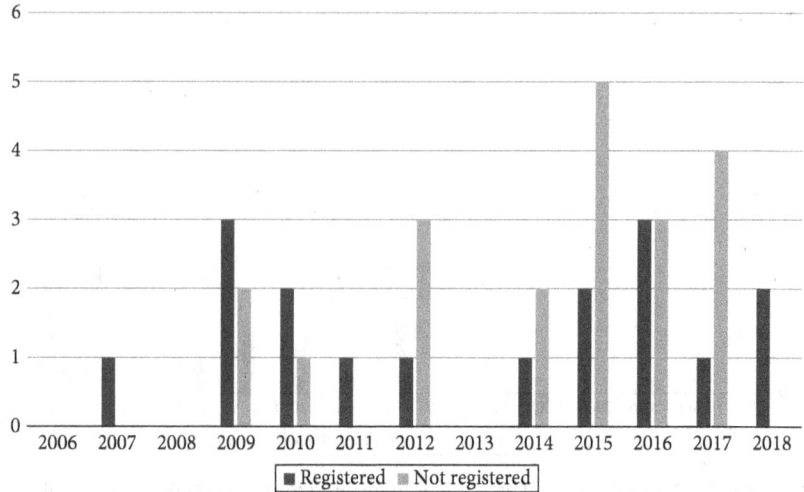

Figure 6.6 Claims Registered versus Not Registered for the AfDB's Accountability Mechanism, 2004–2018.

Transparent

Until recently most mechanisms did not record requests that did not meet the eligibility requirements although these were sometimes mentioned in annual reports. The Inspection Panel stands alone in transparently identifying all claims from its inception on its online public registry, including those it did not register and why. From 2010 the Inter-American Development Bank began to include the cases it has not processed or registered on its case registry, although the reason why is often missing. The Asian Development Bank only began to record the claims it did not register from 2012 and only released that information publicly in 2016, although why claims were rejected is also often missing. Unlike the other mechanisms, between 2004 and 2011 the Accountability Mechanism was "registering" claims that did not meet its eligibility criteria and were later rejected for procedural reasons, but it was also "prescreening" requests it deemed ineligible from 2003 (OSPF 2006: 5, ADB 2016b). As with the other accountability mechanisms, the Asian Development Bank's Special Project Facilitator had discretion as to what was registered and what was not recorded (Park 2015: 461). The Accountability Mechanism now uses the registration process to determine eligibility, as per the other mechanisms. In comparison, the CAO only referred to cases it did not register in an ad hoc way in its annual reports until 2008, when it began to provide a full log of claims received, but with no information as to why they were rejected (CAO 2008: 57–61, 2014). While earlier annual reports mention nonregistrable submissions for the European Bank for Reconstruction and Development's mechanisms, there is not a full account of its nonregistered cases or why they were rejected. A full list of unregistered claims was provided by the African Development Bank in June 2016.

Registered claims for all the accountability mechanisms are now placed on their online public case registries, which enables them to be tracked as to whether they are accepted or rejected for problem solving or compliance investigation or both. The Inspection Panel, the CAO, and both of the European and African Banks' mechanisms, show all registered claims, but there is no public case registry for the early iterations of the Inter-American and Asian Development Banks' mechanisms (the Independent Investigation Mechanism and the Inspection Function).[11] Through the board-mandated reviews, all of the mechanisms would increasingly provide more public information as cases unfolded, including how far a claim has progressed. This is not to say that all documents are now available to the public. A significant number of documents are missing from the Asian, African, Inter-American, and World Bank Group case registries. Over time, the process has also improved to keep claimants informed of the process. As noted previously, the Inspection Panel introduced a procedure for returning to the requestors at the conclusion of a case to inform them of the outcome. All the mechanisms now enable claimants to provide input into the process such as commenting on management's response to their claim. In short, all the accountability mechanisms have become more transparent over time, which enhances their credibility and legitimacy although some were starting at a much lower base than others. Most importantly all the accountability mechanisms now provide claimants with templates for how to submit claims and, as previously noted, have become more responsive to project-affected people throughout the claims process.

Transparency is important for being able to identify how many claims the accountability mechanisms are receiving and how many are deemed eligible for problem solving or compliance investigation. Unsurprisingly, relatively few claims were made during the initial formulation of the mechanisms. The banks were concerned with the accountability mechanisms undertaking outreach to inform people in developing countries of their existence in case this might drum up business. Thus, a claimant would need to know who was financing the project leading to harm, but also know of the accountability mechanism's existence, and to know which MDB policy was being violated that had led to harm or the threat of harm and present this material in the order requested by the accountability mechanism. Initially some mechanisms expected claims to be written in a specific language such as English (the Asian Development Bank) and sent by post (Inspection Panel). Once their claim was submitted, requestors would then have to wait to be informed as to whether their claim was accepted and what the outcome of the investigation was. Scholars therefore argue that the limited number of claims might not be an accurate indicator of the need for the accountability mechanisms (Naude Fourie 2012: 129).

Does Accountability as Justice Influence Bank Behavior?

The MDBs routinely invoke the accountability mechanisms as evidence that they are trying to meet their environmental and social protection standards. As this section shows, the norm occasionally sparks change in the MDBs' operations and policies. However, the norm is a corrective rather than preemptive norm for ensuring justice in international development, with little overall impact on the banks' lending operations. The number of claims from project-affected people registered by the accountability mechanisms constitute between 0.45 and 1.8 percent of the banks' annual lending portfolios (Table 6.1). Over the 24-year period we can see how few claims are registered as meeting the accountability mechanism criteria. As detailed in the last chapter, a much smaller percentage go on to problem solving and an agreement between the parties, or a compliance investigation, with an even smaller number leading to a monitoring of the banks activities to rectify the issues raised by claimants (see Figure 5.7, in chapter 5). Given the small numbers of claims investigated, it is an open question as to whether increasing the monitoring powers of the mechanisms could pressure the banks to systematically provide remedies for bank-financed harm.

Over time, the norm morphed from a formal sanctioning of bank policy non-compliance contributing to harm to include problem solving. Problem solving may address a complainant's concerns but is limited to a willingness of all parties to engage in mediation, and before the damage has become irreversible. It may also divert attention from whether the Bank was not compliant with its own policies contributing to harm. All the banks have engaged in a strategy of Bank defiance in refuting compliance investigation findings. Bank management continues to resist the mechanisms, and staff are wary and distrustful of being investigated. As noted by the Inspection Panel's first chair, the effect of the Panel on the Bank was the development of a Bank staff attitude, described as "panel-proofing." This "may mean—positively—that they take policies and procedures seriously and ensure that the quality of operations is consistent with the Bank's high standards, possibly also that policy-makers also reassess the realism and implementability of policies. . . . On the negative side . . . it may mean that staff and managers will become more conservative and bureaucratically protective."[12]

This negatively highlights the importance of addressing environmental and social issues. All the banks update their policies periodically, including identifying which policies were investigable by the accountability mechanisms in the

2000s. In 2018 the World Bank introduced a new Environmental and Social Framework to better harmonize its policies throughout its operations. NGOs argue the new framework created large loopholes for avoiding environmental and social protections (CIEL 2016). Some suggest that the Inspection Panel may still be able to operate but may face even more challenges from management and borrowers (Passoni et al. 2016).

There is little evidence that using accountability as a corrective can lead to positive change in the banks. Although the banks have institutionalized the norm, the lack of learning from their case histories remains stark. While some argue that the norm can have a "preventive and curative impact, positively influencing the direction of the Bank[s]" (Boisson de Chazournes, cited in Inspection Panel 2009: 106), there is little evidence that lessons have been "mainstreamed" in terms of changing project approval or implementation practices. In part this stems from the fact that those charged with responding to findings of noncompliance were those who did not comply with the Bank's policies in the first place (Bridgeman and Hunter 2008). It also does little to alter the focus on lending over loan performance.

The MDBs share a common apolitical, economistic culture that fosters technical project expertise and confidentiality, based on financial contracts with borrower governments and companies, not individuals. Their banking culture reflects the fact that they are dominated by development economists who make decisions based on financial prudence and economic modeling. All have been identified as having internal incentive structures that reward staff for lending volumes rather than supervising project performance, including when harm arises (Sud and Olmstead-Rumsey 2012). For example, an internal World Bank report found that "many projects with substantial environmental and social impacts remain of concern primarily because of inadequate supervision and follow-up" (World Bank 2010: 1). More significantly, the World Bank identified an increase in projects triggering the involuntary resettlement policy, but without knowing what happened to people being resettled (World Bank 2015). This led President Kim to announce an Action Plan to improve Bank systems, staffing, and implementation of its Involuntary Resettlement policy in 2015.

As the previous chapters have shown, management continues to resist being held accountable for justice, and this is supported by some borrowers who may be subject to claims in their territory. However, evidence does suggest that the norm can affect the banks' lending practices, although this is limited. Buntaine has identified that borrower's receiving concessional loans tend to receive less environmentally risky projects for up to five years after an accountability mechanism claim (2016). The norm could also contribute to improving shareholder oversight for allocating bank loans by taking possible harm in account.[13] However, given board turnover and the difficulties they have in overseeing the banks (see chapter 2), it is unclear whether member states are able to take advantage of the norm in this way. The accountability mechanisms have only been able to impact on the banks' policies because of high-profile cases resulting from egregious harm. Although some of the banks (such as the World Bank, the Asian Development Bank, and the World Bank Group) now track complaints internally, this does not ameliorate conditions that lead to harm. Here I outline the piecemeal changes triggered by specific claims as a means of highlighting how little has changed.

Changes to the MDB's environmental and social policies have resulted from high-profile accountability mechanism cases. For the World Bank, one Inspection Panel case prompted the introduction of a Bank-wide Natural Resource Management Framework. A claim in 2009 revealed that the Bank was noncompliant in relation to a land administration project in Cambodia, which contributed to the forcible eviction of thousands of people from their homes (Land Management and Administration Project, Panel claim 60). Failure to stop the evictions led World Bank President Zoellick to suspend lending to Cambodia for five years while reviewing Bank operations in the forestry sector. The revised Natural Resource Management Framework now addresses land tenure rights for communities living in and around forests (Inspection Panel 2009: 90; World Bank 2010: 37).[14] After the hiatus, the Bank resumed lending to Cambodia, while some evictees continued to protest the project. While this is a major policy shift, it does not address the Bank's focus on lending over project performance.

In comparison, there is little evidence that the accountability mechanism has shaped Inter-American Development Bank's policies or procedures. Only one case shows how MICI was able to influence broader Bank policy (the Argentina Agrifood Health and Quality Management Program [CCLIP], request MICI-AR-2012-035). In this case, the ombudsman facilitated an Agreement of Understanding over mitigating the impact of agrichemicals on human health and the environment. This was facilitated between the Bank, the requestor (an environmental attorney) and the government. The Agreement provided a basis for how agrochemicals would be used in relation to Argentina's laws and the Bank's policies according with best international practice and international environmental agreements (ICIM 2012b). The case was preemptive in addressing the potential health and environmental impacts of an Inter-American Development Bank project.

In contrast, the Asian Development Bank's Accountability Mechanism has not changed Bank policy per se, but it has "played a role in appropriately raising the bar for safeguard compliance." The focus on the safeguard compliance is a direct result of its early investigations (Samut Prakarn, STDP, and Chashma claims), which "reinforced the preoccupation of ADB staff and Management with procedural compliance." (ADB 2006: 29).[15] This reaffirms staff risk-aversion to being investigated (Buntaine 2016: 137–138). An Asian Development Bank evaluation of its Involuntary Resettlement Safeguard is worth quoting:

> As acknowledged by many staff interviewed, the perceived threat of the repercussions of compliance reviews to investigate noncompliance with ADB policies drives much of the current focus on safeguards . . . aside from the more general concerns of "getting things right." (ADB 2006: 29)

Overall, the Asian Development Bank states that the Accountability Mechanism has contributed to "strengthening procedural policy compliance with the Bank's safeguard policy statement" (ADB 2016b: 5, 15). In terms of procedures, the Bank "introduced the requirement to establish project level [grievance redress mechanisms] GRMs," with the operations departments identifying that 80 percent of complaints are now being dealt with at the project level. The Office of the Special Project Facilitator also established a Projects Complaints Tracking System in 2013, which is a process for "logging, classifying, monitoring, and acting on project-specific complaints" (ADB 2016a: 3). Both actions seek to improve the Bank's responsiveness to project-affected people while preempting the need for claimants to submit requests to the Accountability Mechanism. This improves how the Bank deals with complaints, but it does not alter the process through which projects are approved and financed.

The most immediate impact of the CAO on the IFC stemmed from a 2007 claim against its involvement in the Wilmar Corporation in Indonesia (Wilmar Group-01/West Kalimantan (25532 & 26271). Recall that while the CAO was engaged in mediation with stakeholders, the CAO triggered a compliance audit, which found IFC noncompliant with its policies. Public outcry against the project led then World Bank Group President Zoellick to first suspend all IFC lending in the palm oil sector, before extending the suspension to the entire World Bank and World Bank Group. This led to a World Bank Group–wide review of palm oil lending with public consultation, leading to new sectoral guidelines in 2011. As Balaton-Chines and Haines point out, this is evidence of significant institutional learning in terms of how to address problems within the palm oil sector. However, such "achievements will be limited to incremental changes that facilitate adaptation but not transformation of the institution's modus operandi" because it is not within the CAO's purview to challenge the Bank's dominant lending paradigm (2015: 452).

The CAO is the only accountability mechanism to have been given an advisory function from its inception. The CAO's initial work included advising the World Bank Group on how to incorporate ideas of sustainability into its investment decisions; providing advice on the Extractive Industries Review (2001–2003); and advising the World Bank Group on how the World Commission on

Dams final report might be applicable to its investments and guarantees. An independent review of the CAO in 2003 found that it had contributed to the increased knowledge and improvement of World Bank Group functions, while recommending further environmental and social integration (Dysart et al. 2003: 1–14).

The CAO argues that the "positive impact of CAO's work on social and environmental performance has been incremental and cumulative" (2006a: 30). It provided feedback on the updating of the IFC's safeguard policies to performance standards in 2006, with a 2006 review of the CAO noting that its advice had been taken. The CAO also reviewed MIGA's use of its Environmental and Social Review Procedures (ESRP) in 2003, and its shift to environmental and social performance standards in 2007. MIGA increasingly focused on its social impact after the CAO reviewed its Environmental and Social Review Procedures in 2002, although it did not respond to CAO's advice on its extractive industries practices (CAO 2006a: 27–28).

In 2008 the CAO published advisory notes on the World Bank Group's impact on local development; on establishing project-level grievance mechanisms; and on participatory water monitoring (CAO 2008). All advisory notes present "upstream" advice learned from the ombudsman's case work, which management agreed to formally respond to from 2009 (CAO 2009: 2). The CAO also provided input into the IFC's 2012 Sustainability Framework. The Internal Evaluation Group of the World Bank Group highlights that the CAO has identified systemic policy gaps within the World Bank Group regarding the application of its performance standards to the supply chain of its clients (World Bank 2010: 37). The CAO now identifies World Bank Group responses to its recommendations through its Management Tracking Action Record (CAO 2014: 21).

Mechanisms with strong monitoring power also have the capacity to institute broader policy change. The European Bank for Reconstruction and Development's Project Complaint Mechanism has been used to improve the internal processes of the Bank. While the Independent Recourse Mechanism's first investigation (the Vlore thermal project, request 2007/01) found evidence of noncompliance with the Bank's 2003 Environmental Policy, there is no evidence that this fed into the conversion of the Bank's Environmental Performance Standards in 2006. Under the Project Complaint Mechanism's Rules of Procedure, it had the power to monitor the implementation of the Bank's policies and procedures. Three cases triggered the Bank's Performance Requirement 6 (PR6) on Biodiversity Assessment (Boskov Most Hydro Power Project request 2011/05; Ombla Hydro Power project request 2011/06, Paravani Hydro Power Project 2012/01). The findings from all three would feed into the Bank's 2014 updated Environment and Social Policy, and the monitoring reports provide the most tangible evidence of holding the Bank to account for improving its internal policies and procedures (PCM 2014d: 3; PCM 2016: 5; PCM 2016b). The on-going monitoring reports are therefore used to ensure the Bank has stringent internal procedures for upholding its Environment and Social Policy.

Recognizably, the African Development Bank has the weakest Environmental and Social Policy procedures of all the banks. A safeguard unit was established in 2008, and prior to that "there was very little institutional ability" to "ensure the proper implementation of the safeguard policies" (Buntaine 2016: 103). In its compliance investigations the Independent Review Mechanism identified that there were gaps and a lack of clarity in its environmental and social poli-cies, making findings of compliance or noncompliance difficult. This contrib-uted to the need for revising the Bank's policies, leading the Bank to introduce an Integrated Safeguard System in 2013. The Integrated Safeguard System is a much more comprehensive conversion of the Bank's policies and now includes an Integrated Safeguard Policy Statement and five Operational Safeguards cov-ering environmental and social assessment, involuntary resettlement, biodiver-sity, pollution prevention, and labor conditions, including health and safety.

Of specific mention in the lessons learned section of the Independent Review Mechanism's monitoring review of the first compliance investigation (the Bujugali hydropower project claim, RQ 2007/1) was the need for establishing procedures to collect baseline data, particularly with regard to resettlement, to be able to assess Bank compliance (IRM 2012d: 11). This was incorporated into the Integrated Safeguard System (AfDB 2013: 34). The second compliance investiga-tion (the South African Medupi power project, RQ 2010/2) identified the need to improve Bank action regarding project supervision, environmental management plans, public consultation, regional impact assessments, and integrated water re-source management policy. The findings all fed into the Integrated Safeguard System. In this way the Independent Review Mechanism has contributed to the Bank having more rigorous environmental and social policies. In 2015 the Independent Review Mechanism was given advisory powers, which may further contribute to improving the Bank's practices.

In sum, the banks have had to address the cases coming before the account-ability mechanisms, but the overall impact on the banks' lending operating and culture has been limited. The nature of the norm as a corrective to Bank behavior rather than as a preemptive norm that can change the conditions that contribute to harm in the lending process means that the norm sits uneasily alongside the banks' preexisting lending practices. Infrequently there are egregious cases that do have broader Bank impacts, as is evident in the World Bank and World Bank Group. In the cases of the Asian, African, and European banks, there is evidence that giving the accountability mechanisms monitoring powers can be used to feed into strengthening environmental and social policies, with the aim of influ-encing future Bank operations. In one case, the Inter-American Development

Bank's accountability mechanism was used to shape how the Bank understood its responsibility in relation to environmental and health impacts preemptively. This means that there can be recourse for harm for project-affected people, but the broader impacts on the management are piecemeal.

Conclusion

This chapter provided insights into how the accountability as justice norm has strengthened over time in terms of their provision of recourse for project-affected people. They have been able to become more independent, accessible, and transparent, which gives them greater legitimacy and credibility in providing justice. The second part of the chapter then looked at instances where cases have impacted on management, arguing that the norm has had a piecemeal effect on the management' policies and procedures. This reveals little evidence of changes to the managements' operations or organizational culture. This means that the accountability mechanisms can affect the managements' practices, but in very circumscribed circumstances.

7

Norm Diffusion within the MDBs and Insights beyond the Banks

Within a decade all the multilateral development banks (MDBs) would have accountability mechanisms that provide recourse for project-affected people. This book argues that the mechanisms embody a norm of accountability as justice that incorporates two components within a single formal sanctioning process: first, efforts to determine whether the banks acts or omissions contributed to harm via evaluations, auditing, and monitoring, and second, recourse for project-affected people for damaging behavior. The book argues that the norm looks the way it does and not otherwise for two reasons: first, because of the relationship between the United States and the banks. The United States has a long history of trying to control the banks through accountability processes to ensure their obedience and efficiency through evaluations, auditing, and monitoring. Second, evidence of injustice emerged during debates over how to improve the banks after revelations of their underperformance and inefficiency. Ultimately the United States advocated for a norm that incorporated its efforts to control the banks and its demand for the provision of recourse. This chapter recounts the main findings of the book to make three points: First, that the banks used a range of strategies for resisting a norm that threatened their autonomy and lending-imperative culture. This included compromise over the design of the accountability mechanisms, acquiescence to periodic accountability mechanism reviews, avoidance in designing the mechanisms and responding to investigations, defiance in rejecting allegations of wrongdoing, and manipulation over the process, staff, and project-affected people. Despite bank (and sometimes board) resistance, the norm is now a feature of the banks' governance structures. Second, that persistent efforts by the United States using the power of the purse, voice, and vote may be used to shape the practices of other international organizations but ideas remain paramount to their likely success. Third, that once a process had been instituted to establish and oversee the accountability mechanisms, the review process enabled other actors like the accountability officers and activists and consultants to help strengthen the norm. This demonstrates a powerful state not just pushing for a norm but also enabling others to work to improve it over time.

The book demonstrates how powerful states can generate international norms that become accepted behavior. The United States championed the idea that the

The Good Hegemon. Susan Park, Oxford University Press. © Oxford University Press 2022.
DOI: 10.1093/oso/9780197626481.003.0007

MDBs should be held to account for their actions to those they affect from 1993. Since the 1960s the United States has demanded the establishment of auditing and reporting requirements to oversee and direct the operations of the MDBs. In the 1990s the United States created more monitoring and evaluation tools to better ensure the banks' efficiency and effectiveness. The trigger for US norm entrepreneurship was increasing scrutiny of the bank's operations after reviews into their portfolios documented overinflated expectations and underperforming loans at the same time as harm to communities was revealed in relation to large-scale World Bank–financed projects. Within the context of debates over MDB inefficiency and ineffectiveness, the United States sought to convince member states to add concerns of justice to the typical means it uses to control the banks. While other donors initially raised the issue of harm as evidence unfolded from transnational advocacy campaigns, US norm entrepreneurship ultimately not only created the World Bank Inspection Panel but also enabled it to be independent from World Bank management while ensuring that it provided due process for project-affected people. The United States would then demand that the other MDBs follow.

The norm created new ways of thinking, new actors, and new categories of action. It acknowledged that MDB-financed development projects can lead to environmental and social harm and that the banks should address it. It created accountability mechanism officers that independently investigate the MDBs. It created "problem solving" to address community grievances, and "compliance audits" to assess whether bank policy noncompliance led to harm. The norm is regulative such that management and member states on the boards of executive directors must now respond to findings of bank noncompliance resulting in harm.

US efforts can be understood through a relational and interpretivist approach to power. On the one hand, US actions could be seen as upholding the reputation of the banks that it helped create, fund, and from which it benefits, and with no cost to the United States for pursuing such a norm. This fits power-based explanations of strategic material interests and rational action. On the other hand, this does not explain why the United States would choose to go beyond the World Bank and World Bank Group, the targets of significant opposition for their environmental and social impact, to advance the norm for all the MDBs. A relational and interpretivist understanding of power shows how ideas help constitute states interest such that the United States continued to pursue the norm for all banks even when activist and other member states' interest in doing so was absent or muted.

Ideas drove the United States' demand for accountability mechanisms for all the MDBs. Locus for change came from the US Congress, where congressional members became concerned about the negative impact of MDB funding on people at development project sites. Congress can intervene in international organizations owing to the United States' domestic political structure, which gives it the power to approve US financing for multilateral institutions. Ongoing concern for project-affected people revealed by transnational advocacy campaigns explains why the United States went beyond advocating for their creation to ensure that they worked.

The tools available to the United States to exert influence depend on the institutional structure of the international organization and its relations with other member states. All the banks except the African Development Bank were created with the US imprimatur. The banks are similarly governed with similar development financing functions operating in the same policy space. The United States has influence in the MDBs, which derives from its predominant shares in the banks, which also translate into preeminent voting rights. The United States can use its financial position in the banks to allocate resources and to promote certain ideas and practices, which influence other shareholders and the MDBs. Strategies to advance ideas can be ideational or material. In this case, the United States used three strategies to advance the norm: its "power of the purse," its "vote" on the banks' boards, and its "voice." In using the "power of the purse" the United States linked new ideas to commitments to replenish the banks' capital; it used its "vote" on the banks' boards to support new ideas; and it used its "voice" to persuade other member states and the banks to agree with the norm. As the book documents, the power of the purse was an important lever for pressing for the accountability as justice norm for the World Bank, World Bank Group, and African, Asian, and Inter-American Development Banks. The voice mechanism is invoked by the United States across all the MDBs to garner consensus for the norm to be taken up and defended, while the vote was used across all the banks except the European Bank for Reconstruction and Development.

Despite resistance from management, the United States was able to advance the accountability as justice norm across the MDBs through gaining multilateral support to do so. Member states agreed to establish the norm of accountability as justice to constitute and regulate MDB behavior. The United States was able to promote the accountability as justice norm because the idea the United States advocates matters. US power is not absolute, and it does not always get its own way in the banks. The United States was able to garner consensus from other large shareholder member states to create the norm because the idea being promulgated was accepted as a legitimate concern for the MDBs. This compares with previous US efforts for example, to introduce human rights, which was seen as going beyond the apolitical technical mandate of the banks.

Despite this, some borrower member states were concerned with how accountability mechanism operations would affect their lending and sovereignty (Park 2015), with specific instances of borrower resistance to investigations evident in the World Bank (India and Ethiopia) and the Asian Development Bank (Thailand and China). Opposition is also evident at the Inter-American Development Bank, where the borrower-dominated Board has routinely chosen not to accept accountability mechanism recommendations for compliance investigations. Borrowers have three concerns: the cost and delays stemming from an investigation in terms of completing a project, whether this has a negative impact on states' future borrowing, and how investigations infringe on their sovereignty (when investigators enter a borrower's territory). Borrowers on the boards have therefore been skeptical of how the norm operates in practice, often viewing accountability mechanism investigations as investigating the borrower, not the bank.

More specific to the Inter-American Development Bank is the perception that compliance investigations should be avoided at all costs. The banks and their boards favored the introduction of problem-solving processes that avoid any allocation of blame in favor of solving grievances. While again this can be thought of in purely material and rational terms, it should also be pointed out that accountability as a word does not translate into most languages (Dubnick 2014) and attempts to hold actors to account for their actions to an authority holder in this way stem from public renderings of accountability derived from Western liberal democratic structures (Mashaw 2006). Taking a Western liberal idea and seeking to locate it in a broader global context is not without problems, because it exports a concept from one social context to another. Although borrowers agreed that people should have some form of recourse for harm, the initial structures were designed to be investigative and focused on compliance rather than evaluative or focused on performance (Grigorescu 2008: 289). Therefore, it is not surprising that many borrowers were uncomfortable with how the norm operated in practice. Indeed, the shift toward problem solving for all the MDBs took place after the Asian Development Bank reviewed its mechanism. Communities in the Asia Pacific wanted the opportunity to resolve the issue at the project level with the Bank, borrower, and executing agency rather than engage with an adversarial process that apportions blame, which most of the other banks followed. For the World Bank Group, it was considered better to move away from the quasi-judicial approach of the Inspection Panel in favor of a mediation-style ombuds process for the private sector. Nonetheless, the banks' institutional structures continued to allow borrowers to limit the norm in practice, such as refusing to allow investigations to proceed (Park 2015).

The second aim of the book was to investigate how the banks responded to the norm. Owing to their dependence on member states for resources, decision-making, and normative support, the MDBs had no choice but to do as they were bid. The banks were forced to meet US demands to create accountability units that give member states greater oversight of their actions with ramifications for their lending practices. For the banks, the accountability mechanisms are time consuming, costly, and may result in investigations that damage their reputation. Five resistance strategies are evident across the banks: compromise, acquiescence, avoidance, defiance, and manipulation. First, once the MDBs realized that the accountability as justice norm was consolidating, they engaged in a strategy of compromise by seeking to bargain with member states over what the mechanisms would look like. This enabled them to design mechanisms that gave a greater role for management and limited the accountability mechanisms' independence.

The Inspection Panel initially demanded by the United States gave the World Bank little room for reinterpreting members' demands to better fit with their operations and organizational culture. However, even with strong US oversight, the other MDBs were able bargain for a greater role for management in the investigation process (excluding the World Bank Group). Beyond the World Bank and World Bank Group, two factors enabled the accountability as justice norm to be operationalized with less accountability mechanism independence: First, institutional dynamics at the banks' boards supported management having oversight of the accountability mechanisms, including the power to approve accountability mechanism investigations into their own behavior. Moreover, the initial designs of most of the mechanisms omitted giving the accountability mechanisms monitoring or enforcement powers over bank management's development of remedies after findings of noncompliance. This constrained the ability of the mechanisms to enact and enforce accountability as justice. Second, none of the other MDBs faced as much public scrutiny as the World Bank and World Bank Group for their negative environmental and social impact, sharpening the demand for independent investigation procedures for those banks.

Second, acquiescence is a passive strategy, evident with the banks accepting the periodic reviews of the accountability mechanisms structures and operations as demanded by the United States. Third, Bank management engaged in avoidance by creating accountability mechanisms with a variety of technical exclusion criteria that prevented project-affected people's claims from being "registered" or eligible for assessment. Many of the criteria were beyond the capacity of project-affected people to ascertain. Avoidance is evident in management providing ceremonial information in response to investigations to argue that they were compliant with their own policies despite evidence to the contrary. Avoidance is further evident in management failures to respond to findings of bank noncompliance with remedies to improve the plight of people negatively affected by a bank-financed project.

All the banks engaged in a fourth strategy of defiance by dismissing and challenging the norm. Management consistently denied claims from affected people were legitimate and refuted any wrongdoing, frequently seeking to undermine the investigation process. This included preempting and circumventing investigations by establishing their own remedial management action plans to eliminate the need for an investigation into their activities. Finally, Bank resistance was evident in efforts to manipulate responses to the norm. In some cases, management would seek to influence the standards by which they would be evaluated. For example, the World Bank management sought to influence the definition of what constitutes a "project" that could be investigated. A more extreme form of manipulation is when the banks seek to control the investigation process. This included management supporting staff that withheld evidence of wrongdoing in investigations, and staff that sought to persuade affected people not to make claims. The United States would use the same power of the purse, vote, and voice mechanisms to overhaul the accountability mechanisms in egregious cases.

Ongoing efforts to improve the mechanisms have over time have procured greater independence for them, which has enhanced their credibility. These have resulted from periodic reviews into their practices, which the United States demanded when they were established. The banks acquiesced to US demands by complying with regular, iterative reviews of the accountability mechanisms. The results of the reviews are that the mechanisms now share similar features, demonstrating a form of mimicry or institutional isomorphism at work. As documented throughout, the banks look to the last MDB accountability mechanism reviewed to identify what member states will accept. All the mechanisms now include a problem-solving function to directly address people's grievances through mediation. The addition of problem-solving processes may weaken the formal sanctioning process because it takes the focus off whether it was bank compliance or noncompliance with its own social and environmental policies that led to harm. On the other hand, member states have also given the mechanisms greater monitoring powers over bank responses to findings of noncompliance leading to harm and enhanced their advisory powers, which could precipitate transformational change within the MDBs in the future (Streek and Thelen 2005).

Although the norm has been institutionalized within the banks' governing structures, it is clear that the banks raise obstacles to recourse for project-affected people. The book documents tensions and begrudging support by the MDBs as the United States continued its efforts to institutionalize accountability as justice. While opposition to the norm remained, it became accepted that if one had to have an accountability mechanism, then it should be able to operate according to its mandate. While they do not challenge the banks' operations and organizational culture, the accountability mechanisms have been incorporated into the institutional governance of the MDBs, with high-profile cases occasionally sparking policy change in the banks. The argument propounded here, therefore, is that the operations of the mechanisms and their strengthened powers is evidence that the MDBs have institutionalized the norm but that it does not affect the banks' prioritization of lending over project performance. Despite management resistance, the accountability as justice norm is now taken for granted in terms of the established practices of the accountability mechanisms and their growing caseloads. Moreover, ongoing improvements in the operations of the accountability mechanisms generated by US efforts, the periodic reviews, and actions by the accountability mechanism officers, all contribute to making the mechanisms more accessible, transparent, and responsive to project-affected people.[1] More research into how norms emerge among IOs and strengthen over time is warranted.

The various strategies invoked by the banks demonstrate ongoing organizational hypocrisy: providing information of how they act in conformity with the norm while opposing it in practice. The more active resistance strategies of defiance and manipulation reinforce that the banks do not view adherence to the norm as fundamental to their mandate and operations. It also reinforces the internal perception of their own understanding of how to undertake international development finance beyond the findings and recommendations of the accountability mechanisms. The adversarial nature of the compliance investigations also enables the banks to reject the claimant's allegations and the accountability mechanism's findings. This routinizes bank resistance in acceptable ways that the boards have tolerated. However, failure to provide remedies, the provision of ceremonial information in investigations, and efforts at manipulating staff and project-affected people have led the banks Boards to give accountability mechanisms more power to monitor the banks' practices, which may yet curb the banks' active resistance strategies.

What does this mean for understanding US influence beyond the banks? The United States used all three mechanisms to press for the accountability as justice norm. The United States used its voice to advocate for the accountability as justice norm across the banks through garnering multilateral support and by reviewing drafts of the mechanisms by management. The United States used capital replenishments as the arena for generating consensus, and by using future financing as both threats and incentives to make the idea attractive. And it voted on the banks' boards to bring the mechanisms into existence. However, it used its voice alone for the European Bank for Reconstruction and Development in 2003. Hence, the only outlier of the United States using all three mechanisms together is the European Bank. Structurally the European Bank for Reconstruction and Development does not have a soft-loan facility so that was not an option for pressing for change. Yet the general capital increase beginning in 1997 was not invoked either, because at that stage there was not enough donor support for it. The United States was able to use its voice to advocate for the norm in the early

2000s because by then there was general agreement among the donors that all the MDBs should have accountability mechanisms. In the end it did not even need to vote in favor of its creation for it to come into existence: having pressed for its creation, the United States abstained from the vote owing to its lack of independence from management.

Are all three strategies necessary for the norm? Yes, if they are understood as a single case where the mechanisms operated in sequence, with the power of the purse, vote, and voice operating at the beginning of the sequence for five of the banks, followed by just voice for the European Bank. To explain: The United States used the capital replenishment processes as platforms for advocating the norm in the early 1990s and then, with consensus resulting from its voice, voted them into existence. This resulted in the banks creating the mechanisms like falling dominos. By the time accountability as justice was being debated within the European Bank for Reconstruction and Development in the early 2000s the norm had consolidated. This means that member states agreed that having accountability mechanisms was appropriate for all the MDBs, including those like the World Bank Group that lend primarily to the private sector. Seemingly this cannot explain why the United States then had to rely on all three strategies to establish the accountability mechanism for the African Development Bank in 2004. Arguably this is because of the sequence in which the debate entered the African Bank: The accountability as justice norm entered the African Development Bank Board debates in 1994—during the initial generation of the idea by the United States. The norm then languished for a decade while the Bank managed its financial crisis. As a result, the strategies creating it were begun much earlier than for the European Bank for Reconstruction and Development, when the power of the purse, vote, and voice were necessary to bring the norm into existence.

Can the United States use these strategies for other international organization? There is reason to suggest that scholars could benefit from examining states', particularly the United States', use of power of the purse, vote, and voice in seeking to create new norms for international organizations. The United States continues to provide significant asymmetric resources for a plethora of international organizations, although the structure of the payments and voting are qualitatively different and may lead the United States to use different mechanisms to achieve change. For example, many international organizations such as those within the UN family are built on voluntary versus core contributions from member states, which affects how the organization can function to achieve its mandate (Graham 2015). But using financial levers has opened up new research into how other states seek to direct IOs through trust funds, thus circumventing the institutional structures that lock in powerful states' control over international organizations (Reinsburg et al. 2017;

Strand and Trevathan 2016). Few international organizations, however, compare to the MDBs in having such stark asymmetric voting structures based on the weighted subscriptions (except the IMF). Currently the focus is on how the United States has informal governance within the IMF to override the normal decision-making when its interests are threatened (Stone 2011) rather than how it promotes new norms (for an exception, see Momani 2010). Moreover, in general, the UN agencies have a one country, one vote institutional structure, as does the World Trade Organization (WTO), although the latter is consensus-based, which could enable voice to play a stronger role.

It would be fertile ground to examine whether the United States uses all or some of the strategies to achieve change within international organizations with different funding and voting rules, including if these are invoked in sequence. Research would need to focus on how the United States uses its power of the purse (by contribution type), vote, and voice as a means of financial incentives for positive change rather than for punishing international organizations for not doing what the United States wants (see Lyon 2016). For example, in 1977 the United States withdrew from being a member of the International Labour Organization (ILO) after using its power of the purse to protest other member states' decision-making (Melanson 1979: 50; Joyner 1978). There is evidence that US withdrawal from United Nations Educational, Scientific and Cultural Organization (UNESCO) in 1984 was, in part, because of the US failure to garner consensus around its understanding of freedom of communication and media (Singh 2011: 17), but its 2017 decision to withdraw seeks to punish UNESCO rather than seeking to advance new ideas.[2] The United States withdrew from UN Industrial Development Organization (UNIDO) in 1995 after claiming that it had an unclear mandate and was ineffective, rather than seeking to instill new norms. The US withdrawal from the World Health Organization during the global pandemic in 2020 under the Trump administration also sought to punish the international organization for not doing what it wanted.[3] Scholars have focused on examining exit as a strategy in international organizations (Lavelle 2007). In short, the three strategies identified here could be analytically useful to explain the relationship between the United States, other member states, and other international organizations, but would need to be assessed in terms of whether the United States seeks to bring about normative change, documenting US efforts given the differing institutional structures, and the extent to which it used the strategies, and in what sequence. While the United States dominates many international organizations, an analysis of the strategies other influential states use in the organizations that they dominate is also necessary, such as financial levers and collusion (Dijkstra 2017). As argued throughout this book, what is equally, if not more, important is to examine which ideas they promote promulgate change.

Notes

Chapter 1

1. The accountability mechanisms provide recourse for environmental and social harm, which is distinct from other internal monitoring and evaluation units. Practitioners call them the independent accountability mechanisms (IAMs), but because they differ in their independence from their banks, the term "accountability mechanism" is used throughout.

2. IOs are defined as "an organization that has representatives from three or more states supporting a permanent secretariat to perform ongoing tasks related to a common purpose" (Barnett and Finnemore 2004: 177).

3. The World Bank Group includes the International Centre for Settlement of Investment Disputes, which is not a lending body and is therefore excluded. IFC and MIGA have the same member states as the World Bank on their boards but have different voting weights, and decisions for IFC and MIGA are made separately from the World Bank and from each other. Over the last decade there has been a concerted effort to bring their work together, but the institutional structures remain separate.

4. The World Bank only lends to sovereign states.

5. Hydro remains the most prevalent source of (renewable) energy generation globally.

6. Norms are "collective expectations about proper behaviour for a given identity" (Finnemore and Sikkink 1998: 891).

7. Member states are the MDBs' shareholders, and these terms are used interchangeably.

8. "Project-affected people" (PAP) refers to two or more individuals adversely affected by an MDB-financed project either in the project area or nearby.

9. See: Grant and Keohane 2005; Grigorescu 2008; Held and Keonig-Archibugi 2005; Woods 2001, 2003; Woods and Narlikar 2001; Ebrahim and Weisband 2007; Florini 2007; Moravcsik 2004; Kahler 2004; cf. Dubnick 2014; for a critique, see Dahl 1999.

10. These are not mutually exclusive purposes, nor if applied to IOs, do they alter the relationship between states and IOs, or IOs and other actors.

11. Since then, there has been an increase in international conventions and agreements that promote access to justice in environmental matters as a right (Park 2020).

12. Grant and Keohane 2005; Grigorescu 2008, 2016; Held and Keonig-Archibugi 2005; Woods 2001, 2003; Woods and Narlikar 2001; Ebrahim and Weisband 2007.

13. As is the rational design framework (Koremenos et al. 2004).

14. See Hoffman and Megret 2005 on the UN.

15. The United States is a unitary actor in terms of its position within the MDBs, but when tracing how ideas enter IOs and their impacts it is recognized that both states and IOs are composed of multiple actors (for example, the US Congress versus the

executive and bank management compared with operations staff and the accountability mechanism officers).

16. See Mason and Ascher 1973; Watanabe 1977; Tussie 1995; Menkveld 1991; English and Mule 1996. The AfDB became dependent on donors for its economic survival from 1982, after the oil and debt crises (Mingst 1990).

17. And increase borrowing from the Andean Development Corporation (CAF) rather than the World Bank and IDB (Humphrey and Michaelowa 2013). The G7 comprises the United States, United Kingdom, Canada, France, Italy, Germany, and Japan.

18. Even non-US financial institutions like the European Investment Bank have accountability mechanisms. Owing to its different institutional structure, this bank is not examined here.

19. The chapters are segmented to allow people interested in just one bank to read the book that way.

20. "Claimants" and "requestors" are used interchangeably throughout.

Chapter 2

1. A hegemon is a state that occupies a central role in international relations and can influence other states ideas, interests, and preferences. Influence is "the capacity of one actor to modify the behaviour of another" (Woods 2003: 95). It "benefits from material capabilities but is not a function of them" (Reich and Lebow 2014: 6).

2. Except the African Development Bank, which sought US support when it realized it needed extraregional funding (English and Mule 1996).

3. While hegemonic stability theory argues that the international order is predicated on the interest and resources of the hegemon to maintain it (Gilpin 1987). Meanwhile, Goldstein and Keohane (1993) add ideas as a residual explanation of state actions to material power.

4. Realism, rationalism, and poststructuralism have been criticized for presuming intention and rational action from outcomes (Elster 1989).

5. In relation to all the banks except the borrower-dominated African Development Bank and the newer European Bank for Reconstruction and Development.

6. Ideas are accorded status for explaining the internal decision-making within IOs, not in terms of how states create and maintain international norms and institutions. Kaya pays attention to states' normative motivations empirically but not theoretically (2015: 46–47).

7. Alesina and Dollar show that traditional donors' bilateral aid allocation and recipient UN General Assembly voting alignment results from historical colonial linkages. They argue this is evidence of common agreement (shared understanding) between states rather than donors buying inconsequential votes in the General Assembly (2000: 46). Quantitatively Neumayer identifies colonial experience, exports, and strategic interests (identified as recipients of US military grants) shape aid allocation (2003), while Stone (2004) demonstrates that Britain and France have intervened in

the IMF to assist former African colonies. Meanwhile Dreher and Sturm find evidence that as states become more democratic, they align with the G7 in the UNGA (2012: 375). This supports evidence that states' ideology matters (Potrafke 2009).

8. This builds on Neumayer (2003b), who argued that Asian and African Development Banks (but not the Inter-American Development Bank) provide loans on the basis of need by per capita income.

9. On US influence in the IMF, see Thacker 1999; Barro and Lee 2005; Dreher and Jensen 2007; Stone 2011, 2004; Copelovitch 2010.

10. A utility maximization approach derived from economics cannot hold because power is not fungible in the same way money is: "it does not provide a standardised measure of economic value" to assess how utility is maximized (Baldwin 1993: 21). However, bartering, as in the case of Vreeland and Dreher (2014), is possible (Guzzini 2013: 49–50).

11. Lim and Vreeland (2013) find a strong correlation between the size of loans states receive from the Asian Development Bank with when they sit on the UN Security Council (and this is even larger when Japan is an elected member). However, there is less evidence of US "informal" influence over loan disbursements within the Inter-American Development Bank (Bland and Kilby 2015; Hernandez 2013).

12. Kaya does not rule out legitimacy as an explanation (2015: 45).

13. As discussed further in the chapter, the International Development Association (IDA) is a soft-loan financing facility that the World Bank disperses. Andersen et al. argue that the United States may not actively use its influence in IDA allocations to the poorest developing states as a means to divert from IDA lending criteria for its own ends, but suggests there is anecdotal evidence that it has "has sometimes influenced the allocation criteria" (2006: 777).

14. Hurd defines legitimacy as "an actor's normative belief that a rule or institution ought to be obeyed," which is both subjective and intersubjective (2007: 7–8). On legitimacy, see Franck 1990; Scharpf 1999.

15. While specific US administrations under Presidents George W. Bush and Donald Trump tried to divest from multilateralism, they have not dismantled the wide array of multilateral institutions the United States helped create.

16. Legitimacy and public support is also used to explain Japan's behavior in the Asian Development Bank and UN Security Council (Lim and Vreeland 2013: 43).

17. This compares with the stronger link between voter interest and the IMF and is discussed in chapter 3 (see Broz and Hawes 2006; Oatley and Yakee 2004).

18. Thacker (1999); Barro and Lee (2005); Dreher and Jensen (2007).

19. On the indeterminacy and arbitrariness of structural accounts of power, see Guzzini (2013: chapter 3).

20. Stone strips all normativity from the concept of legitimacy. Legitimacy is voluntary participation, which depends on the existence of a social contract between weak states consenting to being governed by the powerful rather than when the United States or the IMF ought to be obeyed. For critiques of legitimacy based on consent, see Hurd 2007 and Williams 2005: 204–210.

21. US interests are predicated on five proxies: US foreign aid, exports, bank exposure, affinity for US voting in the UN General Assembly, and alliance patterns (Stone 2011: 209).
22. This is after a project or program has been approved by the World Bank's board of executive directors on which member states sit.
23. Important votes are those determined by the US State Department as such.
24. Kilby (2011) also shows that there is an increase in the disbursement of loans from the Asian Development Bank if recipients support the United States and Japan in important UN General Assembly votes. Dreher and Sturm (2012) also show that there is a strong correlation between borrowers aligning with G7 votes in the UN General Assembly and receiving IMF programs and World Bank loans.
25. Which may then become internalized to constitute an actor's identity (Bukanovsky 2002).
26. The debate over providing official development assistance for idealistic reasons or strategic interests overlooks the stability of rules, norms, and conventions on the oughtness and means for providing aid (Lumsdaine 1993).
27. As discussed in the next chapter, the banks' inefficiencies and ineffectiveness became apparent in the 1990s (International Financial Institutions Advisory Commission 2000). Since then, donor states began their own evaluations of development IO effectiveness (Easterly and Pfutze 2008).
28. In the World Bank, nonborrowers are called Part I members, Part II are borrowers.
29. The banks have never had to draw on members' callable capital.
30. The United States demanded specific IMF governance arrangements to exert national control, which was emulated for the World Bank (Cowhey 1992: 171–172).
31. Owing to the MDBs' opacity, there is no means of tracing subscription and voting levels across the banks over time.
32. See Gwin 1994; Krasner 1981; Mingst 1990: chapter 10; Sanford 1982; Woods 2003: 34–36; Babb 2009.
33. Inter-American Development Bank proposals foreshadowed the World Bank (Mason and Asher 1973: 15).
34. The Asian Development Bank collapsed its soft-loan lending into its OCR in January 2017.
35. Some argue the United States remains the dominant member of the World Bank because no other state has chosen to challenge it (Kapur 2002: 64). This ignores the US refusal to allow Japan to exceed its voting power in the World Bank (Wan 2001) and the United States' withholding IMF reforms for five years that would increase rising powers' allocations in the IMF, with implications for World Bank subscriptions and voting. These were only approved in December 2015, leading to a World Bank instantiation of its own capital subscriptions and voting allocations separate from the IMF.
36. The United States has used its exit option in relation to the ILO in 1977 and UNESCO in 2017. It has threatened to withdraw from many IOs, and it instigated leaving UNESCO and the UN Human Rights Council, under the Trump administration.
37. Other member states look to see how much the United States will commit to determine their own contributions for the soft-loan facilities. This is complicated because

many donors approve three years of funding at once, while the US legislature approves every year of a three-year IDA replenishment round separately. Other donors have turned to trust funds to channel funding outside ordinary lending, but this does not affect subscriptions or voting (Strand and Trevathan 2016; Reinsberg et al. 2017)).

38. All the MDBs requested GCIs to provide financing for borrowers affected by the 2008 global financial crisis.

39. The IDA recommended removing the pro rata provision for IDA-15, which was approved in 2008 (IDA 2007: 17; IDA 2008: 34).

40. See Culpeper 1997: 33. The top donor generally directs the policy agenda through the IDA replenishment round. Up to the early 2000s the United States was the top IDA donor. This was not the case for IDA-15, IDA-17 (Bank Information Centre 2017), and IDA-19.

41. See Droesse 2011: 198. Apart from the FSO for the Inter-American Development Bank, the soft-loan facilities are not linked to the capital and voting structure of the MDBs. This changed in 2017 for the Asian Development Bank.

42. The European Bank for Reconstruction and Development does not have a soft-loan facility.

43. Although IFC and MIGA operate separately from the World Bank and IDA, the latter is still used as a platform to signal US intentions, given their same membership.

44. Despite reducing its paid-in capital, the United States was able to retain its influence in the World Bank by minimizing the veto required from 20 to 15 percent during a 1988 GCI (Babb 2009: 25, 137), as it did in the IMF (Stone 2011: 54).

45. This could undermine its relational power in the African Bank because it is the only executive director that does not have to negotiate and engage with other states in its constituency. This means it does not get a sense of what is important to other member states, especially as the US executive director has not been permanently located at AfDB headquarters since the 2011 Arab Spring.

46. Lavelle 2011: 27; except in the Inter-American Development Bank's FSO, where the United States has a veto.

47. Germany recently surpassed the United States as the second-largest shareholder in the African Development Bank (2021: Annexes).

48. The World Bank admits to lending for political reasons during the Cold War (World Bank 2012).

49. As earmarking violated the Inter-American Development Bank's charter this could not occur but the conflict did lead to the instatement of a new bank president.

50. Owing to the dominance of studies on the United States there is less known about the behavior of other shareholders. For example, US government officials argue that contra other directors, the US executive directors actively seeks out more information than their counterparts, maintain the same coherent policy across all the banks, and are backed by a single bureaucracy (US Treasury) (Interview with former US Treasury staff, November 4, 2013).

51. Menkveld 1991: 61; Sanford 1982: 8; Strand 2003: 127, fn 14; White 1970: 63; Wilson 1987: 9; Woods 2003: 111; Shaw 1991: 542.

52. Interview with a World Bank executive director March 6, 2009 (Interview 200949). The same has been said of the IMF, see Thacker 1999.
53. An organization's culture is its "system of meaning that governs staff expectations and behaviour" (Chwieroth 2008: 133).
54. Subcultures may develop in units of the IO with different professions, but these react to the dominant culture.
55. As IOs the MDBs are immune under international law.
56. While the United States takes a strong stance on the accountability mechanism, not all executive directors know what the mechanisms do. Coalitions in reaction to accountability mechanism findings are not stable (Nelson 2000), or necessarily based on developed or developing status. Rather executive directors tend to react to investigation findings based on their knowledge of the mechanisms, for example after experiencing them at another MDB (Interview with EBRD staff 4 October 2017). For this reason, recognizing power as social not just material is important for analyzing how member states react to the norm.

Chapter 3

1. Specific Congressional members are discussed later.
2. United States Congress. House. Committee on Appropriations. Subcommittee on Foreign Operations, Export Financing, and Related Programs Appropriations for 1996. 104th Congress, First Session. Washington, DC: US Government Printing Office, 1996. P. 173.
3. The United States also used its power of the purse in the UN pending financial reforms in the 1980s and 1990s (Grigorescu 2008: 288; Hoffman and Megret 2005: 52, 60). Later, a report by the former UN inspector general recommended strengthening the World Bank's internal oversight mechanisms, leading to the creation of the Department of Institutional Integrity (Thornburgh et al. 2000). The Department of Institutional Integrity examines cases of unethical conduct such as fraud, corruption, and staff misconduct. Attempts to strengthen internal oversight mechanisms were pushed by the United States and backed by "influential democracies," and in turn were adopted by the other MDBs (Grigorescu 2008: 289–290, 305).
4. United States Congress. House. Committee on Financial Services. 115th Congress, Second Session. Washington, DC. https://www.congress.gov/bill/115th-congress/house-bill/3326.
5. See Caporoso 2003; Zweifel 2006; Florini 2007; Clark et al. 2003; Fox and Brown 1998.
6. The EBRD had only just been created.
7. The reviews are detailed in the sections on the different MDBs.
8. Interviews 200946 and 200947.
9. Interviews with former World Bank staff, September–October 2013 (Interviews 201335, 201331).

10. Letter from Bradford Morse and Thomas Berger to World Bank President Lewis Preston "Sardar Sarovar Independent Review," dated October 13, 1992. On file with author.

11. Statement of US-ED Pat Coady to the World Bank Board of Executive Directors "India: Sardar Sarovar (Narmada) Projects, Review of Current Status and Next Steps," dated October 23, 1992 (R92–168). On file with author.

12. The nationality of the executive director is indicated here, although many of them represent mixed constituencies.

13. Anonymous notes from the Meeting of the World Bank Board of Executive Directors "India: Sardar Sarovar (Narmada) Projects, Review of Current Status and Next Steps," dated October 23, 1992. On file with author. An idea was also floated to give the job to the Operations Evaluation Department (now Independent Evaluation Group) but the mandate of the post hoc project evaluation department could not be stretched to include investigating harm from project operations. Interview with former World Bank staff member, October 10, 2013.

14. Statement of US-ED Pat Coady to the World Bank Board of Executive Directors "India: Sardar Sarovar (Narmada) Projects, Review of Current Status and Next Steps," dated October 23, 1992 (R92–168). On file with author.

15. "Independent Panel Rips Bank Role in Indian Dam," *World Bank Watch* 2, no. 25: 1. Dated: June 29, 1992.

16. Udall and Hunter worked with the Sierra Club, the National Wildlife Federation, Friends of the Earth, and the Bank Information Centre in advocating greater transparency and accountability for the Bank (van Putten 2008: 74).

17. United States Congress. House of Representatives. Hearing before the Subcommittee on International Development, Finance, Trade and Monetary Policy of the Committee on Banking, Finance and Urban Affairs, One Hundred Third Congress, First Session, May 5, 1993. Serial No 103–36. Appendix V, "Proposal for an Independent Appeals Commission for the World Bank," by Environmental Defense Fund and the Centre for International Environmental Law, pp. 235–240.

18. Interviews 200947 and 201333.

19. World Bank, 2013, "Transcript of the Interview: John H Cosgrove, Executive Director Western Pacific 1991–1995 by Jochen Kraske and William Becker," The World Bank Group Historians Office, Oral History Project, May 3, 1995.

20. The Chilean Executive director was sympathetic to NGO concerns over Narmada and the lack of bank accountability, having come from an NGO background and with Chile facing environmental opposition to the IFC-funded Bio Bio dam (Park 2010a: 134–144). This is discussed further in the chapter. The Malaysian executive director was also concerned, owing to the environmental and social campaign against their Pakmun dam. Both recognized the need to create an accountability mechanism to verify practices on the ground for the Board. Much of the discussion among executive directors took place informally. Email correspondence with Eveline Herfkins, dated August 6 and 24, 2013.

21. International Bank for Reconstruction and Development, "Operations Inspection in the Bank: Issues and Options," From the Vice President and Secretary to the Board of Executive Directors, June 10, 1993, R93-122. On file with author.

22. George Graham, "Developing a More Worldly Bank: Plans at the World Bank for Improving Its Project Management," *Financial Times*, July 2, 1993, p. 8; International Bank for Reconstruction and Development, "Operations Inspection in the Bank: Issues and Options," From the Vice President and Secretary to the Board of Executive Directors, June 10, 1993, R93-122, Appendix I, p. 1. On file with author.

23. Interview 200949. Summary of Discussion at the Meeting of the Executive Directors of the Bank and IDA in a Committee of the Whole, August 26 and 27, 1993, from T. T. Thahane Vice President and Secretary World Bank to the Board of Executive Directors, September 16, 1993. On file with author.

24. Summary of Discussion at the Meeting of the Executive Directors of the Bank and IDA in a Committee of the Whole, August 26 and 27, 1993, from T. T. Thahane Vice President and Secretary World Bank to the Board of Executive Directors, September 16, 1993. On file with author.

25. This section, unless otherwise stated is from Lavelle 2011: 24–27.

26. The committees' names change over time but are referred to as House or Senate, authorizing or appropriation committees and their subcommittees where appropriate (Babb 2009: 267).

27. Lori Udall, memo to the Narmada Action Committee and International NGOs, dated October 11, 1993. On file with author.

28. United States Congress. House of Representatives. Statement of Lori Udall before the Subcommittee on International Development, Finance, Trade and Monetary Policy, Committee on Banking, finance and Urban Affairs, One Hundred Third Congress. Second Session. Serial Number 103–146, June 21, 1994. Appendix IV, Proposed Rules of Procedure for the World Bank Inspection Panel, June 17, 1994.

29. International Bank for Reconstruction and Development, "Operations Inspection in the Bank: Issues and Options," From the Vice President and Secretary to the Board of Executive Directors, June 10, 1993, R93-122. On file with author.

30. Bradlow had also testified at the Canadian House of Commons Standing Committee on Finance (Bradlow 1993) and had presented his ideas to the World Bank's Board, Interview, March 5, 2009. Bank management's earlier endorsement of an ombudsman came from Bradlow's proposal.

31. George Graham, "Developing a More Worldly Bank: Plans at the World Bank for Improving Its Project Management," *Financial Times*, July 2, 1993, p. 8.

32. George Graham, "Panel to Review Rules Complaints" *Financial Times*, September 27, 1993, p. 3.

33. US Congress, House of Representatives, Subcommittee on International Development, Finance, Trade and Monetary Policy of the Banking, Finance and Urban Affairs Committee, Draft International Development and Debt Relief Act of 1993 (May 26, 1993). On file with author.

34. Congressional Record 103rd Congress (1993–1994), Foreign Operations, Export Financing, and Related Programs Appropriations Act, 1994 (House of Representatives—June 17, 1993), p. H3,753.

35. A. Taylor, "House Panel Cuts Contribution to Put Heat on World Bank: International Lender Chided for Secrecy, Urged to Tighten Up Its Operations," *Congressional Quarterly*, September 25, 1993, p. 2530.

36. Now-retired Congressman Frank reiterated this statement at a public address celebrating the World Bank Inspection Panel's twentieth anniversary, World Bank, September 27, 2013.

37. Letter from Patrick Leahy Chairman of the Foreign Operations Subcommittee on Appropriations, United States Senate to World Bank President Lewis Preston, June 1, 1993. On file with author.

38. Congressional Record Daily, Proceedings and Debates of the 103rd Congress, First Session, September 28, 1993, volume 139, no. 129 p. H7159. Until the Trump administration, Congress never funded the full amount requested by the executive (Treasury), see Babb 2009: 68. Between 2000 and 2010, appropriations "amounted to about 86 percent of amount requested" (Anderson 2012:5).

39. Interview 200955.

40. International Bank for Reconstruction and Development, "Operations Inspection in the Bank: Issues and Options," From the Vice President and Secretary to the Board of Executive Directors, June 10, 1993, R93–122. On file with author.

41. United States International Development and Debt Relief Act, 1993, Title 1 International Development Association: Section 101 Tenth Replenishment, June 10 1993 (HR 3063). This included the mark-up from the House of Representatives Committee on Banking, Finance and Urban Affairs. Section 1620 "Avocation of Certain Policies" of the bill includes that the Treasury must instruct the US ED of the World Bank to use its voice and vote to vigorously encourage the Bank to (point 2): "include affected populations, local governments and non-government organizations in all phases of the project cycle, from project identification to post project evaluation." The section concludes with a report to be presented by Treasury to the House of Representatives Committee on Banking, Finance and Urban Affairs and the Senate Committee on Foreign Relations on the efforts made to pursue section 1620 by September 30, 1994.

42. International Bank for Reconstruction and Development, "Operations Inspection in the Bank: Issues and Options," From the Vice President and Secretary to the Board of Executive Directors, June 10, 1993, R93–122, p. 8. On file with author.

43. Interviews 200945 and 200954.

44. Summary of Discussion at the Meeting of the Executive Directors of the Bank and IDA in a Committee of the Whole, August 26 and 27, 1993, from T. T. Thahane Vice President and Secretary World Bank to the Board of Executive Directors, September 16, 1993. On file with author. Many of the ED statements are not attributed in this document.

45. Ibid.

46. Interview with Professor David Hunter, May 15, 2009; Email correspondence with Eveline Herfkins, August 6, 2013.

47. Interview with Professor Daniel Bradlow, October 28, 2013.

48. World Bank, 2013, "Transcript of the Interview: John H Cosgrove, Executive Director Western Pacific 1991–1995 by Jochen Kraske and William Becker," The World Bank Group Historians Office, Oral History Project, May 3, 1995. On file with author.

49. International Development and Debt Relief Act of 1993, November 22, 1993, House of Representatives Committee on Banking Finance and Urban Affairs (H.R 3063), 103rd Congress, First Session, Report 103-411. Pp. 9–10.

50. During this period, NGOs and Congress set the terms of the US–World Bank relationship (Pincus and Winters 2002: 6).

51. International Development and Debt Relief Act of 1993, November 22, 1993, House of Representatives Committee on Banking Finance and Urban Affairs (H.R 3063), 103rd Congress, First Session, Report 103–411. p. 14.

52. Fax from Jonathan Sanford Congressional Research Service to Chad Dobson, Bank Information Centre, "Congressional Intent and Implementation of the Pelosi Amendment Regarding Environmental Impact Assessments of Proposed MDB Projects: Draft for Comment," dated August 1, 1994. On file with author.

53. The Board of Governors relies on the advice and knowledge of the executive director., Interview with an IDB executive director, October 17, 2013.

54. United States Congress. House. Committee on Appropriations. Subcommittee on Foreign Operations, Export Financing, and Related Programs Appropriations for 1996. 104th Congress, First Session. Washington, DC: US Government Printing Office, 1995. P. 173.

55. Letter from Kay Treakle, Bank Information Centre to Lawrence Summers, Undersecretary for International Affairs, United States Treasury, date October 11, 1994.

56. Inter-American Development Bank, "The Independent Investigation Mechanism," From the Secretary to the Board of Executive Directors, March 28, 1994, (GN-1830) p. 1. On file with author.

57. United States Congress. House. Committee on Appropriations. Hearing on the Inter-American Development Bank before the Subcommittee on International Development, Finance, Trade, and Monetary Policy. 103rd Congress. Second Session. Government Printing Office, 1995. Serial No. 103–137. P. 1.

58. Inter-American Development Bank, "The Independent Investigation Mechanism," From the Secretary to the Board of Executive Directors, March 28, 1994, (GN-1830) p. 1. On file with author.

59. Ibid.

60. United States Congress. House. Committee on Appropriations. Subcommittee on Foreign Operations, Export Financing, and Related Programs Appropriations for 1996. 104th Congress, First Session. Washington. DC: US Government Printing Office, 1995. P. 173

61. Former Bank staff could be appointed to the roster, and their appointment would not preclude future employment. This is a conflict of interest.

62. International Development and Debt Relief Act of 1993, November 22, 1993, House of Representatives Committee on Banking Finance and Urban Affairs (H.R 3063), 103rd Congress, First Session, Report 103–411, page unclear.

63. Prepared statement by Lawrence H Summers, Undersecretary of the Treasury for International Affairs. United States Congress. House of Representatives. Committee on Banking and Financial Services. Sub-Committee on Domestic and International Monetary Policy. "Administrations Plan for Authorization of FY96 Funding for the International Financial Institutions" 104th Congress. First Session. May 2, 1995. P. 63. United States Congress. House. Committee on Appropriations. Subcommittee on Foreign Operations, Export Financing, and Related Programs Appropriations for 1996. 104th Congress, First Session. Washington, DC: US Government Printing Office, 1996. P. 192.

64. United States Congress. House. Committee on Appropriations. Subcommittee on Foreign Operations, Export Financing, and Related Programs Appropriations for 1997 and Supplemental for 1996: Hearings before a Subcommittee of the Committee on Appropriations, House of Representatives, One Hundred Fourth Congress, Second Session. Washington, DC: US Government Printing Office, 1996. P. 192.

65. United States Congress. House. Committee on Appropriations. Subcommittee on Foreign Operations, Export Financing, and Related Programs Appropriations for 1998: Justification of Budget Estimates Committee on Appropriations, House of Representatives, One Hundred Fifth Congress. First Session. Washington, DC: US Government Printing Office, 1997. P. 133.

66. Statement by Lawrence H Summers, Undersecretary of the Treasury for International Affairs. United States Congress. House of Representatives. Committee on Banking and Financial Services. Sub-Committee on Domestic and International Monetary Policy. "Administrations Plan for Authorization of FY96 Funding for the International Financial Institutions" One Hundred Fourth Congress. First Session. May 2, 1995. P. 3.

67. Vice President and Secretary of the World Bank, "Review of the Inspection Panel Function: Background Documents: Annex III, The Inspection Mechanisms of Two Regional Development Financial Institutions (IDB and ADB)," to the World Bank Board of Executive Directors, INSP/SecM96-9, February 23, 1996. On file with author.

68. Additionally, the ADB differs from the World Bank in undertaking private sector projects; it was initially decided to exclude these from being eligible for investigation by the Inspection Function owing to the difference in lending processes (this was later included for reasons discussed in the next section; McGill 2001: 197).

69. International Development and Debt Relief Act of 1993. United States Congress. House. Committee on Banking Finance and Urban Affairs (H.R 3063), One Hundred Third Congress, First Session, November 22, 1993, Report 103–411, p. 11.

70. This section, unless otherwise stated, comes from Park 2010a: 133–139.

71. Letter from President Wolfensohn to GABB dated December 6, 1995. On file with author.

72. Secretary of the Committee on Development Effectiveness, "Proposed Inspection Mechanism for Private Sector Projects: IFC and MIGA Inspection Panel," World Bank, IFC and MIGA June 27 1996, CODE96-40. On file with author. CODE is a committee of the Board of Executive Directors charged with examining the development effectiveness of the World Bank Group including its governance and accountability.

73. Secretary for Committee on Development Effectiveness "Minutes of the Meeting held on July 8, 1996: Proposed Inspection Mechanism for Private Sector Projects: IFC and MIGA Inspection Panel," World Bank, IFC and MIGA, August 26, 1996, CODEM96-11. On file with author.

74. Ibid.

75. IFC, "Consultation Paper for Inspection Mechanism for IFC and MIGA," September 10, 1996. On file with author.

76. Dana Clark and David Hunter of CIEL, "Extension of the Inspection Panel to IFC/MIGA Operations," report to CODE, the World Bank, IFC and MIGA, July 3, 1996; Friends of the Earth, 'Friends of the Earth's Comments on the Draft Operational Guidelines for the Office of the Compliance Advisor/Ombudsman at IFC/MIGA,' manuscript, no date; Letter from Kay Treakle from BIC, Claudia Saladin of CIEL and Doug Norlen from the Pacific Environment and Resources Center, to Meg Taylor, the CAO, on the Draft Operational Guidelines for the Office of the Compliance Advisor Ombudsman, March 2, 2000. On file with author.

77. Secretary of the Committee on Development Effectiveness, "Proposed Inspection Mechanism for Private Sector Projects: IFC and MIGA Inspection Panel," World Bank, IFC and MIGA, June 27 1996, CODE96-40. On file with author.

78. Dana Clark and David Hunter of CIEL, "Talking Points on IFC/MIGA Inspection Mechanism," September 10, 1996, on file with author; CIEL "Discussion Paper Revised: Extension of the Inspection Panel to IFC/MIGA Operations," October 1, 1996. On file with author.

79. Email from Andrea Durbin, Friends of the Earth, "Update on IFC Issues (Inspection Panel and Biobio/Hair Report), to MDB Colleagues," January 15, 1997. On file with author.

80. CIEL and FoE, "Proposal for an Independent Review Panel for the International Finance Corporation and the Multilateral Investment Guarantee Agency," August 15, 1997. On file with author.

81. Secretary of the Committee on Development Effectiveness, "Consultations with Private Sector Clients and Co-financiers on the Possible Establishment of an Inspection Mechanism for IFC and MIGA," World Bank, IFC and MIGA, August 9, 1997, CODE97-50. On file with author.

82. The World Bank Group was under pressure during this period to have enforceable environmental and social standards the same or similar to the World Bank. Indeed, IFC was in process of upgrading its environmental and social safeguard policies at this time (Park 2010a).

83. This section unless otherwise noted is from Park 2010a: 167.

84. Statement by US-ED Jan Piercy, "Consultations with private Sector on IFC/MIGA Inspection Function," World Bank Committee on Development Effectiveness (CODE) meeting, October 8, 1997; emphasis added. On file with author.

85. Letter from US-ED Jan Piercy to Bill Schuerch, "CODE Meeting on IFC/MIGA Inspection Mechanism," October 14, 1997. On file with author.

86. United States Congress. House. Committee on Appropriations. Subcommittee on Foreign Operations, Export Financing, and Related Programs Appropriations for 2000. Committee on Appropriations, House of Representatives, One Hundred Fifth Congress, Second Session. Washington, DC: US Government Printing Office, 1999. p.197, p. 205.

87. Speech by Peter Woicke, former EVP of the IFC, Session IV Accountability and the Private Sector, Challenges of International Accountability: Lessons from Independent Accountability Mechanisms, Hosted by American University College of Law and the World Bank Inspection Panel, June 24 2001, American University, Washington, DC. On file with author.

88. Industry/NGO Joint Consensus Statement on IFC/MIGA Consultation Procedures and Extension of Panel Mechanism, Draft for comment by Business Members of the Working Group, October 20, 1997. On file with author.

89. Report from the Secretary, CODE, "Options to Enhance Environmental and Social Compliance and Accountability in IFC and MIGA," World Bank, IFC and MIGA, March 4, 1998, CODE98-12, p. 5. On file with author.

90. Ibid.

91. The origin of the idea of an ombudsman was promoted by the IFC's executive vice president, general counsel, and a member of the Bankers Advisory Group, Sir David Scholey, because it would be "less rigid and punitive than an inspection panel" (Dysart, Murphy, and Chayes 2003: 1; CAO 2010: 14).

92. Report from the Secretary, CODE, "Options to Enhance Environmental and Social Compliance and Accountability in IFC and MIGA," World Bank, IFC and MIGA, March 4,1998, CODE98-12, p. 5. On file with author.

93. Report from the Secretary, CODE, "Integrated Accountability Mechanism for IFC and MIGA," World Bank, IFC and MIGA, late 1998, date and report code unspecified. On file with author. US-ED Jan Piercy was prepared to accept the CAO model and see how it worked (Interview with accountability activist, May15, 2009).

94. United States Congress. House. Committee on Appropriations. Subcommittee on Foreign Operations, Export Financing, and Related Programs Appropriations for 2000. Committee on Appropriations, House of Representatives, One Hundred Fifth Congress, Second Session. Washington, DC: US Government Printing Office, 1999. P. 187.

95. International Development Association, "Additions to IDA Resources, Twelfth Replenishment: A Partnership for Poverty Reduction," December 23, 1998, p. 27, para 77, Washington DC, World Bank.

96. The following section, unless otherwise noted, is from Park 2010a: 168.

97. President's Recommendation to the EBRD Board of Executive Directors, April 29, 2003, p. 8.

98. United States Congress. House. Committee on Appropriations. Subcommittee on Foreign Operations, Export Financing, and Related Programs Appropriations for 1998: Justification of Budget Estimates. Committee on Appropriations, House of Representatives, One Hundred Fifth Congress. First Session. Washington, DC: US Government Printing Office, 1997. P. 145.

99. United States Congress. House. Committee on Appropriations. Subcommittee on Foreign Operations, Export Financing, and Related Programs Appropriations for 2004: Justification of Budget Estimates. Committee on Appropriations, House of Representatives, One Hundred Eighth Congress. First Session. Washington, DC: US Government Printing Office, 2003. P. 200.

100. President's Recommendation to the EBRD Board of Executive Directors, April 29, 2003, p. 7.

101. Friends of the Earth copy of the ADB's Inspection Function proposal dated January 18, 1995. On file with author.

102. United States Congress. House. Committee on Appropriations. Subcommittee on Foreign Operations, Export Financing, and Related Programs Appropriations for 2003: Justification of Budget Estimates. Committee on Appropriations, House of Representatives, One Hundred Seventh Congress. Second Session. Washington, DC: US Government Printing Office, 2002. P. 221.

103. President's Recommendation to the EBRD Board of Executive Directors, April 29, 2003. This was later posted on the EBRD's website. On file with author.

104. United States Congress. House. Committee on Appropriations. Subcommittee on Foreign Operations, Export Financing, and Related Programs Appropriations for 2004: Justification of Budget Estimates. Committee on Appropriations, House of Representatives, One Hundred Eighth Congress. First Session. Washington, DC: US Government Printing Office, 2003. p. 203.

105. Written comments on the draft policy were received from two former World Bank Inspection Panel Chairs (Richard Bissell and Jim MacNeil).

106. BIC, CIEL, and CEE Bankwatch, 2003, "Joint Comments for the EBRD's Proposed Independent Recourse Mechanism," January 29. On file with author.

107. EBRD, October 2002, Draft Policy, "The Independent Recourse Mechanism at the EBRD," EBRD, London. On file with author.

108. EBRD, President's Recommendation to the EBRD Board of Executive Directors, April 29, 2003, EBRD, London, pp. 3–4. This was later posted on the Bank's website. On file with author.

109. United States Congress. House. Committee on Appropriations. Subcommittee on Foreign Operations, Export Financing, and Related Programs Appropriations for 2005: Justification of Budget Estimates. Committee on Appropriations, House of Representatives, One Hundred Eighth Congress. Second Session. Washington, DC: US Government Printing Office, 2004. Pp. 220–221.

110. EBRD, January 2003, "IRM organizational flow chart," EBRD, London; EBRD, October 2002, Draft Policy, "The Independent Recourse Mechanism at the EBRD," EBRD, London. On file with author.

111. African Development Bank and African Development Fund, "The Independent Review Mechanism," Board Resolution B/BD/2004/9-F/BD/2004/7, June 30 2004. On file with author. The subregional MDBs have since established similar mechanisms including the Norwegian Investment Bank, the Caribbean Development Bank, and the Black Sea Trade and Development Bank.

112. Friends of the Earth copy of the ADB's Inspection Function proposal dated January18, 1995. On file with author.

113. Memo from Eric Meyer, Office of the Multilateral Development Banks, US Treasury to Chad Dobson, Bank Information Center, "Discussion of the Proposed African Development Bank Inspection Panel" October 28, 1994. On file with author.

114. United States Congress. House of Representatives. Committee on Financial Services. Sub-Committee on International Monetary Policy and Trade. "US Policy towards the African Development Bank and Fund." 107th Congress. First Session. P. 5.

115. Memo from David Hunter to Jon Elter, "African Development Bank Update," March 18, 1996. On file with author.

116. United States Congress. House. Committee on Appropriations. Subcommittee on Foreign Operations, Export Financing, and Related Programs Appropriations for 1998: Justification of Budget Estimates. Committee on Appropriations, House of Representatives, One Hundred Fifth Congress. First Session. Washington, DC: US Government Printing Office, 1997. P. 141.

117. Memo from David Hunter to Jon Elter, "African Development Bank Update," March 18, 1996. On file with author.

118. United States Congress. House. Committee on Financial Services. Hearing before the Subcommittee on International Monetary Policy and Trade. US Policy towards the African Development Bank and the African Development Fund. April 25, 2001. One Hundred Seventh Congress. First Session. Washington, DC: US Government Printing Office, 2001. Serial no. 107–10.

119. United States Congress. House. Committee on Appropriations. Subcommittee on Foreign Operations, Export Financing, and Related Programs Appropriations for 2003: Justification of Budget Estimates. Committee on Appropriations, House of Representatives, One Hundred Seventh Congress. Second Session. Washington, DC: US Government Printing Office, 2002. P. 193.

120. United States Congress. House. Committee on Appropriations. Subcommittee on Foreign Operations, Export Financing, and Related Programs Appropriations for 2004: Justification of Budget Estimates. Committee on Appropriations, House of Representatives, One Hundred Eighth Congress. First Session. Washington, DC: US Government Printing Office, 2003. Pp. 105, 170.

121. African Development Bank and African Development fund, "The Independent Review Mechanism," Board Resolution B/BD/2004/9-F/BD/2004/7, June 30 2004. On file with author. The IRM covers both public lending to sovereign states and private sector financing.

Chapter 4

1. Lori Udall, March 1994, "Memorandum Regarding the World Bank's Inspection Panel," Bank Information Centre. On file with author.
2. This is common to all the accountability mechanisms. Member states do not want them to drum up business, although they all provide public information through outreach events.
3. Throughout chapters 4 to 6, specific cases are invoked when they impact the dynamics of the mechanisms, the Board, and management. The loan number or accountability mechanism claim number is provided to enable the reader to find and examine the specifics of the case. Arun Concerned Group, *Request for Inspection*, submitted to the World Bank Inspection Panel, October 24, 1994. http://web.worldb ank.org/WBSITE/EXTERNAL/EXTINSPECTIONPANEL/0,,contentMDK:22515 755~pagePK:64129751~piPK:64128378~theSitePK:380794,00.html.
   On details of specific cases, see Naude Fourie 2016.
4. Letter from Lori Udall IRN and David Hunter CIEL to World Bank President James Wolfensohn, July 6, 1995.
5. Ibid.
6. See the nonattributed discussion of the World Bank's Board of Directors. Summary of Discussion at the Meeting of the Executive Directors of the Bank and IDA in a Committee of the Whole, August 26 and 27, 1993, from T. T. Thahane, Vice President and Secretary World Bank to the Board of Executive Directors, September 16, 1993. On file with author.
7. Statement by Jean-Daniel Gerber, Executive Director, *Review of the Inspection Panel Function*, February 26, 1996, EDS96-58. On file with author.
8. Ibid.
9. Vice President and Secretary of the World Bank, "Review of the Inspection Panel Experience: Annex I, The World Bank Inspection Panel: A Background Paper on Its Historical, Legal and Operational Aspects by Ibrahim Shihata," to the World Bank Board of Executive Directors, SecM97-873, November 6, 1997, p. 24.
10. World Bank, "Resolution Establishing the Inspection Panel," September 22, 1993, Resolution No. IBRD 93–10, Resolution No. IDA 93–6, para. 27.
11. Statement of Lori Udall Regarding the World Bank Inspection Panel: Update and Recommendations for Reform in the Context of the Fifteenth Replenishment of the International Development Association, before the Committee on Financial Services, House of Representatives, 110th Congress, Second Session, Serial 110–121, June 18, 2008, p. 76, fn 17. Udall argues that the clarifications weakened the Panel by making "a clear reading of the resolution impossible."
12. Secretary of the Committee of Development Effectiveness, Minutes of the Meeting held June 7, 1996, Revised, to the World Bank Board of Executive Directors, CODE96-8(Rev), August 28, 1996. On file with author.
13. Vice President and Secretary, "Review of the World Bank Inspection Function: Working Paper Prepared by the Inspection Panel," to the World Bank Board of Executive Directors, INSP/R95-3, November 27, 1995.

14. Vice President and Secretary of the World Bank, "Review of the Inspection Panel Experience: Annex I, The World Bank Inspection Panel: A Background Paper on Its Historical, Legal and Operational Aspects by Ibrahim Shihata," to the World Bank Board of Executive Directors, SecM97-873, November 6, 1997, p. 13.

15. Vice President and Secretary, "Review of the Inspection Panel Experience: Annex I, The World Bank Inspection Panel: A Background Paper on Its Historical, Legal and Operational Aspects by Ibrahim Shihata," to the World Bank Board of Executive Directors, SecM97-873, November 6, 1997, p. 18.

16. Ibid.

17. Oxfam International, *The World Bank Inspection Panel: Analysis and Recommendations for Review, Summary Paper*, February 1996, pp. 4 and 7. On file with author.

18. Vice President and Secretary of the World Bank, "Review of the Inspection Panel Function: Background Documents: Annex II," to the World Bank Board of Executive Directors, INSP/SecM96-9, February 23, 1996. On file with author.

19. Vice President and Secretary, "Review of the Inspection Panel Experience: Annex I, The World Bank Inspection Panel: A Background Paper on Its Historical, Legal and Operational Aspects by Ibrahim Shihata," to the World Bank Board of Executive Directors, SecM97-873, November 6, 1997, p. 7.

20. Ibid.

21. India, Argentina, and Brazil are three of the World Bank's top seven borrowers (Guven 2012).

22. Secretary of the World Bank, "Second Review of the Inspection Panel Experience," to the World Bank Board of Executive Directors, SecM98-8, January 7, 1998. On file with author.

23. Vice President and Secretary, "Review of the Inspection Panel Experience, to the World Bank Board of Executive Directors," SecM97-873, November 6, 1997. On file with author.

24. World Bank Press Release, "World Bank Board Approves Clarifications to the Inspection Panel Process," April 20, 1999, Washington DC, World Bank.

25. Letter from the Dean of the Board of Executive Directors of the World Bank to Civil Society, March 2, 1999, On File with Author. During this period the Board rejected another Inspection Panel recommendation for investigation regarding the 1998 India Ecodevelopment Project (Loan Number 29160-IN).

26. Phillips, Michael, "World Bank Board Agrees to Weaken Watchdog Panel," *Wall Street Journal*, Interactive Edition, Business and Finance Asia, April 21, 1999.

27. BIC, "Analysis of IDA-12 Agreement," February 1999. On file with author.

28. World Bank, 1999, "1999 Clarification of the Board's Second Review of the Inspection Panel." http://siteresources.worldbank.org/EXTINSPECTIONPANEL/Resources/1999ClarificationoftheBoard.pdf.

29. Zawada, Adrian, "World Bank Approves Changes to Independent Inspection Panel," *Bloomberg*, April 20, 1999, Washington DC.

30. World Bank Press Release, "Conclusions of the Board's Second Review of the Inspection Panel," April 20, 1999. http://web.worldbank.org/archive/website01541/WEB/0__C-681.HTM

31. Broder was previously president of the European Investment Bank and had strong connections to the European executive directors.

32. World Bank president appointments are political, while most management are career bankers.

33. Inspection Panel, "Discussion Draft: Revised Operating Procedures," September 20 2001, Washington DC, World Bank. On file with author. Interview with World Bank staff, August 23, 2013.

34. The Inspection Panel Chair refused to pass on the names of the individual staff involved in misconduct. Nonetheless, the fallout of the case was the widely held belief that the Inspection Panel can ruin one's career.

35. Letter from US Congressional members Barney Frank and Maxine Waters (Democrat) to World Bank President Kim, September 14, 2012.

36. New operating procedures were needed. For example, the Panel only accepted written not electronic requests for inspection (Inspection Panel 2009: 23).

37. In 2020 the Inspection Panel was changed to incorporate the dispute resolution service into its operations.

38. Letter from David Hunter and Dana Clark, CIEL to President Enrique Iglesias IDB, dated August 15, 1997. On file with author.

39. Walter Leal Filho was an expert on the Roster of Investigators of the mechanism. Angel Rene Rios was its coordinator from 2000 to 2005.

40. Unlike the World Bank's Inspection Panel, the experts could resume work for the IDB two years after serving on the roster, complicating the integrity of the accountability mechanism (Bradlow 2005: 421).

41. Inter-American Development Bank, "The Independent Investigation Mechanism," From the Secretary to the Board of Executive Directors, March 28, 1994, (GN-1830) pp. 4–5. On file with author.

42. Inter-American Development Bank, "The Independent Investigation Mechanism," from the Secretary to the Board of Executive Directors, March 28, 1994, (GN-1830) p. 1. On file with author. Nowhere in the documents is it clear what the Bank's formally adopted norms are.

43. For example, the World Bank Inspection Panel and the CAO. The ADB dropped this requirement in 2003. In 2010 the IDB would also. This was not required for the European Bank for Reconstruction and Development (EBRD) or the African Development Bank (AfDB)'s mechanisms.

44. This was co-financed by the World Bank and subject to two Inspection Panel claims in 1996 and again in 2002. The 1996 Inspection Panel investigation also proceeded as a review as determined by the World Bank's Board prior to the Inspection Panel Resolution's second clarification.

45. IIM, 1997, Yacyreta Hydroelectric Project: Report of the Review Panel, September 15, 1997. On file with author.

46. IIM, 1997, *Board of Directors Cover Memorandum to Accompany the Report of the Review Panel and IDB management Comments* (*Regarding the Yacyreta Hydroelectric Project: Report of the Review Panel,* September 15. On file with author.

47. IIM, 1997, *Yacyreta Hydroelectric Project: Report of the Review Panel,* September 15, 1997. On file with author.

48. Ibid.

49. IIM, *Board of Directors Cover Memorandum to Accompany the Report of the Review Panel and IDB management Comments* (*Regarding the Yacyreta Hydroelectric Project: Report of the Review Panel,* September 15, 1997. On file with author. Emphasis added.

50. Letter from David Hunter and Dana Clark, CIEL to President Enrique Iglesias IDB, dated August 15, 1997. On file with author.

51. Letter from Natalie Bridgeman, Accountability Counsel to Ana-Mita Betancourt, IIM Coordinator for the IDB, Comments on the Inter-American Development Bank Proposed Independent Consultation and Investigation Mechanism, dated June 26, 2009. On file with author.

52. For other claims deemed ineligible for investigation see IDB 2012b.

53. Letter from Marcos A. Orellana, Center for International Environmental Law to President Iglesias IDB, dated February 21, 2003.

54. See for example, IIM, 1997, *Yacyreta Hydroelectric Project: Report of the Review Panel,* September 15, 1997. On file with author.

55. United States Congress. House. Committee on Appropriations. Subcommittee on Foreign Operations, Export Financing, and Related Programs Appropriations for 2005: Justification of Budget Estimates. Committee on Appropriations, House of Representatives, One Hundred Eighth Congress. Second Session. Washington, DC: US Government Printing Office, 2004. p. 164.

56. Consultation or problem solving are used interchangeably here. These are distinct from mediation, which is a deeper level of engagement with establishing rules of interaction and promoting common solutions as the CAO undertakes (outlined in chapter 5). The other banks all undertake problem solving and specifically do not use the term "mediation."

57. Statement of Lori Udall Regarding the World Bank Inspection Panel: Update and Recommendations for Reform in the Context of the Fifteenth Replenishment of the International Development Association, before the Committee on Financial Services, House of Representatives, 110th Congress, Second Session, Serial 110–121, June 18, 2008, p. 74.

58. Unprecedentedly, all of the MDBs officially sought general capital increases in 2009 in light of the 2008 global financial crisis.

59. The IDB sought an $180 billion general capital increase after losing $1.9 billion in the global financial crisis (BIC 2009).

60. Letter from the US Secretary of the Treasury Timothy Geithner to the IDB President Luis Alberto Moreno dated May 21, 2009. On file with author.

61. From the Secretary to the Committee of the Board of Governors, "First Working Paper. Review of the need for a General Capital Increase of the Ordinary Capital and

Replenishment of the Fund for Special Operations: Progress and Next Steps,"CA-501, June 18, 2009, Washington, DC, Inter-American Development Bank. https://publi cations.iadb.org/en/review-need-general-capital-increase-ordinary-capital-and-replenishment-fund-special-operations.

62. Like the Asian Development Bank's Accountability Mechanism, MICI would later cover private sector projects also (IDB 2012b: 7; ICIM 2014b).

63. The Ombudsman also rejected consultation on the grounds that it would not be fruitful because of the lawsuit. The compliance review panel expended significant time unraveling four possible legal actions in relation to the case before determining that the claim was eligible for a compliance review (ICIM 2013).

64. Betancourt left four months after being appointed executive secretary. The post was filled by the project ombudsman and then another staffer until a replacement was appointed in April 2011.

65. The project ombudsman argued that the consultation phase faced a high caseload plus a high administrative burden in its first year with only a few junior staff (IDB 2013a: Part II, p. 1).

66. The report could also be seen as a challenge to the reputation and integrity of the Panel chair himself (Werne Kiene, a former World Bank Inspection Panel chair; see IDB 2012b: 13, 2013: Part III, p. 2).

67. Interviews with IDB staff, October 2013.

68. Udall had also been on the CAO's Strategic Advisors Group and undertaken its 2010 review, and had consulted the ADB during the 2003 revision of their mechanism.

69. Letter from NGOs to IDB President Moreno and the Board of Executive Directors, "Concerns regarding the Independent Consultation and Investigation Mechanism (MICI)," dated September 16, 2011. San Fancisco, Accountability Counsel. On File with Author.

70. Mr Angel Rene Rios, no date, *Comments to the Proposed Policy of the Independent Consultation and Investigation Mechanism (ICIM) of the Inter-American Development Bank (IADB)*. On file with author.

71. Like the IDB these experts could work for the Asian Development Bank after serving on the roster after five years (not two like the IIM).

72. No executive director has ever exercised this right.

73. As with the IDB, the Inspection Function would be administratively supported by the Bank's Office of the Secretary, thus undermining its independence from management (ADB 2002e: 32).

74. The Inspection Function could go beyond the World Bank Inspection Panel in making recommendations as to how to correct Bank noncompliance not just present its findings. Later iterations of the MDB accountability mechanisms were also given this prerogative: the IDB's MICI, and both the AfDB's and the EBRD's mechanisms (Oxfam Australia 2011: 18).

75. The Bank noted that it took 117 days for the Inspection Function to notify claimants as to whether a request had been accepted for investigation (ADB 2002e: 33).

76. The complex diagram of the claims process, involving three separate but interlinked processes with multiple steps, is outlined in ADB 1995b: Annex I.

77. This was not mandatory for the World Bank Inspection Panel (Naude Fourie 2009: 259) or the CAO. The Asian Development Bank dropped this requirement in 2003 (ADB 2003: 26). As noted previously, the IDB would also drop it in later MICI iterations.

78. The Asian Development Bank called it the Accountability Mechanism. Lowercase denotes MDB accountability mechanisms in general.

79. This section unless otherwise noted is from Park 2015.

80. United States Congress. House. Committee on Appropriations. Subcommittee on Foreign Operations, Export Financing, and Related Programs Appropriations for 2003: Justification of Budget Estimates. Committee on Appropriations, House of Representatives, One Hundred Seventh Congress. Second Session. Washington, DC: US Government Printing Office, 2002. P. 16.

81. ADB, 2002, *Inspection Function Review: Notes from Meeting with ADB Executive Directors*, Confidential—March 13, 2002, Not for Circulation. On file with author.

82. United States Congress. House. Committee on Appropriations. Subcommittee on Foreign Operations, Export Financing, and Related Programs Appropriations for 2004: Justification of Budget Estimates. Committee on Appropriations, House of Representatives, One Hundred Eighth Congress. First Session. Washington, DC: US Government Printing Office, 2003. P. 190.

83. United States Congress. House. Committee on Appropriations. Subcommittee on Foreign Operations, Export Financing, and Related Programs Appropriations for 2005: Justification of Budget Estimates. Committee on Appropriations, House of Representatives, One Hundred Eighth Congress. Second Session. Washington, DC: US Government Printing Office, 2004. Pp. 20 and 203.

84. United States Treasury, 2013, "Report to Congress from the Chairman of the National Advisory Council on the International Monetary and Financial Policies," Department of Treasury, Office of the Multilateral Development Banks. https://www.treasury.gov/resource-center/international/development-banks/Pages/congress-index.aspx.

85. The Special Project Facilitator also delayed a visit for facilitation after the Cambodian government requested more time to work with the Bank's resident mission to correct problems with the Phnom Penh to Ho Chi Minh City Highway Project (Loan Number: 1659-CAM (SF)). NGOs saw this as a developing member country refusing a site visit and thus undermining the Office of the Special Project Facilitator (Oxfam Australia 2011: 14). In response, the Asian Development Bank then provided a technical assistance loan to aid claimants and the Special Project Facilitator closed the claim without facilitation (OSPF 2010).

86. In practice the budget has been approved by IFC's budget committee not the Office of the President (Fairman, Joscelyne and Udall 2010: 8).

87. The ombudsman was criticized for doing so in the MICI review (IDB 2012b).

88. The CAO now conducts a compliance appraisal first, which may lead to a compliance desk review or a full-blown compliance audit. Full audits are now undertaken by an independent Panel of Experts (CAO 2011: 18–19).

89. The CAO's Reference Group became a small external group of "Strategic Advisors" to provide informal advice on dispute resolution design and accountability (CAO 2011: 10).

90. For example, the CAO process was still taking 10 days longer than the 120 days specified in its 2007 operational guidelines (Fairman et al. 2010: 28).

91. Both the ADB's Accountability Mechanism after 2012 and the IDB's MICI after 2014 allowed claimants to choose.

92. Wilmar's palm oil operations in Indonesia would trigger three claims: Wilmar Group-01/West Kalimantan (25532 & 26271), Wilmar Group-02/Sumatra (25532 & 26271), and Wilmar Group-03/Jambi (25532 & 26271).

93. Although the current review recommends placing the CAO under IFC/MIGA Boards, which could enable Bank avoidance strategies (Woicke 2020).

94. While experts have three-year renewable terms, they cannot work for the Bank once they have completed their service (EBRD 2004: 21).

95. The CAO only examines environmental and social impacts and lack of information disclosure.

96. Investments under 10 million Euro do not need Board approval in order to expedite financing. Derogations of Bank policies are also allowed.

97. BIC, CIEL, and CEE Bankwatch Network, "Joint Comments on the EBRD's Proposed Independent Recourse Mechanism," dated January 29, 2003. On file with author.

98. Letter from Richard Bissell and Jim McNeill, former Chairs of the World Bank Inspection Panel to EBRD President Jean Lemierre, dated January15, 2003.

99. The registration procedure is discussed in chapter 6.

100. Professor Edith Brown Weiss, a former World Bank Inspection Panel chair also acted as a senior advisor in the early stages of the 2009 review process.

101. Comments by Eduardo G. Abbott on the EBRD's Project Complaint Mechanism Draft Rules of Procedure, February 12, 2009, London, EBRD. On File with Author. Eduardo Abbott was the first secretary of the World Bank Inspection Panel.

102. Of note, the Project Complaint Mechanism process for determining eligibility for a compliance review under the 2014 policy states that assessors must consider whether the claim "relates to more than a technical violation of the Relevant EBRD Policy unless such a technical violation is alleged to have caused harm" (EBRD 2014b: 4). Like the Inspection Panel, the EBRD is very legalistic in how it assesses compliance.

103. This does not seem to have been a major concern to date.

104. This section unless otherwise noted is from IRM 2014: 20.

105. Memorandum from Daniel Bradlow and Richard Bissell, Independent Review Mechanism Panel of Experts, to the AfDB Board of Directors, January 19, 2012, "Review of Problem Solving Report Request No. 2010/01 Request for Compliance Review and Problem Solving Project: Construction of the Marrakech Agadir Motorway Morocco. http://www.afdb.org/fileadmin/uploads/afdb/Documents/ Compliance-Review/IRM%20Experts%20Memo%20to%20Boards%20re%20elig ibility%20of%20Marrakesh%20-%20Agadir%20Motorway%20Web_01.pdf.

106. Another three compliance reviews are in the eligibility assessment phase (cases RQ2014/01, RQ2015/03 and RQ2015/03-bis).

107. The Board would accept a compliance review of four of six of the issues recommended by the Compliance Review Panel in relation to Medupi (Independent Review Mechanism 2011: 5).

Chapter 5

1. The World Bank Inspection Panel only established its Dispute Resolution Service as part of the panel in 2020 and so is excluded here.

2. Four cases were being investigated in mid-2019. The Panel's first case, Arun III, was canceled (see chapter 4), and in only one case did the Panel determine that a claim was already being addressed by management in another claim. Yet both would be monitored by the Panel to ensure management rectified the problem (Panel claims 110 and 113).

3. In 1996, 2001, 2009, and 2011.

4. The title of the project or its accountability mechanism case number are provided when discussing the cases so they can be identified (Park 2019).

5. This also reflects an increase of program lending in the World Bank's portfolio.

6. Panel cases 30, 39, and 66.

7. As seems evident in claims regarding a natural resource project in Afghanistan (Panel cases 83) and a water project in Egypt (Panel case 85).

8. The findings of the most recent cases have yet to be released. In the very first compliance investigation Arun III in 1994 the Panel made no specific finding as to the World Bank's compliance.

9. Positive improvements on the ground may also emerge even when the Inspection Panel rejects or defers an investigation.

10. Subsequent cases would also require ongoing oversight in this way.

11. Two of these claims would also be rejected because legal action was also underway.

12. A sixth case was accepted but transferred to MICI.

13. See the MICI Case Registry: http://www.iadb.org/en/mici/complaint-detail-2014,1804.html?id=BO-MICI001-2011.

14. Eleven cases would go through both problem solving and a compliance investigation.

15. Compliance Review Panel, August 27, 2012, *PN-MICI001-2010 Final Review Report: Panama Pando Monte-Lirio Hydroelectric Project (2266/OC-PN)*, ICIM, Washington, DC. On file with author.

16. Victoria Márquez-Mees, ICIM Secretaria Ejecutiva, December 12, 2012, *PN-MICI001-2010 "Pando-Monte Lirio Hydroelectric Power Plant Project" (Loan 2266/OC-PN): Final Decision of the Board of Executive Directors regarding the Compliance Review Report for Case PN-MICI001-2010*, ICIM, Washington, DC. On file with author.

17. IDB, January 2013, *Pando-Monte Lirio Hydroelectric Power Project (2266/OC-PN)—Panama: Management's Proposed Action Plan in Response to the Independent Consultation and Investigation Mechanism's Compliance Review Report*, IDB, Washington, DC. On file with author.

18. Victoria Márquez-Mees, ICIM Executive Secretary, July 12, 2013, *PR-MICI002-2010 "Program to Improve Highway Corridors in Paraguay" (Loan 933 A/OC-PR): Final Decision by the Board of Executive Directors regarding the Compliance Review Report for Case PR-MICI002-2010*, ICIM, Washington, DC. http://idbdocs.iadb.org/wsdocs/getdocument.aspx?docnum=37893902.

19. Under the 2010 MICI policy (IDB 2010b) the Compliance Review Panel can investigate claims up to 24 months after the final disbursement, but the claim took approximately 3 years to make a finding of noncompliance from the date of the claim. See the MICI public registry: http://www.iadb.org/en/mici/complaint-detail-2014,1804.html?id=PN%2DMICI001%2D2010.

20. The OSPF cases are: request 2004/01, request 2004/02; request 2009/01, request 2011/01, request 2011/03. It is unclear from the documents which OSPF claim regarding the Cambodia Railway project went from the OSPF to the OCRP, as the offices have different case numbers. It may have been OSPF request 2012/01. See Park 2019.

21. Up until mid-2019, nine cases would go through both problem solving and compliance investigation.

22. Again, there are no trends in reasons for rejecting claims for compliance investigation.

23. As discussed later, claims can go from mediation to a compliance audit.

24. This includes five being assessed.

25. In relation to claims regarding projects Agrokasa-01/Ica (26821) and Avianca-01/Colombia (25899), for example. See http://www.cao-ombudsman.org/.

26. Lesley Wroughton, 2009, "World Bank's IFC Suspends Palm Oil Investments," *US and International News*, Business and Financial News, September 9. Reuters.

27. As CEE Bankwatch points out, the number of claims against the BTC pipeline raises questions about more systemic project implementation and Bank oversight practices (2008: 8). Meanwhile the CAO accepted 27 of 33 claims in relation to the pipeline.

28. The project was a joint financing arrangement with the World Bank and the European Investment Bank. These financiers engaged much earlier in the project design, which was finalized by the time EBRD began financing. Problem solving would not have been able to address the project's design.

29. Three more problem-solving initiatives were underway by mid-2019.

30. Another settlement is still being facilitated for another problem-solving initiative.

31. The 2008 Environmental and Social Policy (ESP) adopted by the Bank was modeled on the IFC's 2006 Performance Standards to accord with policies on environmental and social assessment (PS1), biodiversity (PS6), and land acquisition and involuntary resettlement (PS5), among others (see Park 2010b; IFC updated its Environmental and Social Performance Standards in 2012). Updated in 2014, the EBRD now labels these Performance Requirements (for example PR6 on biodiversity).

32. See the case documents: http://www.ebrd.com/work-with-us/project-finance/project-complaint-mechanism/pcm-register.html.

33. Owing to the noncompliance of PR6, the Bank was in technical violation of two further policies, but this stemmed from being in breach of the biodiversity assessment and therefore only one noncompliance breach is recorded (PCM 2014b).

34. See the case documents: http://www.ebrd.com/work-with-us/project-finance/proj ect-complaint-mechanism/pcm-register.html.

35. Unlike the EBRD's PCM, these tend to be in sequence, with problem solving attempted first and then the CRMU director makes a recommendation to the Independent Review Mechanism, which then makes a determination for compliance investigation or not. The Independent Review Mechanism's 2014 annual report (IRM 2014: 20) identifies three cases where it has undertaken both problem solving and compliance review. The compliance outcomes are addressed in the subsequent section.

36. Another three assessments for problem solving were underway in the middle of 2019.

37. Memorandum from Daniel Bradlow and Richard Bissell, Independent Review Mechanism Panel of Experts, to the AfDB Board of Directors, January 19, 2012, "Review of Problem Solving Report Request No. 2010/01 Request for Compliance Review and Problem Solving Project: Construction of the Marrakech Agadir Motorway Morocco." http://www.afdb.org/fileadmin/uploads/afdb/Documents/ Compliance-Review/IRM%20Experts%20Memo%20to%20Boards%20re%20elig ibility%20of%20Marrakesh%20-%20Agadir%20Motorway%20Web_01.pdf.

38. This section, unless otherwise noted, is from IRM 2014: 20.

39. National Association of Professional Environmentalists, *Letter to the Director of the Compliance Review and Mediation Unit, Request (Claim) on the Proposed Bujugali Hydropower and Interconnection Project in Uganda*, May 5, 2007. https://www.afdb. org/en/independent-review-mechanism/management-of-complaints/registered-requests/rq-20071-uganda.

40. A fourth compliance investigation by the IRM found the AfDB non-compliant in relation to the Bank's 2016 project in Guinea (the Multinational—Road Development and Transport Facilitation Programme Within the Manu River Union (Guinea Section) RQ2106/3) regarding the Bank's environmental and social assessment procedures for public sector projects, its environmental policy, and involuntary resettlement policy.

Chapter 6

1. There has not been any public concern with the integrity and professionalism of accountability officers in undertaking their operations, although bias in favor of the MDB over project-affected people has been raised by claimants in some cases and reviews. Timeliness is an issue in terms of the speed of responding to claimants and the length of the process, which all the mechanisms are trying to address while ensuring due process.

2. The data was compiled from the accountability mechanisms' online case registries and annual reports (Park 2019).

3. See their operating procedures: World Bank 2014, IDB 2014, CAO 2013b, EBRD 2014b, ADB 2012e, AfDB 2015.
4. The number of projects has ramped up since the 2009 general capital increase to approximately 600 (IDB 2016). Author calculation from the Inter-American Development Bank website and annual reports 2001–2015.
5. This figure includes requests triggered by the CAO, the World Bank Group president, and the IFC's executive vice president.
6. Taking into account that the IFC generally invests less than 25 percent of a company undertaking a project. Only 5 percent of cases are about MIGA alone, 8 percent are for joint IFC/MIGA investments and guarantees. And 87 percent of cases concern IFC activities (CAO 2015: 73).
7. Note the 15 languages available on its website: http://www.cao-ombudsman.org/ compared with 12 on the Inspection Panel: http://ewebapps.worldbank.org/apps/ip/ Pages/Panel-In-Brief-More-Languages.aspx, 4 for the Inter-American Development Bank's MICI: http://www.iadb.org/en/mici/mici,1752.html; 3 at the European Development Bank's Project Complaint Mechanism: https://www.afdb.org/en/inde pendent-review-mechanism-irm; and English only for the Asian Development Bank: http://www.adb.org/site/accountability-mechanism/main and two for the African Development Bank.: https://www.afdb.org/en/independent-review-mechan ism-irm. More languages make more sense for the global World Bank and World Bank Group.
8. See the simple template letter for lodging a complaint with the CAO (CAO 2013b: 32).
9. Data from the African Development Bank's annual reports.
10. The government then chose not to proceed with the project, thus ending the Independent Review Mechanism's involvement.
11. Both the Inter-American Development Bank's Independent Investigation Mechanism annual reports and case registry were deleted from the Inter-American Development Bank's website when the accountability mechanism was reviewed in 2013. The 2001 and 2004 mechanism Annual Reports were not publicly available on-line in early 2013, and a public information request to access missing reports went unanswered.
12. Vice President and Secretary, "Review of the World Bank Inspection Function: Working Paper Prepared by the Inspection Panel," to the World Bank Board of Executive Directors, INSP/R95-3, November 27, 1995.
13. As the United States does in its voting in the MDBs.
14. Some cases have led to national regulatory changes such as Panel claims 54, 55, and 63. For example, as a result of the review by the Inspection Panel, the Democratic Republic of Congo acknowledged the Pygmie people as Indigenous (Inspection Panel 2009: 86).
15. The compliance investigation into the Pakistan highway (STDP) also led to a change in domestic legislation as well as procedures for land acquisition and compensation (Park 2015).

Chapter 7

1. The regime complex literature examines how international organizations increasingly interact, but not the drivers of norms for international organizations in the regime complex (Alter and Raustiala 2018; Keohane and Victor 2011).

2. Eli Rosenberg and Carol Morello, "U.S. Withdraws from UNESCO, the U.N.'s Cultural Organization, Citing Anti-Israel Bias," Washington Post online, October 12, 2017. https://www.washingtonpost.com/news/post-nation/wp/2017/10/12/u-s-withdraws-from-unesco-the-u-n-s-cultural-organization-citing-anti-israel-bias/?noredirect=on&utm_term=.ee902ef3370d.

3. E. Rauhala, K. Demirjian, and T. Olorunnipa, 2020, "Trump Administration Sends Letter Withdrawing U.S. from World Health Organization over Coronavirus Response," *Washington Post*, July 8, 2020.

Bibliography

Abbott, K., and D. Snidal, 1998, "Why States Act through Formal International Organizations," *Journal of Conflict Resolution* 42 (1): 3–32.

Accountability Counsel, 2011, *Briefing Paper: A Critique of Inter-American Development Bank's Independent Consultation and Investigation Mechanism (MICI)*, August 3, 2011. http://www.accountabilitycounsel.org/wp-content/uploads/2012/02/8.3.11-IADB-MICI-Briefing-Paper_2.pdf.

Accountability Counsel, n.d., "2010–2012 ADB AM Policy Review." http://www.accoun tabilitycounsel.org/policy/existing-mechanisms/adb/past-policy-initiatives/.

Accountability Mechanism, 2015, *Accountability Mechanism Annual Report 2015*, Manila, ADB. http://www.adb.org/site/accountability-mechanism/publications.

Accountability Mechanism, 2014, *Strengthening Partnerships Annual Report 2014*, Manila, ADB. http://www.adb.org/site/accountability-mechanism/publications.

Accountability Mechanism, 2013, *Improving Outcomes Annual Report 2013*, Manila, ADB. http://www.adb.org/site/accountability-mechanism/publications.

Accountability Mechanism, 2012, *Accountability Mechanism Annual Report 2012*, Manila, ADB. http://www.adb.org/site/accountability-mechanism/publications.

Accountability Mechanism, 2008, *The Urban and Environmental Improvement Project: Learning from an Ineligible Complaint from Nepal*, Manila, ADB. http://www. adb.org/sites/default/files/ueip-brochure.pdf.

ADB (Asian Development Bank), 2016a, *Accountability Mechanism Complaint Receiving Officer's Complaints Registry*, Manila, ADB. http://www.adb.org/sites/default/files/ page/161873/adb-am-complaints-registry.pdf.

ADB, 2016b, *2016 Learning Report on the Implementation of the Accountability Mechanism Policy*, Manila, ADB.

ADB, 2014a, *ADB's Accountability Mechanism: Strengthening Partnerships*, Manila, ADB. http://www.adb.org/sites/default/files/publication/148715/adb-accountability-mechanism-partnerships.pdf.

ADB, 2014b, *Ten Years of the Accountability Mechanism*, Manila, ADB. http://www.adb. org/publications/10-years-accountability-mechanism.

ADB, 2015, *Proposed Remedial Action Plan* India: Mundra Ultra Mega Power Project: Appendix 2*, Manila, ADB. http://compliance.adb.org/dir0035p.nsf/attachme nts/R44-15%20(as%20posted%203%20July%202015).pdf/$FILE/R44-15%20(as%20 posted%203%20July%202015).pdf.

ADB, 2012a, *Annual Report 2011*, Manila, ADB. http://www.adb.org/sites/default/files/ adb-ar2011-v1.pdf#page=125.

ADB, 2012b, *Asian Development Fund XI Donors' Report: Empowering Asia's Most Vulnerable*, Manila, ADB.

ADB, 2012c, "Compliance Review Panel." http://www.compliance.adb.org/dir0035p.nsf/ alldocs/RDIA-83N79X?OpenDocument.

ADB, 2012d, *Review of the Accountability Mechanism Policy*, Manila, ADB. http://beta. adb.org/documents/review-accountability-mechanism-policy-r-paper

ADB, 2012e, *Accountability Mechanism Policy*, Manila, ADB.

ADB, 2011. *Further Strengthening the Accountability Mechanism*, Manila, ADB. www.adb. org/Documents/Policies/Accountability-Mechanism-Review/am-review-first-draft. pdf

ADB, 2006, *Special Evaluation Study on Involuntary Resettlement Safeguards*, Manila, ADB, Operations Evaluation Department. https://www.adb.org/sites/default/files/eva luation-document/35442/files/sst-reg-2006-14.pdf.

ADB, 2004, *Samut Prakarn Wastewater Management Project Fourth Semiannual Report to the Board of Directors on Implementation of the Recommendations of the Board Inspection Committee as Adopted on 25 March 2002*, April 2004, Manila, ADB.

ADB, 2003, *Review of the Inspection Function: Establishment of a New ADB Accountability Mechanism*. Manila, ADB. http://www.adb.org/Documents/Policies/ADB_Accountab ility_Mechanism/ADB_accountability_mechanism.pdf.

ADB, 2002a, *Report and Recommendation of the Inspection Committee to the Board of Executive Directors of the Asian Development Bank on Inspection Request: Samut Prakarn Wastewater Management Project, Thailand (ADB Loan Nos. 1410-THA [7 December 1995] and 1646-THA [3 December 1998])*, February 28, 2002. Manila, ADB. On File with Author.

ADB, 2002b, *Board of Directors' Decision on Inspection Request–Samut Prakarn Wastewater Management Project (Loan Nos. 1410-THA and 1646-THA)*. Manila, ADB. On File with Author.

ADB, 2002c, *Annual Report of the Inspection Committee of the Board 2001–2002*, September 12, 2002. Manila, ADB. On File with Author.

ADB, 2002d, *Review of the Inspection Function*, Second Draft of Working Paper, July 31, 2002. Manila, ADB.

ADB, 2002e, *Review of the Inspection Function*, First Draft of Working Paper, May 3, 2002. Manila, ADB.

ADB, 2002f, *Inspection Function Review: Notes from Meeting with ADB Executive Directors*, Confidential—March 13, 2002, Not for Circulation. On file with author.

ADB, 2001, *Report of the Inspection Committee to the Board of Directors Asian Development Bank on Samut Prakarn Wastewater Management Project, Samut Prakarn Thailand (ADB Loan Nos. 1410-THA [7 December 1995] and 1646-THA [3 December 1998])*, June 20, 2001. Manila, ADB. On file with author.

ADB, 2000, *ADF VIII Donor's Report: Fighting Poverty in Asia*, Seventh Replenishment of the Asian Development Fund (ADF VIII), Manila, ADB.

ADB, 1997, *Emerging Asia: Changes and Challenges*, Manila, ADB.

ADB, 1995a, *Establishment of an Inspection Function*, Board of Executive Directors Report R225, November 1995. On File with Author.

ADB, 1995b, *Establishment of an Inspection Function*, Manila: ADB, December 1995.

ADB, 1994, *Report on the Task Force on Improving Project Quality*, Philippines, Manila, ADB.

AfDB (African Development Bank), 2021, *2019 Annual Report*, Abidjan, AfDB. https:// www.afdb.org/en/documents/annual-report-2019.

AfDB, 2015, *The African Development Bank Group: The Independent Review Mechanism Resolution*, January 2015, Tunis, AfDB. http://www.afdb.org/en/about-us/organizatio nal-structure/independent-review-mechanism-irm/.

AfDB, 2013, *AfDB's Integrated Safeguard System: Policy Statement and Operational Safeguards*. http://www.afdb.org/en/topics-and-sectors/topics/quality-assurance-resu lts/safeguards-and-sustainability-series/.

AfDB, 2010a, *African Development Bank and African Development Fund Board of Directors Resolution B/BD/2010/10—F/BD/2010/04 the Independent Review Mechanism,* Adopted at the 831st Meeting of the Board of Directors of the Bank and the 765th Meeting of the Board of Directors of the Fund, June 16, 2010, Abidjan, AfDB. www.afdb.org.

AfDB, 2010b, *Compliance Review and Mediation Unit of the Independent Review Mechanism Operating Rules and Procedures,* Tunis, AfDB. www.afbd.org.

AfDB, 2009, *Summary of Public Comments and Proposals on IRM Review,* Tunis, AfDB. www.afbd.org.

AfDB, 2007, *AfDB Management Response to the Request for Compliance Review of the Uganda Bujugali Hydropower Project (Private Sector) and the Interconnection Project (Public Sector),* June 2007. Tunis, AfDB. www.afbd.org.

AfDB, 2006, *Compliance Review and Mediation Unit of the Independent Review Mechanism Operating Rules and Procedures,* Tunis, AfDB. www.afbd.org.

AfDB, 2004a, *African Development Bank Annual Report,* Abidjan, AfDB. www.afbd.org.

AfDB, 2004b, *Stepping Up to the Future: An Independent Evaluation of AfDF VII, VIII, and IX,* Abidjan, AfDB, Operations Evaluation Department.

AfDB, 2004c, *African Development Bank and African Development Fund Board of Directors Resolution B/BD/2004/9—F/BD/2004/7 the Independent Review Mechanism,* Adopted at the 608th Meeting of the Board of Directors of the Bank and the 539th Meeting of the Board of Directors of the Fund, on June 30, 2004. Tunis, AfDB. www.afdb.org.

AfDB, 1994, *The Quest for Quality: Report of the Task Force on Project Quality for the African Development Bank,* Abidjan, AfDB.

AfDF (African Development Fund), 2014, "Voting Powers of Executive Directors as at 31 December 2014." http://www.afdb.org/fileadmin/uploads/afdb/Documents/Boards-Documents/ADF_VotingPowers_31_December_2014.pdf.

AfDF, 2011, "Total Resources Mobilized for AfDF 11." http://www.afdb.org/en/about-us/african-development-fund-adf/adf-11/total-resources-mobilized/.

AIIB (Asian Infrastructure Investment Bank), 2016, "Enhancing AIIB's Accountability: The Project-Affected People's Mechanism," Beijing, AIIB. https://www.aiib.org/en/policies-strategies/_download/consultation/draft-AIIB-complaint-handling-mechanism.pdf.

Alesina, A., and D. Dollar, 2000, "Who Gives Foreign Aid to Whom and Why?," *Journal of Economic Growth* 5 (1): 33–63.

Alter, K., and K. Raustiala, 2018, "The Rise of International Regime Complexity," *Annual Review of Law and Social Science* 14: 329–349.

Andersen, T., H. Hansen, and T. Markussen, 2006, "US politics and World Bank IDA-Lending," *Journal of Development Studies* 42 (5): 772–794.

Anderson, D., 2012, "Multilateralism and US Interagency Economic Development Efforts," Colonel Arthur D. Simons Centre, Fort Leavenworth Texas, Working Paper 12-01. http://thesimonscenter.org/iae-12-01-january-2012/.

Ascher, W., 1992, "The World Bank and US Control," in M. Karns and K. Mingst (eds.), *The United States and Multilateral Institutions,* London and New York, Routledge: 115–141.

Babb, Sarah, 2009, *Behind the Development Banks,* Chicago, Chicago University Press.

Bachrach, P., and M. Baratz, 1970, *Power and Poverty: Theory and Practice,* New York, Oxford University Press.

Balaton Chrimes, S., and F. Haines, 2015, "The Depoliticisation of Accountability Processes for Land Based Grievances, and the IFC CAO," *Global Policy* 6 (4): 445–454.

Balboa, C., 2015, "The Accountability and Legitimacy of International NGOs," in W. DeMars and D. Dijkzeul (eds.), *The NGO Challenge for International Relations Theory*, London and New York, Routledge: 159–186.

Baldwin, D. A. (ed.), 1993, *Neorealism and Neoliberalism: The Contemporary Debate*, New York, Columbia University Press.

Bank Information Centre (BIC), 2017, *International Development Association Replenishment*, Washington, DC, BIC. http://www.bankinformationcenter.org/our-work/international-development-association-ida-replenishment/.

Bank Information Centre (BIC), 2009, "A Serious Crisis Should Never Go to Waste: IDB Rush to Increase Capital Fails Stress Test," in *Civil Society Concept Note: Conditions for a 9th Recapitalization of the Inter-American Development Bank*, October 1, 2009, Washington, DC, BIC.

Barnett, M., and L. Coleman, 2005, "Designing Police: Interpol and the Study of Change in International Organizations," *International Studies Quarterly* 49 (4): 593–620.

Barnett, M., and M. Finnemore, 2004, *Rules for the World: International Organizations in Global Politics*, Ithaca and London, Cornell University Press.

Barro, R., and J. Lee, 2005, "IMF Programs: Who Is Chosen and What Are the Effects?," *Journal of Monetary Economics*, 57 (2): 1245–1269.

Beach, D., and R. Peterson, 2013, *Process Tracing Methods: Foundations and Guidelines*, Ann Arbor, University of Michigan Press.

Bello, W., 2002, "Philippine Power Scandal Illustrates Flaws in ADB's Privatisation Strategy," in *Creating Poverty: The ADB in Asia, Focus on the Global South*, Bangkok, Chulalongkorn University: 27–38.

Ben-Artzi, R., 2016, *Regional Development Banks in Comparison: Banking Strategies versus Development Goals*, Cambridge, Cambridge University Press.

Bissell, R., 1997, "Recent Practice of the Inspection Panel of the World Bank," *American Journal of International Law* 91 (4): 741–744.

Bissell, R., and S. Nanwani, 2009a, "Multilateral Development Bank Accountability Mechanisms: Developments and Challenges," *Central and European Journal of International and Security Studies* 3 (2): 154–197.

Bissell, R., and S. Nanwani, 2009b, "Multilateral Development Bank Accountability Mechanisms: Developments and Challenges," *Michigan Journal of International Economic Law* 6 (1): 2–55.

Bland, E., and C. Kilby, 2015, "Informal Influence on Multilateral Lending: The Case of the Inter-American Development Bank," in B. Arvin and B. Lew (eds.), *Handbook on the Economic of Foreign Aid*, Cheltenham, Edward Elgar: 255–279.

Blanton, T., 2007, "The Struggle for Openness in the International Financial Institutions," in A. Florini (ed.), *The Right to Know: Transparency in an Open World*, New York, Columbia University Press: 243–278.

Bosshard, P., D. Hunter, and L. Udall, 1993, *Creating an Independent Appeals Commission at the World Bank*, August 26, 1993. Erklarung von Berne, Centre for International Environmental Law, and Environmental Defense Fund. On file with author.

Bowles, I., and C. Kormos, 1999, "The American Campaign for Environmental Reforms at the World Bank," *Fletcher Forum of World Affairs* 23 (1): 211–225.

Bradlow, D., 2005, "Private Complainants and International Organizations: A Comparative Study of the Independent Inspection Mechanisms of International Financial Institutions," *Georgetown International Law Journal* 36: 403–494.

Bradlow, D., 1994, "International Organizations and Private Complaints: The Case of the World Bank Inspection Panel," *Virginia Journal of International Law* 34: 551–613.

Bradlow, D., 1993, "Opening Statement to the Subcommittee on Financial Institutions of the Canadian House of Commons Standing Committee on Finance," February 18.

Bradlow, D., and A. Naudé Fourie, 2011, "Independent Accountability Mechanisms at Regional Development Banks," in Thomas Hale and David Held (eds.), *Handbook of Innovations in Transnational Governance*, London, Polity Press: 122–138.

Bradlow, D., and S. Schlemmer-Schulte, 1994, "The World Bank's New Inspection Panel: A Constructive Step in the Transformation of the International Legal Order," *Zeitschrift für ausländisches öffentliches Recht / The Heidelberg Journal of International Law (ZaöRV)* 54 (2): 353–415.

Braaten, B., 2016, "Ambivalent Engagement: Human Rights and the Multilateral Development Banks," in S. Park and J. Strand (eds.), *Global Economic Governance and the Development Practices of the Multilateral Development Banks*, London, Routledge: 99–118.

Bridgeman, N., and D. Hunter, 2008, "Narrowing the Accountability Gap: Toward a New Foreign Investor Accountability Mechanism," *Georgetown International Environmental Law Review* 20: 187–236.

Bronstone, A., 1999, *The European Bank for Reconstruction and Development*, Manchester, Manchester University Press.

Brown, B., 1992, *The United States and the Politicization of the World Bank*, London and New York, Kegan Paul International.

Broz, J. L., 2008, "Congressional Voting on Funding the International Financial Institutions," *Review of International Organizations* 3: 351–374.

Broz, J., and M. Hawes, 2006, "Congressional Politics of Financing the International Monetary Fund," *International Organization* 60: 367–399.

Bukovansky, M. 2002. *Legitimacy and Power Politics: The American and French Revolutions in International Political Culture*, Princeton, NJ, Princeton University Press.

Buntaine, M., 2016, *Giving Aid Effectively*, Oxford, Oxford University Press.

CAO (Compliance Advisor/Ombudsman), 2015, *Annual Report 2015*, Washington, DC, IFC.

CAO, 2014, *Annual Report 2014*, Washington, DC, IFC.

CAO, 2013a, *Annual Report 2013*, Washington, DC, IFC.

CAO, 2013b, *Operational Guidelines*, Washington, DC, IFC.

CAO, 2013c, *Dispute Resolution Conclusion Report - Wilmar 3*, Washington, DC, IFC. http://www.cao-ombudsman.org/cases/default.aspx?region_id=1.

CAO, 2012a, *Annual Report 2012*, Washington, DC, IFC.

CAO, 2012b, *Comments Submitted: CAO Operational Guidelines Consultation 2012*, Washington, DC, IFC.

CAO, 2011, *Annual Report 2011*, Washington, DC, IFC.

CAO, 2010, *The CAO at 10: Annual Report FY2010 and Review FY2000–2010*, Washington, DC, IFC.

CAO, 2009, *Annual Report 2008–2009*, Washington, DC, IFC.

CAO, 2008, *Annual Report 2007–2008*, Washington, DC, IFC.

CAO, 2007a, *CAO Operational Guidelines*, Washington, DC, IFC.

CAO, 2007b, *Annual Report 2006–2007*, Washington, DC, IFC.

CAO, 2006a, *A Retrospective Analysis of CAO Interventions, Trends, Outcomes and Effectiveness*, Washington, DC, IFC.

CAO, 2006b, *Annual Report: 2005–2006*, Washington, DC, IFC and MIGA, CAO.

CAO, 2006c, *The Pangue Complaint Settlement Agreement between CAO and UNIMACH*, February 9, 2006. www.cao-ombudsman.org.

CAO, 2005, *Annual Report: 2004–2005*, Washington, DC, IFC and MIGA, CAO.

CAO, 2004, *Annual Report: 2003–2004*, Washington, DC, IFC and MIGA, CAO.

CAO, 2003, *Annual Report: 2002–2003*, Washington, DC, IFC and MIGA, CAO.

CAO, 2002, *Annual Report: 2001–2002*, Washington, DC, IFC and MIGA, CAO.

CAO, 2001, *Annual Report: 2000–2001*, Washington, DC, IFC and MIGA, CAO.

CAO, 2000, *CAO Operational Guidelines*, Washington, DC, IFC and MIGA, CAO.

CAO, 1999, *Terms of Reference*, Washington, DC, IFC. http://www.cao-ombudsman.org/about/whoweare/.

Caporoso, James, 2003, "Democracy, Accountability, and Rights in Supranational Governance," in M. Kahler and D. A. Lake (eds.), *Governance in a Global Economy: Political Authority in Transition*, Princeton and Oxford, Princeton University Press: 361–385.

Carnegie, A., 2015, *Power Plays: How International Institutions Reshape Coercive Diplomacy*, Cambridge, Cambridge University Press.

Carter, D., and R. Stone, 2015, "Democracy and Multilateralism: The Case of Vote Buying in the UN General Assembly," *International Organization* 68 (1): 1–33.

Caufield, C., 1996, *Masters of Illusion: The World Bank and the Poverty of Nations*, New York, Henry Holt.

CEE Bankwatch Network, 2008, *The EBRD Independent Recourse Mechanism: CEE Bankwatch Network's Comments on the Existing IRM*, June 2008, Prague, Czech Republic, CEE Bankwatch.

CEE Bankwatch Network, 2007, *The Independent Recourse Mechanism: Three Years on and the Question Remains—Who Is It For? The EBRD or Those Affected by EBRD Projects?* June 2007, Prague, Czech Republic, CEE Bankwatch.

CEE Bankwatch Network, 2001, *Empowering People: The Need for an EBRD Appeals/Compliance Mechanism*. Prague, Czech Republic, CEE Bankwatch. www.bankwatch.org.

Center for Ecology and Sustainable Development (CEKOR), 2015, *Comments on the Draft of the Compliance Review Report and the Management Action Plan on the EPS Emergency Power Sector Reconstruction Loan, EPS Power II and EPS Kolubara Environmental Improvement projects*, October 29, 2015, London, EBRD. https://www.ebrd.com/documents/occo/kolubara-map-comments.pdf

Chorev, N., 2012, *The World Health Organization Between North and South*, Ithaca, Cornell University Press.

Christensen, E., 1990, *Green Appeal: A proposal for an Independent Commission of Inquiry at the World Bank*, Washington, DC, Natural Resources Defense Council,.

Chwieroth, J., 2008, "Normative Change 'From Within': The International Monetary Fund's Approach to Capital Account Liberalization," *International Studies Quarterly* 52: 129–158.

CIEL, 2016, "NGO Response: Proposed World Bank Safeguards Represent Dangerous Set-Back to Key Environmental and Social Protections," Press Release, July 22. http://www.ciel.org/news/safeguard-policy-endangers-rights/.

Clark, D., J. Fox, and K. Treakle, 2003, *Demanding Accountability: Civil-Society Claims and the World Bank Inspection Panel*, Lanham, Rowman and Littlefield.

Connell, J., 2015, "Is "Good" Resettlement Policy Unimplementable?† Learning from Advocacy in Cambodia," *Development in Practice* 25 (5): 655–672.

Copelovitch, M., 2010, *The International Monetary Fund in the Global Economy: Banks, Bonds, and Bailouts*, Cambridge, Cambridge University Press.

Cowhey, P., 1992, "Elect Locally—Order Globally: Domestic Politics and Multilateral Cooperation," in J. Ruggie (ed.), *Multilateralism Matters: The Theory and Praxis of an Institutional Form*, New York, Columbia University Press: 157–200.

Crippa, L., and M. Keffer, 2009, "Comments and Recommendations on the IDB's Proposed Independent Consultation and Investigation Mechanism," Indian Law Resource Centre. http://www.indianlaw.org/sites/default/files/2009-09-30%20C omments%20ICIM%20FINAL%20ENG.pdf.

CRP (Compliance Review Panel), 2016, *Second Annual Monitoring Report to the Board of Directors on the Implementation of Remedial Actions for the Greater Mekong Subregion Rehabilitation of the Railway in Cambodia Project (Supplementary) in the Kingdom of Cambodia*, June 20, 2016, Manila, ADB. http://compliance.adb.org/dir0035p.nsf/atta chments/CAM-2ndMonitoringReport-For%20Web.pdf/$FILE/CAM-2ndMonitorin gReport-For%20Web.pdf.

CRP, 2015, *Third Annual Monitoring Report to the Board of Directors on the Implementation of Remedial Actions for the Visayas Base-Load Power Development Project in the Republic of the Philippines*, August 14, 2015, Manila, ADB. http://www.compliance.adb. org/dir0035p.nsf/attachments/FINAL-CRP%203rd%20MonitoringRpt-Visayas_17 Aug-withPCPdisclosure.pdf/$FILE/FINAL-CRP%203rd%20MonitoringRpt-Visayas_ 17Aug-withPCPdisclosure.pdf.

CRP, 2014, *Compliance Review Final Report Greater Mekong Subregion: Rehabilitation of the Railway in Cambodia Project (Supplementary) in the Kingdom of Cambodia*, January14, 2014, Manila, ADB. http://compliance.adb.org/dir0035p.nsf/attachments/ Cambodia-FinalReport-13Jan2014_OSEC%20Submission.pdf/$FILE/Cambodia-FinalReport-13Jan2014_OSEC%20Submission.pdf.

CRP, 2014b, *Decision of the Board of Directors of the Asian Development Bank*, January 31, 2014, Manila, ADB. http://compliance.adb.org/dir0035p.nsf/attachments/Board%20D ecision%20on%20CRP%20Final%20Report%20(R114)_31%20January%202014_ 7Feb.pdf/$FILE/Board%20Decision%20on%20CRP%20Final%20Report%20(R1-14)_31%20January%202014_7Feb.pdf.

CRP, 2013, *Decision of the Board of Directors of the Asian Development Bank*, January 31, 2014, Manila, ADB. http://compliance.adb.org/dir0035p.nsf/attachments/Cambodia-FinalReport-13Jan2014_OSEC%20Submission.pdf/$FILE/Cambodia-FinalReport-13Jan2014_OSEC%20Submission.pdf.

CRP, 2012, *Compliance Review Final Report Compliance Review Panel request No. 2011/1 on the Visayas Base-Load Power Development Project in the Republic of the Philippines*, March 12, 2012, Manila, ADB. http://www.compliance.adb.org/dir0035p.nsf/atta chments/PHI%20FINAL%20REPORT%20FINAL%20APPROVED%20BY%20BOD. pdf/$FILE/PHI%20FINAL%20REPORT%20FINAL%20APPROVED%20BY%20 BOD.pdf.

CRP, 2004, *Southern Development Transport Project CRP Request: New Evidence*, December 2, 2004, Manila, ADB, Office of the Compliance Review Panel. http://ocrp. asiandevbank.org/dir0035p.nsf/attachments/STDP-NewEvidence.pdf/$FILE/STDP-NewEvidence.pdf.

CRP, 2004b, *Appendix 3: Executive Summary of the Panel's Report*, August 19, 2004. Manila, ADB, Office of the Compliance Review Panel. http://compliance.adb.org/dir00 35p.nsf/alldocs/BDAO-7XW4XE?OpenDocument.

Culpeper, R., 1997, *Titans or Behemoths? Multilateral Development Banks*, Series No. 5, London, Intermediate Technology Publications and Lynne Rienner,

Culpeper, R., 1990, "Crossroads or Cross-Purposes? Inter-American Development Bank at 31," *Briefing Paper* 25, Review Outlook: An Annual Publication of the North South Institute, Ottawa Canada, n.p.

Dahl, R. 1999, "Can International Organizations Be Democratic? A Skeptic's View," in I. Shapiro and C. Hacker-Cordon (eds.), *Democracy's Edges*, Cambridge, Cambridge University Press: 19–36.

Darrow, M., 2003, *Between Light and Shadow: The World Bank, the International Monetary Fund and International Human Rights Law*, Oxford, and Portland, OR, Hart Publishing.

Dell, S., 1972, *The Inter-American Development Bank: A Study in Development Financing*, New York, Praeger.

DeWitt, R. P., 1977, *The Inter-American Development Bank and Political Influence: With Special Reference to Costa Rica*, New York and London, Praeger.

Dijkstra, H., 2017, "Collusion in International Organizations: How States Benefit from the Authority of Secretariats," *Global Governance* 23 (4): 601–618.

DiMaggio, P., and W. Powell. 1983. "The Iron Cage Revisited: Institutional Isomorphism and Collective Rationality in Organizational Fields," *American Sociological Review* 48 (2): 147–160.

Dowdle, M., 2006, *Public Accountability: Designs, Dilemmas and Experiences*, Cambridge: Cambridge University Press.

Downing, T., 1996, "A Participatory Interim Evaluation of the Pehuen Foundation," International Finance Corporation 2067, AGRA Earth and Environment, Downing and Associates.

Dreher, A., and N. Jensen, 2007, "Independent Actor or Agent? An Empirical Analysis of the Impact of US Interests on IMF Conditions," *Journal of Law and Economics*, 50(1): 105–124.

Dreher, A., and J.-E. Sturm, 2012, "Do the IMF and the World Bank Influence Voting in the UN General Assembly?," *Public Choice* 151: 363–397.

Dreher, A., J. Sturm, and J. Vreeland, 2009, "Development Aid and International Politics: Does Membership on the UN Security Council Influence World Bank Decisions?," *Journal of Development Economics* 88: 1–18.

Droesse, G. (ed.), 2011, *Funds for Development: Multilateral Channels of Concessional Financing*, Manila, ADB. http://www.adb.org/sites/default/files/pub/2011/funds-for-development.pdf.

Dubnick, M., 2014, "Accountability as a Cultural Keyword," in M. Bovens, R. Goodin, and T. Schillermans (eds.), *The Oxford Handbook of Public Accountability*, Oxford, Oxford University Press: 23–38.

Dysart, B., T. Murphy, and A. Chayes, 2003, "Beyond Compliance? An External Review Team Report on the Compliance Advisor/Ombudsman Office of IFC/MIGA," prepared for Meg Taylor, IFC/MIGA Compliance Advisor Ombudsman, July 24, 2003, Washington, DC, The World Bank Group.

Easterly, W., 2001, *The Elusive Quest for Growth*, Cambridge, MIT Press.

Easterly, W., and T. Pfutze, 2008, "Where Does the Money Go? Best and Worst Practices in Foreign Aid," *Journal of Economic Perspectives* 22 (2): 29–52.

Ebrahim, A., and E. Weisband (eds.), 2007, *Global Accountabilities: Participation, Pluralism and Public Ethics*, Cambridge, Cambridge University Press.

EBRD (European Bank for Reconstruction and Development), 2020, *Project Accountability Policy*, London, EBRD. https://www.ebrd.com/work-with-us/project-finance/project-complaint-mechanism/pcm-evolution.html.

EBRD, 2015a, *Project Complaint Mechanism Annual Report*, London, EBRD. http://www.ebrd.com/work-with-us/project-finance/project-complaint-mechanism.html.

EBRD, 2015b, *Annual Report*, London, EBRD. https://www.ebrd.com/news/publications/annual-report/annual-report-2015.html

EBRD, 2014a, "Compliance." http://www.ebrd.com/pages/about/integrity/compliance.shtml.

EBRD, 2014b, *Project Complaint Mechanism: Rules of Procedure*, London, EBRD.

EBRD, 2009a, *Project Complaint Mechanism: Rules of Procedure*, London, EBRD.

EBRD, 2009b, *Project Complaint Mechanism: Report on the Invitation to the Public to Comment and Bank Responses*, London, EBRD. http://www.ebrd.com/pages/project/pcm.shtml.

EBRD, 2006, *Basic Documents of the European Bank for Reconstruction and Development*, London, EBRD. http://www.ebrd.com/pubs/insti/basics.pdf.

EBRD, 2004, *Independent Recourse Mechanism: Rules of Procedure*, Approved by the Board, April 6, 2004, London, EBRD.

EBRD, 2003, *Independent Recourse Mechanism: Summary of Staff Responses to Public Comments*, London, EBRD.

Einhorn, J., 2006, "Reforming the World Bank," *Foreign Affairs* 85 (1): 17–22.

Elster, J., 1989, *Nuts and Bolts for the Social Sciences*, Cambridge, Cambridge University Press.

English, E. P., and H. M. Mule, 1996, *The African Development Bank*, Intermediate Technology Publishing, Boulder, CO, Lynne Rienner.

Faini, R., and E. Grilli, 2004, "Who Runs the IFIs?," Working Paper 4666, London, Centre for Economic Policy Research.

Fairman, D., G. Joscelyne, and L. Udall, 2010, *Internal Review of CAO Terms of Reference, Operational Guidance and Operational Practices, Final Report*, Washington, DC, IFC and MIGA, CAO.

Filho, W. L., and R. Rios, 2007, *Accountability Issues in International Development Projects*, Frankfurt am Main, Peter Lang.

Finnemore, M., and K. Sikkink, 2001, "Taking Stock: The Constructivist Research Program in International Relations and Comparative Politics," *Annual Review of Political Science* 4: 391–416.

Finnemore, M., and K. Sikkink, 1998, "International Norm Dynamics and Political Change," *International Organization* 52 (4): 887–917.

Fleck, R., and C. Kilby, 2006, "World Bank Independence: A Model and Statistical Analysis of U.S. Influence," *Review of Development Economics* 10(2): 224–240.

Florini, A., 2007, *The Right to Know: Transparency for an Open World*, New York, Columbia University Press.

Foot, R., S. Neil, and M. Mastanduno (eds.), 2003, *US Hegemony and International Organizations*, Oxford, Oxford University Press.

Fox, J., 2000, "The World Bank Inspection Panel: Lessons from the First Five Years," *Global Governance* 6 (3): 279–318.

Fox, J. and D. L. Brown (eds.), 1998, *The Struggle for Accountability: The World Bank, NGOs and Grassroots Movements*, Cambridge, MA, MIT Press.

Franck, T., 1990. *The Power of Legitimacy among Nations*, New York: Oxford University Press.

Friends of the Earth International, 2003, *FoEI Comments on the Proposal for an Independent Recourse Mechanism at the EBRD*. Amsterdam, FoEI. http://bankwatch. org/documents/comm_irm_foei_1_03.pdf.

Fukuda, Kenji, 2003, "Critical Analysis of the New Accountability Mechanism of the Asian Development Bank," in D. Guerrero (ed.), *Focus Asien No. 16: A Handbook on the Asian Development Bank: The ADB and Its Operations in Asia and the Pacific Region*, Essen, Asienstiftung/Asienhaus: 31–38.

Gardiner, R., and J. Pickett, 1984, *The African Development Bank: 1964–84*, Abidjan, AfDB.

Gilpin, R., 1987, *The Political Economy of International Relations*, Princeton, Princeton University Press.

Goldstein, J., and R. Keohane, 1993, *Ideas and Foreign Policy: Beliefs, Institutions, and Political Change*, Ithaca, Cornell University Press.

Government Accountability Project, 2013, "The Inter-American Development Bank," Government Accountability Project Website. \http://www.whistleblower.org/prog ram-areas/international-reform/regional-development-banks/the-inter-american-development-bank.

Graham, E., 2015, "Money and Multilateralism: How Funding Rules Constitute IO Governance," *International Theory* 7 (1): 162–194.

Grant, R., and R. Keohane, 2005, "Accountability and Abuses of Power in World Politics," *American Political Science Review* 99 (1): 29–43.

Greenhill, B., 2010, "The Company You Keep: International Socialization and the Diffusion of Human Rights Norms," *International Studies Quarterly* 54: 127–145.

Griffith-Jones, S., H. W. Singer, A. Puyana, and C. Stevens, 1994, "Assessment of the IDB Lending Programme, 1979–1992," *IDS Research Report 25*, Sussex, UK, Sussex University, Institute of Development Studies.

Grigorescu, A., 2016, *Democratic Intergovernmental Organizations? Normative Pressures and Decision-Making Rules*, Cambridge, Cambridge University Press.

Grigorescu, A., 2010, "The Spread of Bureaucratic Oversight Mechanisms across Intergovernmental Organizations," *International Studies Quarterly* 54, 871–886.

Grigorescu, A., 2008, "Horizontal Accountability in Intergovernmental Organizations," *Ethics and International Affairs* 22 (3): 285–308.

Group of Seven (G7), 2000, "Strengthening the International Financial Architecture," Report of the G7 Finance Ministers to the Heads of State and Government, Fukuoka, Japan, July 8, 2000. http://www.g8.utoronto.ca/finance/fm20000708-st.html#23-36.

Group of Seven (G7), 2001, "Strengthening the International Financial System and the Multilateral Development Banks," Report of the G7 Finance Ministers and Central Bank Governors, July 7, 2001, Rome, Italy. http://www.g8.utoronto.ca/finance/fm010 707.htm.

Gruber, L., 2001, "Power Politics and the Free Trade Bandwagon," *Comparative Political Studies* 34 (7): 703–741.

Grupo de Action por el BioBio (GABB), 1995, "The BioBio Dams in Chile: Violations of World Bank Policies and Lack of Accountability at the International Finance Corporation," Claim before the Inspection Panel and Petition before the IFC Board of Executive Directors, Chile, GABB.

Gutner, T., 2005a, "Explaining the Gaps between Mandate and Performance: Agency Theory and World Bank Environmental Reform," *Global Environmental Politics* 5 (2): 10–37.

Gutner, T., 2005b, "World Bank Environmental Reform: Revisiting Lessons from Agency Theory," *International Organization* 59: 773–783.

Gutner, T., 2002, *Banking on the Environment: Multilateral Development Banks and Their Environmental Performance in Central and Eastern Europe*, Cambridge, MIT Press.

Guven, 2012, "The IMF, the World Bank, and the Global Economic Crisis: Exploring Paradigm Continuity," *Development and Change* 43 (4): 869–898.

Guzzini, S., 2013, *Power, Realism, and Constructivism*, London and New York, Routledge.

Gwin, C., 1994, *US Relations with the World Bank 1945–92*, Brookings Occasional Papers, Washington, DC, The Brookings Institute.

Haas, E., 1990, *When Knowledge Is Power: Three Models of Change in International Organizations*, Berkeley, University of California Press.

Hair, J., 1997, "Pangue Hydroelectric Project (Chile): An Independent Review of the International Finance Corporation's Compliance with Applicable World Bank Group Environment and Social Requirements," IFC Internal Review, Washington, DC, IFC.

Hansungule, M., 2009, *Review of the IRM, Finding and Recommendations*, Tunis, AfDB.

Hawkins, D., and W. Jacoby, 2006, "How Agents Matter," in D. Hawkins, D. Lake, D. Nielson, and M. Tierney (eds.), *Delegation to International Organizations*, Cambridge, Cambridge University Press: 199–228.

Hawkins, D., D. Lake, D. Nielson, and M. Tierney, 2006, *Delegation to International Organizations*, Cambridge, Cambridge University Press.

Held, D., and M. Koenig-Archibugi, 2005, *Global Governance and Public Accountability*, Malden, Oxford, and Carlton, Blackwell.

Hernandez, D. 2013, "Does Inclusion Guarantee Institutional Autonomy? The Case of the Inter-American Development Bank," University of Heidelberg Department of Economics Discussion Paper 541.

Hlobil, Petr, 2002, "Bank Accountability Redux: The Campaign for Compliance and Appeal Mechanisms at the European Development Banks," *Multinational Monitor* 23 (5): 17–20.

Hoffman, F., and F. Megret, 2005, "Fostering Human Rights Accountability: An Ombudsman for the United Nations," *Global Governance* 11: 43–63.

Hug, S., 2003, "Endogenous Preference and Delegation in the European Union," *Comparative Politics Studies* 36 (1/2): 41–74.

Huijstee, M., K. Genovese, C. Daniel, and S. Singh, 2016, *Glass Half Full: The State of Accountability in Development Finance*, Report by 11 NGOs, Amsterdam, SOMO. https://www.somo.nl/glass-half-full-2/.

Humphrey, C., 2016, "The 'Hassle Factor' of MDB Lending and Borrower Demand in Latin America," in S. Park and J. Strand (eds.), *Global Economic Governance and the Development Practices of the Multilateral Development Banks*, London, Routledge: 92–112.

Humphrey, C., and K. Michaelowa, 2013, "Shopping for Development: Multilateral Lending, Shareholder Composition and Borrower Preferences," *World Development* 44: 142–155.

Hunter, D., 2008, "Civil Society Networks and the Development of Environmental Standards at International Financial Institutions," *Chicago Journal of International Law* 8 (2): 437–177.

Hurd, I., 2007, *After Anarchy: Legitimacy and Power in the UN Security Council*, Princeton, Princeton University Press.

ICIM (Independent Consultation and Investigation Mechanism), 2015a, *Annual Report 2014*, Washington, DC, IDB. http://idbdocs.iadb.org/wsdocs/getdocument.aspx?doc num=39678430.

ICIM, 2015b, *PN-MICI002-2011Compliance Panel Review Report: Panama Canal Expansion Program PN-L1032*, August 4, 2015, Annex II. Washington, DC, IDB. http:// idbdocs.iadb.org/wsdocs/getdocument.aspx?docnum=39766242.

ICIM, 2014a, *Annual Report 2013*, Washington, DC, IDB. http://idbdocs.iadb.org/wsd ocs/getdocument.aspx?docnum=38733586.

ICIM, 2014b, *Policy of the Independent Consultation and Investigation Mechanism*, December 17, 2014. Washington, DC, IDB.

ICIM, 2013, *Document of the Independent Consultation and Investigation Mechanism ME-MICI002-2012: Determination of Eligibility for the Compliance Review Phase, Mexico. Marena Renovable Wind Project*, September 8, 2013. Washington, DC, IDB. http://idbd ocs.iadb.org/wsdocs/getdocument.aspx?docnum=38068277.

ICIM, 2012, *Annual Report 2011*, IDB. http://www.iadb.org/en/mici/publicati ons,1768.html.

ICIM, 2012b, *Assessment and Consultation Phase Report Agrifood Health and Quality Management Program in Argentina (AR-ICIM004-2012)*. Washington, DC, IDB. http:// idbdocs.iadb.org/wsdocs/getdocument.aspx?docnum=37066269.

ICIM, 2011, *Annual Report 2010*, Washington, DC, IDB. http://www.iadb.org/en/mici/ publications,1768.html.

IDA (International Development Association), 2008, "Report from the Executive Directors of the International Development Association to the Board of Governors 'Additions to IDA Resources: Fifteenth Replenishment IDA: The Platform for Achieving Results at the Country Level,' Approved by the Executive Directors of IDA on February 28, 2008," Washington, DC, World Bank.

IDA, 2007, *IDA15 Financing Framework, IDA Resource Mobilization*, Washington, DC, World Bank.

IDB (Inter-American Development Bank), 2020, *Paraguay Project "Downtown Redevelopment, Modernization of Metropolitan Public Transport and Government Offices," MICI-BID-PR-2016-0101 Action Plan of the IDB Administration to Address the ICIM Compliance Review Report Recommendations of the Case of the Project "Downtown Redevelopment, Modernization of Metropolitan Public Transport and Government Offices"(PR-L1044)*, Revised Version, Washington, DC, IDB. https://idbd ocs.iadb.org/wsdocs/getdocument.aspx?docnum=EZSHARE-33351106-1461.

IDB, 2016, "Projects." http://www.iadb.org/en/projects/projects,1229.html.

IDB, 2014, *Policy of the Independent Consultation and Investigation Mechanism of the Inter-American Development Bank*, December 17, 2014. Washington, DC, IDB.

IDB, 2013a, *ICIM's Response to the Evaluation of the Independent Consultation and Investigation Mechanism*, Independent Consultation and Investigation Mechanism, Washington, DC, IDB.

IDB, 2013b, *Report of the Chairpersons of the Policy and Evaluation and of the Organization, Human Resources and Board Matters Committees, Evaluation of the Independent Consultation and Investigation Mechanism (RE-416-1)*, Board of Executive Directors, Washington, DC, IDB.

IDB, 2013c, *Annual Report 2013*, Washington, DC, IDB.

IDB, 2013d, *Mechanismo Indepdendiente de Consulta e Investigacion Proceso de Consulta Publica 2013—Etapa I*, Washington, DC, IDB [This document includes Spanish, Portuguese, and English public submissions in their original].

IDB, 2012a, *Approach Paper—Evaluation of the Independent Consultation and Investigation Mechanism*, Document RE-416, July 2012, Office of Evaluation and Oversight, Washington, DC, IDB.

IDB, 2012b, *Corporate Evaluation: Evaluation of the Independent Consultation and Investigation Mechanism*, December 2012, Office of Evaluation and Oversight, Washington, DC, IDB.

IDB, 2012c, *Corporate Evaluation: Evaluation of the Independent Consultation and Investigation Mechanism Annexes*, December 2012, Office of Evaluation and Oversight, Washington, DC, IDB.

IDB, 2010, *Policy Establishing the Independent Consultation and Investigation Mechanism of the Inter-American Development Bank*, February 17, 2010. Washington, DC, IDB.

IDB, 2010a, *Report on the Ninth General Capital Increase in the Resources of the Inter-American Development Bank*, Document AB-2764, May 21, 2010. Washington, DC, IDB. http://publications.iadb.org/handle/11319/2201?locale-attribute=en.

IDB, 2010b, *Policy establishing the Independent Consultation and Investigation Mechanism*, Document GN-1830-49, February 4, 2010. Washington, DC, IDB.

IDB, 2010c, *The Cancun Declaration*, Document AB-2728, March 21, 2010. Washington, DC, IDB. http://idbdocs.iadb.org/wsdocs/getdocument.aspx?docnum=35121613.

IDB, 2009a, *Evaluation Findings Regarding IDB-8 Guidance and Implications for Future Capital Increase Agreements*, Document RE-354, Office of Evaluation and Oversight, Washington, DC, IDB.

IDB, 2000, *Annual Report*, Washington, DC, IDB.

IDB, 1996, *Agreement Establishing the Inter-American Development Bank*, Amended July 31, 1995, Washington, DC, IDB. http://www.iadb.org/leg/documents/pdf/convenio-eng.pdf.

IDB, 1994, *Annual Report*, Washington, DC, IDB.

IDB, 1993, *Managing for Effective Development: Report of the Task Force on Portfolio Management for the Inter-American Development Bank*, Washington, DC, IDB.

IDBWatch, 2008, *A Publication of Civil Society Groups Working to Reform the Inter-American Development Bank*, Issue 1, April 4, 2008.

IFC (International Finance Corporation), n.d., "IFC and IDA," News and Events, Washington, DC, IFC. www.ifc.org.

IFC, 2006a, "Strategic Directions Implementation Update and FY 07–09 Outlook," *Report to the Board of Directors*, April 11, 2006. Washington, DC, IFC. www.ifc.org.

IFC, 2006b, *Sustainability Report 2005*, Washington, DC, IFC.

IFC, 1999, *IFC Annual Report 1999*, Washington, DC, IFC.

IFC, 1992, "IFC Board Approves Pangue Dam," IFC Press Release No 92/32, Washington, DC, IFC.

IIM, 1997, *Yacyreta Hydroelectric Project: Report of the Review Panel*, September 15, 1997. On file with author.

IIM (Independent Investigation Mechanism), 2009, *Annual Report 2008*, Washington, DC, IDB. http://www.iadb.org/en/mici/publications,1768.html.

IIM, 2008, *Annual Report 2007*, Washington, DC, IDB. http://www.iadb.org/en/mici/publications,1768.html.

IIM, 2007, *Annual Report 2006*, Washington, DC, IDB. http://www.iadb.org/en/mici/publications,1768.html.

IIM, 2006, *Annual Report 2005*, Washington, DC, IDB. http://www.iadb.org/en/mici/publications,1768.html.

IIM, 2004, *Annual Report 2003*, Washington, DC, IDB. http://www.iadb.org/iim/iim2 003.pdf.

IIM, 2003, *Annual Report 2002*, Washington, DC, IDB. http://www.iadb.org/en/mici/ publications,1768.html.

IIM, 2001, *Annual Report 2000*, Washington, DC, IDB. http://www.iadb.org/en/mici/ publications,1768.html.

Independent Recourse Mechanism, 2004–2005, *Report of the Chief Compliance Officer*, London, EBRD.

Independent Recourse Mechanism, 2008, *Annual Report for 2008*, London, EBRD.

Independent Recourse Mechanism, 2007, *Annual Report for 2007*, London, EBRD.

Independent Recourse Mechanism, 2006, *Annual Report for 2006*, London, EBRD.

Independent Review Mechanism, 2016a, *Register of Unregistered Claims, 2009–2015*, Tunis, AfDB. http://www.afdb.org/fileadmin/uploads/afdb/Documents/Compliance-Review/4th%20Monitoring%20Report-Uganda%20Bujagali%20Hydropower%20 Project%20and%20Bujagali%20Interconnection%20Project.pdfhttp://www.afdb.org/ fileadmin/uploads/afdb/Documents/Compliance-Review/ENG_REGISTER_OF_UN REGISTERED_REQUESTS.pdf.

Independent Review Mechanism, 2016b, *Management Response on the Request Filed on the Diversification of the Activities of the Modern Mills Project (Moulins Modernes du Mali) in Mali*, Tunis, AfDB. https://www.afdb.org/fileadmin/uploads/afdb/Docume nts/Compliance-Review/Management_Response_on_the_request_filed_on_the_di-versification_of_the_activities_of_the_modern_Mills_project__Moulins_Modern es_du_Mali__in_Mali.pdf.

Independent Review Mechanism, 2014a, *Annual Report for 2014*, Tunis, AfDB.

Independent Review Mechanism, 2014b, *IRM Problem Solving Report Request RQ2012/01 Road Sector Support Project II, Tanzania, February 2014*, Tunis, AfDB, Tunisia. http:// www.afdb.org/fileadmin/uploads/afdb/Documents/Compliance-Review/Tanzania_-_Tanzania_Road_Support_Project_II_ -_Problem-Solving_Report_-_Request_N__ RQ2012-1.pdf.

Independent Review Mechanism, 2012a, *Annual Report for 2012*, Tunis, AfDB.

Independent Review Mechanism, 2012b, *Daniel Bradlow and Richard Bissell, IRM Panel of Experts, Review of "Problem Solving Report": Request 2010/01 Request for Compliance Review and Problem Solving Project: Marrakech-Agadir Motorway Morocco to the AfDB Board of Directors*, January 19, 2012. Tunis, AfDB. http://www.afdb.org/fileadmin/uplo ads/afdb/Documents/Compliance-Review/IRM%20Experts%20Memo%20to%20Boa rds%20re%20eligibility%20of%20Marrakesh%20-%20Agadir%20Motorway%20Web _01.pdf.

Independent Review Mechanism, 2012c, *Request Register RQ2010/02 Republic of South Africa, Medupi Power Project*. Tunis, AfDB. http://www.afdb.org/fileadmin/uploads/ afdb/Documents/Compliance-Review/Request_Register__2012_06_28_.pdf.

Independent Review Mechanism, 2012d, *Fourth Monitoring Report on the Implementation of Findings of Non-Compliance and Related Actions to be Undertaken by AfDB Management on the Bujugali Hydropower and Interconnection Projects*, September 2012, Tunis, AfDB.

Independent Review Mechanism, 2011a, *Annual Report for 2011*, Tunis, AfDB.

Independent Review Mechanism, 2011b, *Compliance Review Report: Medupi Power Project, Republic of South Africa, Compliance Review Request 2010/02*, December 19, 2011, Tunis, AfDB. http://www.afdb.org/fileadmin/uploads/afdb/Documents/Com pliance-Review/Medupi%20Power%20Project%20Q20102%20%20%281%29.pdf.

Independent Review Mechanism, 2010, *Annual Report for 2010*, Tunis, AfDB.

Independent Review Mechanism, 2009, *Annual Report for 2009*, Tunis, AfDB.

Independent Review Mechanism, 2008, *Annual Report for 2008*, Tunis, AfDB.

Independent Review Mechanism, 2007a, *Annual Report for 2007*, Tunis, AfDB.

Independent Review Mechanism, 2007b, *Eligibility Report for Compliance Review: Bujugali Hydropower Project and the Bujugali Interconnection Project, Uganda. RQ2007/01.24*, August 2007. Tunis, AfDB. http://www.afdb.org/fileadmin/uploads/afdb/Documents/Generic-Documents/19836283-EN-NOTICE-OF-REGISTRAT ION-2007-06-04.PDF.

Independent Review Mechanism, 2006, *Annual Report for 2006*, Tunis, AfDB.

Inspection Panel, 2014, *World Bank Inspection Panel Response to Amnesty International's Briefing Paper on Badia East, September 2014, and Amnesty International's Comments on the Inspection Panels Responses, 5 November 2014*, Washington, DC, World Bank. http://www.refworld.org/pdfid/54608abb4.pdf.

Inspection Panel, 2013a, *Final Report and Recommendation Lebanon: Greater Beirut Water Supply Project (IBRD Loan No. 7967-LB)*, April 8, 2013, Washington, DC, World Bank. http://web.worldbank.org/WBSITE/EXTERNAL/EXTINSPECTIONPANEL/ 0,,contentMDK:22761665~menuPK:64129250~pagePK:64129751~piPK:64128 378~theSitePK:380794~isCURL:Y,00.html.

Inspection Panel, 2013b, *Inspection Panel Investigation of Ethiopia: Promoting Basic Service Phase III Initial Investigation Plan (August 2013)*, Washington, DC, World Bank. http://siteresources.worldbank.org/EXTINSPECTIONPANEL/Resources/ InvestigationPlan_EthiopiaPBSIII_August7_2013.pdf.

Inspection Panel, 2011a, *Report Follow-Up to Board Decision of March 10, 2011, Lebanon: Greater Beirut Water Supply Project (IBRD Loan No. 7967-LB)*, July 29, 2011. Washington, DC, World Bank. http://ewebapps.worldbank.org/apps/ip/PanelCases/ 71-Inspection%20Panel%20Report%20-%20Follow-up%20to%20Board%20Decis ion%20of%20March%2010,%202011.pdf.

Inspection Panel, 2011b, *Final Report and Recommendation CHILE: Quilleco Hydropower Project (Trust Fund No. TF056272-CL)*, August 31, 2011, Washington, DC, World Bank. http://ewebapps.worldbank.org/apps/ip/PanelCases/67-Final%20Report%20 and%20Recommendation%20(English).pdf.

Inspection Panel, 2009a, *Accountability at the World Bank: The Inspection Panel at 15 Years*, Washington, DC, World Bank.

Inspection Panel, 2009b, *Statement of Mr. Werner Kiene, Chairman of the Inspection Panel*, September 14, 2009, Yemen to the World Bank Board of Directors, Washington, DC, World Bank. http://ewebapps.worldbank.org/apps/ip/PanelCases/57-Statement%20 of%20the%20Panel%20Chairman%20to%20the%20Board%20(English).pdf.

Inspection Panel, 2007, *Final Eligibility Report and Recommendation Brazil: Paraná Biodiversity Project (GEF TF 051007)*, March 1, 2007, Washington, DC, World Bank. http://ewebapps.worldbank.org/apps/ip/PanelCases/41-Final%20Eligibility%20Rep ort%20(English).pdf.

Inspection Panel, 2006, *Eligibility Assessment Report: Report and Recommendation On Request for Inspection Brazil: Paraná Biodiversity Project (PBP)(GEF TF 051007)*, September 11, 2006, Washington, DC, World Bank. http://ewebapps.worldbank.org/ apps/ip/PanelCases/41-Eligibility%20Report%20(English).pdf.

Inspection Panel, 2003, *Accountability at the World Bank: The Inspection Panel 10 Years On*, Washington, DC, World Bank.

Inspection Panel, 2002, *The Inspection Panel Investigation Report for the Chad-Cameroon Petroleum Pipeline Project (Loan No. 4558-CD); Petroleum Sector Management Capacity Building Project (Credit No. 3373-CD); and Management of the Petroleum Economy (Credit No. 3316-CD)*, Washington, DC, World Bank. http://web.worldbank.org/ WBSITE/EXTERNAL/EXTINSPECTIONPANEL/0,,contentMDK:22515234~pag ePK:64129751~piPK:64128378~theSitePK:380794,00.html.

Inspection Panel, 1995, *Proposed Arun III Hydroelectric Project and Credit 2029-NEP Investigation Report*, June 21, 1995. Washington, DC, World Bank. http://web.worldb ank.org/WBSITE/EXTERNAL/EXTINSPECTIONPANEL/0,,contentMDK:22515 755~pagePK:64129751~piPK:64128378~theSitePK:380794,00.html.

Inspection Panel and the World Bank, 2011, *Joint Statement from World Bank Management and the Inspection Panel: World Bank Board Discusses Request for Inspection in Lebanon*, News Release, March 10, 2011. Washington, DC, World Bank. http://ewebapps.worldb ank.org/apps/ip/PanelCases/71-Press%20Release%20(English).pdf.

International Financial Advisory Commission, 2000, *Report of the International Financial Advisory Commission*, United States Congress. http://www.house.gov/jec/imf/melt zer.pdf.

Johnson, T., 2014, *Organizational Progeny: Why Governments are Losing Control over the Proliferating Structures of Global Governance*, Oxford, Oxford University Press.

Johnston, A., 2001, "Treating International Institutions as Social Environments," *International Studies Quarterly* 45: 487–515.

Johnston, B., and T. Turner, 1998, *The Pehuenche, the World Bank Group and Endesa S.A.: Violations of Human Rights in the Pangue and Ralco Dam Projects on the Bio River in Chile*, Report of the Committee for Human Rights, American Anthropological Association.

Joyner, C., 1978, "The United States' Withdrawal from the ILO: International Politics in the Labor Arena," *The International Lawyer*, 12 (4): 721–739.

Kahler, M., 2004, "Defining Accountability Up: The Global Economic Multilaterals," *Government and Opposition* 39 (2): 132–158.

Kaja, A., and E. Werker, 2010, "Corporate Governance at the World Bank and the Dilemma of Global Governance," *World Bank Economic Review* 24 (2): 171–198.

Kapur, D., 2002, "The Changing Anatomy of Governance at the World Bank," in J. R. Pincus and J. A. Winters (eds.), *Reinventing the World Bank*, Ithaca and London, Cornell University Press: 54–75.

Kapur, D., J. Lewis, and R. Webb (eds.), 1997, *The World Bank: Its First Half Century*, Vol. 1, Washington, DC, Brookings Institute.

Karns, M., and K. Mingst, 2002, "The United States as Deadbeat? US Policy and the UN Financial Crisis," in S. Patrick and S. Forman (eds.), *Multilateralism and US Foreign Policy*, Boulder and London, Lynne Rienner: 267–294.

Karns, M., and K. Mingst, 1990, *The United States and Multilateral Institutions*, London and New York, Routledge.

Kaya, A., 2015, *Power and Global Economic Institutions*, Cambridge, Cambridge University Press.

Keck, M., and K. Sikkink, 1998, *Activists beyond Borders: Advocacy Networks in International Politics*, Ithaca and London, Cornell University Press.

Kelley, J., 2004, "International Actors on the Domestic Scene: Membership Conditionality and Socialisation by International Institutions," *International Organization* 58: 425–457.

Keohane, R.O, 1984, *After Hegemony: Cooperation and Discord in the World Political Economy*, Princeton, NJ, Princeton University Press.

Keohane, R. O., and D. G. Victor, 2011, "The Regime Complex for Climate Change," *Perspectives on Politics*, 9 (1): 7–23.

Keonig-Archibugi, M., 2004, "Transnational Corporations and Public Accountability," *Government and Opposition* 39 (2): 234–259.

Khagram, S., 2004, *Dams and Development: Transnational Struggles for Water and Power*, Ithaca, Cornell University Press.

Kiewiet, D. R., and M. McCubbins, 1991, *The Logic of Delegation: Congressional Parties and the Appropriations Process*, Chicago and London, University of Chicago Press.

Kilby, C., 2013, "An Empirical Assessment of Informal Influence in the World Bank," *Economic Development and Cultural Change* 61 (2): 431–464.

Kilby, C., 2011, "Informal Influence in the Asian Development Bank," *Review of International Organizations* 6: 223–267.

Kilby, C., 2009, "An Empirical Assessment of Informal Influence in the World Bank," Villanova, PA, Villanova School of Business, Department of Economics and Statistics Working Paper #9. http://repec.library.villanova.edu/workingpapers/VSBEcon9.pdf.

Koenig-Archibugi, M., 2004, "Transnational Corporations and Public Accountability," *Government and Opposition* 39 (2): 234–259.

Koremenous, B., C. Lipson, and D. Snidal, 2004, *The Rational Design of International Institutions*, Cambridge, Cambridge University Press.

Koslowski, R., and F. Kratochwil, 1994, "Understanding Change in International Politics: The Soviet Empire's Demise and the International System," *International Organization* 48 (2): 215–247.

Kramarz, T., and S. Park, 2016, "Accountability in Global Environmental Governance: A Meaningful Tool for Action?," *Global Environmental Politics*, 16 (2): 1–21.

Krasner, S., 1981, "Power Structures and Regional Development Banks," *International Organization* 35 (2): 303–328.

Kratochwil, F., 1982, "On the Notion of 'Interest' in International Relations," *International Organization*, 36 (1): 1–30.

Lardone, M., 2010, "New Public Management on the Ground: A Comparative Analysis of the World Bank Experience in Chile and Argentina," in S. Park and A. Vetterlein (eds.), *Owning Development: Creating Policy Norms in the IMF and the World Bank*, Cambridge, Cambridge University Press: 204–223.

Lavelle, K., 2011, *Legislating International Organization: The US Congress, the IMF and the World Bank*, Oxford, Oxford University Press.

Lavelle, K., 2007, "Exit, Voice, and Loyalty in International Organizations: US Involvement in the League of Nations," *Review of International Organizations* 2: 371–393.

Lewis, K., 2012, "Citizen-Driven Accountability for Sustainable Development: Giving Affected People a Voice 20 Years On," A Paper by the Independent Accountability Mechanisms Network. http://siteresources.worldbank.org/EXTINSPECTIONPA NEL/Resources/Rio20_IAMs_Contribution.pdf.

Lim, D., and J. Vreeland, 2013, "Regional Organizations and International Politics: Japanese Influence over the Asian Development Bank and the UN Security Council," *World Politics* 65 (1): 34–72.

Lombardi, D., 2008, "The Governance of the World Bank: Lessons from the Corporate Sector," *Review of International Organizations* 3: 287–323.

Lori Udall, M., 1994, "Memorandum Regarding the World Bank's Inspection Panel," Bank Information Centre. On file with author.

Lowery, C., 2013, "A Proposal for IDA-17: Instead of an Income Transfer, Direct the IFC to Invest Its Time, Resources, and Expertise in IDA Countries," Centre for Global Development Brief, Washington, DC, Centre for Global Development. cgdev.org.

Luck, E., 1999, *Mixed Messages: American Politics and International Organization 1919–1999*. Washington, DC, Brookings Institute, Century Foundation.

Lumsdaine, D., 1993, *Moral Vision in International Politics: The Foreign Aid Regime 1949–1989*, Princeton, NJ, Princeton University Press.

Lyon, A., 2016, *US Politics and the United Nations: A Tale of Dysfunctional Dynamics*, Boulder, CO, Lynne Rienner.

Mahoney, J., and K. Thelen (eds.), 2010, *Explaining Institutional Change: Agency, Ambiguity and Power*, Cambridge, Cambridge University Press.

Martin, L., and B. Simmons, 1998, "Theories and Empirical Studies of International Institutions," *International Organization* 52: 729–757.

Mashaw, J., 2006, "Accountability in Institutional Design: Some Thoughts on the Grammar of Governance," in M. D. Dowdle (ed.), *Public Accountability: Designs, Dilemmas and Experiences*, Cambridge, Cambridge University Press: 115–156.

Mason, E. S., and R. E. Asher, 1973, *The World Bank since Bretton Woods*, Washington, DC, Brookings Institute.

Matecki, B. E., 1957, *Establishment of the International Finance Corporation and United States Policy: A Case Study of International Organization*, London, Thames and Hudson.

McCawley, P., 2017, *Banking on the Future of the Asia Pacific: 50 Years of the Asian Development Bank*, Manila, ADB.

McCubbins, M., and T. Schwartz, 1984, "Congressional Oversight Overlooked: Police Patrols versus Fire Alarms," *American Journal of Political Science* 28: 165–179.

McGill, E., 2001, "The Inspection Policy of the Asian Development Bank," in G. Alfredsson and R. Ring (eds.), *The Inspection Panel of the World Bank: A Different Complaints Procedure*, Leiden, Martinus Nijhoff: 191–209.

McKeown, T., 2009, "How U.S Decision-Makers Assessed their Control of Multilateral Organizations 1957-1982," *Review of International Organizations* 4: 269–291.

McIntyre, O., and S. Nanwani (eds.), 2020, *The Practices of the Independent Accountability Mechanisms: Towards Good Governance in Development Finance*, Leiden and Boston, Brill Njihoff.

Melansen, R., 1979, "Human Rights and the American Withdrawal from the ILO," *Universal Human Rights*, 1 (1): 43–61.

Menkveld, Paul, 1991, *The Origin and Role of the European Bank for Reconstruction and Development*, London, Graham and Trotman.

Meyer, J., and B. Rowan, 1977, "Institutionalized Organizations: Formal Structure as Myth and Ceremony," *American Journal of Sociology* 83 (2): 340–363.

Meyer, J., and B. Rowan, 1991, "Institutional Organizations: Formal Structures as Myth and Ceremony," in W. W. Powell and P. DiMaggio (eds.), *The New Institutionalism in Organizational Analysis*, Chicago, Chicago University Press: 141–162.

Miller, G., 2001, "The Independent Investigation Mechanism of the Inter-American Development Bank," in G. Alfredsson and R. Ring (eds.), *The Inspection Panel of the World Bank: A Different Complaints Procedure*, Leiden, Martinus Nijhoff: 209–218.

Milner, H., and D. Tingley, 2011, "Who Supports Global Economic Engagement? The Sources of Preferences in American Foreign Economic Policy," *International Organization* 65: 37–68.

Milner, H., and D. Tingley, 2013, "The Choice for Multilateralism: Foreign Aid and American Foreign Policy," *Review of International Organizations* 8: 313–341.

Mingst, K., 1990, *Politics and the African Development Bank*, Lexington, University of Kentucky Press.

Mingst, K., 1987, "Inter-Organizational Politics: The World Bank and the African Development Bank," *Review of International Studies* 13: 281–293.

Mistry, P., 1995, *Multilateral Development Banks: An Assessment of Their Financial Structures, Policies and Practices*, The Hague, FONDAD.

Momani, B., 2010, "Internal or External Norm Champions: The IMF and Multilateral Debt Relief," in S. Park and A. Vetterlein (eds.), *Owning Development: Creating Policy Norms in the IMF and the World Bank*, Cambridge, Cambridge University Press: 29–47.

Moravcsik, A., 2004, "Is There a 'Democratic Deficit' in World Politics? A Framework for Analysis," *Government and Opposition* 39 (2): 336–363.

Morse, B., and T. Berger, 1992, *The Independent Review of the Sardar Sarovar Projects*, Ottawa, Resource Futures International.

Mulgan, R., 2000, "Accountability: An Ever-Expanding Concept?," *Public Administration* 78 (3): 555–573.

Nanwani, S., 2010, "Accountability Mechanisms of Multilateral Development Banks: Powers, Complications, Enhancements," in A. Perry-Kessaris (ed.), *Law in the Pursuit of Development: Principles into Practice*, London and New York, Routledge: 110–130.

Nash, N., 1992, "On a Remote Chilean River, Fight over Dam," *New York Times*, p. 8.

Naude Fourie, A., 2016, *World Bank Accountability—In Theory and in Practice*. The Hague: Eleven International Publishing.

Naude Fourie, A., 2012, "The World Bank Inspection Panel's Normative Potential: A Critical Assessment and a Restatement," *Netherlands International Law Review* 59: 199–234.

Naude Fourie, A., 2009, *The World Bank Inspection Panel and Quasi-Judicial Oversight*, Utrecht, Eleven.

Nelson, P., 2000, "Whose Civil Society—Whose Governance—Decisionmaking and Practice in the New Agenda at the Inter-American Development Bank and the World Bank," *Global Governance* 6: 405–431.

Nelson, S., 2014, "Playing Favorites: How Shared Beliefs Shape the IMF's Lending Decisions," *International Organization* 68 (2): 297–328.

Nelson, R., 2015, *Multilateral Development Banks: Overview and Issues for Congress*. Congressional Research Service Report for Members and Committees of Congress, R41170, US Government.

Nelson, R., and M. Weiss, 2013, *Multilateral Development Banks: How the United States Makes and Implements Policy*, Congressional Research Service Report for Members and Committees of Congress, R41537, US Government.

Nelson, S., 2014, "Playing Favorites: How Shared Beliefs Shape the IMF's Lending Decisions," *International Organization* 68 (2): 297–328.

Neumayer, E., 2003a, *Explaining the Pattern of Aid Giving—The Impact of Good Governance on Development Assistance*, London, Routledge.

Neumayer, E., 2003b, "The Determinants of Aid Allocation by Regional Multilateral Development Banks and United Nations Agencies," *International Studies Quarterly* 47, 101–122.

NGO Forum on the ADB, 2011, *Holding ADB Accountable: A Look at the Present Accountability Mechanism,* Quezon City, Philippines, http://forum-adb.org/docs/AM-briefer.pdf.

Nielson, D., and M. Tierney, 2005, "Theory, Data and Hypothesis Testing: World Bank Environmental Reform Redux," *International Organization* 59: 785–800.

Nielson, D., and M. Tierney, 2003, "Delegation to International Organizations: Agency Theory and World Bank Environmental Reform," *International Organization* 57 (2): 241–276.

Nielson, D., M. Tierney, and Weaver, C., 2006, "Bridging the Rationalist-Constructivist Divide: Re-Engineering the Culture at the World Bank," *Journal of International Relations and Development* 9: 107–139.

Oately, T., and J. Yakee, 2004, "American Interests and IMF Lending," *International Politics* 41: 415–429.

OCRP (Office of the Compliance Review Panel), 2011, *2011 Annual Report: The Compliance Review Panel,* Manila, ADB. http://www.adb.org/publications/series/compliance-review-panel-annual-reports.

OCRP. 2009, *2009 Annual Report: The Compliance Review Panel,* Manila, ADB. http://www.adb.org/site/accountability-mechanism/publications.

OCRP. 2008, *2008 Annual Report: The Compliance Review Panel,* Manila: ADB. http://www.adb.org/publications/series/compliance-review-panel-annual-reports.

OCRP. 2007, *2007 Annual Report: The Compliance Review Panel,* Manila: ADB. http://www.adb.org/publications/series/compliance-review-panel-annual-reports.

Oehlers, A., 2006, "A Critique of ADB Policies towards the Greater Mekong Sub-Region," *Journal of Contemporary Asia* 36 (4): 464–478.

Organization for Economic Cooperation and Development (OECD), 2018, *Multilateral Development Finance: Towards a New Pact on Multilateralism to Achieve the 2030 Agenda Together,* Geneva, OECD. http://www.oecd.org/dac/financing-sustainable-development/development-finance-topics/Multilateral-Development-Finance-Highlights-2018.pdf.

Oliver, C., 1991, "Strategic Responses to Institutional Processes," *Academy of Management Review* 16 (1): 145–179.

Orchard, P., 2014, *A Right to Flee: Refugees, States, and the Construction of International Cooperation,* Cambridge, Cambridge University Press.

OSPF (Office of the Special Project Facilitator), 2012, *Final Report of the Special Project Facilitator: Integrated Citarum Water Resources Management Investment Program,* February 2012, Manila, ADB. http://www.adb.org/sites/default/files/page/42458/ino-complaint-final-report-1-2011.pdf.

OSPF, 2010, *Final Report of the Special Project Facilitator on the Phnom Penh to Ho Chi Minh City Highway Project in Cambodia ADB Loan 1659-CAM(SF) (15 December 1998),* Complaint Received July 30, 2007, Manila, ADB.

OSPF, 2009, *Annual Report of the OSPF,* Manila, ADB. http://www.adb.org/site/accountability-mechanism/publications.

OSPF, 2006, *Annual Report,* Manila: ADB. http://www.adb.org/site/accountability-mechanism/problem-solving-function/publications.

OSPF, 2005, *Final Report of the Special Project Facilitator on the Southern Transport Development Project, Sri Lanka,* March 2005. Manila, ADB. http://www.adb.org/sites/default/files/page/42458/sf-sri-1711.pdf.

Oxfam Australia, 2011, *ADB Accountability Mechanism Review 2011: Oxfam Australia Submission to the ADB on Consultation Paper February 2011*, April 1, 2011, Melbourne, Oxfam Australia.

Park, S., 2020, *Environmental Recourse at the Multilateral Development Banks*, Cambridge, Cambridge University Press.

Park, S., 2019, "Claims Submitted to the Multilateral Development Bank Accountability Mechanisms 1994–2019," Database Version 2, Sydney, University of Sydney. doi: 10.25910/5bdb90e22bf46.

Park, S., 2015, "Assessing Accountability in Practice: The Asian Development Bank's Accountability Mechanism," *Global Policy* 6 (4): 455–465.

Park, S., 2014, "Institutional Isomorphism and the Asian Development Bank's Accountability Mechanism: Something Old, Something New; Something Borrowed, Something Blue?," *Pacific Review* 27 (2): 1–23.

Park, S., 2017, "Accountability as Justice for the Multilateral Development Banks? Borrower Opposition and Bank Avoidance to US Power and Influence," *Review of International Political Economy* 24 (5): 776–801.

Park, S., 2010a, *The World Bank Group and Environmentalists: Changing International Organization Identities*, London, Manchester University Press.

Park, S., 2010b, "The World Bank's Global Safeguard Policy Norm?," in S. Park and A. Vetterlein (eds.), *Owning Development: Creating Global Policy Norms in the IMF and the World Bank*, Cambridge, Cambridge University Press: 181–203.

Park., S., 2021, "Policy Norms, the Development Finance Regime Complex, and Holding the EBRD to Account," *Global Policy* 12 (4): 90–100.

Park, S., and J., Strand (eds.), 2016, *Global Economic Governance and the Development Practices of the Multilateral Development Banks*, London, Routledge.

Park, S., and A. Vetterlein, 2010, *Owning Development: Creating Global Policy Norms in the IMF and the World Bank*, Cambridge, Cambridge University Press.

Pascha, W., 2000, "The Asian Development Bank in the Context of Rapid Regional Development," in R. Tilley and P. J. J. Welfens (eds.), *Economic Globalization, International Organization and Crisis Management*, Berlin, Sringer: 155–184.

Passoni, C., A. Rosenbaum, and E. Vermunt, 2016, *Empowering the Inspection Panel: The Impact of the World Bank's Safeguards Review*, Report, New York University School of Law. http://www.iilj.org/publications/empowering-the-inspection-panel/.

Patrick, S., and S. Forman (eds.), 2002, *Multilateralism and US Foreign Policy*, Boulder, CO, and London, Lynne Rienner.

Payne, R., and N. Samhat, 2004, *Democratizing Global Politics: Discourse Norms, International Regimes and Political Community*, Albany, SUNY Press.

PCM (Project Complaint Mechanism), 2016a, *Compliance Review Monitoring Report IV: Ombla HPP Project, Request Number 2011/06*. London, EBRD.

PCM, 2016b, *Compliance Review Monitoring Report V: Paravani Hydropower Project: Request 2012/01*, November 2016, EBRD Project Complaints Mechanism Registry, London, EBRD.

PCM, 2015a, *Annual Report 2015*, London, EBRD. http://www.ebrd.com/pages/project/pcm/about.shtml.

PCM, 2015b, *Compliance Review Report EPS Kolubara Environmental Improvement Project Request 2012/04 and EPS Emergency Power Sector Reconstruction Plan 2013/03*, Publicly Released October 29, 2015. London, EBRD. http://www.ebrd.com/work-with-us/project-finance/project-complaint-mechanism/pcm-register.html.

PCM, 2014a, *Annual Report 2014*, London, EBRD. http://www.ebrd.com/pages/project/pcm/about.shtml.

PCM, 2014b, *Compliance Review Report Ombla Hydro Power Project Request 2011/06*, London, EBRD. http://www.ebrd.com/work-with-us/project-finance/project-complaint-mechanism/pcm-register.html.

PCM, 2014c, *Compliance Review Report Paravani Hydro Power Project Request 2012/01*, Publicly Released January 2, 2014. London, EBRD. http://www.ebrd.com/work-with-us/project-finance/project-complaint-mechanism/pcm-register.html.

PCM, 2014d, *Compliance Review Monitoring Report 1: Boskov Most Hydro Power, Request Number 2011/05*, London, EBRD.

PCM, 2013, *Annual Report 2013*, London, EBRD. http://www.ebrd.com/pages/project/pcm/about.shtml.

PCM, 2012, *Annual Report 2012*, London, EBRD. http://www.ebrd.com/pages/project/pcm/about.shtml.

PCM, 2011, *Annual Report 2011*, London, EBRD. http://www.ebrd.com/pages/project/pcm/about.shtml.

PCM, 2011b, *Compliance Review Report Boskov Most Hydro Power Project 2011/05*, London, EBRD. http://www.ebrd.com/work-with-us/project-finance/project-complaint-mechanism/pcm-register.html.

Pierson, J., 1987, "The Inter-American Development Bank: Rethinking America's Role," *The Backgrounder* no. 586, June 15, The Heritage Foundation.

Pincus, J. R., and J. A. Winters, 2002 (eds.) *Reinventing the World Bank*, Ithaca and London, Cornell University Press.

Pop-Eleches, G. 2009, "Public Goods or Political Pandering: Evidence from IMF Programs in Latin America and Eastern Europe," *International Studies Quarterly* 53 (3): 787–816.

Potrafke, N., 2009, "Does Government Ideology Influence Political Alignment with the US? An Empirical Analysis of Voting in the UN General Assembly," *Review of International Organizations* 4: 245–268.

Pouliot, V., 2007, "'Sobjectivism': Toward a Constructivist Methodology," *International Studies Quarterly* 51 (2): 359–384.

Rathbun, B., 2012, *Trust in International Cooperation, International Security Institutions, Domestic Politics, and American Multilateralism*, Cambridge, Cambridge University Press.

Reich, S., and R. Lebow, 2014, *Good-Bye Hegemony! Power and Influence in the Global System*, Princeton, NJ, Princeton University Press.

Reinsberg, B., K. Michealowa, and S. Knack, 2017, "Trust Funds as a Lever of Influence at International Development Organizations," *Global Policy* 8 (5): 85–95.

Rich, B. 1994, *Mortgaging the Earth: The World Bank, Environmental Impoverishment and the Crisis of Development*, Boston, Beacon Press.

Risse, T., S. Ropp, and K. Sikkink (eds.), 1999, *The Power of Human Rights: International Norms and Domestic Change*, Cambridge, Cambridge University Press.

Rodrigues, M. G., 2003, *Global Environmentalism and Local Politics: Transnational Advocacy Networks in Brazil, Ecuador, and India*, New York, SUNY Press.

Ruggie, J. G, 1982, "International Regimes, Transactions, and Change: Embedded Liberalism in the Postwar Economic Order," *International Organization* 36 (2): 379–415.

Sanford, J., 1982, *US Foreign Policy and Multilateral Development Banks*, Boulder, CO, Westview Press.

Scharpf, F. 1999. *Governing in Europe: Effective and Democratic?* Oxford: Oxford University Press.

Schedler, A., 1999, "Conceptualising Accountability," in A. Schedler, L. Diamond, and M. Plattner (eds.), *The Self-Restraining State: Power and Accountability in New Democracies*, Boulder, CO, Lynne Rienner: 13–28.

Schimmelfennig, F., 2000, "International Socialisation in the New Europe: Rational Action in an Institutional Environment," *European Journal of International Relations* 6 (1): 109–139.

Schoultz, L., 1982, "Politics, Economics and US Participation in Multilateral Development Banks," *International Organization* 36 (3): 537–574.

Schweller, R., and Priess, D., 1997, "A Tale of Two Realisms: Expanding the Institutions Debate," *Mershon International Studies Review* 41: 1–32.

Seabrooke, 2014, "Epistemic Arbitrage: Transnational Professional Knowledge in Action," *Journal of Professions and Organization* 1 (1): 49–64.

Sharma, P., 2013, "Bureaucratic Imperatives and Policy Outcomes: The origins of World Bank Structural Adjustment Lending," *Review of International Political Economy* 20 (4): 667–686.

Shaw, C., 1991, "Par Iter Paribus: The Nature of Power in Cooperation: Lessons (for the United States) From the African Development Bank," *African Affairs* 90: 537–558.

Shihata, I., 2000, *The World Bank Inspection Panel: In Practice*, 2nd ed., Washington, DC, World Bank and Oxford University Press.

Shihata, I., 1994, *The World Bank Inspection Panel*, Washington, DC, World Bank and Oxford University Press.

Singh, J., 2011, *United Nations Educational Scientific and Cultural Organization*, Routledge, London and New York.

Singh, S., 2009, "World Bank–Directed Development? Negotiating Participation in the Nam Theun 2 Hydropower Project in Laos," *Development and Change*, 40 (3): 487–507.

Stern, N., and F. Ferreira, 1997, "The World Bank as 'Intellectual Actor,'" in D. Kapur, J. P. Lewis, and R. Webb (eds.) *The World Bank: Its First Half Century, Volume 2: Perspectives*. Washington, DC, Brookings Institution: 523–609.

Stone, R., 2011, *Controlling Institutions: International Organizations and the Global Economy*, Cambridge, Cambridge University Press.

Stone, R., 2004, "The Political Economy of IMF Lending in Africa," *American Political Science Review* 98 (4): 577–592.

Strand, J., 2003, "Measuring Voting Power in an International Institution: The United States and the Inter-American Development Bank," *Economics of Governance* 4 (1): 19–36.

Strand, J., 2001, "Institutional Design and Power Relations in the African Development Bank," *Journal of African and Asian States* 36 (2): 203–223.

Strand, J., 1999, "State Power in a Multilateral Context: Voting Strength in the Asian Development Bank," *International Interactions* 25 (3): 53–74.

Strand, J., and D. Rapkin, 2011, "Weighted Voting in the United Nations Security Council: A Simulation," *Simulation and Gaming* 42 (8): 772–802.

Strand J., and M. Trevathan, 2016, "Implications of Accommodating Rising Powers for the Regional Development Banks," in S. Park and J. Strand (eds.), *Global Economic Governance and the Development Practices of the Multilateral Development Banks*, London, Routledge: 121–143.

Strand, J., and T. Zappile, 2015, "Always Vote for Principle, Though You May Vote Alone: Explaining United States Political Support for Multilateral Development Loans," *World Development* 72: 224–239.

Streek, W., and K. Thelen, 2005, *Beyond Continuity: Institutional Change in Advanced Political Economies*, Oxford: Oxford University Press.

Sud, I., and J. Olmstead-Rumsey, 2012, "Development Outcomes of World Bank Projects: Real or Illusory Improvements?," IGIS Working Paper, Washington, DC, Institute for Global and International Studies, George Washington University. http://www.gwu.edu/~igis/assets/docs/working_papers/sud_olmstead-rumsey.pdf.

Suzuki, E., and S. Nanwani, 2006, "Responsibility of International Organizations: The Accountability Mechanisms of Multilateral Development Banks," *Michigan Journal of International Law* 27: 177–255.

Tadem, T., 2003, "Thai Social Movements and the Anti-ADB Campaign," *Journal of Contemporary Asia*, 33 (3): 377–398.

Tallberg, J., T. Sommerer, T. Squatrito, and C. Jönsson, 2013, *The Opening Up of International Organizations: Transnational Access in Global Governance*, New York: Cambridge University Press.

Thacker, S., 1999, "The High Politics of IMF Lending," *World Politics* 52: 38–75.

Thompson, A., 2006, "Coercion through IOs: The Security Council and the Logic of Information Transmission," *International Organization* 60 (1): 1–34.

Thornburgh, D., R. Gainer, and C. Walker, 2000, "Report to Shengman Zhang, Managing Director and Chairman of the Oversight Committee on Fraud and Corruption, The World Bank: Concerning Mechanisms to Address Problems of Fraud and Corruption," January 21, 2000, Washington, DC, World Bank.

Tussie, D., 1995, *The Inter-American Development Bank*, Boulder, CO, Lynne Rienner.

Udall, L., 2008, Testimony to the United States House of Representatives Committee on Financial Services, Hearing on the International Development Association (IDA) and the 11th Replenishment of the African Development Bank 110th Congress, Second session, June 18, 2008, Serial no. 110–121.

Udall, L., 1997, *The World Bank Inspection Panel: A Three Year Review*, Washington, DC, Bank Information Center.

Udall, L., 1994, "Memorandum Regarding the World Bank's Inspection Panel," Bank Information Centre. March. On file with author.

Udall, L., and D. Hunter. 1993. *Proposal for an Independent Appeals Commission*. Environmental Defense Fund and Center for International Environmental Law, Washington, DC.

Umana, A., 1998, *The World Bank Inspection Panel: The First Four Years (1994–1998)*, Inspection Panel, Washington, DC, World Bank.

United Nations, 2016, *Sustainable Development Goals*. http://www.un.org/sustainable development/sustainable-development-goals/.

United Nations, 2012, *Guiding Principles on Business and Human Rights: Implementing the United Nations "Protect, Respect and Remedy" Framework*, Geneva, United Nations. http://www.ohchr.org/Documents/Publications/GuidingPrinciplesBusinessHR_EN.pdf.

UNICEF, 1997, *Development with a Human Face: Experiences in Social Achievement and Economic Growth*, edited by S. Mehrotra and R. Jolly, Oxford, Oxford University Press.

United States Government and Accounting Office (GAO), 1995, "Multilateral Development Banks: Financial Condition of the African Development Bank," Briefing

Report to the Chairman, Committee on the Budget, House of Representatives. Report number GAO-NSIAD-95-143BR.

United States Treasury, 2016, "2015 Report to Congress by Chairman of the National Advisory Council on International Monetary and Financial Policies." https://www.treasury.gov/resource-center/international/development-banks/Documents/NAC%20Report%20(Issued%20March%202016).pdf.

United States Treasury, 2013, "Report to Congress from the Chairman of the National Advisory Council on the International Monetary and Financial Policies," Department of Treasury, Office of the Multilateral Development Banks. https://www.treasury.gov/resource-center/international/development-banks/Pages/congress-index.aspx.

United States Treasury, 2010, "2009 Report to Congress by the National Advisory Council on International Monetary and Financial Policies." http://www.treasury.gov/resource-center/international/development-banks/Pages/congress-index.aspx.

Upton, B., 2000, *The Multilateral Development Banks: Improving U.S Leadership*, Westport, CT, Praeger.

van Putten, M., 2008, *Policing the Banks: Accountability Mechanisms for the Financial Sector*, Montreal, Kingston, and London, McGill-Queens University Press.

Vaubel, R., 2006, "Principal-Agent Problems in International Organizations," *Review of International Organizations* 1 (2): 125–138.

Vreeland, J., and A. Dreher, 2014, *The Political Economy of the United Nations Security Council*, Cambridge, Cambridge University Press.

Wade, R., 2009, "Accountability Gone Wrong: the World Bank, Non-Governmental Organizations and the US Government in a Fight over China," *New Political Economy* 14 (1): 25–48.

Wade, R., 1997, "Greening the Bank: The Struggle over the Environment 1970–1995," in D. Kapur, J. Lewis, and R. C, Webb (eds.), *The World Bank: Its First Half Century*, Washington, DC, Brookings Institute: 611–734.

Wan, M., 2001, *Japan between Asia and the West: Economic Power and Strategic Balance*, Armonk, NY, M. E. Sharpe.

Wapenhans, W., et al., 1992, *Effective Implementation: Key to Development Impact*, Portfolio Management Task Force, Washington, DC, World Bank.

Watanabe, T., 1977, *Towards a New Asia*, Manila, ADB.

Weaver, C., 2008, *The Hypocrisy Trap: The World Bank and the Poverty of Reform*, Princeton, NJ, Princeton University Press.

Weaver, C. 2007, "The World's Bank and the Bank's World," *Global Governance* 13 (4): 493–512.

Weber, M., (1980 [1921–2]), *Wirtschaft und Gesellschaft. Grundriss der verstehenden Soziologie*, 5th rev. edn. Tubingen : J. C. B. Mohr (Paul Siebeck).

Weber, S., 1994, "Origins of the European Bank for Reconstruction and Development," *International Organization* 48 (1): 1–38.

Wendt, A., 1999, *Social Theory of International Politics*, Cambridge, Cambridge University Press.

White, J., 1970, *Regional Development Banks: A Study of Institutional Style*, London, Overseas Development Institute.

Wiener, A. 2009. "Enacting Meaning-in-Use: Qualitative Research on Norms and International Relations," *Review of International Studies*, 35 (1): 175–193.

Wihtol, R., 1988, *The Asian Development Bank and Rural Development*, Oxford, Macmillan Press.

Williams, M. 2005. *The Realist Tradition and the Limits of International Relations.* Cambridge: Cambridge University Press.

Wilson, D., 1987, *A Bank for Half the World: The Story of the Asian Development Bank 1966–1986*, Manila, Asian Development Bank.

Winston, C., 2018, "Norm Structure, Diffusion, and Evolution: A Conceptual Approach," *European Journal of International Relations*, 24 (3): 638–661.

Wodie, F., 1984, "The African Development Bank and the African Development Fund," in D. Mazzeo (ed.), *African Regional Organizations*, Cambridge, Cambridge University Press: 85–102.

Woicke, P., 2020, *External Review of IFC/MIGA E&S Accountability, including CAO's Role and Effectiveness: Report and Recommendations*, World Bank Group. https://www.worldbank.org/en/about/leadership/brief/external-review-of-ifc-miga-es-accountability.

Wold, C., and D. Zaelke, 1992, "Establishing an Independent Review Board at the European Bank for Reconstruction and Development: A Model for Improving MDB Decision-Making," *Duke Environmental Law and Policy Forum* 2: 59–78.

Woods, N., 2006, *The Globalizers: The IMF, the World Bank and Their Borrowers*, Ithaca, New York, Cornell University Press.

Woods, N., 2003, "The United States and the International Financial Institutions: Power and Influence within the World Bank and the IMF," in R. Foot, S. N. MacFarlane, and M. Mastanduno (eds.), *US Hegemony and International Organizations*, Oxford, Oxford University Press: 92–114.

Woods, Ngaire, 2001, "Making the IMF and the World Bank More Accountable," *International Affairs* 77 (1): 83–100.

Woods, N., and D. Lombardi, 2006, "Uneven Patterns of Governance: How Developing Countries are Represented in the IMF," *Review of International Political Economy* 13 (3): 480–515.

Woods, Ngaire, and A. Narlikar, 2001, "Governance and the Limits of Accountability: The WTO, the IMF and the World Bank," *International Social Science Journal* 53 (170): 569–583.

World Bank, 2017, "Grievance Redress Service," Washington, DC, World Bank. http://www.worldbank.org/en/projects-operations/products-and-services/grievance-redress-service#4.

World Bank, 2016a, "The New Environmental and Social Framework," Safeguards, World Bank website. http://web.worldbank.org/WBSITE/EXTERNAL/PROJECTS/EXTPOLICIES/EXTSAFEPOL/0,,menuPK:584441~pagePK:64168427~piPK:64168435~theSitePK:584435,00.html.

World Bank, 2016b, "Grievance Redress Service," Project Operations, World Bank. http://www.worldbank.org/en/projects-operations/products-and-services/grievance-redress-service#1.

World Bank, 2016c, "Overview: Program for Results Financing," November 3, 2016. Washington, DC, World Bank. http://www.worldbank.org/en/programs/program-for-results-financing.

World Bank, 2016d, "World Bank Projects," Washington, DC, World Bank. http://www.worldbank.org/projects.

World Bank, 2016e, *Overview of Status of Implementation of Management Action Plans: Prepared in Response to Inspection Panel Eligibility and Investigation Reports*, Washington, DC, World Bank. http://ewebapps.worldbank.org/apps/ip/Documents/Tracking%20Management%20Action%20Plan%20-%20April%202016.pdf.

World Bank, 2015, "World Bank Acknowledges Shortcomings in Resettlement Projects, Announces Action Plan to Fix Problems," Press Release, March 4. http://www.worldb ank.org/en/news/press-release/2015/03/04/world-bank-shortcomings-resettlement-projects-plan-fix-problems.

World Bank, 2014, *The Inspection Panel at the World Bank: Operating Procedures April 2014, with Annex Two Added February 2016.* http://ewebapps.worldbank.org/apps/ip/PanelMandateDocuments/2014%20Updated%20Operating%20Procedures.pdf.

World Bank, 2013, "Investment, Development Policy and Program-for-Results Operations," Projects and Operations, World Bank. http://web.worldbank.org/WBS ITE/EXTERNAL/PROJECTS/0,,contentMDK:20120732~menuPK:268725~pag ePK:41367~piPK:51533~theSitePK:40941,00.html.

World Bank, 2012, "Projects and Lending: Frequently Asked Questions." http://web. worldbank.org/WBSITE/EXTERNAL/EXTSITETOOLS/0,,contentMDK:20264 002~menuPK:534379~pagePK:98400~piPK:98424~theSitePK:95474,00.html#6.

World Bank, 2011, "Use of Country Systems for Environmental Safeguards, 2010 Environment Strategy, Analytical Background Paper," February 22, 2011, World Bank Group.   http://siteresources.worldbank.org/EXTENVSTRATEGY/Resources/6975 692-1289855310673/20110222-Use-of-Country-Systems.pdf.

World Bank, 2010, *Safeguards and Sustainability Policies in a Changing World: An Independent Evaluation of World Bank Group Experience,* Washington, DC, Independent Evaluation Group, World Bank.

World Bank, 2008, *Environmental Sustainability: An Evaluation of World Bank Group Support,* Washington, DC, Independent Evaluation Group, World Bank.

World Bank, 2007, *Bank Management Response to the Request for Inspection Panel Review of the Albania: Integrated Coastal Zone Management and Clean-Up Project (IDA Credit No. 4083-ALB).* http://ewebapps.worldbank.org/apps/ip/PanelCases/47-Managem ent%20Response%20(English).pdf.

World Bank, 2006, *Annual Report,* Washington, DC, World Bank.

World Bank, 2004, "Bank Management Response to Request for Inspection Panel Review of the India-Mumbai Urban Transport Project (IBRD LOAN No. 4665-IN; IDA CREDIT No. 3662-IN)." http://ewebapps.worldbank.org/apps/ip/PanelCases/32-First%20Management%20Response%20(English).pdf.

World Bank, 2001, *Adjustment Lending Retrospective,* Operations Policy and Country Services, June 15, 2001. http://siteresources.worldbank.org/PROJECTS/Resources/ALR06_20_01.pdf.

World Bank, 1998, *Additions to IDA Resources: Twelfth Replenishment, A Partnership for Poverty Reduction,* December 23, 1998, International Development Association.

World Bank, 1997a, *India: NTPC Power Generation Project (Loan 3632-IN), Management Response to Inspection Panel,* June 3. http://ewebapps.worldbank.org/apps/ip/PanelCa ses/10-Management%20Response%20(English).pdf.

World Bank, 1997b, *Management Response to Request for Inspection Panel Review of Itaparica Resettlement and Irrigation Project Loan 2883-BR.* http://ewebapps.worldb ank.org/apps/ip/PanelCases/9-Management%20Response%20(English).pdf.

World Bank, 1995, *Tanzania - Power VI Project (Credit 2489-TA), Management Response to Request for Inspection.* http://ewebapps.worldbank.org/apps/ip/PanelCases/3-Man agement%20Response%20(English).pdf.

World Bank, 1994, *Nepal, Arun III: Management Response to Request for Inspection,* November   22.   http://ewebapps.worldbank.org/apps/ip/PanelCases/1-Managem ent%20Response%20(English).pdf.

World Bank, 1993, *The East Asian Miracle: Economic Growth and Public Policy*, Oxford, Oxford University Press.

World Bank Group, 2009, From Jyrki Koskelo to Meg Taylor: "Final IFC Management Group Response to CAO's Audit Report on Wilmar," August 4, 2009, Office Memorandum. http://www.cao-ombudsman.org/.

World Bank Group, 2008, *IFC Response to the CAO Audit Report on Kazakhstan: Karachaganak*, April 4, 2008. http://www.cao-ombudsman.org/.

World Bank Group, 2005, Letter from Rashad Kaldary, Director COCDR to Meg Taylor, CAO VP "CAO Assessment Report: Complaint Regarding Lukoil Overseas Project (Karachaganak Oil and Gas Field) Burlisky District, Western Kazakhstan Oblast, Kazakhstan," June 1. Office Memorandum. http://www.cao-ombudsman.org/.

Wroughton, L., 2009, "World Bank's IFC Suspends Palm Oil Investments," *US and International News*, Business and Financial News, September 9, Reuters.

Zappile, T., 2016, "Sub-Regional Development Banks: Development as Usual?," in S. Park and J. R. Strand (eds.), *Global Economic Governance and the Development Practices of the Multilateral Development Banks*, Abingdon, Routledge: 187–211.

Zweifel, T., 2006, *International Organizations and Democracy: Accountability, Politics, and Power*, Boulder, CO, Lynne Rienner.

Index

Inspection Panel (*cont.*)
    general capital increases (GCIs), 54–55, 71–73, 117–18
    soft-loan financing, 71–72
  purposes of, 1
  resistance to accountability mechanisms, 110–24
    generally, 110–11, 227–28
    avoidance, 112–14
    Board, by, 111–17
    borrowers, by, 111–17
    challenging rules, 204–5
    compromise, 10
    defiance, 114, 115, 179
    Independent Consultation and Investigation Mechanism (MICI), 117–20, 175, 178–80
    manipulation, 47, 97–98
  Tapoma (Qureshi) Report, 58, 72–73
  transparency and, 216–17
  US and
    "accountability as control," 54–55
    funding from, 73
    norm entrepreneurship, 51–52
    pressure from, 54–55, 57, 70–73, 74–75
    relationship with, 22, 29–32, 33, 34
    Treasury Department, role of, 71, 74
    "voice" and, 41
    voting in, 36, 37–38
  World Bank and
    comparison, 78
    influence of, 70–71, 72, 73
International Bank for Reconstruction and Development. *See* World Bank
International Centre for Settlement of Investment Disputes, 235n.3
International Development Association (IDA)
  generally, 71, 237n.13
  Inspection Panel and, 63–67, 68, 69, 105
  signaling and, 239n.43
  US funding of, 33–34, 35, 55–57, 59–60
  World Bank Group and, 85
International Finance Corporation (IFC). *See also* World Bank Group *for general provisions*
  generally, 235n.3
  accountability and, 78
  "accountability as justice" in, 80–87
  accountability mechanisms in, 80–87
  activism regarding, 79
  avoidance, 192–93
  CAO and, 104–5, 139–40 (*see also* World Bank Group)

  compliance investigations, 145, 191, 193, 205
  Corporate Risk Committee, 193–94
  EBRD compared, 88–89, 90
  environmental and social policy, 79–80, 82, 85, 86, 193, 222
  Financial Intermediaries, 194
  Hair Report, 82
  harm caused by projects, 1–2, 79–80
  Inspection Panel, applicability of, 84, 104–5, 192
  investment by, 260n.6
  lending by, 88, 139, 212–13
  lesser role of Board, 205
  mediation, 145
  monitoring of, 78–79
  "power of the purse" and, 83–84
  private sector lending by, 139
  purposes of, 1
  resistance to accountability mechanisms, 192–93
  safeguard policies, 222
  Sustainability Framework, 194, 222
  US and, 79, 83–84
  World Bank compared, 212–13
International Labour Organization (ILO), 233, 238n.36
International Monetary Fund (IMF)
  correlation between voting and assistance, 22–23, 238n.24
  informal governance of US in, 232–33
  power in, 21
  subscriptions, 28
  US and
    generally, 39–40, 232–33
    influence of, 24
    pressure from, 59
    resistance to reform, 9, 238n.35
    veto power, 24
investigation process. *See also specific institution*
  generally, 17, 166–67
  continuation of projects during, 17
  defiance of, 16–17, 229–30
  improvement of accountability mechanisms and, 166–67
  Inspection Panel and, 70
  manipulation of, 12, 16–17, 229–30
  "organizational hypocrisy" and, 231
  resistance to, 227–28

Japan
  ADB and, 22, 34, 37–38, 237n.16
  AfDB and, 34
  IMF, influence on, 24